Programming Google App Engine with Python

Dan Sanderson

Beijing · Boston · Farnham · Sebastopol · Tokyo

Programming Google App Engine with Python

by Dan Sanderson

Printed in the United States of America.

Published by O'Reilly Media, Inc., 1005 Gravenstein Highway North, Sebastopol, CA 95472.

O'Reilly books may be purchased for educational, business, or sales promotional use. Online editions are also available for most titles (*http://safaribooksonline.com*). For more information, contact our corporate/institutional sales department: 800-998-9938 or *corporate@oreilly.com*.

Editors: Meghan Blanchette and Brian Anderson	**Proofreader:** Charles Roumeliotis
Acquisition Editor: Mike Loukides	**Indexer:** Judy McConville
Production Editors: Colleen Lobner and Kara Ebrahim	**Interior Designer:** David Futato
Copyeditor: Jasmine Kwityn	**Cover Designer:** Ellie Volckhausen
	Illustrator: Rebecca Demarest

June 2015:   First Edition

Revision History for the First Edition
2015-06-17:   First Release

See *http://oreilly.com/catalog/errata.csp?isbn=9781491900253* for release details.

978-1-491-90025-3

[LSI]

Table of Contents

Preface

On the Internet, popularity is swift and fleeting. A mention of your website on a popular news site can bring 300,000 potential customers your way at once, all expecting to find out who you are and what you have to offer. But if you're a small company just starting out, your hardware and software aren't likely to be able to handle that kind of traffic. You've sensibly built your site to handle the 30,000 visits per hour you're actually expecting in your first six months. Under heavy load, such a system would be incapable of showing even your company logo to the 270,000 others that showed up to look around. And those potential customers are not likely to come back after the traffic has subsided.

The answer is *not* to spend time and money building a system to serve millions of visitors on the first day, when those same systems are only expected to serve mere thousands per day for the subsequent months. If you delay your launch to build big, you miss the opportunity to improve your product by using feedback from your customers. Building big early risks building something your customers don't want.

Historically, small companies haven't had access to large systems of servers on day one. The best they could do was to build small and hope that meltdowns wouldn't damage their reputation as they try to grow. The lucky ones found their audience, got another round of funding, and halted feature development to rebuild their product for larger capacity. The unlucky ones, well, didn't.

These days, there are other options. Large Internet companies such as Amazon.com, Google, and Microsoft are leasing parts of their high-capacity systems by using a pay-per-use model. Your website is served from those large systems, which are plenty capable of handling sudden surges in traffic and ongoing success. And because you pay only for what you use, there is no up-front investment that goes to waste when traffic is low. As your customer base grows, the costs grow proportionally.

Google's offering, collectively known as Google Cloud Platform, consists of a suite of high-powered services and tools: virtual machines in a variety of sizes, multiple forms of reliable data storage, configurable networking, automatic scaling infrastructure, and even the big data analysis tools that power Google's products. But Google Cloud Platform does more than provide access to Google's infrastructure. It encapsulates best practices for application architecture that have been honed by Google engineers for their own products.

The centerpiece of Google Cloud Platform is Google App Engine, an application hosting service that grows automatically. App Engine runs your application so that each user who accesses it gets the same experience as every other user, whether there are dozens of simultaneous users or thousands. Your application code focuses on each individual user's experience. App Engine takes care of large-scale computing tasks—such as load balancing, data replication, and fault tolerance—automatically.

The scalable model really kicks in at the point where a traditional system would outgrow its first database server. With such a system, adding load-balanced web servers and caching layers can get you pretty far, but when your application needs to write data to more than one place, you face a difficult problem. This problem is made more difficult when development up to that point has relied on features of database software that were never intended for data distributed across multiple machines. By thinking about your data in terms of Cloud Platform's model up front, you save yourself from having to rebuild the whole thing later.

Often overlooked as an advantage, App Engine's execution model helps to distribute computation as well as data. App Engine excels at allocating computing resources to small tasks quickly. This was originally designed for handling web requests from users, where generating a response for the client is the top priority. Combining this execution model with Cloud Platform's task queue service, medium-to-large computational tasks can be broken into chunks that are executed in parallel. Tasks are retried until they succeed, making tasks resilient in the face of service failures. The execution model encourages designs optimized for the parallelization and robustness provided by the platform.

Running on Google's infrastructure means you never have to set up a server, replace a failed hard drive, or troubleshoot a network card. You don't have to be woken up in the middle of the night by a screaming pager because an ISP hiccup confused a service alarm. And with automatic scaling, you don't have to scramble to set up new hardware as traffic increases.

Google Cloud Platform and App Engine let you focus on your application's functionality and user experience. You can launch early, enjoy the flood of attention, retain customers, and start improving your product with the help of your users. Your app grows with the size of your audience—up to Google-sized proportions—without having to rebuild for a new architecture. Meanwhile, your competitors are still putting out fires and configuring databases.

With this book, you will learn how to develop web applications that run on Google Cloud Platform, and how to get the most out of App Engine's scalable execution model. A significant portion of the book discusses Google Cloud Datastore, a powerful data storage service that does not behave like the relational databases that have been a staple of web development for the past decade. The application model and the datastore together represent a new way of thinking about web applications that, while being almost as simple as the model we've known, requires reconsidering a few principles we often take for granted.

A Brief History of App Engine

If you read all that, you may be wondering why this book is called *Programming Google App Engine* and not *Programming Google Cloud Platform*. The short answer is that the capabilities of the platform as a whole are too broad for one book. In particular, Compute Engine, the platform's raw virtual machine capability, can do all kinds of stuff beyond serving web applications.

By some accounts (mine, at least), App Engine started as an early rendition of the Cloud Platform idea, and evolved and expanded to include large-scale and flexible-scale computing. When it first launched in 2008, App Engine hosted web applications written in Python, with APIs for a scalable datastore, a task queue service, and services for common features that lay outside of the "container" in which the app code would run (such as network access). A "runtime environment" for Java soon followed, capable of running web apps based on Java servlets using the same scalable infrastructure. Container-ized app code, schemaless data storage, and service-oriented architecture proved to be not only a good way to build a scalable web app, but a good way to make reliability a key part of the App Engine product: no more pagers.

App Engine evolved continuously, with several major functionality milestones. One such milestone was a big upgrade for the datastore, using a new Paxos-based replication algorithm. The new algorithm changed the data consistency guarantees of the API, so it was released as an opt-in migration (including an automatic migration tool). Another major milestone was the switch from isolated request handlers billed by CPU usage to long-running application instances billed by instance uptime. With the upgraded execution model, app code could push "warm-up" work to occur outside of user request logic and exploit local memory caches.

Google launched Compute Engine as a separate product, a way to access computation on demand for general purposes. With a Compute Engine VM, you can run any 64-bit Linux-based operating system and execute code written in any language compiled to (or interpreted by) that OS. Apps—running on App Engine or otherwise—can call into Compute Engine to start up any number of virtual machines, do work, and either shut down machines when no longer needed or leave them running in traditional or custom configurations.

App Engine and Compute Engine take different approaches to provide different capabilities. But these technologies are already starting to blend. In early 2014, Google announced Managed VMs, a new way to run VM-based code in an App Engine-like way. (This feature is not fully available as I write this, but check the Google Cloud Platform website (*https://cloud.google.com*) for updates.) Overall, you're able to adopt as much of the platform as you need to accomplish your goals, investing in flexibility when needed, and letting the platform's automaticity handle the rest.

This book is being written at a turning point in App Engine's history. Services that were originally built for App Engine are being generalized for Cloud Platform, and given REST APIs so you can call them from off the platform as well. App Engine development tools are being expanded, with a new universal Cloud SDK and Cloud Console. We're even seeing the beginnings of new ways to develop and deploy software, with integrated Git-based source code revision control. As with any book about an evolving technology, what follows is a snapshot, with an emphasis on major concepts and long-lasting topics.

The focus of this book is building web applications using App Engine and related parts of the platform, especially Cloud Datastore. We'll discuss services currently exclusive to App Engine, such as those for fetching URLs and sending email. We'll also discuss techniques for organizing and optimizing your application, using task queues and offline processes, and otherwise getting the most out of Google App Engine.

Using This Book

Programming Google App Engine with Python covers App Engine's runtime environment for the Python programming language. The Python runtime environment provides a fast interpreter for the Python language, and includes Python libraries for all of App Engine's features. It is compatible with many major open source web application frameworks, such as Django and Flask.

App Engine supports three other runtime environments: Java, PHP, and Go. Java support includes a complete Java servlet environment, with a JVM capable of running bytecode produced by compilers for Java and other languages. The PHP environment runs a native PHP interpreter with the standard library and many extensions enabled, and is capable of running many off-the-shelf PHP applications such as WordPress and Drupal. With the Go runtime environment, App Engine compiles your Go code on the server and executes it at native CPU speeds.

The information contained in this book was formerly presented in a single volume, *Programming Google App Engine*, which also covered Java. To make it easy to find the information you need for your language, that book has been split into language-specific versions. You are reading the Python version. *Programming Google App Engine with Java* covers the same material using the Java language, as well as Java-specific topics.

We are considering PHP and Go versions of this book as a future endeavor. For now, the official App Engine documentation (*https://cloud.google.com/appengine/*) is the best resource for using these languages on the platform. If you're interested in seeing versions of this book for PHP or Go, let us know by sending email to *bookquestions@oreilly.com*.

The book is organized so you can jump to the subjects that are most relevant to you. The introductory chapters provide a lay of the land, and get you working with a complete example that uses several features. Subsequent chapters are arranged by App Engine's various features, with a focus on efficient data storage and retrieval, communication, and distributed computation. Project life cycle topics such as deployment and maintenance are also covered.

Cloud Datastore is a large enough subject that it gets multiple chapters to itself. Starting with Chapter 6, datastore concepts are introduced alongside Python APIs related to those concepts. Python examples use the ndb data modeling library, provided in the Cloud SDK. Data modeling gets its own chapter, in Chapter 9.

Here's a quick look at the chapters in this book:

Chapter 1, Introducing Google App Engine
> A high-level overview of Google App Engine and its components, tools, and major features, as well as an introduction to Google Cloud Platform as a whole.

Chapter 2, Creating an Application
> An introductory tutorial in Python, including instructions on setting up a development environment, using template engines to build web pages, setting up accounts and domain names, and deploying the application to App Engine. The tutorial application demonstrates the use of several App Engine features—Google Accounts, the datastore, and memcache—to implement a pattern common to many web applications: storing and retrieving user preferences.

Chapter 3, Configuring an Application
> A description of how App Engine handles incoming requests, and how to configure this behavior. This introduces App Engine's architecture, the various features of the frontend, app servers, and static file servers. We explain how the frontend routes requests to the app servers and the static file servers, and manages secure connections and Google Accounts authentication and authorization. This chapter also discusses quotas and limits, and how to raise them by setting a budget.

Chapter 4, Request Handlers and Instances

A closer examination of how App Engine runs your code. App Engine routes incoming web requests to request handlers. Request handlers run in long-lived containers called instances. App Engine creates and destroys instances to accommodate the needs of your traffic. You can make better use of your instances by writing threadsafe code and enabling the multithreading feature.

Chapter 5, Using Modules

Modules let you build your application as a collection of parts, where each part has its own scaling properties and performance characteristics. This chapter describes modules in full, including the various scaling options, configuration, and the tools and APIs you use to maintain the modules of your app.

Chapter 6, Datastore Entities

The first of several chapters on Cloud Datastore, a scalable object data storage system with support for local transactions and two modes of consistency guarantees (strong and eventual). This chapter introduces data entities, keys and properties, and Python APIs for creating, updating, and deleting entities from App Engine.

Chapter 7, Datastore Queries

An introduction to Cloud Datastore queries and indexes, and the Python APIs for queries. This chapter describes the features of the query engine in detail, and how each feature uses indexes. The chapter also discusses how to define and manage indexes for your application's queries. Advanced features like query cursors and projection queries are also covered.

Chapter 8, Datastore Transactions

How to use transactions to keep your data consistent. Cloud Datastore uses local transactions in a scalable environment. Your app arranges its entities in units of transactionality known as entity groups. This chapter attempts to provide a complete explanation of how the datastore updates data, and how to design your data and your app to best take advantage of these features.

Chapter 9, Data Modeling with ndb

How to use the Python ndb data modeling library to enforce invariants in your data schema. The datastore itself is schemaless, a fundamental aspect of its scalability. You can automate the enforcement of data schemas by using App Engine's data modeling interface.

Chapter 10, Datastore Administration

Managing and evolving your app's datastore data. The Cloud Console, SDK tools, and administrative APIs provide a myriad of views of your data, and information about your data (metadata and statistics). You can access much of this information programmatically, so you can build your own administration panels. This chapter also discusses how to use the Remote API, a proxy for building administrative tools that run on your local computer but access the live services for your app.

Chapter 11, Using Google Cloud SQL with App Engine

Google Cloud SQL provides fully managed MySQL database instances. You can use Cloud SQL as a relational database for your App Engine applications. This chapter walks through an example of creating a SQL instance, setting up a database, preparing a local development environment, and connecting to Cloud SQL from App Engine. We also discuss prominent features of Cloud SQL such as backups, and exporting and importing data. Cloud SQL complements Cloud Datastore and Cloud Storage as a new choice for persistent storage, and is a powerful option when you need a relational database.

Chapter 12, The Memory Cache

App Engine's memory cache service ("memcache"), and its Python APIs. Aggressive caching is essential for high-performance web applications.

Chapter 13, Fetching URLs and Web Resources

How to access other resources on the Internet via HTTP by using the URL Fetch service. Python applications can call this service using a direct API as well as via Python's standard library.

Chapter 14, Sending and Receiving Email Messages

How to use App Engine services to send email. This chapter covers receiving email relayed by App Engine by using request handlers. It also discusses creating and processing messages by using tools in the API.

Chapter 15, Sending and Receiving Instant Messages with XMPP

How to use App Engine services to send instant messages to XMPP-compatible services (such as Google Talk), and receive XMPP messages via request handlers. This chapter discusses several major XMPP activities, including managing presence.

Chapter 16, Task Queues and Scheduled Tasks

How to perform work outside of user requests by using task queues. Task queues perform tasks in parallel by running your code on multiple application servers. You control the processing rate with configuration. Tasks can also be executed on a regular schedule with no user interaction.

Chapter 17, Optimizing Service Calls

A summary of optimization techniques, plus detailed information on how to make asynchronous service calls, so your app can continue doing work while services process data in the background. This chapter also describes AppStats, an important tool for visualizing your app's service call behavior and finding performance bottlenecks.

Chapter 18, The Django Web Application Framework

How to use the Django web application framework with the Python runtime environment. This chapter discusses setting up a project by using the Django 1.5 library included in the runtime environment, and using Django features such as component composition, URL mapping, views, and templating. It also discusses how to use a newer version of Django than what is built into the runtime environment. The chapter introduces WTForms, a web form framework with special features for integrating with App Engine's `ndb` data modeling library.

Chapter 19, Managing Request Logs

Everything you need to know about logging messages, browsing and searching log data in the Cloud Console, and managing and downloading log data. This chapter also introduces the Logs API, which lets you manage logs programmatically within the app itself.

Chapter 20, Deploying and Managing Applications

How to upload and run your app on App Engine, how to update and test an application using app versions, and how to manage and inspect the running application. This chapter also introduces other maintenance features of the Cloud Console, including billing. The chapter concludes with a list of places to go for help and further reading.

Conventions Used in This Book

The following typographical conventions are used in this book:

Italic

Indicates new terms, URLs, email addresses, filenames, and file extensions.

`Constant width`

Used for program listings, as well as within paragraphs to refer to program elements such as variable or function names, databases, data types, environment variables, statements, and keywords.

`Constant width bold`

Shows commands or other text that should be typed literally by the user.

`Constant width italic`

Shows text that should be replaced with user-supplied values or by values determined by context.

This icon signifies a tip, suggestion, or general note.

This icon indicates a warning or caution.

Safari® Books Online

 *Safari Books Online* is an on-demand digital library that delivers expert content in both book and video form from the world's leading authors in technology and business.

Technology professionals, software developers, web designers, and business and creative professionals use Safari Books Online as their primary resource for research, problem solving, learning, and certification training.

Safari Books Online offers a range of plans and pricing for enterprise, government, education, and individuals.

Members have access to thousands of books, training videos, and prepublication manuscripts in one fully searchable database from publishers like O'Reilly Media, Prentice Hall Professional, Addison-Wesley Professional, Microsoft Press, Sams, Que, Peachpit Press, Focal Press, Cisco Press, John Wiley & Sons, Syngress, Morgan Kaufmann, IBM Redbooks, Packt, Adobe Press, FT Press, Apress, Manning, New Riders, McGraw-Hill, Jones & Bartlett, Course Technology, and hundreds more. For more information about Safari Books Online, please visit us online.

How to Contact Us

Please address comments and questions concerning this book to the publisher:

O'Reilly Media, Inc.

1005 Gravenstein Highway North

Sebastopol, CA 95472

800-998-9938 (in the United States or Canada)

707-829-0515 (international or local)

707 829-0104 (fax)

We have a web page for this book, where we list errata, examples, and any additional information. You can access this page at *http://bit.ly/google-app-python*.

You can download extensive sample code and other extras from the author's website at *http://www.dansanderson.com/appengine*.

To comment or ask technical questions about this book, send email to *bookquestions@oreilly.com*.

For more information about our books, courses, conferences, and news, see our website at *http://www.oreilly.com*.

Find us on Facebook: *http://facebook.com/oreilly*

Follow us on Twitter: *http://twitter.com/oreillymedia*

Watch us on YouTube: *http://www.youtube.com/oreillymedia*

Acknowledgments

I am indebted to the App Engine team for their constant support of this book since its inception in 2008. The number of contributors to App Engine has grown too large for me to list them individually, but I'm grateful to them all for their vision, their creativity, and their work, and for letting me be a part of it.

Programming Google App Engine, from which this book is derived, was developed under the leadership of Paul McDonald and Pete Koomen. Ryan Barrett provided many hours of conversation and detailed technical review. Max Ross and Rafe Kaplan contributed material and provided extensive review to the datastore chapters. Thanks to Matthew Blain, Michael Davidson, Alex Gaysinsky, Peter McKenzie, Don Schwarz, and Jeffrey Scudder for reviewing portions of the first edition in detail, as well as Sean Lynch, Brett Slatkin, Mike Repass, and Guido van Rossum for their support.

For the second edition, I want to thank Peter Magnusson, Greg D'alesandre, Tom Van Waardhuizen, Mike Aizatsky, Wesley Chun, Johan Euphrosine, Alfred Fuller, Andrew Gerrand, Sebastian Kreft, Moishe Lettvin, John Mulhausen, Robert Schuppenies, David Symonds, and Eric Willigers.

Substantial effort was required to separate the original book into two books. My thanks to Mike Fotinakis for reviewing the Python version, and to Amy Unruh and Mark Combellack for reviewing the Java version.

Thanks also to Sahala Swenson, Steven Hines, David McLaughlin, Mike Winton, Andres Ferrate, Dan Morrill, Mark Pilgrim, Steffi Wu, Karen Wickre, Jane Penner, Jon Murchinson, Tom Stocky, Vic Gundotra, Bill Coughran, and Alan Eustace.

At O'Reilly, I'd like to thank Michael Loukides, Meghan Blanchette, and Brian Anderson for giving me this opportunity and helping me see it through to the end, three times over.

I dedicate this book to Google's site reliability engineers. It is they who carry the pagers, so we don't have to. We are forever grateful.

## CHAPTER 1

Introducing Google App Engine

Google App Engine is a web application hosting service. By "web application," we mean an application or service accessed over the Web, usually with a web browser: storefronts with shopping carts, social networking sites, multiplayer games, mobile applications, survey applications, project management, collaboration, publishing, and all the other things we're discovering are good uses for the Web. App Engine can serve traditional website content too, such as documents and images, but the environment is especially designed for real-time dynamic applications. Of course, a web browser is merely one kind of client: web application infrastructure is well suited to mobile applications, as well.

In particular, Google App Engine is designed to host applications with many simultaneous users. When an application can serve many simultaneous users without degrading performance, we say it *scales*. Applications written for App Engine scale automatically. As more people use the application, App Engine allocates more resources for the application and manages the use of those resources. The application itself does not need to know anything about the resources it is using. x Unlike traditional web hosting or self-managed servers, with Google App Engine, you only pay for the resources you use. Billed resources include CPU usage, storage per month, incoming and outgoing bandwidth, and several resources specific to App Engine services. To help you get started, every developer gets a certain amount of resources for free, enough for small applications with low traffic.

App Engine is part of Google Cloud Platform, a suite of services for running scalable applications, performing large amounts of computational work, and storing, using, and analyzing large amounts of data. The features of the platform work together to host applications efficiently and effectively, at minimal cost. App Engine's specific role on the platform is to host web applications and scale them automatically. App Engine apps use the other services of the platform as needed, especially for data storage.

An App Engine web application can be described as having three major parts: application instances, scalable data storage, and scalable services. In this chapter, we look at each of these parts at a high level. We also discuss features of App Engine for deploying and managing web applications, and for building websites integrated with other parts of Google Cloud Platform.

The Runtime Environment

An App Engine application responds to web requests. A web request begins when a client, typically a user's web browser, contacts the application with an HTTP request, such as to fetch a web page at a URL. When App Engine receives the request, it identifies the application from the domain name of the address, either a custom domain name you have registered and configured for use with the app, or an *.appspot.com* subdomain provided for free with every app. App Engine selects a server from many possible servers to handle the request, making its selection based on which server is most likely to provide a fast response. It then calls the application with the content of the HTTP request, receives the response data from the application, and returns the response to the client.

From the application's perspective, the runtime environment springs into existence when the request handler begins, and disappears when it ends. App Engine provides several methods for storing data that persists between requests, but these mechanisms live outside of the runtime environment. By not retaining state in the runtime environment between requests—or at least, by not expecting that state will be retained between requests—App Engine can distribute traffic among as many servers as it needs to give every request the same treatment, regardless of how much traffic it is handling at one time.

In the complete picture, App Engine allows runtime environments to outlive request handlers, and will reuse environments as much as possible to avoid unnecessary initialization. Each instance of your application has local memory for caching imported code and initialized data structures. App Engine creates and destroys instances as needed to accommodate your app's traffic. If you enable the multithreading feature, a single instance can handle multiple requests concurrently, further utilizing its resources.

Application code cannot access the server on which it is running in the traditional sense. An application can read its own files from the filesystem, but it cannot write to files, and it cannot read files that belong to other applications. An application can see environment variables set by App Engine, but manipulations of these variables do not necessarily persist between requests. An application cannot access the networking facilities of the server hardware, although it can perform networking operations by using services.

In short, each request lives in its own "sandbox." This allows App Engine to handle a request with the server that would, in its estimation, provide the fastest response. For web requests to the app, there is no way to guarantee that the same app instance will handle two requests, even if the requests come from the same client and arrive relatively quickly.

Sandboxing also allows App Engine to run multiple applications on the same server without the behavior of one application affecting another. In addition to limiting access to the operating system, the runtime environment also limits the amount of clock time and memory a single request can take. App Engine keeps these limits flexible, and applies stricter limits to applications that use up more resources to protect shared resources from "runaway" applications.

A request handler has up to 60 seconds to return a response to the client. While that may seem like a comfortably large amount for a web app, App Engine is optimized for applications that respond in less than a second. Also, if an application uses many CPU cycles, App Engine may slow it down so the app isn't hogging the processor on a machine serving multiple apps. A CPU-intensive request handler may take more clock time to complete than it would if it had exclusive use of the processor, and clock time may vary as App Engine detects patterns in CPU usage and allocates accordingly.

Google App Engine provides four possible runtime environments for applications, one for each of four programming languages: Java, Python, PHP, and Go. The environment you choose depends on the language and related technologies you want to use for developing the application.

The Python environment runs apps written in the Python 2.7 programming language, using a custom version of CPython, the official Python interpreter. App Engine invokes a Python app using WSGI, a widely supported application interface standard. An application can use most of Python's large and excellent standard library, as well as rich APIs and libraries for accessing services and modeling data. Many open source Python web application frameworks work with App Engine, such as Django, web2py, Pyramid, and Flask. App Engine even includes a lightweight framework of its own, called webapp.

Similarly, the Java, PHP, and Go runtime environments offer standard execution environments for those languages, with support for standard libraries and third-party frameworks.

All four runtime environments use the same application server model: a request is routed to an app server, an application instance is initialized (if necessary), application code is invoked to handle the request and produce a response, and the response is returned to the client. Each environment runs application code within sandbox restrictions, such that any attempt to use a feature of the language or a library that would require access outside of the sandbox returns an error.

You can configure many aspects of how instances are created, destroyed, and initialized. How you configure your app depends on your need to balance monetary cost against performance. If you prefer performance to cost, you can configure your app to run many instances and start new ones aggressively to handle demand. If you have a limited budget, you can adjust the limits that control how requests queue up to use a minimum number of instances.

I haven't said anything about which operating system or hardware configuration App Engine uses. There are ways to figure this out with a little experimentation, but in the end it doesn't matter: the runtime environment is an abstraction *above* the operating system that allows App Engine to manage resource allocation, computation, request handling, scaling, and load distribution without the application's involvement. Features that typically require knowledge of the operating system are either provided by services outside of the runtime environment, provided or emulated using standard library calls, or restricted in sensible ways within the definition of the sandbox.

Everything stated above describes how App Engine allocates application instances dynamically to scale with your application's traffic. In addition to a flexible bank of instances serving your primary traffic, you can organize your app into multiple "modules." Each module is addressable individually using domain names, and can be configured with its own code, performance characteristics, and scaling pattern— including the option of running a fixed number of always-on instances, similar to traditional servers. In practice, you usually use a bank of dynamically scaling instances to handle your "frontend" traffic, then establish modules as "backends" to be accessed by the frontends for various purposes.

The Static File Servers

Most websites have resources they deliver to browsers that do not change during the regular operation of the site. The images and CSS files that describe the appearance of the site, the JavaScript code that runs in the browser, and HTML files for pages without dynamic components are examples of these resources, collectively known as *static files*. Because the delivery of these files doesn't involve application code, it's unnecessary and inefficient to serve them from the application servers.

Instead, App Engine provides a separate set of servers dedicated to delivering static files. These servers are optimized for both internal architecture and network topology to handle requests for static resources. To the client, static files look like any other resource served by your app.

You upload the static files of your application right alongside the application code. You can configure several aspects of how static files are served, including the URLs for static files, content types, and instructions for browsers to keep copies of the files in a cache for a given amount of time to reduce traffic and speed up rendering of the page.

Frontend Caches

All App Engine traffic goes through a set of machines that know how to cache responses to requests. If a response generated by the app declares that another request with the same parameters should return the same response, the frontend cache stores the response for a period of time. If another matching request comes in, the cache returns the stored response without invoking the application. The resources conserved by exploiting frontend caches can be significant.

App Engine recognizes standard HTTP controls for proxy caches. Do a web search for "HTTP cache control" for more information (Cache-Control, Expires). By default, responses from an app have Cache-Control set to no-cache.

The static file servers can also be configured to serve specific cache controls. These are described by a configuration file. (More on that later.)

Cloud Datastore

Most useful web applications need to store information during the handling of a request for retrieval during a later request. A typical arrangement for a small website involves a single database server for the entire site, and one or more web servers that connect to the database to store or retrieve data. Using a single central database server makes it easy to have one canonical representation of the data, so multiple users accessing multiple web servers all see the same and most recent information. But a central server is difficult to scale once it reaches its capacity for simultaneous connections.

By far the most popular kind of data storage system for web applications in the past two decades has been the relational database, with tables of rows and columns arranged for space efficiency and concision, and with indexes and raw computing power for performing queries, especially "join" queries that can treat multiple related records as a queryable unit. Other kinds of data storage systems include hierarchical datastores (filesystems, XML databases) and object databases. Each kind of database has pros and cons, and which type is best suited for an application depends on the nature of the application's data and how it is accessed. And each kind of database has its own techniques for growing past the first server.

Google Cloud Platform offers several kinds of data storage you can use with an App Engine app, including a relational database (Google Cloud SQL). Most scalable apps use Google Cloud Datastore, or as it is known to App Engine veterans, simply "the datastore."[1] The datastore most closely resembles an object database. It is not a join-query relational database, and if you come from the world of relational database-backed web applications (as I did), this will probably require changing the way you think about your application's data. As with the runtime environment, the design of the App Engine datastore is an abstraction that allows App Engine to handle the details of distributing and scaling the application, so your code can focus on other things.

 If it turns out the scalable datastore does not meet your needs for complex queries, you can use Google Cloud SQL, a full-featured relational database service based on MySQL. Cloud SQL is a feature of Google Cloud Platform, and can be called directly from App Engine using standard database APIs. The trade-off comes from how you intend to scale your application. A Cloud SQL instance behaves like a single MySQL database server, and can get bogged down by traffic. Cloud Datastore scales automatically: with proper data design, it can handle as many simultaneous users as App Engine's server instances can.

Entities and Properties

With Cloud Datastore, an application stores its data as one or more datastore *entities*. An entity has one or more *properties*, each of which has a name, and a value that is of one of several primitive value types. Each entity is of a named *kind*, which categorizes the entity for the purpose of queries.

At first glance, this seems similar to a relational database: entities of a kind are like rows in a table, and properties are like columns (fields). However, there are two major differences between entities and rows. First, an entity of a given kind is not required to have the same properties as other entities of the same kind. Second, an entity can have a property of the same name as another entity has, but with a different type of value. In this way, datastore entities are "schemaless." As you'll soon see, this design provides both powerful flexibility as well as some maintenance challenges.

Another difference between an entity and a table row is that an entity can have multiple values for a single property. This feature is a bit quirky, but can be quite useful once understood.

Every datastore entity has a unique key that is either provided by the application or generated by App Engine (your choice). Unlike a relational database, the key is not a

---

1 Historically, the datastore was a feature exclusive to App Engine. Today it is a full-fledged service of Google Cloud Platform, and can be accessed from Compute Engine VMs and from apps outside of the platform using a REST API. App Engine apps can access Cloud Datastore using the App Engine datastore APIs and libraries.

"field" or property, but an independent aspect of the entity. You can fetch an entity quickly if you know its key, and you can perform queries on key values.

An entity's key *cannot* be changed after the entity has been created. The entity's kind is considered part of its key, so the kind cannot be changed either. App Engine uses the entity's key to help determine where the entity is stored in a large collection of servers. (No part of the key guarantees that two entities are stored on the same server, but you won't need to worry about that anyway.)

Queries and Indexes

A datastore query returns zero or more entities of a single kind. It can also return just the keys of entities that would be returned for a query. A query can filter based on conditions that must be met by the values of an entity's properties, and can return entities ordered by property values. A query can also filter and sort using keys.

In a typical relational database, queries are planned and executed in real time against the data tables, which are stored just as they were designed by the developer. The developer can also tell the database to produce and maintain indexes on certain columns to speed up certain queries.

Cloud Datastore does something dramatically different. *Every* query has a corresponding index maintained by the datastore. When the application performs a query, the datastore finds the index for that query, locates the first row that matches the query, then returns the entity for each consecutive row in the index until the first row that doesn't match the query.

Of course, this requires that Cloud Datastore know ahead of time which queries the application is going to perform. It doesn't need to know the values of the filters in advance, but it does need to know the kind of entity to query, the properties being filtered or sorted, and the operators of the filters and the orders of the sorts.

Cloud Datastore provides a set of indexes for simple queries by default, based on which properties exist on entities of a kind. For more complex queries, an app must include index specifications in its configuration. The App Engine developer tools help produce this configuration file by watching which queries are performed as you test your application with the provided development web server on your computer. When you upload your app, the datastore knows to make indexes for every query the app performed during testing. You can also edit the index configuration manually.

When your application creates new entities and updates existing ones, the datastore updates every corresponding index. This makes queries very fast (each query is a simple table scan) at the expense of entity updates (possibly many tables may need updating for a single change). In fact, the performance of an index-backed query is not affected by the number of entities in the datastore, only the size of the result set.

It's worth paying attention to indexes, as they take up space and increase the time it takes to update entities. We discuss indexes in detail in Chapter 7.

Transactions

When an application has many clients attempting to read or write the same data simultaneously, it is imperative that the data always be in a consistent state. One user should never see half-written data or data that doesn't make sense because another user's action hasn't completed.

When an application updates the properties of a single entity, Cloud Datastore ensures that either every update to the entity succeeds all at once, or the entire update fails and the entity remains the way it was prior to the beginning of the update. Other users do not see any effects of the change until the change succeeds.

In other words, an update of a single entity occurs in a *transaction*. Each transaction is *atomic*: the transaction either succeeds completely or fails completely, and cannot succeed or fail in smaller pieces.

An application can read or update multiple entities in a single transaction, but it must tell Cloud Datastore which entities will be updated together when it creates the entities. The application does this by creating entities in *entity groups*. Cloud Datastore uses entity groups to control how entities are distributed across servers, so it can guarantee a transaction on a group succeeds or fails completely. In database terms, the datastore natively supports *local transactions*.

When an application calls the datastore API to update an entity, the call returns only after the transaction succeeds or fails, and it returns with knowledge of success or failure. For updates, this means the service waits for all entities to be updated before returning a result. The application can call the datastore asynchronously, such that the app code can continue executing while the datastore is preparing a result. But the update itself does not return until it has confirmed the change.

If a user tries to update an entity while another user's update of the entity is in progress, the datastore returns immediately with a contention failure exception. Imagine the two users "contending" for a single piece of data: the first user to commit an update wins. The other user must try her operation again, possibly rereading values and calculating the update from fresh data. Contention is expected, so retries are common. In database terms, Cloud Datastore uses *optimistic concurrency control*: each user is "optimistic" that her commit will succeed, so she does so without placing a lock on the data.

Reading the entity never fails due to contention. The application just sees the entity in its most recent stable state. You can also read multiple entities from the same entity group by using a transaction to ensure that all the data in the group is current and consistent with itself.

In most cases, retrying a transaction on a contested entity will succeed. But if an application is designed such that many users might update a single entity, the more popular the application gets, the more likely users will get contention failures. It is important to design entity groups to avoid a high rate of contention failures even with a large number of users.

It is often important to read and write data in the same transaction. For example, the application can start a transaction, read an entity, update a property value based on the last read value, save the entity, and then commit the transaction. In this case, the save action does not occur unless the entire transaction succeeds without conflict with another transaction. If there is a conflict and the app wants to try again, the app should retry the entire transaction: read the (possibly updated) entity again, use the new value for the calculation, and attempt the update again. By including the read operation in the transaction, the datastore can assume that related writes and reads from multiple simultaneous requests do not interleave and produce inconsistent results.

With indexes and optimistic concurrency control, Cloud Datastore is designed for applications that need to read data quickly, ensure that the data it sees is in a consistent form, and scale the number of users and the size of the data automatically. While these goals are somewhat different from those of a relational database, they are especially well suited to web applications.

The Services

The datastore's relationship with the runtime environment is that of a service: the application uses an API to access a separate system that manages all its own scaling needs separately from application instances. Google Cloud Platform and App Engine include several other self-scaling services useful for web applications.

The memory cache (or *memcache*) service is a short-term key-value storage service. Its main advantage over the datastore is that it is fast—much faster than the datastore for simple storage and retrieval. The memcache stores values in memory instead of on disk for faster access. It is distributed like the datastore, so every request sees the same set of keys and values. However, it is not persistent like the datastore: if a server goes down, such as during a power failure, memory is erased. It also has a more limited sense of atomicity and transactionality than the datastore. As the name implies, the memcache service is best used as a cache for the results of frequently performed queries or calculations. The application checks for a cached value, and if the value isn't there, it performs the query or calculation and stores the value in the cache for future use.

Google Cloud Platform provides another storage service specifically for very large values, called Google Cloud Storage.[2] Your app can use Cloud Storage to store, manage, and serve large files, such as images, videos, or file downloads. Cloud Storage can also accept large files uploaded by users and offline processes. This service is distinct from Cloud Datastore to work around infrastructure limits on request and response sizes between users, application servers, and services. Application code can read values from Cloud Storage in chunks that fit within these limits. Code can also query for metadata about Cloud Storage values.

For when you really need a relational database, Google Cloud SQL provides full-featured MySQL database hosting. Unlike Cloud Datastore or Cloud Storage, Cloud SQL does not scale automatically. Instead, you create *SQL instances*, virtual machines running managed MySQL software. Instances are large, and you only pay for the storage you use and the amount of time an instance is running. You can even configure instances to turn themselves off when idle, and reactivate when a client attempts to connect. Cloud SQL can be the basis for an always-on web app, or a part of a larger data processing solution.

Yet another storage service is dedicated to providing full-text search infrastructure, known simply as the Search service.[3] As Cloud Datastore stores entities with properties, the Search service stores *documents* with *fields*. Your app adds documents to *indexes*. Unlike the datastore, you can use the Search service to perform faceted text searches over the fields of the documents in an index, including partial string matches, range queries, and Boolean search expressions. The service also supports stemming and tokenization.

App Engine applications can access other web resources using the URL Fetch service. The service makes HTTP requests to other servers on the Internet, such as to retrieve pages or interact with web services. Because remote servers can be slow to respond, the URL Fetch API supports fetching URLs in the background while a request handler does other things, but in all cases the fetch must start and finish within the request handler's lifetime. The application can also set a deadline, after which the call is canceled if the remote host hasn't responded.

App Engine applications can send email messages using the Mail service. The app can send email on behalf of the application itself or on behalf of the user who made the request that is sending the email (if the message is from the user). Many web applications use email to notify users, confirm user actions, and validate contact information.

---

2 An earlier version of this service was known as App Engine's "Blobstore" service. Both Blobstore and Cloud Storage are still available, with similar features. For new projects, prefer Cloud Storage. See the book's website (*http://www.dansanderson.com/appengine*) for a free bonus chapter about the Blobstore service.

3 The Search service is currently exclusive to App Engine.

An application can also receive email messages. If an app is configured to receive email, a message sent to the app's address is routed to the Mail service, which delivers the message to the app in the form of an HTTP request to a request handler.

App Engine applications can send and receive instant messages to and from chat services that support the XMPP protocol. An app sends an XMPP chat message by calling the XMPP service. As with incoming email, when someone sends a message to the app's address, the XMPP service delivers it to the app by calling a request handler.

You can accomplish real-time two-way communication directly with a web browser using the Channel service, a clever implementation of the Comet model of browser app communication. Channels allow browsers to keep a network connection open with a remote host to receive real-time messages long after a web page has finished loading. App Engine fits this into its request-based processing model by using a service: browsers do not connect directly to application servers, but instead connect to "channels" via a service. When an application decides to send a message to a client (or set of clients) during its normal processing, it calls the Channel service with the message. The service handles broadcasting the message to clients, and manages open connections. Paired with web requests for messages from clients to apps, the Channel service provides real-time browser messaging without expensive polling. App Engine includes a JavaScript client so your code in the browser can connect to channels.

Google Accounts, OpenID, and OAuth

App Engine integrates with Google Accounts, the user account system used by Google applications such as Google Mail, Google Docs, and Google Calendar. You can use Google Accounts as your app's user authentication system, so you don't have to build your own. And if your users already have Google accounts, they can sign in to your app using their existing accounts, with no need to create new accounts just for your app.

Google Accounts is especially useful for developing applications for your company or organization using Google Apps for Work (or Google Apps for Education). With Google Apps, your organization's members can use the same account to access your custom applications as well as their email, calendar, and documents. You can add your App Engine application to a subdomain of your Apps domain from your Google Apps dashboard, just like any other Google Apps feature.

Of course, there is no obligation to use Google Accounts. You can always build your own account system, or use an OpenID provider. App Engine includes special support for using OpenID providers in some of the same ways you can use Google Accounts. This is useful when building applications for the Google Apps Marketplace, which uses OpenID to integrate with enterprise single sign-on services.

App Engine includes built-in support for OAuth, a protocol that makes it possible for users to grant permission to third-party applications to access personal data in another service, without having to share their account credentials with the third party. For instance, a user might grant a mobile phone application access to her Google Calendar account, to read appointment data and create new appointments on her behalf. App Engine's OAuth support makes it straightforward to implement an OAuth service for other apps to use. Note that the built-in OAuth feature only works when using Google Accounts, not OpenID or a proprietary identity mechanism.

There is no special support for implementing an OAuth client in an App Engine app, but most OAuth client libraries work fine with App Engine. For Google services and APIs, the easiest way is to use the Google APIs Client Libraries, which are known to run from App Engine and are available for many languages.

Google Cloud Endpoints

APIs are an essential part of the modern Web. It is increasingly common for browser-based web applications to be implemented as rich JavaScript clients: the user's first visit downloads the client code to the browser, and all subsequent interactions with the server are performed by structured web requests issued by the JavaScript code (as XMLHttpRequests, or XHRs). Nonbrowser clients for web apps, especially native mobile apps running on smartphones and tablets, are also increasingly important. Both kinds of clients tend to use REST (Representational State Transfer) APIs provided by the web app, and tend to need advanced features such as OAuth for authenticating calls.

To address this important need, Google Cloud Platform provides a service and a suite of tools called Google Cloud Endpoints. Endpoints make it especially easy for a mobile or rich web client to call methods on the server. Endpoints includes libraries and tools for generating server functionality from a set of methods in Python and Java, and generating client code for Android, iOS, and browser-based JavaScript. The tools can also generate a "discovery document" that works with the Google APIs Client Libraries for many client languages. And OAuth support is built in, so you don't have to worry about authentication and can just focus on the application logic.

Task Queues and Cron Jobs

A web application must respond to web requests very quickly, usually in less than a second and preferably in just a few dozen milliseconds, to provide a smooth experience to the user sitting in front of the browser. This doesn't give the application much time to do work. Sometimes there is more work to do than there is time to do it. In such cases, it's usually OK if the work gets done within a few seconds, minutes, or hours, instead of right away, as the user is waiting for a response from the server. But the user needs a guarantee that the work will get done.

For this kind of work, an App Engine app uses *task queues*. Task queues let you describe work to be done at a later time, outside the scope of the web request. Queues ensure that every task gets done eventually. If a task fails, the queue retries the task until it succeeds.

There are two kinds of task queues: push queues and pull queues. With push queues, each task record represents an HTTP request to a request handler. App Engine issues these requests itself as it processes a push queue. You can configure the rate at which push queues are processed to spread the workload throughout the day. With pull queues, you provide the mechanism, such as a custom computational engine, that takes task records off the queue and does the work. App Engine manages the queuing aspect of pull queues.

A push queue performs a task by calling a request handler. It can include a data payload provided by the code that created the task, delivered to the task's handler as an HTTP request. The task's handler is subject to the same limits as other request handlers, with one important exception: a single task handler can take as long as 10 minutes to perform a task, instead of the 60-second limit applied to user requests. It's still useful to divide work into small tasks to take advantage of parallelization and queue throughput, but the higher time limit makes tasks easier to write in straightforward cases.

An especially powerful feature of task queues is the ability to enqueue a task within a Cloud Datastore transaction, when called via App Engine. This ensures that the task will be enqueued only if the rest of the datastore transaction succeeds. You can use transactional tasks to perform additional datastore operations that must be consistent with the transaction eventually, but that do not need the strong consistency guarantees of the datastore's local transactions. For example, when a user asks to delete a bunch of records, you can store a receipt of this request in the datastore and enqueue the corresponding task in a single transaction. If the transaction fails, you can report this to the user, and rest assured that neither the receipt nor the task are in the system.

App Engine has another service for executing tasks at specific times of the day: the scheduled tasks service. Scheduled tasks are also known as "cron jobs," a name borrowed from a similar feature of the Unix operating system. The scheduled tasks service can invoke a request handler at a specified time of the day, week, or month, based on a schedule you provide when you upload your application. Scheduled tasks are useful for doing regular maintenance or sending periodic notification messages.

We'll look at task queues, scheduled tasks, and some powerful uses for them in Chapter 16.

Namespaces

Cloud Datastore, Cloud Storage, memcache, Search, and task queues all store data for an app. It's often useful to partition an app's data across all services. For example, an app may be serving multiple companies, where each company sees its own isolated instance of the application, and no company should see any data that belongs to any other company. You could implement this partitioning in the application code, using a company ID as the prefix to every key. But this is prone to error: a bug in the code may expose or modify data from another partition.

To better serve this case, these storage services provide this partitioning feature at the infrastructure level. An app can declare it is acting in a *namespace* by calling an API. All subsequent uses of any of the data services will restrict itself to the namespace automatically. The app does not need to keep track of which namespace it is in after the initial declaration.

The default namespace has a name equal to the empty string. This namespace is distinct from other namespaces. (There is no "global" namespace.) In the services that support it, all data belongs to a namespace.

Developer Tools

Google provides a rich set of tools and libraries for developing for Cloud Platform and App Engine. The main tool suite is the Cloud SDK, which, among other things, includes a package installer and updater for the other tools. You will use this installer to acquire the App Engine SDK for Python, and other components you might need. If you're using Windows or Mac OS X, you can also get a windowed "launcher" application that offers many common tasks for App Engine developers in an easy-to-use visual app. All of the tools are scriptable, so you can integrate them into deployment scripts and other parts of your development environment.

One of the most useful parts of the SDK is the development web server. This tool runs your application on your local computer and simulates the runtime environment and services. The development server automatically detects changes in your source files and reloads them as needed, so you can keep the server running while you develop the application.

The development server's simulated datastore can automatically generate configuration for query indexes as the application performs queries, which App Engine will use to prebuild indexes for those queries. You can turn this feature off to test that queries have appropriate indexes in the configuration.

The development web server includes a built-in browser-based developer console for inspecting and prodding your app. You use this console to inspect and modify the contents of the simulated data storage services, manage task queue interactions, and simulate nonweb events such as incoming email messages.

You also use the toolkit to interact with App Engine directly, especially to deploy your application and run it on Cloud Platform. You can download log data from your live application, and manage the live application's datastore indexes and service configuration.

With a provided library, you can add a feature to your application that lets you access the running app's environment programmatically. This is useful for building administrative tools, uploading and downloading data, and even running a Python interactive prompt that can operate on live data.

But wait, there's more! The SDK also includes libraries for automated testing, and for gathering reports on application performance. We'll cover one such tool, AppStats, in Chapter 17.

The Cloud Console

When your application is ready for its public debut, you create a *project*, then deploy your app's code to the project using a tool in the Cloud SDK. The project contains everything related to your app, including your App Engine code, data in all of Cloud Platform's data services, any Compute Engine VMs you might create with the app, and project-related settings and permissions. All of this is managed in a browser-based interface known as the Google Developers Console, or just "Cloud Console."

You sign in to the Cloud Console using your Google account. You can use your current Google account if you have one. You may also want to create a Google account just for your application, which you might use as the "from" address on email messages. Once you have created a project in Cloud Console, you can add additional Google accounts to the project. Each account has one of three possible roles: *owners* can change settings and manage permissions for other accounts, *editors* can change settings (but not permissions), and *viewers* can read (but not change) settings and project information.

The Console gives you access to real-time performance data about how your application is being used, as well as access to log data emitted by your application. You can query Cloud Datastore and other data services for the live application by using a web interface, and check on the status of datastore indexes and other features.

When you upload new code for your application, the uploaded version is assigned a version identifier, which you specify in the application's configuration file. The version used for the live application is whichever major version is selected as the "default." You control which version is the "default" by using the Cloud Console. You can access nondefault versions by using a special URL containing the version identifier. This allows you to test a new version of an app running on App Engine before making it official.

You use the Console to set up and manage the billing account for your application. When you're ready for your application to consume more resources beyond the free amounts, you set up a billing account using a credit card and Google Accounts. The owner of the billing account sets a *budget*, a maximum amount of money that can be charged per calendar day. Your application can consume resources until your budget is exhausted, and you are only charged for what the application actually uses beyond the free amounts.

Getting Started

You can start developing applications for Google App Engine without creating an account. All you need to get started is the Cloud SDK, which is a free download from the Cloud Platform website:

https://cloud.google.com/sdk/

For a brief guided tour of creating an App Engine app with some sample code, see this quick-start guide (sign-in required):

https://console.developers.google.com/start/appengine

And while you're at it, be sure to bookmark the official App Engine documentation, which includes tutorials, articles, and reference guides for all of App Engine's features:

https://cloud.google.com/appengine/

In the next chapter, we'll describe how to create a new project from start to finish, including how to create an account, upload the application, and run it on App Engine.

## CHAPTER 2

Creating an Application

The App Engine development model is as simple as it gets:

1. Create the application.
2. Test the application on your own computer by using the web server software included with the App Engine development kit.
3. Deploy the finished application to App Engine.

In this chapter, we'll walk through the process of creating a new application, testing it with the development server, registering a new project ID with Google Cloud Platform, setting up a domain name, and uploading the app to App Engine. We'll look at some of the features of the Python software development kit (SDK) and the Cloud Console. We'll also discuss the workflow for developing and deploying an app.

We will take this opportunity to demonstrate a common pattern in web applications: managing user preferences data. This pattern uses several App Engine services and features.

Setting Up the Cloud SDK

To develop an App Engine app in Python, you need several unsurprising things on your local computer:

- Python, version 2.7.x
- Your favorite programming text editor or IDE for Python
- The Google Cloud SDK

The Google Cloud SDK is a collection of tools and libraries for developing, testing, and deploying software for the Cloud Platform, including App Engine. The centerpiece of the suite is the gcloud command, a multifunction tool which you use to install and update components, perform deployment and maintenance tasks, and otherwise interact with Cloud Platform as an administrator. The App Engine component provides tools for running your app locally on your computer for testing, and for deploying the app. The Cloud SDK works on any platform that can run Python, including Windows, Mac OS X, and Linux.

The development server and app maintenance features are all available through command-line tools. You can use these tools from a command prompt or otherwise integrate them into your development environment as you see fit. For example, it's common to automate the deployment process with scripts that run the deployment tool and manage application versions and testing.

On Windows and Mac OS X, you can install a "launcher" application that makes it especially easy to create, edit, test, and upload an app, using a simple graphical interface. Paired with a good programming text editor (such as Notepad++ for Windows, or Sublime Text for Mac OS X), the launcher provides a fast and intuitive Python development experience.

Some professional Python IDEs, such as JetBrains PyCharm, have built-in support for creating App Engine applications, and provide another alternative to the command line for invoking the App Engine SDK tools.

In the next few sections, we'll install the Cloud SDK and components related to Python app development.

Installing Python

The App Engine SDK for the Python runtime environment is compatible with any computer that runs Python 2.7. If you are using Mac OS X or Linux, or if you have used Python previously, you may already have Python on your system. You can test whether Python is installed on your system and check which version is installed by running the following command at a command prompt (in Windows, Command Prompt; in Mac OS X, Terminal):

```
python -V
```

(That's a capital "V.") If Python is installed, it prints its version number, like so:

```
Python 2.7.5
```

You can download and install Python 2.7 for your platform from the Python website (*https://www.python.org/*).

Be sure to get Python version 2.7 (such as 2.7.8) from the Downloads section of the site. As of this writing, the latest major version of Python is 3.4, and the latest 2.x-compatible release is 2.7.[1]

 App Engine Python does not yet have a dedicated Python 3 runtime environment. Python 3 includes several new language and library features that are not backward compatible with earlier versions. As we'll see in a minute, you specify the runtime environment for your application using configuration, so your app always runs with the same major version of Python, even as new major versions become available.

Installing the Cloud SDK

There are several easy ways to install the Cloud SDK, depending on your operating system and personal preferences.

For Windows, visit the Cloud SDK website, select the Windows installation instructions, then click the "Download" button:

https://cloud.google.com/sdk/

Run *GoogleCloudSDKInstaller.exe* and follow the instructions. By default, the installer puts the SDK in *C:\Program Files\Google\Cloud SDK*, and offers to create appropriate shortcuts on the desktop. One of these shortcuts, the Google Cloud SDK Shell, opens a command prompt with its command lookup path amended to include the Cloud SDK commands.

For Mac OS X or Linux, open a command prompt and run the following command:

```
curl https://sdk.cloud.google.com | bash
```

This downloads the Cloud SDK archive, unpacks it, and runs an interactive installation routine. If you'd rather invoke these steps manually, you can download the archive from the Cloud SDK website. The installation routine is this shell script: `./google-cloud-sdk/install.sh`.

Either way you do it, the result is a *google-cloud-sdk* directory, which you can put in a convenient place. The installation script attempts to add the Cloud SDK commands to your command prompt's search path by amending your environment. If you're using a shell other than `bash`, you may need to finish this step manually. You can

---

1 If you're developing an old App Engine Python application using Python 2.5, you can continue to do so. However, you will need Python 2.7 to run the Cloud SDK tools. Your Python 2.5 code will work with the Python 2.7 interpreter locally. Upgrading to the Python 2.7 runtime environment is strongly recommended.

always invoke the Cloud SDK commands using their full path in the *google-cloud-sdk* directory.

Close and reopen your command prompt to pick up the changes to the command search path.

On all platforms, confirm that the SDK was installed successfully by running the gcloud command like so:

```
gcloud -h
```

The command will print some help text describing its various features. If instead the command prompt reports that the command is not found, double-check that the SDK is on the command path. In Windows, this is set up by the "SDK Shell," or the *cloud_env.bat* script in the main SDK folder. In Mac OS X and Linux, make sure you have restarted your command prompt to pick up the environment changes to your shell startup scripts, and that the *google-cloud-sdk/bin* directory is on your search path.

The Cloud SDK politely keeps all of its stuff in the *google-cloud-sdk* directory. To uninstall it, simply delete the directory, and undo the command search path modifications.

Authenticating with the Cloud SDK

Before doing anything else, run this command:

```
gcloud auth login
```

This opens a browser window for the Google authentication sequence. Sign in using your Google account (or register for a free account if you don't have one yet), then authorize the Google Cloud SDK to access Cloud services on your behalf.

The gcloud command remembers the authentication credentials it receives and uses them with subsequent commands that you run from your computer. To revoke these credentials (to "sign out" of gcloud), run this command:

```
gcloud auth revoke
```

You can use gcloud auth login to sign in with multiple accounts. Credentials for all accounts are remembered until revoked, and you can switch between them without signing in again. To add an account, simply gcloud auth login again with the new account. To list all accounts with stored credentials and see which account is currently active:

```
gcloud auth list
```

To switch the active account to another one with stored credentials:

```
gcloud config set account your.email@gmail.com
```

Installing the App Engine SDK

The Cloud SDK installation process already asked you if you wanted to install an App Engine SDK. If you answered in the affirmative and requested the App Engine SDK for "Python and PHP," then you're all set. (The Python SDK and the PHP SDK are the same component.)

If you have not yet installed the App Engine SDK for Python, you can do so with this command:

```
gcloud components update gae-python
```

You can test that the App Engine SDK is installed by running the following command:

```
dev_appserver.py --help
```

You will use the `dev_appserver.py` command to start a local development server running a test version of your app. With the `--help` argument, the command simply prints help text and exits.

Windows users, if when you run this command, a dialog box opens with the message "Windows cannot open this file... To open this file, Windows needs to know what program created it," you must tell Windows to use Python to open the file. In the dialog box, choose "Select the program from a list," and click OK. Click Browse, then locate your Python installation (such as *C:\Python27*). Select *python* from this folder, then click Open. Select "Always use the selected program to open this kind of file." Click OK. A window will open and attempt to run the command, then immediately close. You can now run the command from the Command Prompt.

You use the `gcloud components` command to install, update, and manage the various components of the Cloud SDK. To see a list of all available components and which ones are installed, run this command:

```
gcloud components list
```

To update all components that need updating:

```
gcloud components update
```

Developing the Application

It's time to write our first App Engine application!

So what is an App Engine app? An App Engine app is software that responds to web requests. It does so by calling *request handlers*, routines that accept request parameters and return responses. App Engine determines which request handler to use for a given request from the request's URL, using a configuration file included with the app that maps URLs to handlers.

An app can also include static files, such as images, CSS stylesheets, and browser Java-Script. App Engine serves these files directly to clients in response to requests for corresponding URLs without invoking any code. The app's configuration specifies which of its files are static, and which URLs to use for those files.

The application configuration includes metadata about the app, such as its project ID and version number. When you deploy the app to App Engine, all of the app's files, including the code, configuration files, and static files, are uploaded and associated with the project ID and version number mentioned in the configuration. An app can also have configuration files specific to the services, such as for datastore indexes, task queues, and scheduled tasks. These files are associated with the app in general, not a specific version of the app.

In the next few sections, we create the files needed for a simple application, and look at how to use the tools and libraries included with the SDK.

The User Preferences Pattern

The application we create in this section is a simple clock. When a user visits the site, the app displays the current time of day according to the server's system clock. By default, the app shows the current time in the Coordinated Universal Time (UTC) time zone. The user can customize the time zone by signing in using Google Accounts and setting a preference.

This app demonstrates three App Engine features:

- The datastore, primary storage for data that is persistent, reliable, and scalable
- The memory cache (or *memcache*), secondary storage that is faster than the datastore, but is not necessarily persistent in the long term
- Google Accounts, the ability to use Google's user account system for authenticating and identifying users

Google Accounts works similarly to most user account systems. If the user is not signed in to the clock application, she sees a generic view with default settings (the UTC time zone) and a link to sign in or create a new account. If the user chooses to sign in or register, the application directs her to a sign-in form managed by Google Accounts. Signing in or creating an account redirects the user back to the application.

Of course, you can implement your own account mechanism instead of using Google Accounts. Using Google Accounts has advantages and disadvantages—the chief advantage being that you don't have to implement your own account mechanism. If a user of your app already has a Google account, the user can sign in with that account without creating a new account for your app.

If the user accesses the application while signed in, the app loads the user's preferences data and uses it to render the page. The app retrieves the preferences data in two steps. First, it attempts to get the data from the fast secondary storage, the memory cache. If the data is not present in the memory cache, the app attempts to retrieve it from the primary storage (the datastore), and if successful, it puts it into the memory cache to be found by future requests.

This means that for most requests, the application can get the user's preferences from memcache without accessing the datastore. While reading from the datastore is reasonably fast, reading from the memcache is much faster and avoids the cost of a datastore call. The difference is substantial when the same data must be accessed every time the user visits a page.

Our clock application has two request handlers. One handler displays the current time of day, along with links for signing in and out. It also displays a web form for adjusting the time zone when the user is signed in. The second request handler processes the time zone form when it is submitted. When the user submits the preferences form, the app saves the changes and redirects the browser back to the main page.

The application gets the current time from the application server's system clock. It's worth noting that App Engine makes no guarantees that the system clocks of all its web servers are synchronized. Because two requests for this app may be handled by different servers, different requests may see different clocks. The server clock is not consistent enough as a source of time data for a real-world application, but it's good enough for this example.

A Simple App

The simplest Python application for App Engine is a single directory with two files: a configuration file named *app.yaml*, and a file of Python code for a request handler. The directory containing the *app.yaml* file is the application root directory. You'll refer to this directory often when using the tools.

Create a directory named *clock* to contain the project. Using your favorite text editor, create a file inside this directory named *app.yaml* similar to Example 2-1.

Example 2-1. The app.yaml configuration file for a simple application, using the Python 2.7 runtime environment

```
application: clock
version: 1
runtime: python27
api_version: 1
threadsafe: yes

handlers:
- url: .*
```

```
script: main.application

libraries:
- name: webapp2
  version: "2.5.2"
```

This configuration file is in a format called YAML, an open format for configuration files and network messages. You don't need to know much about the format beyond what you see here.

In this example, the configuration file tells App Engine that this is version 1 of an application called `clock`, which uses version 1 (`api_version`) of the Python 2.7 runtime environment. Every request for this application (every URL that matches the regular expression `.*`, which is all of them) is to be handled by an application object defined in the `application` variable of a Python module named `main`.

Next, create a file named *main.py* similar to Example 2-2, in the same directory as *app.yaml*.

Example 2-2. A simple Python web application, using the webapp2 framework

```
import datetime
import webapp2

class MainPage(webapp2.RequestHandler):
    def get(self):
        message = '<p>The time is: %s</p>' % datetime.datetime.now()
        self.response.out.write(message)

application = webapp2.WSGIApplication([('/', MainPage)],
                                     debug=True)
```

This simple Python web application uses a web application framework called "webapp2," which is included with App Engine. This framework conforms to a common standard for Python web application frameworks known as the Web Server Gateway Interface (WSGI). You don't need to know much about WSGI, except that it's a Python standard, there are many useful frameworks to choose from, and it's easy to port a WSGI application to other application hosting environments using various adapters (such as a WSGI-to-CGI adapter). webapp2 is a simple example of a WSGI framework. Django, a popular open source web app framework for Python that's also included with App Engine, is another.

We'll walk through this example in a moment, but first, let's get it running. From a command prompt, run the `dev_appserver.py` command, specifying the path to the project directory (*clock*) as an argument:

```
dev_appserver.py clock
```

If your current working directory is the *clock* directory you just created, you can run the command using a dot (.) as the path to the project:

```
dev_appserver.py .
```

Test your application by visiting the server's URL in a web browser:

http://localhost:8080/

The browser displays a page similar to Figure 2-1.

Figure 2-1. The first version of the clock application viewed in a browser

You can leave the web server running while you develop your application. The web server notices when you make changes to your files, and reloads them automatically as needed.

The server starts up and prints several messages to the console. You can safely ignore warnings that say things like "Could not initialize images API." These are expected if you have followed the installation steps so far. The last message should look something like this:

```
INFO ... Starting module "default" running at: http://localhost:8080
INFO ... Starting admin server at: http://localhost:8000
```

This message indicates the server started successfully. If you do not see this message, check the other messages for hints, and double-check that the syntax of your *app.yaml* file is correct.

Introducing the webapp Framework

App Engine's Python 2.7 runtime environment uses WSGI as the interface between your application and the server instance running the application. Typically, you would not write the code that implements this interface. Instead, you would use a *framework*, a suite of libraries and tools that form an easy way to think about building web applications and perform common web tasks.

There are dozens of web frameworks written in Python, and several are mature, well documented, and have active developer communities. Django, Flask, web2py, and Pyramid are examples of well-established Python web frameworks that work well with App Engine. We'll discuss how to use Django with App Engine in Chapter 18.

The webapp2 framework is intended to be small and easy to use. It doesn't have the features of more established frameworks, but it's good enough for small projects. For simplicity, most of the Python examples in this book use the webapp2 framework. We'll introduce some of its features here.

Let's take a closer look at our simple web application, line by line:

```
import datetime
import webapp2
```

This loads the libraries we intend to use in the main module. We use datetime to get the system time for our clock. The webapp2 framework is in the webapp2 module:

```
class MainPage(webapp2.RequestHandler):
    def get(self):
        message = '<p>The time is: %s</p>' % datetime.datetime.now()
        self.response.out.write(message)
```

webapp2 applications consist of one or more *request handlers*, units of code mapped to URLs or URL patterns that are executed when a client (or other process) requests a URL. As we saw earlier, the first URL mapping takes place in *app.yaml*, which associates the request URL with its WSGI application object in a Python module. The webapp2 application maps this to a RequestHandler class.

To produce the response, webapp2 instantiates the class and then calls a method of the class that corresponds to the HTTP method of the request. When you type a URL into your browser's address bar, the browser uses the HTTP GET method with the request, so webapp2 calls the get() method of the request handler. Similarly, when you submit a web form, the browser uses the HTTP POST method, which would attempt to call a post() method.

The code can access the request data and produce the response data, using attributes of the instance. In this case, we prepared a response string (message), then used the output stream of the response attribute to write the message. You can also use the response attribute to set response headers, such as to change the content type. (Here, we leave the content type at its default of text/html.)

```
application = webapp2.WSGIApplication([('/', MainPage)],
                                       debug=True)
```

The application module global variable contains the object that represents the WSGI application. This value is created when the main module is imported for the first time, and stays in memory for the lifetime of the application instance. (App Engine creates and destroys application instances as needed to serve your app's traffic. More on that later.) App Engine knows which module and variable to use based on the mapping in the *app.yaml* file.

The application object is an instance of the WSGIApplication class provided by the webapp2 module. The constructor is called with two values. The first is a list of URL pattern and RequestHandler class pairs. When the application is called to handle a request, the URL is tested against each pattern in the order it appears in the list. The first to match wins. The URL pattern is a regular expression.

In this case, our application simply maps the root URL path (/) to MainPage. If the application is asked to handle any other URL path (any path that doesn't match), webapp2 serves an HTTP 404 error page. Notice that the *app.yaml* file maps all URL paths to this application, effectively putting webapp2 in charge of serving 404 errors. (If a URL does not match any pattern in *app.yaml*, App Engine serves its own 404 error.)

The WSGIApplication constructor is also given a debug=True parameter. This tells webapp2 to print detailed error messages to the browser when things go wrong. webapp2 knows to only use this in the development server, and to disable this feature when it is running on App Engine, so you can just leave it turned on.

A single WSGIApplication instance can handle multiple URLs, routing the request to different RequestHandler classes based on the URL pattern. But we've already seen that the *app.yaml* file maps URL patterns to handler scripts. So which URL patterns should appear in *app.yaml*, and which should appear in the WSGIApplication? Many web frameworks include their own URL dispatcher logic, and it's common to route all dynamic URLs to the framework's dispatcher in *app.yaml*. With webapp2, the answer mostly depends on how you'd like to organize your code. For the clock application, we will create a second request handler as a separate script to take advantage of a feature of *app.yaml* for user authentication, but we could also put this logic in *main.py* and route the URL with the WSGIApplication object.

Templates, Users, and Google Accounts

So far, our clock shows the same display for every user. To allow users to customize the display and save their preferences for future sessions, we need a way to identify the user making a request. An easy way to do this is with Google Accounts, aka the Users service.

Before we make the user interface of our app more elaborate, let's introduce a templating system to manage our HTML. Mixing markup and code for the browser in your server-side code gets messy fast. It's nearly always better to use a library that can represent the user interface code separately from your app code, using templates. The app code calls the templating system to fill in the blanks with dynamic data and render the result.

For this example, we'll use the Jinja2 templating system. Jinja2 is an open source templating system written in Python, based on the templating system included with the Django web application framework. App Engine will provide this library to your app if you request it in the *app.yaml* file.

Edit *app.yaml*, and add these lines to the libraries: section near the bottom:

```
libraries:
# ...
- name: jinja2
  version: "2.6"
- name: markupsafe
  version: "0.15"
```

The libraries: section of *app.yaml* tells App Engine to add certain Python libraries to the runtime environment when it runs the app. We used this feature to request version 2.5.2 of webapp2. These new lines add Jinja2 (and its related library markupsafe) to the environment. App Engine supports a short but useful list of third-party libraries in this way, so you do not have to add the library to your application code.

To run your app locally, you must have these libraries installed. For historical reasons, webapp2 is provided for us by the App Engine SDK, but Jinja2 is not, so we must install it in the local development environment. App Engine does not include every library in the SDK because it would have to include every supported version of every library, and that could get large.

There are several ways to install Python packages. Your Python installation may already have the `easy_install` command, and if it doesn't, you can get it by downloading and installing setuptools (*https://pypi.python.org/pypi/setuptools*). A newer more featureful alternative is pip (*https://pip.pypa.io/*). Both `easy_install` and `pip` get packages from the Python Package Index (PyPi) and install them in your Python installation's *site-packages* collection.

To install Jinja2 (and its helper package `markupsafe`) using `pip`:

```
pip install jinja2 markupsafe
```

In Mac OS X or Linux, if you're installing these packages in the system's main Python installation, you must run this command via `sudo` and enter an administrative password when prompted:

```
sudo pip install jinja2 markupsafe
```

Windows users, there is a `pip.exe` command you can add to your command path (in *C:\Python27\Scripts*), but you can also just invoke it with the `python` command:

```
python -m pip install jinja2 markupsafe
```

Let's add something to our app's home page that indicates whether the user is signed in, and provides links for signing in and signing out of the application. Edit *main.py* to resemble Example 2-3.

Example 2-3. A version of main.py that invites the user to sign in with Google Accounts, using a Jinja2 template

```python
import datetime
import jinja2
import os
import webapp2

from google.appengine.api import users

template_env = jinja2.Environment(
    loader=jinja2.FileSystemLoader(os.getcwd()))

class MainPage(webapp2.RequestHandler):
    def get(self):
        current_time = datetime.datetime.now()
        user = users.get_current_user()
        login_url = users.create_login_url(self.request.path)
        logout_url = users.create_logout_url(self.request.path)

        template = template_env.get_template('home.html')
        context = {
            'current_time': current_time,
            'user': user,
            'login_url': login_url,
```

```
            'logout_url': logout_url,
        }
        self.response.out.write(template.render(context))

application = webapp2.WSGIApplication([('/', MainPage)],
                                     debug=True)
```

Next, create a new file in the same directory named *home.html*, and edit it to resemble Example 2-4. This is the Jinja2 template.

Example 2-4. The HTML template for the home page, using the Jinja2 template system

```
<html>
  <head>
    <title>The Time Is...</title>
  </head>
  <body>
  {% if user %}
    <p>
      Welcome, {{ user.email() }}!
      You can <a href="{{ logout_url }}">sign out</a>.
    </p>
  {% else %}
    <p>
      Welcome!
      <a href="{{ login_url }}">Sign in or register</a> to customize.
    </p>
  {% endif %}
    <p>The time is: {{ current_time }}</p>
  </body>
</html>
```

Reload the page in your browser. The new page resembles Figure 2-2.

We've added a few new things to *main.py*:

```
import jinja2
import os

# ...

from google.appengine.api import users
```

You import the Jinja2 library the same way you would with a typical installation on your computer. The libraries: section of *app.yaml* puts Jinja2 on the library search path when running on App Engine.

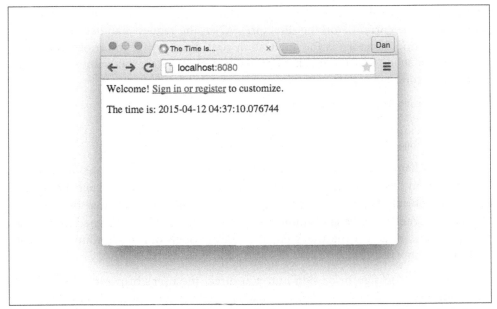

Figure 2-2. The clock app with a link to Google Accounts when the user is not signed in

We also import the os module to use in the next part, as well as the API for the Users service:

```
template_env = jinja2.Environment(
    loader=jinja2.FileSystemLoader(os.getcwd()))
```

One way to configure Jinja2 is with an Environment object. This object maintains aspects of the template system that are common across your app. In this case, we use the Environment to declare that our template files are loaded from the filesystem, using the FileSystemLoader.

We store the Jinja2 Environment object in a module global variable because we only need to create this object once in the lifetime of the application instance. As with the WSGIApplication object, the constructor is called when the module is imported, and the object stays resident in memory.

 Remember that we've turned on concurrent requests using the threadsafe: true line in *app.yaml*. This tells App Engine to use one instance to process multiple requests simultaneously. These requests will share global module variables, and may interleave instructions. This is fine for most common read-only uses of global variables, such as configuration data, compiled regular expressions, or the Jinja2 Environment object.

The os.getcwd() value passed to the FileSystemLoader constructor tells it to find templates in the current working directory. When the request handler is called, the current working directory is the application root directory. If you move your templates into a subdirectory (and that's probably a good idea), this value needs to be modified accordingly:

```
current_time = datetime.datetime.now()
user = users.get_current_user()
login_url = users.create_login_url(self.request.path)
logout_url = users.create_logout_url(self.request.path)
```

The request handler code calls the Users service API by using functions in the users module from the google.appengine.api package. users.get_current_user() returns an object of class users.User that represents the user making the request if the user is signed in, or None (Python's null value) if the user is not signed in. You can use this value to access the user's email address, which our application does from within the template.

To allow a user to sign in or sign out, you direct the user's browser to the Google Accounts system "login" or "logout" URLs. The app gets these URLs using the users.create_login_url() and users.create_logout_url() functions, respectively. These functions take a URL path for your application as an argument. Once the user has signed in or signed out successfully, Google Accounts redirects the user back to your app using that URL path. For this app, we direct the user to sign in or sign out by presenting her with links to click. (In other situations, redirecting the user might be more appropriate.)

```
template = template_env.get_template('home.html')
context = {
    'current_time': current_time,
    'user': user,
    'login_url': login_url,
    'logout_url': logout_url
}
self.response.out.write(template.render(context))
```

Here, we load the *home.html* template, set the dynamic data in the template's "context," render the template with the context values into the text of the page, and finally write it to the response.

Within the template, we use a conditional section to display a different welcome message depending on whether the user is signed in or not. `{% if user %}` is true if the context value we set to `'user'` is considered true in Python, which it would be if `users.get_current_user()` returned a `User` object. The `{% else %}` and `{% endif %}` directives delimit the sections of the template to render, based on the condition. `{{ user.email() }}` calls the `email()` method of the object, and interpolates its return value into the template as a string. Similarly, `{{ logout_url }}`, `{{ login_url }}`, and `{{ current_time }}` interpolate the generated URLs we set in the context.

 For more information about Jinja2 template syntax and features, see the Jinja2 website (*http://jinja.pocoo.org/*).

If you click the "Sign in or register" link with the app running in the development server, the link goes to the development server's simulated version of the Google Accounts sign-in screen, as shown in Figure 2-3. At this screen, you can enter any email address, and the development server will proceed as if you are signed in with an account that has that address.

If this app were running on App Engine, the login and logout URLs would go to the actual Google Accounts locations. Once signed in or out, Google Accounts redirects back to the given URL path for the live application.

Click "Sign in or register," then click the Login button on the simulated Google Accounts screen, using the default test email address (*test@example.com*). The clock app now looks like Figure 2-4. To sign out again, click the "sign out" link.

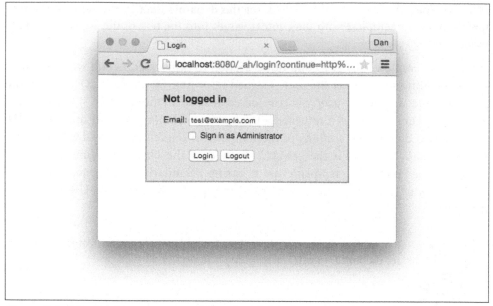

Figure 2-3. The development server's simulated Google Accounts sign-in screen

Using Python Virtual Environments

When we installed the Jinja2 library earlier, we added it directly to the collection of libraries available to Python on our local computer. This is convenient for writing software that's meant to be run on your local computer, but not so convenient when writing software that will be run elsewhere. It can be tricky to keep track of all of the packages your software depends on, and ensure that those packages are installed—or can be installed—in the environment where the software is to run. And if two projects depend on different versions of a package, your computer's site packages are no help, because they can only contain one at a time.

The App Engine development server is smart about isolating your app under test from packages you have installed locally that won't be available in the live runtime environment. If we didn't specify `jinja2` in the `libraries:` region of *app.yaml*, the `import jinja2` statement would have failed in the development server even if we had the `jinja2` package installed. Similarly, importing a module that's installed locally but would not otherwise be available on App Engine will fail locally.

Figure 2-4. The clock app, with the user signed in

This is great, but it isn't a complete solution. App Engine lets you request a specific version of a library in *app.yaml*, and when your app is running on App Engine, exactly that version will be loaded. In the development server, the requested version is ignored, and it just imports whatever you have installed. If your app needs Django 1.3 but you have Django 1.5 installed, the development server will use Django 1.5, no matter what *app.yaml* says. If you're developing multiple projects on your computer and two projects need different versions of the same library, site packages are insufficient.

The solution is to use a *virtual environment*. A virtual environment is a Python environment that is isolated from your main Python installation's site packages. The environment starts out clean, as if you installed Python for the first time. You can add libraries to the virtual environment, and these will not affect the main Python installation. And you can install different versions of the same libraries in different environments. These environments are "virtual" because they share the same Python interpreter and standard library as your main installation, and use tools to manipulate the Python library load path to isolate your app.

Virtual environments are a good practice for Python development in general, and App Engine in particular. Let's take a quick look at how to use them.

To get started, install the `virtualenv` library in your main Python installation:

```
pip install virtualenv
```

As before, Mac OS X and Linux users will need `sudo pip install virtualenv` to install this to the system's Python, and Windows users may prefer `python -m pip install virtualenv`.

Installing this package adds the `virtualenv` command to your system. In Mac OS X and Linux, this is typically at */usr/local/bin/virtualenv*. In Windows, it's *C:\Python27\Scripts\virtualenv.exe*, or you can use `python -m virtualenv`.

A virtual environment lives in a new directory. To create a new virtual environment, change the current working directory to where you want this new environment directory to live, then run the `virtualenv` command with a name for the new environment:

```
virtualenv myapp_env
```

The command creates the directory and populates it with tools and its own *site-packages* directory. To use the environment, you *activate* it. The process is only slightly different between Mac OS X/Linux and Windows.

In Mac OS X or Linux, you use the shell's `source` directive for this, like so:

```
source ./myapp_env/bin/activate
```

Similarly, in Windows, you activate a virtual environment with the `activate.bat` script that `virtualenv` created in the environment's *Scripts* directory:

```
myapp_env\Scripts\activate.bat
```

The command prompt changes to include the name of the active environment, like so:

```
(myapp_env)~/
```

While the environment is active, the environment's *bin/* directory (or *Scripts* directory in Windows) is at the beginning of your command path. This includes special versions of `python`, `easy_install`, and `pip` that know how to use the virtual environment. If you use any of these commands at the prompt, you'll be using these environment-specific versions.

Let's do so now. Use `pip` to install Jinja2, like we did earlier:

```
pip install jinja2 markupsafe
```

Mac and Linux users, notice that `sudo` is not necessary as it was before, because we're modifying our own environment, not the system-wide Python installation.

You can now start the development server from the command line as usual, and it will use the virtual environment for its libraries:

```
dev_appserver.py clock
```

In addition to taking package names on the command line, `pip` can read a list of packages to install from a *requirements file*. This is a simple text file that lists the packages to install. It can also request specific versions of the packages. For example, say you had a file named *requirements.txt* with the following contents:

```
jinja2==2.6
markupsafe==0.15
```

To install the modules listed in this file, pass the filename to `pip install` using the `-r` flag:

```
pip install -r requirements.txt
```

Using a requirements file that matches the `libraries:` section of *app.yaml* makes it easy for you and other members of your team to set up a virtual environment that looks exactly like the App Engine runtime environment for the app. Store this file in your source control repository with the rest of your code.

To deactivate the environment and restore your command path, run the `deactivate` command:

```
deactivate
```

To use a third-party library that is *not* provided by the runtime environment, you must add the library to your application directory along with your application files. This only works with "pure Python" libraries, and not libraries that depend on natively compiled extensions. You can use `pip` to install these libraries as well, but notice the key difference. Here, we used `pip` to install libraries in a local virtual environment to emulate what App Engine provides. When you install a library into your app directory, you are adding the library's Python code files to the app itself. These files are uploaded to App Engine along with your app code.

To install a library into your app directory, use the `-t` flag with a path to a subdirectory that will contain it. It's a good idea to reserve a *lib/* directory in the app root for this purpose:

```
pip install -t lib WTForms WTForms-Appengine
```

This creates the *lib/* directory if needed, downloads the library packages, then installs them. Once completed, *lib/* contains directories ending in *-info/* that are only used during installation. You can delete these to reduce the number of files that get uploaded. The installed libraries reside in separate directories (such as *lib/wtforms*).

To use these libraries, you must add the *lib/* directory to the module lookup path. Put this at the top of each module that contains request handler code:

```
import sys
sys.path.append('lib')
```

With this directory on the lookup path, you can import these libraries in the usual way (such as `import wtforms`).

Datastore Models and Web Forms

Now that we know who the user is, we can ask her for her preferred time zone, remember her preference, and use it on future visits.

First, we need a way to remember the user's preferences so future requests can access them. The Google Cloud Datastore provides reliable, scalable storage for this purpose. The Python API includes a data modeling interface that maps Python objects to datastore entities. We can use it to write a `UserPrefs` class.

Create a new file named *models.py*, as shown in Example 2-5.

Example 2-5. The file models.py, with a class for storing user preferences in the datastore

```
from google.appengine.api import users
from google.appengine.ext import ndb

class UserPrefs(ndb.Model):
    tz_offset = ndb.FloatProperty(default=0.0)
    user = ndb.UserProperty(auto_current_user_add=True)

def get_userprefs(user_id=None):
    if not user_id:
        user = users.get_current_user()
        if not user:
            return None
        user_id = user.user_id()

    key = ndb.Key('UserPrefs', user_id)
    userprefs = key.get()
    if not userprefs:
        userprefs = UserPrefs(id=user_id)
    return userprefs
```

The Python data modeling interface is provided by the module `ndb` in the package `google.appengine.ext`. A data model is a class whose base class is `ndb.Model`. The model subclass defines the structure of the data in each object by using class properties. This structure is enforced by `ndb.Model` when values are assigned to instance properties. For our `UserPrefs` class, we define two properties: `tz_offset`, a floating-point number of hours to offset UTC, and user, a User object returned by the Google Accounts API.

Every datastore entity has a primary key. Unlike a primary key in a relational database table, an entity key is permanent and can only be set when the entity is created. A key is unique across all entities in the system, and consists of several parts, including the entity's kind (in this case, UserPrefs). An app can set one component of the key to an arbitrary value, known in the API as the *key name*.

The clock application uses the user's unique ID, provided by the user_id() method of the User object, as the key name of a UserPrefs entity. This allows the app to fetch the entity by key, as it knows the user's ID from the Google Accounts API. Fetching the entity by key is faster than performing a datastore query.

In *models.py*, we define a function named get_userprefs() that gets the UserPrefs object for the user. After determining the user ID, the function constructs a datastore key for an entity of the kind UserPrefs with a key name equivalent to the user ID. If the entity exists in the datastore, the function returns the UserPrefs object.

If the entity does not exist in the datastore, the function creates a new UserPrefs object with default settings and a key name that corresponds to the user. The new object is *not* saved to the datastore automatically. The caller must invoke the put() method on the UserPrefs instance to save it.

Now that we have a mechanism for getting a UserPrefs object, we can make two upgrades to the main page. If the user is signed in, we can get the user's preferences (if any) and adjust the clock's time zone.

Edit *main.py*. With the other import statements, import the models module we just created:

```
import models
```

In the request handler code, call the models.get_userprefs() function, and use the return value to adjust the current_time value. Also, add the userprefs value to the template context:

```
class MainPage(webapp2.RequestHandler):
    def get(self):
        # ...
        userprefs = models.get_userprefs()

        if userprefs:
            current_time += datetime.timedelta(
                0, 0, 0, 0, 0, userprefs.tz_offset)

        template = template_env.get_template('home.html')
        context = {
            # ...
```

```
                  'userprefs': userprefs,
              }
              self.response.out.write(template.render(context))
```

Let's also add a web form to the template so the user can set a time zone preference. You'll need to edit *home.html*, adding the following near the bottom of the template, above the </body>:

```
{% if user %}
  <form action="/prefs" method="post">
    <label for="tz_offset">
      Timezone offset from UTC (can be negative):
    </label>
    <input name="tz_offset" id="tz_offset" type="text"
      size="4" value="{{ userprefs.tz_offset }}" />
    <input type="submit" value="Set" />
  </form>
{% endif %}
```

To enable the preferences form, we need a new request handler to parse the form data and update the datastore. Let's implement this as a new request handler module. (We'll see why in a moment.)

Create a file named *prefs.py* with the contents shown in Example 2-6.

Example 2-6. A new handler module, prefs.py, for the preferences form

```
import webapp2

import models

class PrefsPage(webapp2.RequestHandler):
    def post(self):
        userprefs = models.get_userprefs()
        try:
            tz_offset = float(self.request.get('tz_offset'))
            userprefs.tz_offset = tz_offset
            userprefs.put()
        except ValueError:
            # User entered a value that wasn't a float.  Ignore for now.
            pass

        self.redirect('/')

application = webapp2.WSGIApplication([('/prefs', PrefsPage)],
                                     debug=True)
```

This request handler handles HTTP POST requests to the URL /prefs, which is the URL ("action") and HTTP method used by the form. Because it's an HTTP POST action, the code goes in the post() method (instead of the get() method used in *main.py*). The handler code calls the get_userprefs() function from *models.py* to get the UserPrefs object for the current user, which is either a new unsaved object with default values, or the object for an existing entity. The handler parses the tz_offset parameter from the form data as a float, sets the property of the UserPrefs object, then saves the object to the datastore by calling its put() method. The put() method creates the object if it doesn't exist, or updates the existing object.

If the user enters something other than a floating-point number in the form field, we don't do anything. It'd be appropriate to return an error message, but we'll leave this as is to keep the example simple.

The form handler redirects the user's browser to the / URL. In webapp2, the self.redirect() method takes care of setting the appropriate response headers for redirecting the browser.

Finally, as shown in Example 2-7, edit *app.yaml* to map the handler module to the URL /prefs in the handlers: section.

Example 2-7. A new version of app.yaml mapping the URL /prefs, with login required

```
application: clock
version: 1
runtime: python27
api_version: 1
threadsafe: true

handlers:
- url: /prefs
  script: prefs.application
  login: required

- url: .*
  script: main.application

libraries:
- name: webapp2
  version: "2.5.2"
- name: jinja2
  version: "2.6"
- name: markupsafe
  version: "0.15"
```

The login: required line says that the user must be signed in to Google Accounts to access the /prefs URL. If the user accesses the URL while not signed in, App Engine automatically directs the user to the Google Accounts sign-in page, then redirects her back to this URL afterward. This makes it easy to require sign-in for sections of your site, and to ensure that the user is signed in before the request handler is called.

Be sure to put the /prefs URL mapping before the .* mapping. URL patterns are tried in order, and the first pattern to match determines the handler used for the request. Because the pattern .* matches all URLs, /prefs must come first or it will be ignored.

Reload the page to see the customizable clock in action. Try changing the time zone by submitting the form. Also try signing out, then signing in again using the same email address, and again with a different email address. The app remembers the time zone preference for each user.

The Development Server Console

The development server has a handy feature for inspecting and debugging your application while testing on your local machine: a web-based console. With your development server running, visit the following URL in a browser to access the console:

http://localhost:8000/

(This is the same as the server URL, with a different port number: 8000.)

When the development server console opens for the first time, the Instances panel is shown. At first, only one instance is running locally. The development server is multithreaded, and can simulate an app running with multiple instances on App Engine.

In the left navigation, select datastore viewer. This lets you inspect and manipulate the local simulated instance of Cloud Datastore being used by your app. If you completed and tested the clock app described in this chapter, there should be at least one entity in the viewer, showing its field data and other information. Figure 2-5 shows the datastore viewer in this state.

The Datastore Viewer lets you list and inspect entities by kind, edit entities, and create new ones. You can edit the values for existing properties, but you cannot delete properties or add new ones, nor can you change the type of the value. For new entities, the console makes a guess as to which properties belong on the entity based on existing entities of that kind, and displays a form to fill in those properties. Similarly, you can only create new entities of existing kinds, and cannot create new kinds from the console.

The development server console includes features for managing other aspects of the simulated environment, such as task queues and messaging. We'll look at these when we discuss the corresponding services.

Figure 2-5. The development server console with the datastore viewer selected

Caching with Memcache

The code that gets user preferences data in Example 2-5 calls the `key.get()` method to fetch the `UserPrefs` entity every time a signed-in user visits the site. User preferences are often read and seldom changed, so calling the datastore with every request is more expensive than it needs to be. We can mitigate the cost of reading from primary storage by using a caching layer, secondary storage that's faster to read than the datastore, but less permanent.

We can use the memory cache service (*memcache*) as secondary storage for user preferences data. Using memcache with the datastore this way is so common for App Engine apps, the `ndb` library can do this automatically, and does it by default. We do not need to change our code at all to take advantage of this feature.

To see our app use memcache, open the development server console, then select Memcache Viewer. If you have already tried storing a time zone preference, the console reports that the cache has one item in it. Click the Flush Cache button, and confirm that you want to delete everything from the cache. In a new tab, visit the app in the development server. If you already have a preference stored in the datastore, the app loads it again, and stores it in memcache for future quick reference. (If you don't have a preference stored, store one now.) Go back to the memcache viewer and reload. Memcache once again contains an item, the cached version of the UserPrefs object.

The ndb library knows to delete the object in the cache whenever it updates the object in the datastore. This keeps fresh data in the cache. However, this behavior is not guaranteed. Memcache and the datastore are separate services, and it is possible for the update to the datastore to succeed and the delete from memcache to fail. In this case, memcache has stale data. To mitigate the problem this may cause, memcache only retains values for a limited amount of time. You can adjust the maximum amount of time it will retain a value. You can also disable ndb's use of memcache completely.

Later, in Chapter 9, we'll discuss ndb's use of memcache in detail. In Chapter 12, we'll see how to call the memcache service directly, such as for storing the results of computation or network access.

The Python Interactive Console

An especially useful feature exclusive to the Python development server is the Interactive Console. This feature lets you type arbitrary Python code directly into a web form and see the results displayed in the browser. You can use this to write ad hoc Python code to test and manipulate the datastore, memcache, and global data within the local development server.

Here's an example: run your clock application, sign in with an email address, and then set a time zone preference, such as -8. Now open the development server console, then select Interactive Console. In the lefthand text box, enter the following, where -8 is the time zone preference you used:

```
import models

q = models.UserPrefs.gql("WHERE tz_offset = -8")

for prefs in q:
    print prefs.user
```

Click the Execute button. The code runs, and the email address you used appears below.

Code run in the development server console behaves just like application code. If you perform a datastore query that needs a custom index, the development server adds configuration for that index to the application's *index.yaml* configuration file. Datastore index configuration is discussed in Chapter 7.

Registering the Application

Before you can upload your application to App Engine and share it with the world, you must first register a project ID. It's time to introduce the Cloud Console.

To access the Cloud Console, visit the following URL in your browser, signing in with your Google account if necessary:

https://console.developers.google.com/

Bookmark or memorize this URL, as you'll be back here frequently once your app is live. The Cloud Console is home base for all of your cloud projects.

The home screen lists all of your current projects (if any), and gives you access to your Cloud-related account settings and billing information.[2]

It costs nothing to create a project. You can have up to 25 free projects per Google account, and you can delete projects later. You can have an unlimited number of paid applications. Note that you will be reserving a unique ID when you create a project, and IDs for deleted projects cannot be reclaimed.

In the Projects section, click the Create Project button. When prompted, enter a project name. The Console generates a unique project ID for you, but you can change it to something more memorable if you like. As we're about to see, the ID is used in test URLs and a few other places. If you intend to register a domain name for your web application, you will not need to show your project ID to your users.[3] You cannot change the ID after the project has been created (but you can delete the project and create a new one). Click Create to create the project.

Uploading the Application

In a traditional web application environment, releasing an application to the world can be a laborious process. Getting the latest software and configuration to multiple web servers and backend services in the right order and at the right time to minimize downtime and prevent breakage is often a difficult and delicate process. With App Engine, deployment is as simple as uploading the files with a single click or com-

---

2 The descriptions and screenshots of the Google Developers Console in this book are current as of the time this material was produced. Google improves the Console continuously, and some descriptions may be out of date by the time you read this. Such is life.

3 As of this writing, there is one obscure feature that does not yet support custom domains: incoming XMPP messages. I'm not aware of another case where end users must interact with a project ID when the app has a custom domain.

mand. You can upload and test multiple versions of your application, and set any uploaded version to be the current public version.

Edit your *app.yaml* configuration file, and replace the `application:` value with the project ID you registered in the previous step:

```
application: saucy-boomerang-123
```

From a command prompt, run the `appcfg.py` command as follows, substituting the path to your application directory for *clock*:

```
appcfg.py update clock
```

As with `dev_appserver.py`, `clock` is just the path to the directory. If the current working directory is the *clock/* directory, you can use the relative path, a dot (`.`).

The `appcfg.py` tool uses your Google credentials to communicate with Google. These are the credentials you set up earlier with the `gcloud auth login` command.

 If you intend to use the `gcloud` command to access other Cloud Platform services, you can tell it to use your new project by default using this command:

```
gcloud config set project saucy-boomerang-123
```

To see all of the `gcloud` configuration fields that you can set in this way, use the following command:

```
gcloud config list
```

The upload process determines the project ID and version number from the *app.yaml* configuration file, then uploads and installs the files and configuration as the given version of the app. The app starts running on App Engine immediately.

Testing the App

Every App Engine project gets a free domain name consisting of the project ID followed by `.appspot.com`. For example, if your project ID is `saucy-boomerang-123`, you can access the app at this URL:

```
http://saucy-boomerang-123.appspot.com/
```

Visit your app's URL in a browser, and confirm that it works as expected.

Next, go back to the Cloud Console (*https://console.developers.google.com/*) and select your project. The Overview section now displays graphs representing your test traffic. Figure 2-6 shows an example.

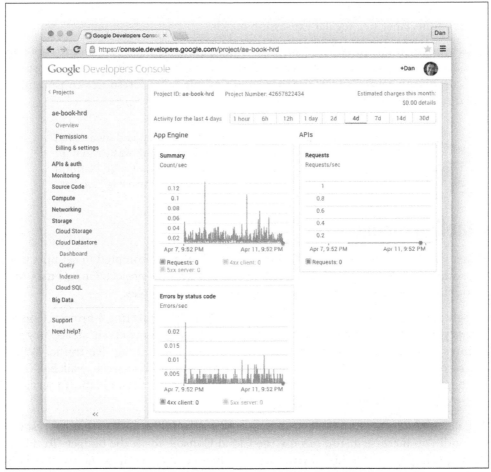

Figure 2-6. The Cloud Console overview screen for a small app (this book's website)

Navigate to Compute, then App Engine, and finally Dashboard. This dashboard shows more detailed graphs than the project overview and is specific to the App Engine part of Cloud Platform. You should see a small spike in the requests-per-second chart, referring to your test traffic. The scale of the chart goes up to the highest point in the chart, so the spike reaches the top of the graph, even though you have only accessed the application a few times.

Next, open Monitoring in the sidebar, then select the Logs panel. All requests served by App Engine are logged with details about the request and the app's response. These records also include all messages logged by the application code during the request. Click a record to expand it for more information. You can scroll up and down to attempt to load more records in either direction on the timeline. You can also filter records by log level (such as to only show requests during which your app logged errors), time, label, or a regular expression match.

Take a moment to browse the Console. Throughout this book, we discuss how an application consumes system resources, and how you can optimize an app for speed and cost effectiveness. You will use the Cloud Console to track resource consumption and diagnose problems.

 Google improves the Cloud Console continuously, and menus and buttons may have changed since the time this book was written. In particular, as features graduate from App Engine to Cloud Platform as a whole, their Console panels may relocate in the navigation bar.

Enabling Billing

When you created the project in Cloud Console, you were prompted to set up a billing account, or associate an existing billing account with the project. Google uses this account's payment information when the project accrues charges.

Google App Engine costs nothing to get started. Simply by creating a project, Google grants you a limited amount of application resources so you can create an app, try the features of the platform, and get your app working and serving live traffic. When you're ready, you can set a spending limit to make more resources available. This limit applies to all resources managed by App Engine. Other Cloud Platform services, such as Compute Engine, are billed separately.

The default budget is zero dollars, and you will not be billed for App Engine resources until you increase it. You can use the Cloud Console to set the budget. To do so, expand Compute in the sidebar nav, then App Engine, then Settings. Adjust the daily budget, then save your preferences.

## CHAPTER 3

Configuring an Application

Many of App Engine's features can be tailored and controlled using configuration files that you deploy alongside your code. A few of these features apply to the entire project's use of a service, such as datastore index configuration (which we'll cover in Chapter 7). The most important configuration file controls how App Engine manages incoming requests, how App Engine runs your code on its scalable servers, and how App Engine routes requests to your code on those servers.

To build an App Engine application, you write code for one or more *request handlers*, and provide configuration describing to App Engine which requests go to which handlers. The life of a request handler begins when a single request arrives, and ends when the handler has done the necessary work and computed the response. App Engine does all the heavy lifting of accepting incoming TCP/IP connections, reading HTTP request data, ensuring that an instance of your app is running on an application server, routing the request to an available instance, calling the appropriate request handler code in your app, and collecting the response from the handler and sending it back over the connection to the client.

The system that manages and routes requests is known generally as the App Engine *frontend*. You can configure the frontend to handle different requests in different ways. For instance, you can tell the frontend to route requests for some URLs to App Engine's static file servers instead of the application servers, for efficient delivery of your app's images, CSS, or JavaScript code. If your app takes advantage of Google Accounts for its users, you can tell the frontend to route requests from signed-in users to your application's request handlers, and to redirect all other requests to the Google Accounts sign-in screen. The frontend is also responsible for handling requests over secure connections, using HTTP over SSL/TLS (sometimes called "HTTPS," the URL scheme for such requests). Your app code only sees the request after it has been decoded, and the frontend takes care of encoding the response.

In this chapter, we take a look at App Engine's request handling architecture, and follow the path of a web request through the system. We discuss how to configure the system to handle different kinds of requests, including requests for static content, requests for the application to perform work, and requests over secure connections. We also cover other frontend features such as custom error pages, and application features you can activate called "built-ins."

We'll also take this opportunity to discuss related features that you manage from the Cloud Console, including setting up custom domain names and SSL/TLS certificates.

The App Engine Architecture

The architecture of App Engine—and therefore an App Engine application—can be summarized as shown in Figure 3-1. (There are some lines missing from this simplified diagram. For instance, frontends have direct access to Cloud Storage for serving large data objects from app URLs. We'll take a closer look at these in later chapters.)

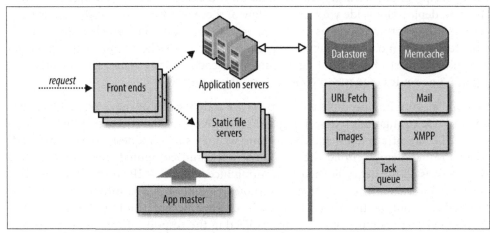

Figure 3-1. The App Engine request handling architecture

The first stop for an incoming request is the App Engine frontend. A load balancer, a dedicated system for distributing requests optimally across multiple machines, routes the request to one of many frontend servers. The frontend determines the app for which the request is intended from the request's domain name, either the associated custom domain or subdomain, or the *appspot.com* subdomain. It then consults the app's configuration to determine the next step.

The app's configuration describes how the frontends should treat requests based on their URL paths. A URL path may map to a static file that should be served to the client directly, such as an image or a file of JavaScript code. Or, a URL path may map to a request handler, application code that is invoked to determine the response for the request. You upload this configuration data along with the rest of your application.

If the URL path for a request does not match anything in the app's configuration, the frontends return an HTTP 404 Not Found error response to the client. By default, the frontends return a generic error response. If you want clients to receive a custom response when accessing your app, such as a friendly HTML message along with the error code, you can configure the frontend to serve a static HTML file. (In the case of Not Found errors, you can also just map all unmatched URL paths to an application handler, and respond any way you like.)

If the URL path of the request matches the path of one of the app's static files, the frontend routes the request to the static file servers. These servers are dedicated to the task of serving static files, with network topology and caching behavior optimized for fast delivery of resources that do not change often. You tell App Engine about your app's static files in the app's configuration. When you upload the app, these files are pushed to the static file servers.

If the URL path of the request matches a pattern mapped to one of the application's request handlers, the frontend sends the request to the app servers. The app server pool starts up an *instance* of the application on a server, or reuses an existing instance if there is one already running. The server invokes the app by calling the request handler that corresponds with the URL path of the request, according to the app configuration.

An instance is a copy of your application in the memory of an application server. The instance is isolated from whatever else is running on the machine, set up to perform equivalently to a dedicated machine with certain hardware characteristics. The code itself executes in a *runtime environment* prepared with everything the request handler needs to inspect the request data, call services, and evaluate the app's code. There's enough to say about instances and the runtime environment that an entire chapter is dedicated to the subject (Chapter 4).

You can configure the frontend to authenticate the user with Google Accounts. The frontend can restrict access to URL paths with several levels of authorization: all users, users who have signed in, and users who are application administrators. The frontend checks whether the user is signed in, and redirects the user to the Google Accounts sign-in screen if needed.

The frontend takes the opportunity to tailor the response to the client. Most notably, the frontend compresses the response data, using the gzip format, if the client gives some indication that it supports compressed responses. This applies to both app responses and static file responses, and is done automatically. The frontend uses several techniques to determine when it is appropriate to compress responses, based on web standards and known browser behaviors. If you are using a custom client that does not support compressed content, simply omit the "Accept-Encoding" request header to disable the automatic gzip behavior. Similarly, for clients that support the SPDY protocol, App Engine will use SPDY instead of HTTP 1.1, automatically and invisibly.

The frontends, app servers, and static file servers are governed by an "app master." Among other things, the app master is responsible for deploying new versions of application software and configuration, and updating the "default" version served on an app's user-facing domain. Updates to an app propagate quickly, but are not atomic in the sense that only code from one version of an app is running at any one time. If you switch the default version to new software, all requests that started before the switch are allowed to complete using their version of the software. If you have an app that makes an HTTP request to itself, you might run into a situation where an older version is calling a newer version or vice versa, but you can manage this in code if needed.

Configuring a Python App

The files for a Python application include Python code for request handlers and libraries, static files, and configuration files. On your computer, these files reside in the application root directory. Static files and application code may reside in the root directory or in subdirectories. Configuration files always reside in fixed locations in the root directory.

You configure the frontend for a Python application using a file named *app.yaml* in the application root directory. This file is in a format called YAML, a concise human-readable data format with support for nested structures like sequences and mappings.

Example 3-1 shows an example of a simple *app.yaml* file. We'll discuss these features in the following sections. For now, notice a few things about the structure of the file:

- The file is a mapping of values to names. For instance, the value `python` is associated with the name `runtime`.
- Values can be scalars (`python`, `1`), sequences of other values, or mappings of values to names. The value of `handlers` in Example 3-1 is a sequence of two values, each of which is a mapping containing two name-value pairs.
- Order is significant in sequences, but not mappings.
- YAML uses indentation to indicate scope.
- YAML supports all characters in the Unicode character set. The encoding is assumed to be UTF-8 unless the file uses a byte order mark signifying UTF-16.

- A YAML file can contain comments. All characters on a line after a # character are ignored, unless the # is in a quoted string value.

Example 3-1. An example of an app.yaml configuration file

```
application: ae-book
version: 1
runtime: python27
api_version: 1
threadsafe: true

handlers:
- url: /css
  static_dir: css

- url: /.*
  script: main.application

libraries:
- name: webapp2
  version: "2.5.2"
```

Runtime Versions

Among other things, this configuration file declares that this application (or, specifically, this version of this application) uses the Python 2.7 runtime environment. It also declares which version of the Python 2.7 runtime environment to use. Currently, there is only one version of this environment, so `api_version` is always 1. If Google ever makes changes to the runtime environment that may be incompatible with existing applications, the changes may be released using a new version number. Your app will continue to use the version of the runtime environment specified in your configuration file, giving you a chance to test your code with the new runtime version before upgrading your live application.

You specify the name and version of the runtime environment in *app.yaml*, using the `runtime` and `api_version` elements, like so:

```
runtime: python27
api_version: 1
```

Google originally launched App Engine with a runtime environment based on Python 2.5. You can use this older environment by specifying a `runtime` of `python`. Note that this book mostly covers the newer Python 2.7 environment. You'll want to use Python 2.7 for new apps, as many recent features only work with the newer environment.

App IDs and Versions

Every App Engine application has an application ID that uniquely distinguishes the app from all other applications. As described in Chapter 2, you can register an ID for a new application using the Cloud Console. Once you have an ID, you add it to the app's configuration so the developer tools know that the files in the app root directory belong to the app with that ID. This ID appears in the `appspot.com` domain name:

> `app-id.appspot.com`

The app's configuration also includes a version identifier. Like the app ID, the version identifier is associated with the app's files when the app is uploaded. App Engine retains one set of files and frontend configuration for each distinct version identifier used during an upload. If you do not change the app version in the configuration before you upload files, the upload replaces the existing files for that version.

Each distinct version of the app is accessible at its own domain name, of the following form:

> `version-id.app-id.appspot.com`

When you have multiple versions of an app uploaded to App Engine, you can use the Cloud Console to select which version is the one you want the public to access. The Console calls this the "default" version. When a user visits your custom domain or the `appspot.com` domain without the version ID, she sees the default version.

The `appspot.com` domain containing the version ID supports an additional domain part, just like the default `appspot.com` domain:

> `anything.version-id.app-id.appspot.com`

 Unless you explicitly prevent it, anyone who knows your application ID and version identifiers can access any uploaded version of your application using the `appspot.com` URLs. You can restrict access to nondefault versions of the application by using code that checks the domain of the request and only allows authorized users to access the versioned domains. You can't restrict access to static files this way.

Another way to restrict access to nondefault versions is to use Google Accounts authorization, described later in this chapter. You can restrict access to app administrators while a version is in development, then replace the configuration to remove the restriction just before making that version the default version.

All versions of an app access the same datastore, memcache, and other services, and all versions share the same set of resources. Later on, we'll discuss other configuration files that control these backend services. These files are separate from the configuration files that control the frontend because they are not specific to each app version.

There are several ways to use app versions. For instance, you can have just one version, and always update it in place. Or you can have a "dev" version for testing and a "live" version that is always the public version, and do separate uploads for each. Some developers generate a new app version identifier for each upload based on the version numbers used by a source code revision control system.

You can have up to 60 active versions, if billing is enabled for the app. You can delete previous versions, using the Cloud Console or the `appcfg.py` command.

Application IDs and version identifiers can contain numbers, lowercase letters, and hyphens.

The application ID and version identifier appear in the *app.yaml* file. The app ID is specified with the name `application`. The version ID is specified as `version`.

Here is an example of *app.yaml* using `dev` as the version identifier:

```
application: ae-book
version: dev
```

This would be accessible using this domain name:

```
http://dev.ae-book.appspot.com/
```

Multithreading

The Python 2.7 runtime environment supports handling multiple requests concurrently within each instance. This is a significant way to make the most of your instances, and is recommended. However, your code must be written with the knowledge that it will be run concurrently, and take the appropriate precautions with shared data. You must declare whether your code is "threadsafe" in your application configuration.

To set this preference, specify the `threadsafe` value in *app.yaml*, either `true` or `false`:

```
threadsafe: true
```

Request Handlers

The app configuration tells the frontend what to do with each request, routing it to either the application servers or the static file servers. The destination is determined by the URL path of the request. For instance, an app might send all requests whose URL paths start with `/images/` to the static file server, and all requests for the site's home page (the path `/`) to the app servers. The configuration specifies a list of patterns that match URL paths, with instructions for each pattern.

For requests intended for the app servers, the configuration also specifies the request handler responsible for specific URL paths. A request handler is an entry point into the application code. With the Python runtime environment, this entry point is an object that conforms to the Web Server Gateway Interface (WSGI). All Python web application frameworks provide this object for use with application containers such as App Engine.

 The URL /form is reserved by App Engine and cannot be used by the app. The explanation for this is historical and internal to App Engine, and unfortunately this is easy to stumble upon by accident. This URL will always return a 404 Not Found error.

All URL paths under /_ah/ are reserved for use by App Engine libraries and tools.

All URL paths for Python apps are described in the *app.yaml* file, using the handlers element. The value of this element is a sequence of mappings, where each item includes a pattern that matches a set of URL paths and instructions on how to handle requests for those paths. Here is an example with four URL patterns:

```
handlers:
- url: /profile/.*
  script: userprofile.application

- url: /css
  static_dir: css

- url: /info/(.*\.xml)
  static_files: datafiles/\1
  upload: datafiles/.*\.xml

- url: /.*
  script: main.application
```

The url element in a handler description is a regular expression that matches URL paths. Every path begins with a forward slash (/), so a pattern can match the beginning of a path by also starting with this character. This URL pattern matches all paths:

```
url: /.*
```

If you are new to regular expressions, here is the briefest of tutorials: the . character matches any single character, and the * character says the previous symbol, in this case any character, can occur zero or more times. There are several other characters with special status in regular expressions. All other characters, like /, match literally. So this pattern matches any URL that begins with a / followed by zero or more of any character.

If a special character is preceded by a backslash (\), it is treated as a literal character in the pattern. Here is a pattern that matches the exact path /home.html:

```
- url: /home\.html
```

See the Python documentation for the re module for an excellent introduction to regular expressions. The actual regular expression engine used for URL patterns is not Python's, but it's similar.

App Engine attempts to match the URL path of a request to each handler pattern in the order the handlers appear in the configuration file. The first pattern that matches determines the handler to use. If you use the catchall pattern /.*, make sure it's the last one in the list, as a later pattern will never match.

To map a URL path pattern to application code, you provide a script element. The value is the Python import path (with dots) to a global variable containing a WSGI application instance.[1] The application root directory is in the lookup path, so in the preceding example, main.application could refer to the application variable in a Python source file named *main.py*:

```
import webapp2

class MainPage(webapp2.RequestHandler):
    def get(self):
        # ...

application = webapp2.WSGIApplication([('/', MainPage)], debug=True)
```

If the frontend gets a request whose path matches a script handler, it routes the request to an application server to invoke the script and produce the response.

In the previous example, the following handler definition routes all URL paths that begin with /profile/ to the application defined in a source file named *userprofile.py*:

```
- url: /profile/.*
  script: userprofile.application
```

The URL pattern can use regular expression groups to determine other values, such as the script path. A group is a portion of a regular expression inside parentheses, and the group's value is the portion of the request URL that matches the characters within (not including the parentheses). Groups are numbered starting with 1 from left to right in the pattern. You can insert the value of a matched group into a script path or other values with a backslash followed by the group number (\1). For example:

---

[1] The word "script" is a misnomer: the value is a Python path to a variable. In the legacy Python 2.5 runtime environment, this is a filesystem path to a Python CGI script. The object path more accurately represents the resident WSGI app.

```
- url: /project/(.*?)/home
  script: apps.project_code.\1.app
```

With this pattern, a request for `/project/registration/home` would be handled by the WSGI application at `apps.project_code.registration.app`.

Static Files and Resource Files

Most web applications have a set of files that are served verbatim to all users, and do not change as the application is used. These can be media assets like images used for site decoration, CSS stylesheets that describe how the site should be drawn to the screen, JavaScript code to be downloaded and executed by a web browser, or HTML for full pages with no dynamic content. To speed up the delivery of these files and improve page rendering time, App Engine uses dedicated servers for static files. Using dedicated servers also means the app servers don't have to spend resources on requests for static files.

Static files are uploaded with your code when you deploy the application. This makes them well suited for web support files like images of icons, but not so well suited for content files like photos to accompany a magazine article. In most cases, content served by your web application belongs in a content management system built into your app that separates the content publishing workflow from the application deployment workflow.

Locally, static files sit with your app code in the app's root directory. You tell the deployment process and the frontend which of the application's files are static files using app configuration. The deployment process reads the configuration and delivers the static files to the dedicated static file servers. The frontend remembers which URL paths refer to static files, so it can route requests for those paths to the appropriate servers.

The static file configuration can also include a recommendation for a cache expiration interval. App Engine returns the cache instructions to the client in the HTTP header along with the file. If the client chooses to heed the recommendation (and most web browsers do), it will retain the file for up to that amount of time, and use its local copy instead of asking for it again. This reduces the amount of bandwidth used, but at the expense of clients retaining old copies of files that may have changed.

To save space and reduce the amount of data involved when setting up new app instances, static files are not pushed to the application servers. This means application code cannot access the contents of static files by using the filesystem.

The files that do get pushed to the application servers are known as "resource files." These can include app-specific configuration files, web page templates, or other static data that is read by the app but not served directly to clients. Application code can access these files by reading them from the filesystem. The code itself is also accessible this way.

We've seen how request handlers defined in the *app.yaml* file can direct requests to scripts that run on the app servers. Handler definitions can also direct requests to the static file servers.

There are two ways to specify static file handlers. The easiest is to declare a directory of files as static, and map the entire directory to a URL path. You do this with the `static_dir` element, as follows:

```
handlers:
- url: /images
  static_dir: myimgs
```

This says that all the files in the directory *myimgs/* are static files, and the URL path for each of these files is `/images/` followed by the directory path and filename of the file. If the app has a file at the path *myimgs/people/frank.jpg*, App Engine pushes this file to the static file servers, and serves it whenever someone requests the URL path `/images/people/frank.jpg`.

Notice that with `static_dir` handlers, the `url` pattern does not include a regular expression to match the subpath or filename. The subpath is implied: whatever appears in the URL path after the URL pattern becomes the subpath to the file in the directory.

The other way to specify static files is with the `static_files` element. With `static_files`, you use a full regular expression for the `url`. The URL pattern can use regular expression groups to match pieces of the path, then use those matched pieces in the path to the file. The following is equivalent to the `static_dir` handler shown earlier:

```
- url: /images/(.*)
  static_files: myimgs/\1
  upload: myimgs/.*
```

The parentheses in the regular expression identify which characters are members of the group. The `\1` in the file path is replaced with the contents of the group when looking for the file. You can have multiple groups in a pattern, and refer to each group by number in the file path. Groups are numbered in the order they appear in the pattern from left to right, where `\1` is the leftmost pattern, `\2` is the next, and so on.

When using `static_files`, you must also specify an `upload` element. This is a regular expression that matches paths to files in the application directory on your computer. App Engine needs this pattern to know which files to upload as static files, because it cannot determine this from the `static_files` pattern alone (as it can with `static_dir`).

While developing a Python app, you keep the app's static files in the application directory along with the code and configuration files. Application code files and static files are separated based on the configuration during the deployment process.

The Python SDK treats every file as either a resource file or a static file. If you have a file that you want treated as both a resource file (available to the app via the filesystem) and a static file (served verbatim from the static file servers), you can create a symbolic link in the project directory to make the file appear twice to the deployment tool under two separate names. The file will be uploaded twice, and count as two files toward the file count limit.

MIME Types

When the data of an HTTP response is of a particular type, such as a JPEG image, and the web server knows the type of the data, the server can tell the client the type of the data by using an HTTP header in the response. The type can be any from a long list of standard type names, known as MIME types. If the server doesn't say what the type of the data is, the client has to guess, and may guess incorrectly.

By default, for static files, App Engine will guess the file type based on the last few characters of the filename (such as *.jpeg*). If the filename does not end in one of several known extensions, App Engine serves the file as the MIME type `application/octet-stream`, a generic type most web browsers treat as generic binary data.

If this is not sufficient, you can specify the MIME type of a set of static files by using the `mime_type` element in the static file handler configuration. For example:

```
- url: docs/(.*)\.ps
  static_files: psoutput/\1.dat
  upload: psoutput/.*\.dat
  mime_type: application/postscript
```

This says that the application has a set of datafiles in a directory named *psoutput/* whose filenames end in *.dat*, and these should be served using URL paths that consist of `docs/`, followed by the filename with the *.dat* replaced with *.ps*. When App Engine serves one of these files, it declares that the file is a PostScript document.

You can also specify `mime_type` with a `static_dir` handler. All files in the directory are served with the declared type.

Cache Expiration

It's common for a static file to be used on multiple web pages of a site. Because static files seldom change, it would be wasteful for a web browser to download the file every time the user visits a page. Instead, browsers can retain static files in a cache on the user's hard drive, and reuse the files when they are needed.

To do this, the browser needs to know how long it can safely retain the file. The server can suggest a maximum cache expiration in the HTTP response. You can configure the cache expiration period App Engine suggests to the client.

To set a default cache expiration period for all static files for an app, you specify a `default_expiration` value. This value applies to all static file handlers, and belongs at the top level of the *app.yaml* file, like so:

```
application: ae-book
version: 1
runtime: python
api_version: 1

default_expiration: "5d 12h"

handlers:
  # ...
```

The value is a string that specifies a number of days, hours, minutes, and seconds. As shown here, each number is followed by a unit (d, h, m, or s), and values are separated by spaces.

You can also specify an expiration value for `static_dir` and `static_files` handlers individually, using an `expiration` element in the handler definition. This value overrides the `default_expiration` value, if any. For example:

```
handlers:
- url: /docs/latest
  static_dir: /docs
  expiration: "12h"
```

If the configuration does not suggest a cache expiration period for a set of static files, App Engine does not give an expiration period when serving the files. Browsers will use their own caching behavior in this case, and may not cache the files at all.

Sometimes you want a static file to be cached in the browser as long as possible, but then replaced immediately when the static file changes. A common technique is to add a version number for the file to the URL, then use a new version number from the app's HTML when the file changes. The browser sees a new URL, assumes it is a new resource, and fetches the new version.

You can put the version number of the resource in a fake URL parameter, such as `/js/code.js?v=19`, which gets ignored by the static file server. Alternatively, in Python, you can use regular expression matching to match all versions of the URL and route them to the same file in the static file server, like so:

```
- handlers:
  url: /js/(.*)/code.js
  static_files: js/code.js
  expiration: "90d"
```

This handler serves the static file `js/code.js` for all URLs such as `/js/v19/code.js`, using a cache expiration of 90 days.

 If you'd like browsers to reload a static file resource automatically every time you launch a new major version of the app, you can use the multiversion URL handler just discussed, then use the `CURRENT_VERSION_ID` environment variable as the "version" in the static file URLs:

```
self.response.out('<script src="/js/' +
                  os.environ['CURRENT_VERSION_ID'] +
                  '/code.js" />')
```

Domain Names

Every app gets a free domain name on *appspot.com*, based on the application ID. Requests for URLs that use your domain name are routed to your app by the frontend:

```
http://app-id.appspot.com/path...
```

But chances are, you want to use a custom domain name with your app. You can register your custom domain name with any Internet domain registrar. With your domain name, you will also need Domain Name Service (DNS) hosting, a service that advertises the destination associated with your name (in this case, App Engine). Name registrars such as Hover (*http://www.hover.com/*) include DNS hosting with the cost of the registration. Alternatively, you can use Google Cloud DNS (*https://cloud.google.com/dns/docs*), a high-performance DNS solution with powerful features.

You can configure your domain name so that all requests for the name (`example.com`) go to App Engine, or so only requests for a subdomain (such as `www.example.com`) go to App Engine. You might use a subdomain if the root domain or other subdomains are pointing to other services, such as a company website hosted on a different service.

 If you intend to support secure web traffic over secure connections (SSL/TLS, aka "HTTPS"), skip ahead to the next section, "Google Apps" on page 64. You must use Google Apps to set up your custom domain to use SSL/TLS with the domain.

The `appspot.com` domain supports SSL/TLS. See "Configuring Secure Connections" on page 67 for more information.

To set up a custom domain, go to Cloud Console, select the project, then select Compute, App Engine, Settings. From the tabs along the top, select "Custom domains." This panel is shown in Figure 3-2.

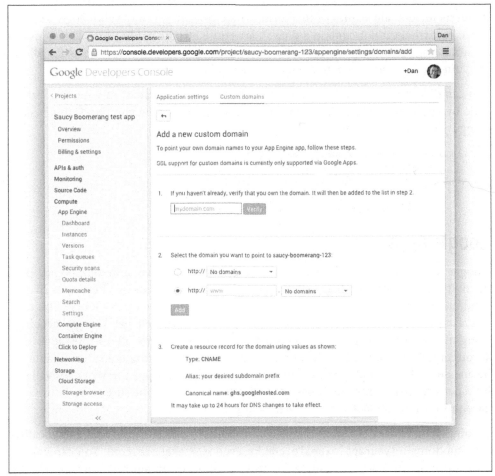

Figure 3-2. The "Custom domains" settings panel

The setup procedure involves three main steps:

1. Verify that you own the domain. You can verify the domain by adding a verification code to the DNS record, or if the domain is already pointing to a web host, by adding a verification code to a file on the web host.

2. Add the domain or subdomain to the project.

3. Configure the DNS record to point to App Engine.

Cloud Console will walk you through these steps with specific instructions.

The `appspot.com` domain has a couple of useful features. One such feature is the ability to accept an additional domain name part:

    anything.app-id.appspot.com

Requests for domain names of this form, where *anything* is any valid single domain name part (that cannot contain a dot, `.`), are routed to the application. This is useful for accepting different kinds of traffic on different domain names, such as for allowing your users to serve content from their own subdomains.

You can determine which domain name was used for the request in your application code by checking the `Host` header on the request. Here's how you check this header using Python and webapp:

```
class MainHandler(webapp2.RequestHandler):
    def get(self):
        host = self.request.headers['Host']

        self.response.out.write('Host: %s' % host)
```

Google Apps

Google Apps is a service that gives your organization its own suite of Google's productivity applications, such as Gmail, Docs, Drive, and Hangouts. These apps live on subdomains of your organization's Internet domain name (such as Google Drive on `drive.example.com`), and your organization's employees all get Google accounts using the domain name (`juliet@example.com`). Access to all of the apps and accounts can be managed by the domain administrator, making the suite suitable for businesses, schools, and government institutions. Google Apps for Work is available for a per user per month fee. If your organization is a school, be sure to look for Google Apps for Education, which is free of charge.

A compelling feature of Google Apps is the ability to add an App Engine application on a subdomain (`yourapp.example.com`, or even `www.example.com`). You can configure App Engine's Google accounts features to support domain accounts specifically, making it easy to built intranet apps that only your organization's members can see. You can also make the app on your domain accessible to the public—with no per-user fee for doing so. (The per-user fee only applies to accounts on the domain. You will still need one administrator account.) You can configure a public app on a domain to accept regular Google accounts, or you can implement your own account mechanism.

Google Apps is currently the only way to use secure connections (SSL/TLS, aka "HTTPS") with custom domains on App Engine. This has the advantage of using the Google Apps SSL/TLS infrastructure. In exchange, you lose the ability to serve the App Engine app from the "naked" domain (`http://example.com/`): all Google Apps applications must be associated with a subdomain (such as `www.example.com`). We'll discuss that next, in "Secure Connections with Custom Domains" on page 69.

Google Apps can perform a redirect from the naked domain to any desired subdomain. For example, you can set the naked domain to redirect to `www`, and put the app on that subdomain.

To get started, go to the Google Apps for Work website (*https://www.google.com/work/apps/business/*), or if you're part of an educational institution, use the Google Apps for Education website (*https://www.google.com/work/apps/education/*).

Follow the instructions to create a Google Apps account. You must already have registered your domain name to set up Google Apps. This process will include the opportunity to create an "administrator" account for the domain, which is a new Google account with an email address on the domain (`your.name@example.com`).

Next, add the App Engine app to the domain, as follows:

1. From the Google Admin console (*https://admin.google.com/*) (the Google Apps console), sign in using the Apps domain's administrator account.

2. Expand the "More controls" panel at the bottom, then locate App Engine Apps and click it. You may need to click the right arrow to find it.

3. Click "Add services to your domain," or click the plus symbol (+).

4. Under Other Services, in the Enter App ID field, enter the project ID for your App Engine app. Click "Add it now." Follow the prompts to accept the terms of service.

5. When prompted, under "Web address," click "Add new URL," and enter the subdomain you wish to use. If you try to use the `www` subdomain and it complains "Already used, please remove previous mapping first," this is likely because Google Sites is configured to use `www`. Navigate to Google Apps, click Sites, then click Web Address Mapping. Check the `www` mapping in this list, then click Delete Mapping(s). Navigate back to App Engine Apps, select the app, then try again.

6. As instructed, in another browser window, go to your domain's DNS service, and create a CNAME record for the subdomain. Set the destination to `ghs.google hosted.com`. Return to the Google Admin panel window, then click "I've comple-

ted these steps." Google verifies your CNAME record. It may take a few minutes for your DNS service to update its records.

Your app can now be accessed using the custom domain, with the subdomain you configured.

While you're here, you should make the Apps domain's administrator account an owner of the app. This is required for setting up secure connections. There are three parts to this: adding the Cloud Console as an "app" that the domain admin can use, inviting the domain admin to be an owner of the app, and finally accepting the invitation as the domain admin. (You must add the Cloud Console as a service before the domain admin can accept the invitation.)

To enable the Cloud Console as a service for the domain:

1. While signed in as the domain administrator, return to the Google Admin console's dashboard.

2. Locate and click Apps, then select Additional Google services.

3. In the list, locate Google Developers Console, then click the pop-up menu icon on the right. Select the "On for everyone" option from the menu. Confirm that you want domain users to be able to access the Google Developers Console.

To make the domain administrator an owner of the app:

1. Sign out of Google, then sign in with the account you used to create the App Engine app.

2. From the Cloud Console (*https://console.developers.google.com/*), select the app, then click Permissions.

3. Add the Apps domain's administrator account as a member, and set its permission to "Is owner."

4. Sign out of Google again, then sign in again using the Apps domain's administrator account.

5. Go to the account's Gmail inbox (*https://mail.google.com/*), find the invitation email, then click the link to accept the invitation to join the project.

App Engine developer invitations do not work well with Google's multiple sign-in feature. If you click an invitation link, it will attempt to accept the invitation on behalf of the first ("primary") account you're using, then fail because the signed-in account is not the intended recipient of the invitation. To perform this self-invitation maneuver, you must sign out of Google completely then sign in again with the invited account. Alternatively, you can use a Chrome Incognito window to sign in with the invited account and visit the invitation link.

If you intend to use the Google accounts features of App Engine with accounts on your organization's domain, go to Cloud Console, then select Compute, App Engine, Settings. Change the Google Authentication option to "Google Apps domain," then click Save. This ensures that only your domain accounts can be authorized with the app via these features. See "Authorization with Google Accounts" on page 71 for more information.

As you can see, Google Apps is a sophisticated service and requires many steps to set up. With Apps on your domain, not only can you run your App Engine app on a subdomain, but you get a customized instance of Google's application suite for your company or organization. Take a deep breath and congratulate yourself on getting this far. Then proceed to the next section.

Configuring Secure Connections

When a client requests and retrieves a web page over an HTTP connection, every aspect of the interaction is transmitted over the network in its final intended form, including the URL path, request parameters, uploaded data, and the complete content of the server's response. For web pages, this usually means human-readable text is flying across the wire, or through the air if the user is using a wireless connection. Anyone else privy to the network traffic can capture and analyze this data, and possibly glean sensitive information about the user and the service.

Websites that deal in sensitive information, such as banks and online retailers, can use a secure alternative for web traffic. With servers that support it, the client can make an HTTPS connection (HTTP over the Secure Socket Layer, or SSL/TLS). All data sent in either direction over the connection is encrypted by the sender and decrypted by the recipient, so only the participants can understand what is being transmitted even if the encrypted messages are intercepted. Web browsers usually have an indicator that tells the user when a connection is secure.

App Engine supports secure connections for incoming web requests. By default, App Engine accepts HTTPS connections for all URLs, and otherwise treats them like HTTP requests. You can configure the frontend to reject or redirect HTTP or HTTPS requests for some or all URL paths, such as to ensure that all requests not using a secure connection are redirected to their HTTPS equivalents. The application code itself doesn't need to know the difference between a secure connection and a standard connection: it just consumes the decrypted request and provides a response that is encrypted by App Engine.

All URL paths can be configured to use secure connections, including those mapped to application code and those mapped to static files. The frontend takes care of the secure connection on behalf of the app servers and static file servers.

App Engine only supports secure connections over TCP port 443, the standard port used by browsers for `https://` URLs. Similarly, App Engine only supports standard connections over port 80. The App Engine frontend returns an error for URLs that specify a port other than the standard port for the given connection method.

The development server does not support secure connections, and ignores the security settings in the configuration. You can test these URLs during development by using the nonsecure equivalent URLs.

To configure secure connections for a URL handler in a Python application, add a `secure` element to the handler's properties in the *app.yaml* file:

```
handler:
- url: /profile/.*
  script: userprofile.py
  secure: always
```

The value of the `secure` element can be `always`, `never`, or `optional`:

- `always` says that requests to this URL path should always use a secure connection. If a user attempts to request the URL path over a nonsecure connection, the App Engine frontend issues an HTTP redirect code telling it to try again using a secure HTTP connection. Browsers follow this redirect automatically.

- `never` says that requests to this URL path should never use a secure connection, and requests for an HTTPS URL should be redirected to the HTTP equivalent. Note that some browsers display a warning when a secure page is redirected to a nonsecure page.

- `optional` allows either connection method for the URL path, without redirects. The app can use the `HTTPS` environment variable to determine which method was used for the request, and produce a custom response.

If you don't specify a `secure` element for a URL path, the default is `optional`.

When configured to allow (or require) SSL, you can access the default version of your app using the HTTPS version of the `appspot.com` URL:

```
https://ae-book.appspot.com/
```

Because HTTPS uses the domain name to validate the secure connection, requests to versioned `appspot.com` URLs, such as `https://3.ae-book.appspot.com/`, will display a security warning in the browser saying that the domain does not match the security certificate, which only applies to the immediate subdomains (`*.app spot.com`). To prevent this, App Engine has a trick up its sleeve: replace the dots (`.`) between the version and app IDs with `-dot-` (that's hyphen, the word "dot," and another hyphen), like this:

```
https://3-dot-ae-book.appspot.com/
```

A request to this domain uses the certificate for `*.appspot.com`, and avoids the security warning.

 Secure connections are an increasingly important part of the Web. Even if you do not collect user data or perform sensitive transactions explicitly, secure connections protect the user transactional data implicit when visiting web pages. They're so important, Google's search engine considers HTTPS a ranking signal when evaluating the quality of a website for appearing in search results.[2]

When possible, use `secure: always`. It's worth it.

Secure Connections with Custom Domains

To enable secure connections over a custom domain for your app, you need to set up Google Apps for the domain, with the app added on a subdomain and the domain administrator account set up as an owner of the app. If you haven't done this yet, see "Google Apps" on page 64.[3]

The protocol for secure connections depends on an *SSL/TLS certificate*,[4] a document that says who you are and that you are responsible for traffic served from the domain. You acquire a certificate from a *certificate authority* (CA). The CA may also be certified, and this certification can be traced back to a list of known CAs built in to your user's web browser. Browsers will only make secure connections with websites whose certificates can be traced back to known authorities, thereby assuring the user that the connection to your app is genuine, and not being intercepted by a third party.

---

2 See HTTPS as a Ranking Signal (*http://googlewebmastercentral.blogspot.com/2014/08/https-as-ranking-signal.html*).

3 The procedure for setting up secure connections via Google Apps is a bit convoluted. If your only interest is to use SSL with a custom domain, check the Cloud Console and the official documentation for an easier way in case one was added since this book was published.

4 TLS, or Transport Layer Security, refers to the latest standard, and is a successor to SSL, or Secure Socket Layer. SSL is still sometimes used as an umbrella term for secure connections.

You can purchase a certificate valid for a limited time from any of a number of CAs, much like registering a domain name from a registrar. CAs offer certificates at different levels of assurance, and some CAs, such as StartSSL (*https://www.startssl.com/*), offer free certificates at the lowest level. Some browsers attempt to communicate the assurance level to the user in various ways. Be sure to follow your CA's procedures for verifying your domain name and adding it to the certificate, and for creating a TLS/SSL certificate for a web server.

For example, StartSSL initially grants you an "S/MIME and Authentication" certificate to authenticate with its website. After you have used the StartSSL website to validate your email address and domain name, you can generate a "Web Server TLS/SSL certificate," with a private key protected by a password. StartSSL then prompts you to copy and paste the encrypted private key into a text file (*ssl.key*), then run the following command to encode it using the RSA method:

```
openssl rsa -in ssl.key -out ssl.key
```

Enter the password you used to encrypt the private key when prompted. The key is decrypted, then encoded using RSA, suitable for uploading to Google.

 The openssl command is installed on most Mac OS X and Linux systems. Windows users can get it from the OpenSSL website (*https://www.openssl.org/*).

Whatever process your CA uses, the end result should be a TLS/SSL certificate associated with your root domain name and your app's subdomain, as well as the unencrypted RSA-encoded private key. You will upload both of these files to Google in the next step.

Before you can complete this process, you must decide which method App Engine should use to serve your secure traffic. There are two choices: Server Name Indication (SNI) or Virtual IP (VIP). SNI associates one or more certificates with your app's domain name. SNI is a relatively new standard, and only modern web clients (most browsers) support it. If you need broader support for SSL-capable clients, Google also offers a virtual IP (VIP) solution, which ties your certificate and application to an IP address. This expensive resource comes with a monthly fee.

You are now ready to activate SSL for your domain, using the Google Apps Admin console:

1. Open the Google Admin console (*https://admin.google.com/*). Expand "More controls" (located at the bottom of the page), then locate and select Security. Select SSL for Custom Domains, clicking "Show more" if necessary to reveal it.

2. In the panel that opens, enter the project ID for the app. This confirms that the app will be responsible for SSL-related computation.

3. On the following screen,[5] click Enable SSL. You are returned to the Google Apps Admin console to complete the process. Now that SSL is enabled, you can get to this screen at any point in the future by navigating to Security, SSL for Custom Domains.

4. If you wish to use SNI for the certificate, click the "Increase SNI certificate slots by 5" button. If you need the VIP solution, look for the Add a VIP button. If it is disabled with a message prompting you to increase the budget for the app, do so in the Cloud Console, under Compute, App Engine, Settings. The VIP option needs a nonzero budget for its resources.

5. Still in the SSL for Custom Domains screen, click Configure SSL Certificates. In the subsequent screen, click "Upload a new certificate." For the "PEM encoded X.509 certificate," select the certificate file. For the "Unencrypted PEM encoded RSA private key," select the *ssl.key* file. Click Upload. The certificate information appears in the window.

6. In the box that has appeared, under "Current state," change "Serving mode" to the method you have chosen, either SNI or VIP. An Assigned URLs section appears. Use it to assign your subdomain to the certificate. For VIP, use your domain's DNS hosting to add a CNAME record with the value shown. (No DNS change is needed for SNI only.)

7. Click "Save changes."

That's it! It was a long haul, but you now have full HTTPS support for your app on a custom domain. Give it a try: visit your subdomain using the `https://` method in your browser. The browser indicates that a secure connection is successful, usually with an icon in the address bar. In Chrome and other browsers, you can click the icon to get more information about the certificate.

Authorization with Google Accounts

Back in Chapter 2, we discussed how an App Engine application can integrate with Google Accounts to identify and authenticate users. We saw how an app can use library calls to check whether the user making a request is signed in, access the user's email address, and calculate the sign-in and sign-out URLs of the Google Accounts

---

5 As of August 2014, this screen appears on *appengine.google.com*, a website we haven't mentioned yet. This is the old App Engine console, the one App Engine launched with in 2008. It is in the process of being replaced by the Cloud Console. Once the last few features (such as this screen) have been moved to Cloud Console, this old site will be decommissioned. For now, you can use either console to access any of these features.

system. With this API, application code can perform fine-grained access control and customize displays.

Another way to do access control is to leave it to the frontend. With just a little configuration, you can instruct the frontend to protect access to specific URL handlers such that only signed-in users can request them. If a user who is not signed in requests such a URL, the frontend redirects the user to the Google Accounts sign-in and registration screen. Upon successfully signing in or registering a new account, the user is redirected back to the URL.

You can also tell the frontend that only the registered developers of the application can access certain URL handlers. This makes it easy to build administrator-only sections of your website, with no need for code that confirms the user is an administrator. You can manage which accounts have developer status in the Cloud Console, in the Developers section. If you revoke an account's developer status, that user is no longer able to access administrator-only resources, effective immediately.

Later on, we will discuss App Engine services that call your application in response to events. For example, the scheduled tasks service (the "cron" service) can be configured to trigger a request to a URL at certain times of the day. Typically, you want to restrict access to these URLs so not just anybody can call them. For the purposes of access control enforced by the frontend, these services act as app administrators, so restricting these URLs to administrators effectively locks out meddling outsiders while allowing the services to call the app.

This coarse-grained access control is easy to set up in the frontend configuration. And unlike access control in the application code, frontend authentication can restrict access to static files as well as application request handlers.

You establish frontend access control for a URL handler with the `login` element in *app.yaml*, like so:

```
handlers:
- url: /myaccount/.*
  script: account.py
  login: required
```

The `login` element has two possible values: `required` and `admin`.

If `login` is `required`, then the user must be signed in to access URLs for this handler. If the user is not signed in, the frontend returns an HTTP redirect code to send the user to the Google Accounts sign-in and registration form.

If `login` is `admin`, then the user must be signed in *and* must be a registered developer for the application.

If no `login` is provided, the default policy is to allow anyone to access the resource, regardless of whether the client represents a signed-in user, and regardless of whether or not the app is set to use a members-only access policy.

You can use the `login` element with both script handlers and static file handlers.

Environment Variables

You can use app configuration to specify a list of environment variables to be set prior to calling any request handlers. This is useful to control components that depend on environment variables, without having to resort to hacks in your code to set them.

To set environment variables, provide the `env_variables` element in *app.yaml* with a mapping value:

```
env_variables:
  DJANGO_SETTINGS_MODULE: 'gnero.prod.settings'
```

Inbound Services

Some App Engine services call an application's request handlers in response to external events. For example, the Mail service can call a request handler at a fixed URL when it receives an email message at an email address associated with the app. This is a common design theme in App Engine: all application code is in the form of request handlers, and services that need the app to respond to an event invoke request handlers to do it.

Each service capable of creating inbound traffic must be enabled in app configuration, to confirm that the app is expecting traffic from those services on the corresponding URL paths. To enable these services, provide the `inbound_services` element in *app.yaml* with a list of service names:

```
inbound_services:
- mail
- warmup
```

Table 3-1 lists the services that can be enabled this way, and where to find more information about each service.

Table 3-1. Services that create inbound traffic for an app, which must be enabled in service configuration

Service	Description	Name	Handler URLs
Channel Presence	Receive channel connection notifications	channel_pres ence	/_ah/channel/.*
Mail	Receive email at a set of addresses; see Chapter 14	mail	/_ah/mail/.*
XMPP Messages	Receive XMPP chat messages; for all XMPP services, see Chapter 15	xmpp_message	/_ah/xmpp/message/chat/
XMPP Presence	Receive XMPP presence notifications	xmpp_presence	/_ah/xmpp/presence/.*
XMPP Subscribe	Receive XMPP subscription notifications	xmpp_sub scribe	/_ah/xmpp/subscription/.*
XMPP Error	Receive XMPP error messages	xmpp_error	/_ah/xmpp/error/
Warmup Requests	Initialize an instance, with warmup requests enabled; see "Warmup Requests" on page 98	warmup	/_ah/warmup

Custom Error Responses

When your application serves a status code that represents an error (such as 403 Forbidden or 500 Internal Server Error) in a response to a browser, it can also include an HTML page in the body of the response. The browser typically shows this HTML to the user if the browser expected to render a full page for the request. Serving an error page can help prevent the user from being disoriented by a generic error message—or no message at all.

There are cases when an error condition occurs before App Engine can invoke your application code, and must return an error response. For example, if none of the request handler mappings in the app's configuration match the request URL, App Engine has no request handler to call and must return a 404 Not Found message. By default, App Engine adds its own generic HTML page to its error responses.

You can configure custom error content to be used instead of App Engine's error page. You provide the response body in a file included with your app, and mention the file in your application configuration.

To set error pages, add an error_handlers element to your *app.yaml*. Its value is a list of mappings, one per error file:

```
error_handlers:
- file: error.html
- error_code: over_quota
  file: busy_error.html
- error_code: dos_api_denial
  file: dos_denial.txt
  mime_type: text/plain
```

The `file` value specifies the path from the application root directory to the error file. The optional `mime_type` specifies the MIME content type for the file, which defaults to `text/html`.

The `error_code` value associates the error file with a specific error condition. If omitted, the file is associated with every error condition that doesn't have a specific error file of its own. Error codes include the following:

over_quota
: The request cannot be fulfilled because the app has temporarily exceeded a resource quota or limit.

dos_api_denial
: The origin of the request is blocked by the app's denial-of-service protection configuration. (See the App Engine documentation for more information about this feature.)

timeout
: The request handler did not return a response before the request deadline.

 Custom error files must be stored on application servers. They must not be static files. Be careful not to configure static file handlers that match these files.

Python Libraries

On your own computer, Python programs run in an environment with access to many libraries of modules. Some of these modules—quite a few, actually—come with Python itself, in the Python standard library. Others you may have installed separately, such as with `pip install` or `easy_install`. Perhaps you use `virtualenv` to create multiple isolated Python environments, each with its own set of available libraries. A Python program can import any module within its environment, and a module must be available in this environment (or elsewhere on the Python library load path) to be importable.

On App Engine, a Python app also runs in an environment with access to libraries. This environment includes a slightly modified version of the Python 2.7 standard library. (The modifications account for restrictions of the App Engine runtime environment, which we'll discuss in Chapter 4.) App Engine adds to this the libraries and tools included with the App Engine SDK, such as APIs for accessing the services (such as `google.appengine.api.urlfetch`), and utilities such as the data modeling libraries (`google.appengine.ext.ndb`).

Naturally, the environment also includes any Python modules you provide in your application directory. In addition to your own code, you might add a copy of a third-party library your app uses to your app directory, where it is uploaded as part of your app. Note that this method only works for "pure Python" libraries, and not libraries that have portions written in C.

For convenience, the Python runtime environment includes several third-party libraries popular for web development. We've already seen Jinja, the templating library. The Django web application framework is also included. You can use NumPy for data processing and numerical analysis. The Python Cryptography Toolkit (PyCrypto) provides strong encryption capabilities.

To use one of the provided third-party libraries, you must declare it in the *app.yaml* file for the app, like so:

```
libraries:
- name: django
  version: "1.3"
```

This declaration is necessary to select the version of the library your app will use. When a new version of a third-party library becomes available, your app will continue to use the declared version until you change it. You'll want to test your app to make sure it's compatible with the new version before making the switch with your live app. With this declaration in place, `import django` will load the requested version of the library. (Without it, the import will fail with an `ImportError`.)

 For more information about using Django with App Engine, see Chapter 18.

You can specify a `version` of `latest` to always request the latest major version of the library. This may be desired for small libraries, where new versions are typically backward compatible. For larger packages like Django, you almost certainly want to select a specific version, and upgrade carefully when a new version is added:

```
libraries:
- name: jinja2
  version: latest
```

```
  - name: markupsafe
    version: latest
```

While the App Engine runtime environment provides these libraries, the Python SDK does not. You must install third-party libraries in your local Python environment yourself, and make sure your version matches the one requested in your *app.yaml*. Installation instructions are specific to each library.

Table 3-2 lists third-party libraries available as of SDK version 1.9.18. Check the official documentation for an up-to-date list.

Table 3-2. Third-party Python libraries available by request in the runtime environment

Library	Description	Name	Versions
Django	A web application framework; see the Django website (*https://www.djangoproject.com/*) for installation instructions	`django`	1.5, 1.4, 1.3, 1.2
Endpoints	The Google Endpoints library	`endpoints`	1.0
Jinja2	A templating library; MarkupSafe is recommended with Jinja2; to install, use: `sudo easy_install jinja2`	`jinja2`	2.6
lxml	An XML parsing and production toolkit; see the lxml website (*http://lxml.de/*) for installation instructions, including the `libxml2` and `libxslt` libraries	`lxml`	2.3.5, 2.3
MarkupSafe	Fast HTML-aware string handler; to install, use: `sudo easy_install markupsafe`	`markupsafe`	0.15
matplotlib	A 2D mathematical plotting package	`matplotlib`	1.2.0
MySQLdb	A common interface to MySQL databases, useful with Google Cloud SQL; see Chapter 11	`MySQLdb`	1.2.4b4
NumPy	Data processing and numerical analysis; see the SciPy website (*http://www.scipy.org/*) for installation	`numpy`	1.6.1
Python Imaging Library (PIL)	Image manipulation toolkit; see the PIL website (*http://www.pythonware.com/products/pil/index.htm*) for installation	`pil`	1.1.7
protorpc	An efficient remote procedure call bundling format, used by Google	`protorpc`	1.0
PyAMF	For manipulating Action Message Format (AMF) messages, used for server messaging from Adobe Flash Player	`PyAMF`	0.6.1

Library	Description	Name	Versions
Python Cryptography Toolkit (PyCrypto)	Cryptographic routines; see the PyCrypto website (*https://www.dlitz.net/software/pycrypto/*) for installation; export restrictions may apply	`pycrypto`	2.6, 2.3
setuptools	For discovering which packages are installed (you don't use this for installing packages)	`setuptools`	0.6c11
webapp2	The webapp2 web application framework	`webapp2`	2.5.2, 2.5.1, 2.3 (deprecated)
WebOb	An object-oriented interface to HTTP requests and responses; used by (and included automatically with) the webapp framework; included in the SDK	`webob`	1.1.1
YAML	Library for parsing the YAML message serialization format; used by the SDK for the config files; included in the SDK	`yaml`	3.10

Built-in Handlers

Some of the utilities included with the Python runtime environment use their own request handlers to provide functionality, such as a web-based administrative UI or web service endpoints. Typically, these handlers map to URLs with paths beginning with /_ah/, which are reserved for App Engine use. Because this code runs within your application, you must enable this functionality by setting up these request handlers.

To make it easy to do (and difficult to do incorrectly), many of these tools are available as "built-ins." You enable a built-in feature by naming it in your *app.yaml* file, in a mapping named `builtins`:

```
builtins:
- appstats: on
- remote_api: on
```

Table 3-3 lists the built-ins available as of SDK version 1.9.18. As usual, check the official documentation for an up-to-date list.

Table 3-3. Built-in features that must be enabled using the built-ins directive in app.yaml

Feature	Description	Name
AppStats	Sets up the AppStats control panel at `/_ah/stats`; see "Visualizing Calls with AppStats" on page 377	`appstats`
Deferred work	Sets up the task queue handler for the `deferred` library; see "Deferring Work" on page 358	`deferred`
Remote API	Establishes the web service endpoint for remote API access; see "Remote Controls" on page 253	`remote_api`

Includes

An *app.yaml* file can get rather large, especially if you use it to route your app's URLs to multiple handlers. You can organize your app's configuration into separate component files by using the `includes` directive. This also makes it easy to write App Engine components that can be installed in other apps, regardless of which frameworks the apps are using.

The `includes` value is a list of file or directory paths, like so:

```
includes:
- lib/component/ae_config.yaml
```

The path can be an absolute path, a path relative to the app root directory, or a path relative to the file that contains the `includes`. If the path is to a file, the file is parsed as a YAML file. If the path is to a directory, the filename is assumed to be *include.yaml* in the given directory.

An included file can contain `builtins`, `includes`, `handlers`, and `admin_console` values. These list values are *prepended* to the list that appears in the current file.

For `handlers`, this means that handler URL patterns from includes are tested before those in the current file. If your main *app.yaml* file has a handler mapped to the URL pattern `/.*`, handlers from includes will be tested first, and only those that don't match will fall to the catch-all handler. Notice that if an included file maps a handler to `/.*`, none of the handlers in the current file (or any file that includes the current file) will ever match a request! So don't do that.

Includes are aggregated in the order they appear in the list. For example, consider this *app.yaml*:

```
handlers:
- url: /.*
  script: main.app

includes:
- lib/component_one
- lib/component_two
```

Here, a request URL will try to match each of the `handlers` in *lib/component_one/include.yaml* in the order they appear in that file, followed by each of the `handlers` in *lib/component_two/include.yaml*, followed by the `/.*` handler in *app.yaml*.

## CHAPTER 4

Request Handlers and Instances

When a request arrives intended for your application code, the App Engine frontend routes it to the application servers. If an instance of your app is running and available to receive a user request, App Engine sends the request to the instance, and the instance invokes the request handler that corresponds with the URL of the request. If none of the running instances of the app are available, App Engine starts up a new one automatically. App Engine will also shut down instances it no longer needs.

The *instance* is your app's unit of computing power. It provides memory and a processor, isolated from other instances for both data security and performance. Your application's code and data stay in the instance's memory until the instance is shut down, providing an opportunity for local storage that persists between requests.

Within the instance, your application code runs in a *runtime environment*. The environment includes the language interpreter, libraries, and other environment features you selected in your app's configuration. Your app can also access a read-only filesystem containing its files (those that you did not send exclusively to the static file servers). The environment manages all the inputs and outputs for the request handler, setting up the request at the beginning, recording log messages during, and collecting the response at the end.

If you have multithreading enabled, an instance can handle multiple requests concurrently, with all request handlers sharing the same environment. With multithreading disabled, each instance handles one request at a time. Multithreading is one of the best ways to utilize the resources of your instances and keep your costs low. But it's up to you to make sure your request handler code runs correctly when handling multiple requests concurrently.

The runtime environment and the instance are abstractions. They rest above, and take the place of, the operating system and the hardware. It is these abstractions that allow your app to scale seamlessly and automatically on App Engine's infrastructure. At no point must you write code to start or stop instances, load balance requests, or monitor resource utilization. This is provided for you.

In fact, you could almost ignore instances entirely and just focus on request handlers: a request comes in, a request handler comes to life, a response goes out. During its brief lifetime, the request handler makes a few decisions and calls a few services, and leaves no mark behind. The instance only comes into play to give you more control over efficiency: local memory caching, multithreading, and warmup initialization. You can also configure the hardware profile and parameters of instance allocation, which involve trade-offs of performance and cost.

In this chapter, we discuss the features of the runtime environments and instances. We introduce a way of thinking about request handlers, and how they fit into the larger notion of instances and the App Engine architecture. We also cover how to tune your instances for performance and resource utilization.

We'll focus this discussion on App Engine's automatic scaling features for the user-facing parts of an application. In the next chapter, we'll branch out into modules and other scaling patterns, and see how to use instances in various ways to build more complex application architecture.

The Runtime Environment

All code execution occurs in the runtime environment you have selected for your app. There are four major runtime environments: Java, Python 2.7, PHP, and Go. For this version of the book, we're focusing on the Python 2.7 environment.

The runtime environment manages all the interaction between the application code and the rest of App Engine. To invoke an application to handle a request, App Engine prepares the runtime environment with the request data, calls the appropriate request handler code within the environment, then collects and returns the response. The application code uses features of the environment to read inputs, call services, and calculate the response data.

The environment isolates and protects your app to guarantee consistent performance. Regardless of what else is happening on the physical hardware that's running the instance, your app sees consistent performance as if it is running on a server all by itself. To do this, the environment must restrict the capabilities normally provided by a traditional server operating system, such as the ability to write to the local file-system.

An environment like this is called a "sandbox": what's yours is yours, and no other app can intrude. This sandbox effect also applies to your code and your data. If a piece of physical hardware happens to be running instances for two different applications, the applications cannot read each other's code, files, or network traffic.

App Engine's services are similarly partitioned on an app-by-app basis, so each app sees an isolated view of the service and its data. The runtime environment includes APIs for calling these services in the form of language-specific libraries. In a few cases, portions of standard libraries have been replaced with implementations that make service calls.

The Sandbox

The runtime environment does not expose the complete operating system to the application. Some functions, such as the ability to create arbitrary network connections, are restricted. This "sandbox" is necessary to prevent other applications running on the same server from interfering with your application (and vice versa). Instead, an app can perform some of these functions using App Engine's scalable services, such as the URL Fetch service.

The most notable sandbox restrictions include the following:

- An app cannot spawn additional processes. All processing for a request must be performed by the request handler's process. Multiple threads within the process are allowed, but when the main thread has returned a response, all remaining threads are terminated. There is a way to create long-lived background threads using modules and manual scaling, but this is an exception. You'll most likely use automatic scaling for handling user traffic, and this is the default.

- An app cannot make arbitrary network connections. Networking features are provided by the App Engine services, such as URL Fetch and Mail.

- The app does not manipulate the socket connection with the client directly. Instead, the app prepares the response data, then exits. App Engine takes care of returning the response. This isolates apps from the network infrastructre, at the expense of preventing some niceties like streaming partial results data.

- An app can only read from the filesystem, and can only read its own code and resource files. It cannot create or modify files. Instead of files, an app can use the datastore to save data.

- An app cannot see or otherwise know about other applications or processes that may be running on the server. This includes other request handlers from the same application that may be running simultaneously.

- An app cannot read another app's data from any service that stores data. More generally, an app cannot pretend to be another app when calling a service, and all services partition data between apps.

These restrictions are implemented on multiple levels, both to ensure that the restrictions are enforced and to make it easier to troubleshoot problems that may be related to the sandbox. For example, some standard library calls have been replaced with behaviors more appropriate to the sandbox.

Quotas and Limits

The sandboxed runtime environment monitors the system resources used by the application and limits how much the app can consume. For the resources you pay for, such as running time and storage, you can lift these limits by allocating a daily resource budget in the Cloud Console. App Engine also enforces several system-wide limits that protect the integrity of the servers and their ability to serve multiple apps.

In App Engine parlance, "quotas" are resource limits that refresh at the beginning of each calendar day (at midnight, Pacific Time). You can monitor your application's daily consumption of quotas using the Cloud Console, in the Quota Details section.

Because Google may change how the limits are set as the system is tuned for performance, we won't state some of the specific values of these limits in this book. You can find the actual values of these limits in the official App Engine documentation. Google has said it will give 90 days' notice before changing limits in a way that would affect existing apps.

Request limits

Several system-wide limits specify how requests can behave. These include the size and number of requests over a period of time, and the bandwidth consumed by inbound and outbound network traffic.

One important request limit is the request timer. An application has 60 seconds to respond to a user request.

Near the end of the 60-second limit, the server raises an exception that the application can catch for the purposes of exiting cleanly or returning a user-friendly error message. In Python, the request timer raises a `google.appengine.run time.DeadlineExceededError`.

If the request handler has not returned a response or otherwise exited after 60 seconds, the server terminates the process and returns a generic system error (HTTP code 500) to the client.

The 60-second limit applies to user web requests, as well as requests for web hooks such as incoming XMPP and email requests. A request handler invoked by a task queue or scheduled task can run for up to 10 minutes in duration. Tasks are a convenient and powerful tool for performing large amounts of work in the background. We'll discuss tasks in Chapter 16.

The size of a request is limited to 32 megabytes, as is the size of the request handler's response.

Service limits

Each App Engine service has its own set of quotas and limits. As with system-wide limits, some can be raised using a billing account and a budget, such as the number of recipients the application has sent emails to. Other limits are there to protect the integrity of the service, such as the maximum size of a response to the URL Fetch service.

In Python, when an app exceeds a service-specific limit or quota, the runtime environment raises a `apiproxy_errors.OverQuotaError` (from the `google.appengine.api.runtime` package).

With a few notable exceptions, the size of a service call and the size of the service response are each limited to 1 megabyte. This imposes an inherent limit on the size of datastore entities and memcache values. Although an incoming user request can contain up to 32 megabytes, only 1 megabyte of that data can be stored using a single datastore entity or memcache value.

The datastore has a "batch" API that allows you to store or fetch multiple data objects in a single service call. The total size of a batch request to the datastore is unlimited: you can attempt to store or fetch as many entities as can be processed within an internal timing limit for datastore service calls. Each entity is still limited to 1 megabyte in size.

The memcache also has a batch API. The total size of the request of a batch call to the memcache, or its response, can be up to 32 megabytes. As with the datastore, each memcache value cannot exceed 1 megabyte in size.

The URL Fetch service, which your app can use to connect to remote hosts using HTTP, can issue requests up to 10 megabytes, and receive responses up to 32 megabytes.

We won't list all the service limits here. Google raises limits as improvements are made to the infrastructure, and numbers printed here may be outdated. See the official documentation for a complete list, including the latest values.

Deployment limits

Two limits affect the size and structure of your application's files. A single application file cannot be larger than 32 megabytes. This applies to resource files (code, configuration) as well as static files. Also, the total number of files for an application cannot be larger than 10,000, including resource files and static files. The total size of all files must not exceed 150 megabytes.

These limits aren't likely to cause problems in most cases, but some common tasks can approach these numbers. Some third-party libraries or frameworks can be many hundreds of files. Sites consisting of many pages of text or images (not otherwise stored in the datastore) can reach the file count limit. A site offering video or software for download might have difficulty with the 32-megabyte limit.

The Python runtime offers two ways to mitigate the application file count limit. If you have many files of Python code, you can store the code files in a ZIP archive file, then add the path to the ZIP archive to sys.path at the top of your request handler scripts. The request handler scripts themselves must not be in a ZIP archive. Thanks to a built-in Python feature called zipimport, the Python interpreter recognizes the ZIP file automatically and unpacks it as needed when importing modules. Unpacking takes additional CPU time, but because imports are cached, the app only incurs this cost the first time the module is imported in a given app instance:

```
import sys
sys.path.insert(1, 'locales.zip')

import locales.es
```

The Python App Engine runtime includes a similar mechanism for serving static files from a ZIP archive file, called zipserve. Unlike zipimport, this feature is specific to App Engine. To serve static files from a ZIP archive, add the zipserve request handler to your *app.yaml*, associated with a URL path that represents the path to the ZIP file:

```
- url: /static/images/.*
  script: $PYTHON_LIB/google/appengine/ext/zipserve
```

This declares that all requests for a URL starting with /static/images/ should resolve to a path in the ZIP file /static/images.zip.

The string $PYTHON_LIB in the script path refers to the location of the App Engine libraries, and is the only such substitution available. It's useful precisely for this purpose, to set up a request handler whose code is in the App Engine Python modules included with the runtime environment. (zipserve is not a configurable built-in because it needs you to specify the URL mapping.)

When using zipserve, keep in mind that the ZIP archive is uploaded as a resource file, not a static file. Files are served by application code, not the static file infrastructure. By default, the handler advises browsers to cache the files for 20 minutes. You can customize the handler's cache duration using the wrapper WSGIApplication. See the source code for *google/appengine/ext/zipserve/__init__.py* in the SDK for details.

An application can only be uploaded a limited number of times per day, currently 1,000. You may not notice this limit during normal application development. If you are using app deployments to upload data to the application on a regular schedule, you may want to keep this limit in mind.

Projects

Each Google account can own or be a member of up to 25 Cloud projects. A Cloud project has exactly one App Engine "app," so you can think of this as being a developer of up to 25 apps. A project includes all of the Cloud resources for a major application, and there isn't much reason to use more than one project toward a single purpose. Features such as App Engine modules (discussed in Chapter 5) and Compute Engine give each project a tremendous amount of flexibility in its architecture and scope. Most services and features that can be used for multiple purposes within a single app have ways of segmenting their data within the app and within the Cloud Console. (For example, you can look at logs for each module and version individually.)

That said, having multiple projects for different purposes is often useful just to keep things organized. Each project has its own billing configuration and list of contributors. A single company that produces multiple web products might have one project per product.

If 25 projects per account is a burden in your case, Google offers more apps with their paid support programs (*https://cloud.google.com/support/*).

Versions

When you deploy your app, it is uploaded as a *version* of your app. The version ID is set either in your *app.yaml* file or as a command-line argument when you deploy. If you deploy an app using the same version ID as a previous deployment, the version is replaced. Otherwise, a new version is created.

All traffic to your live app (on your custom domain or your primary `appspot.com` domain) goes to the *default version*. You can change which version is the default version using the Cloud Console, or with another command-line invocation. Nondefault versions are accessible on separate `appspot.com` domains. This makes versions a valuable part of your deployment workflow: you can deploy a release candidate to a nondefault version ID, test it, then switch the default version to make the upgrade. See Chapter 20 for more details.

With billing enabled, each app can have up to 60 versions at one time. (The limit is 15 if billing is not enabled.) You can delete unused versions from the Cloud Console.

Billable quotas

Every application gets a limited amount of computing resources for free, so you can start developing and testing your application right away. You can purchase additional computing resources at competitive rates. You only pay for what you actually use, and you specify the maximum amount of money you want to spend.

You can create an app by using the free limits without setting up a billing account. Free apps never incur charges, but are constrained by the free quotas.

When you are ready for your app to accept live traffic or otherwise exceed the free quotas, you enable billing for the app, and set a resource budget. Apps with billing enabled get higher free quotas automatically, and you can keep the resource budget at zero dollars to prevent the app from incurring charges. If you're in a position to associate a credit card with your account, you can claim these extra free resources just by enabling billing.

To enable billing, sign in to the Cloud Console with the developer account that is to be the billing account. Select Billing Settings from the sidebar. Click the Enable Billing button, and follow the prompts to enter your payment information. This billing account applies to all Cloud services you use with the project, including App Engine.

When you are ready to grow beyond the free resource limits, you set a maximum daily resource budget for the app. This limit applies to App Engine resources specifically, such as App Engine–managed computation. For now, it also applies to the Cloud Datastore.[1] The budget specifies the amount of money App Engine can "spend" on resources, at the posted rates, over the course of a day. This budget is in addition to the free quotas: the budget is not consumed until after a resource has exceeded its free quota. After the budget for the calendar day is exhausted, service calls that would require more resources raise an exception. If there are not enough resources remaining to invoke a request handler, App Engine will respond to requests with a generic error message. The budget resets at the beginning of each calendar day (Pacific Time).

To set the budget, visit the Console while signed in with the billing account. Select Compute from the sidebar, then App Engine, then Settings. Adjust the "Daily budget" setting, then click Save. A change to your budget takes about 10 minutes to complete, and you will not be able to change the setting again during those 10 minutes. Figure 4-1 shows the Settings panel with a daily budget being set.

---

1 Cloud Datastore was originally a feature exclusive to App Engine, and is now a standalone service with a REST API as well as its original App Engine integration. As of September 2014, Datastore billing is still managed by App Engine's quota system, but this may change in the future.

Figure 4-1. Setting a daily budget in the app's Settings panel

It's worth repeating: you are only charged for the resources your app uses. If you set a high daily resource budget and App Engine only uses a portion of it, you are only charged for that portion. Typically, you would test your app to estimate resource consumption, then set the budget generously so every day comes in under the budget. The budget maximum is there to prevent unexpected surges in resource usage from draining your bank account—a monetary surge protector, if you will. If you're expecting a spike in traffic (such as for a product launch), you may want to raise your budget in advance of the event.

The official documentation includes a complete list of the free quota limits, the increased free quota limits with billing enabled, the maximum allocation amounts, and the latest billing rates. You can view the app's current quota consumption by navigating to Compute, App Engine, "Quota details" in the Console.

The Python Runtime Environment

When an app instance receives a request intended for a Python application, it compares the URL path of the request to the URL patterns in the app's *app.yaml* file. As we saw in "Configuring a Python App" on page 52, each URL pattern is associated with either the Python import path for a WSGI application instance, or a file of Python code (a "script"). The first pattern to match the path identifies the code that will handle the request.

If the handler is a WSGI instance, the runtime environment prepares the request and invokes the handler according to the WSGI standard. The handler returns the response in kind.

If the handler is a file of Python code, the runtime environment uses the Common Gateway Interface (CGI) standard to exchange request and response data with the code. The CGI standard uses a combination of environment variables and the application process's input and output streams to handle this communication.

You're unlikely to write code that uses the WSGI and CGI interfaces directly. Instead, you're better off using an established web application framework. Python developers have many web frameworks to choose from. Django, Pyramid (of the Pylons Project), Flask, and web2py are several "full-stack" frameworks that work well with App Engine. For convenience, App Engine includes Django as part of the runtime environment. You can include other frameworks and libraries with your application simply by adding them to your application directory. As we saw in Chapter 2, App Engine also includes a simple framework of its own, called webapp2.

By the time an app instance receives the request, it has already fired up the Python interpreter, ready to handle requests. If the instance has served a request for the application since it was initialized, it may have the application in memory as well, but if it hasn't, it imports the appropriate Python module for the request. The instance invokes the handler code with the data for the request, and returns the handler's response to the client.

When you run a Python program loaded from a *.py* file on your computer, the Python interpreter compiles the Python code to a compact bytecode format, which you might see on your computer as a *.pyc* file. If you edit your *.py* source, the interpreter will recompile it the next time it needs it. Because application code does not change after you've uploaded your app, App Engine precompiles all Python code to bytecode one time when you upload the app. This saves time when a module or script is imported for the first time in each instance of the app.

The Python interpreter remains in the instance memory for the lifetime of the instance. The interpreter loads your code according to Python's module import semantics. Typically, this means that once a module is imported for the first time on an instance, subsequent attempts to import it do nothing, as the module is already loaded. This is true across multiple requests handled by the same instance.

The Python 2.7 runtime environment uses a modified version of the official Python 2.7 interpreter, sometimes referred to as "CPython" to distinguish it from other Python interpreters. The application code must run entirely within the Python interpreter. That is, the code must be purely Python code, and cannot include or depend upon extensions to the interpreter. Python modules that include extensions written in C cannot be uploaded with your app or otherwise added to the runtime environment. The "pure Python" requirement can be problematic for some third-party libraries, so be sure that libraries you want to use operate without extensions.

A few popular Python libraries, including some that depend on C code, are available within the runtime environment. Refer back to "Python Libraries" on page 75 for more information.

App Engine sets the following environment variables at the beginning of each request, which you can access using os.environ:

APPLICATION_ID

> The ID of the application. The ID is preceded by s~ when running on App Engine, and dev~ when running in a development server.

CURRENT_VERSION_ID

> The ID of the version of the app serving this request.

AUTH_DOMAIN

> This is set to gmail.com if the user is signed in using a Google Account, or the domain of the app if signed in with a Google Apps account; not set otherwise.

SERVER_SOFTWARE

> The version of the runtime environment; starts with the word Development when running on the development server. For example:

```
import os

# ...

    if os.environ['SERVER_SOFTWARE'].startswith('Development'):
        # ... only executed in the development server ...
```

The Python interpreter prevents the app from accessing illegal system resources at a low level. Because a Python app can consist only of Python code, an app must perform all processing within the Python interpreter.

For convenience, portions of the Python standard library whose only use is to access restricted system resources have been disabled. If you attempt to import a disabled module or call a disabled function, the interpreter raises an ImportError. The Python development server enforces the standard module import restrictions, so you can test imports on your computer.

Some standard library modules have been replaced with alternative versions for speed or compatibility. Other modules have custom implementations, such as zipimport.

The Request Handler Abstraction

Let's review what we know so far about request handlers. A request handler is an entry point into the application code, mapped to a URL pattern in the application configuration. Here is a section of configuration for a request handler which would appear in the *app.yaml* file:

```
handlers:
- url: /profile/.*
  script: users.profile.app
```

A source file named *users/profile.py* contains a WSGI application instance in a variable named app. This code knows how to invoke the webapp2 framework to handle the request, which in turn calls our code:

```
import jinja2
import os
import webapp2

from google.appengine.api import users
from google.appengine.ext import ndb
```

```
class UserProfile(ndb.Model):
    user = ndb.UserProperty()

template_env = jinja2.Environment(
    loader=jinja2.FileSystemLoader(os.path.dirname(__file__)))

class ProfileHandler(webapp2.RequestHandler):
    def get(self):
        # Call the Users service to identify the user making the request,
        # if the user is signed in.
        current_user = users.get_current_user()

        # Call the Datastore service to retrieve the user's profile data.
        profile = None
        if current_user:
            profile = UserProfile.query().filter(
                UserProfile.user == current_user).fetch(1)

        # Render a response page using a template.
        template = template_env.get_template('profile.html')
        self.response.out.write(template.render({'profile': profile}))

app = webapp2.WSGIApplication([('/profile/?', ProfileHandler)], debug=True)
```

When a user visits the URL path /profile/ on this application's domain, App Engine matches the request to users.profile.app via the application configuration, and then invokes it to produce the response. The WSGIApplication creates an object of the ProfileHandler class with the request data, then calls its get() method. The method code makes use of two App Engine services, the Users service and the Datastore service, to access resources outside of the app code. It uses that data to make a web page, then exits.

In theory, the application process only needs to exist long enough to handle the request. When the request arrives, App Engine figures out which request handler it needs, makes room for it in its computation infrastructure, and creates it in a runtime environment. Once the request handler has created the response, the show is over, and App Engine is free to purge the request handler from memory. If the application needs data to live on between requests, it stores it by using a service like the datastore. The application itself does not live long enough to remember anything on its own.

Figure 4-2 illustrates this abstract life cycle of a request handler.

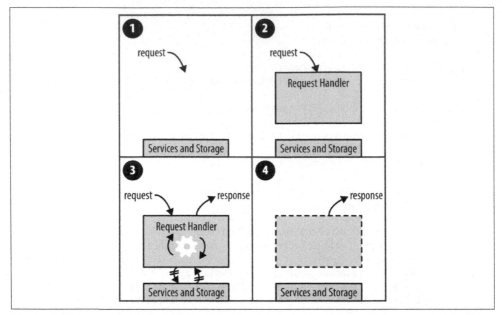

Figure 4-2. Request handlers in the abstract: (1) a request arrives; (2) a request handler is created; (3) the request handler calls services and computes the response; (4) the request handler terminates, the response is returned

On App Engine, a web application can handle many requests simultaneously. There could be many request handlers active at any given moment, in any stage of its life cycle. As shown in Figure 4-3, all these request handlers access the same services.

Each service has its own specification for managing concurrent access from multiple request handlers, and for the most part, a request handler doesn't have to think about the fact that other request handlers are in play. The big exception here is datastore transactions, which we'll discuss in detail in Chapter 8.

The request handler abstraction is useful for thinking about how to design your app, and how the service-oriented architecture is justified. App Engine can create an arbitrary number of request handlers to handle an arbitrary number of requests simultaneously, and your code barely has to know anything about it. This is how your app scales with traffic automatically.

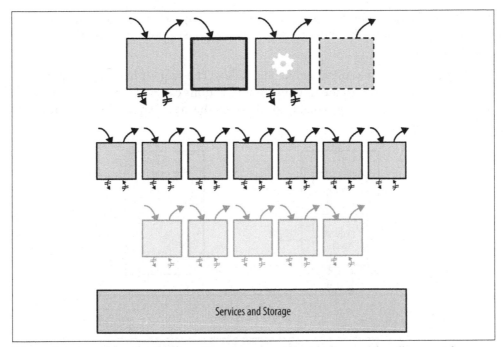

Figure 4-3. A web application handles many requests simultaneously; all request handlers access the same services

Introducing Instances

The idea of a web application being a big pot of bubbling request handlers is satisfying, but in practice, this abstraction fails to capture an important aspect of real-world system software. Starting a program for the first time on a fresh system can be expensive: code is read into RAM from disk, memory is allocated, data structures are set up with starting values, and configuration files are read and parsed. App Engine initializes new runtime environments prior to using them to execute request handlers, so the environment initialization cost is not incurred during the handler execution. But application code often needs to perform its own initialization that App Engine can't do on its own ahead of time. The Python interpreter is designed to exploit local memory, and many web application frameworks perform initialization, expecting the investment to pay off over multiple requests. It's wasteful and impractical to do this at the beginning of every request handler, while the user is waiting.

App Engine solves this problem with *instances*, long-lived containers for request handlers that retain local memory. At any given moment, an application has a pool of zero or more instances allocated for handling requests. App Engine routes new requests to available instances. It creates new instances as needed, and shuts down instances that are excessively idle. When a request arrives at an instance that has already handled previous requests, the instance is likely to have already done the necessary preparatory work, and can serve the response more quickly than a fresh instance.

The picture now looks something like Figure 4-4. The request handler still only lives as long as it takes to return the response, but its actions can now affect instance memory. This instance memory remains available to the next request handler that executes inside the instance.

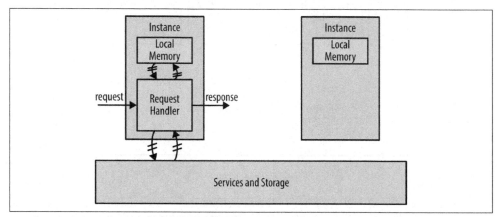

Figure 4-4. An instance handles a request, while another instance sits idle

Keep in mind that instances are created and destroyed dynamically, and requests are routed to instances based purely on availability. While instances are meant to live longer than request handlers, they are as ephemeral as request handlers, and any given request may be handled by a new instance. There is no guarantee that requests of a particular sort will always be handled by the same instance, nor is it assured that an instance will still be around after a given request is handled. Outside of a request handler, the application is not given the opportunity to rescue data from local memory prior to an instance being shut down. If you need to store user-specific information (such as session data), you must use a storage service. Instance memory is only suitable for local caching.

Instances can provide another crucial performance benefit: multithreading. With multithreading enabled in your application configuration, an instance will start additional request handlers in separate threads as local resources allow, and execute them concurrently. All threads share the same instance memory just like any other multithreaded application—which means your code must take care to protect shared memory during critical sections of code. You can use Python's language and library features for synchronizing access to shared memory (such as the Queue module).

Figure 4-5 illustrates an instance with multithreading enabled. Refer to "Multithreading" on page 55 for information on how to enable or disable multithreading in application configuration.

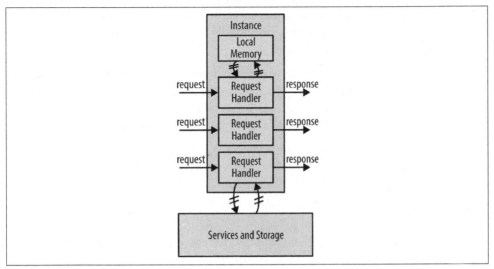

Figure 4-5. A multithreaded instance handles multiple requests concurrently

Instance uptime is App Engine's billable unit for computation, measured in fractions of an *instance hour*. This makes multithreading an important technique for maximizing throughput and minimizing costs. Most request handlers will spend a significant amount of time waiting for service calls, and a multithreaded instance can use the CPU for other handlers during that time.

Request Scheduling and Pending Latency

App Engine routes each request to an available instance. If all instances are busy, App Engine starts a new instance. This is App Engine's *automatic scaling* feature, and is what makes it especially useful for handling real-time user traffic for web and mobile clients.

App Engine considers an instance to be "available" for a request if it believes the instance can handle the request in a reasonable amount of time. With multithreading disabled, this definition is simple: an instance is available if it is not presently busy handling a request.

With multithreading enabled, App Engine decides whether an instance is available based on several factors. It considers the current load on the instance (CPU and memory) from its active request handlers, and its capacity. It also considers historical knowledge of the load caused by previous requests to the given URL path. If it seems likely that the new request can be handled effectively in the capacity of an existing instance, the request is scheduled to that instance.

Incoming requests are put on a *pending queue* in preparation for scheduling. App Engine will leave requests on the queue for a bit of time while it waits for existing instances to become available, before deciding it needs to create new instances. This waiting time is called the *pending latency*.

You can control how App Engine decides when to start and stop instances in response to variances in traffic. App Engine uses sensible defaults for typical applications, but you can tune several variables to your app based on how your app uses computational resources and what traffic patterns you're expecting.

To set these variables, you edit your *app.yaml* file, and add an `automatic_scaling` section, like so:

```
automatic_scaling:
  min_pending_latency: automatic
  max_pending_latency: 30ms
```

The *maximum pending latency* (`max_pending_latency`) is the most amount of time a request will wait on the pending queue before App Engine decides more instances are needed to handle the current level of traffic. Lowering the maximum pending latency potentially reduces the average wait time, at the expense of activating more instances. Conversely, raising the maximum favors reusing existing instances, at the expense of potentially making the user wait a bit longer for a response. The setting is a number of milliseconds, with `ms` as the unit.

The *minimum pending latency* (`min_pending_latency`) specifies a minimum amount of time a request must be on the pending queue before App Engine can conclude a new instance needs to be started. Raising the minimum encourages App Engine to be more conservative about creating new instances. This minimum only refers to creating new instances. Naturally, if an existing instance is available for a pending request, the request is scheduled immediately. The setting is a number of milliseconds (with the unit: `5ms`), or `automatic` to let App Engine adjust this value on the fly as needed (the default).

Warmup Requests

There is a period of time between the moment App Engine decides it needs a new instance and the moment the instance is available to handle the next request off the request queue. During this time, App Engine initializes the instance on the server hardware, sets up the runtime environment, and makes the app files available to the instance. App Engine takes this preparation period into account when scheduling request handlers and instance creation.

The goal is to make the instance as ready as possible prior to handling the first request, so when the request handler begins, the user only waits on the request handler logic, not the initialization. But App Engine can only do so much on its own. Many initialization tasks are specific to your application code. For instance, App Engine can't automatically import every module in a Python app, because imports execute code, and an app may need to import modules selectively.

App-specific initialization potentially puts undue burden on the first request handler to execute on a fresh instance. A "loading request" typically takes longer to execute than subsequent requests handled by the same instance. This is common enough that App Engine will add a log message automatically when a request is the first request for an instance, so you can detect a correlation between performance issues and app initialization.

You can mitigate the impact of app initialization with a feature called *warmup requests*. With warmup requests enabled, App Engine will attempt to issue a request to a specific warmup URL immediately following the creation of a new instance. You can associate a warmup request handler with this URL to perform initialization tasks that are better performed outside of a user-facing request handler.

To enable warmup requests, activate the `warmup` inbound service in your app configuration. (Refer to "Inbound Services" on page 73.) In Python, set this in your *app.yaml* file:

```
inbound_services:
- warmup
```

Warmup requests are issued to this URL path:

```
/_ah/warmup
```

You bind your warmup request handler to this URL path in the usual way.

 There are a few rare cases where an instance will not receive a warmup request prior to the first user request even with warmup requests enabled. Make sure your user request handler code does not depend on the warmup request handler having already been called on the instance.

Resident Instances

Instances stick around for a while after finishing their work, in case they can be reused to handle more requests. If App Engine decides it's no longer useful to keep an instance around, it shuts down the instance. An instance that is allocated but is not handling any requests is considered an *idle instance*.

Instances that App Engine creates and destroys as needed by traffic demands are known as *dynamic instances*. App Engine uses historical knowledge about your app's traffic to tune its algorithm for dynamic instance allocation to find a balance between instance availability and efficient use of resources.

You can adjust how App Engine allocates instances by using two settings: minimum idle instances and maximum idle instances. To adjust these settings, edit your *app.yaml* file, and set the appropriate values in the `automatic_scaling` section, like so:

```
automatic_scaling:
  min_idle_instances: 0
  max_idle_instances: automatic
```

The *minimum idle instances* (`min_idle_instances`) setting ensures that a number of instances are always available to absorb sudden increases in traffic. They are started once and continue to run even if they are not being used. App Engine will try to keep resident instances in reserve, starting new instances dynamically (*dynamic instances*) in response to load. When traffic increases and the pending queue heats up, App Engine uses the resident instances to take on the extra load while it starts new dynamic instances.

Setting a nonzero minimum for idle instances also ensures that at least this many instances are never terminated due to low traffic. Because App Engine does not start and stop these instances due to traffic fluctuations, these instances are not dynamic; instead, they are known as *resident instances*.

You *must* enable warmup instances to set the minimum idle instances to a nonzero value.

Reserving resident instances can help your app handle sharp increases in traffic. For example, you may want to increase the resident instances prior to launching your product or announcing a new feature. You can reduce them again as traffic fluctuations return to normal.

App Engine only maintains resident instances for the default version of your app. While you can make requests to nondefault versions, only dynamic instances will be created to handle those requests. When you change the default version (in the Versions panel of the Cloud Console), the previous resident instances are allowed to finish their current request handlers, then they are shut down and new resident instances running the new default version are created.

Resident instances are billed at the same rate as dynamic instances. Be sure you want to pay for 24 instance hours per day per resident instance before changing this setting. It can be annoying to see these expensive instances get little traffic compared to dynamic instances. But when an app gets high traffic at variable times, the added performance benefit may be worth the investment.

The *maximum idle instances* (`max_idle_instances`) setting adjusts how aggressively App Engine terminates idle instances above the minimum. Increasing the maximum causes idle dynamic instances to live longer; decreasing the maximum causes them to die more quickly. A larger maximum is useful for keeping more dynamic instances available for rapid fluctuations in traffic, at the expense of greater unused (dynamic) capacity. The name "maximum idle instances" is not entirely intuitive, but it opposes "minimum idle instances" in an obvious way: the maximum can't be lower than the minimum. A setting of `automatic` lets App Engine decide how quickly to terminate instances based on traffic patterns.

Instance Classes and Utilization

App Engine uses several factors to decide when to assign a request to a given instance. If the request handlers currently running on an instance are consuming most of the instance's CPU or memory, App Engine considers the instance fully utilized, and either looks for another available instance, leaves the request on the pending queue, or schedules a new instance to be started.

For safety's sake, App Engine also assumes a maximum number of concurrent requests per instance. The default maximum is 10 concurrent request handlers. If you know in advance that your request handlers consume few computational resources on an instance, you can increase this limit to as much as 100. To do so, in the *app.yaml* file, edit the `automatic_scaling` section to include the `max_concurrent_requests` setting:

```
automatic_scaling:
  max_concurrent_requests: 20
```

Naturally, App Engine may consider an instance utilized when fewer request handlers than the maximum are running. The maximum just gives App Engine some guidance as to what's typical, so it can start more instances before the existing instances get too hot.

Another way to fit more concurrent requests onto an instance is to just use instances with more memory and faster CPUs. The *instance class* determines the computational resources available to each instance. By default, App Engine uses the smallest instance class. Larger instance classes provide more resources at a proportionally higher cost per instance hour.

You set the instance class for the app using the `instance_class` setting in *app.yaml*:

```
instance_class: F4
```

With automatic scaling, you can choose from the following instance classes:

F1
    128 MB of memory, 600 MHz CPU (this is the default)

F2
    256 MB of memory, 1.2 GHz CPU

F4
    512 MB of memory, 2.4 GHz CPU

F4_1G
    1024 MB (1 GB) of memory, 2.4 GHz CPU

Instance Hours and Billing

Instance use is a resource measured in instance hours. An instance hour corresponds to an hour of clock time that an instance is alive. An instance is on the clock regardless of whether it is actively serving traffic or is idle, or whether it is resident or dynamic.

Each instance incurs a mandatory charge of 15 minutes, added to the end of the instance's lifespan. This accounts for the computational cost of instance creation and other related resources. This is one reason why you might adjust the minimum pending latency and maximum idle instances settings to avoid excess instance creation.

The free quotas include a set of instance hours for dynamic instances. The free quota for dynamic instances is enough to power one instance of the most basic class ("F1") continuously, plus a few extra hours per day.

Computation is billed by the instance hour. Larger instance classes have proportionally larger costs per instance hour. See the official documentation for the current rates. (This industry is competitive, and prices change more frequently than books do.)

The Instances Console Panel

The Cloud Console includes a panel for inspecting your app's currently active instances. A portion of such a panel is shown in Figure 4-6. In the sidebar navigation, this is the Instances panel under Compute, App Engine.

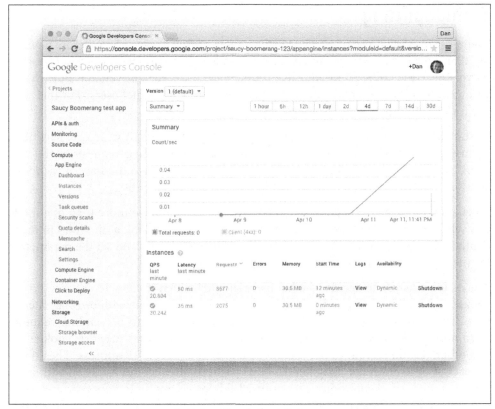

Figure 4-6. The Instances panel of the Cloud Console

You can use this panel to inspect the general behavior of your application code running in an instance. This includes summary information about the number of instances, and averages for QPS, latency, and memory usage per instance over the last minute of activity. Each active instance is also itemized, with its own QPS and latency averages, total request and error counts over the lifetime of the instance, the age of the instance, current memory usage, and whether the instance is resident or dynamic. You can query the logs for requests handled by the individual instance.

You can also shut down an instance manually from this panel. If you shut down a resident instance, a new resident instance will be started in its place, effectively like restarting the instance. If you shut down a dynamic instance, a new instance may or may not be created as per App Engine's algorithm and the app's idle instance settings.

As with several other Console panels, the Instances panel is specific to the selected version of your app. If you want to inspect instances handling requests for a specific app version, be sure to select it from the Console's app version drop-down at the top of the screen.

Traffic Splitting

The most important use of versions is to test new software candidates before launching them to all of your users. You can test a nondefault version yourself by addressing its version URL, while all of your live traffic goes to the default version. But what if you want to test a new candidate with a percentage of your actual users? For that, you use traffic splitting.

With traffic splitting enabled, App Engine identifies the users of your app, partitions them according to percentages that you specify, and routes their requests to the versions that correspond to their partitions. You can then analyze the logs of each version separately to evaluate the candidate for issues and other data.

To enable traffic splitting, go to the Versions panel. If you have more than one module, select the module whose traffic you want to split. (We'll look at modules in more depth in Chapter 5.) Click the "Enable traffic splitting" button, and set the parameters for the traffic split in the dialog that opens.

The dialog asks you to decide whether users should be identified by IP address or by a cookie. Splitting by cookie is likely to be more accurate for users with browser clients, and accommodates cases where a single user might appear to be sending requests from multiple IP addresses. If the user is not using a client that supports cookies, or you otherwise don't want to use them, you can split traffic by IP address. The goal is for each user to always be assigned the same partition throughout a session with multiple requests, so clients don't get confused talking to multiple versions, and your experiment gets consistent results.

Traffic splitting occurs with requests sent to the main URL for the app or module. Requests for the version-specific URLs bypass traffic splitting.

## CHAPTER 5

Using Modules

You can build large web applications using just App Engine's automatically scaling instances, and many have. Automatic scaling is well suited to large scale user traffic and can accommodate real-world traffic spikes with ease. But it isn't long before you want to do more computational tasks with App Engine besides serving user traffic and residual tasks. Other parts of a mature app's architecture, such as batch jobs, long-running computing tasks, and special purpose always-on backend services, don't quite fit the same mold. Performance tuning that's suited to one kind of computation doesn't suit another. Your web traffic may work well with small instance classes and aggressive pending queues, while your nightly data crawl needs more memory on a single instance. And you probably don't want your user traffic instance pool saturated by a batch job.

App Engine lets you define sets of instances for different purposes, called *modules*. Each module can be configured and tuned separately using all of the options we've discussed so far, such as instance classes and automatic scaling parameters. Each module gets its own URL, so it can be addressed individually. You can make a module's URL publicly accessible or just call it internally from other modules. Each module can scale its own instances according to its purpose-specific traffic patterns.

For even greater flexibility, App Engine offers two additional scaling patterns beyond automatic scaling: *manual scaling* and *basic scaling*. With manual scaling, you start and stop instances directly using the Cloud SDK or within the app by calling an API. Basic scaling has the same features as manual scaling, with the addition of a simple configurable scheduler that can start new instances in response to requests and stop idle instances after a period of time. Each module can be configured to use any of the three available scaling strategies.

Modules can also be deployed separately from each other, at separate times and with separate versions. It's easiest to use the same code base for all modules, but this gives you more options as to when software versions are deployed or rolled back.

With modules, you can design an architecture that meets your application's needs, and develop and tune each component separately.

An Example Layout

Let's consider a simple modular architecture for our hypothetical multiplayer game. Refer to Figure 5-1.

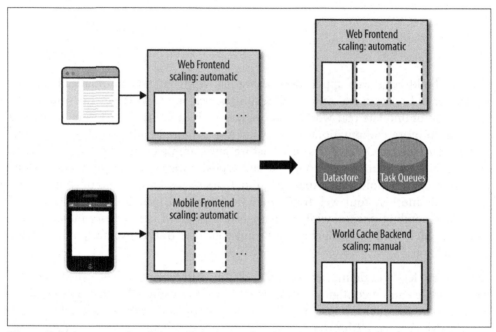

Figure 5-1. An example of an application architecture using modules

In this example, a "web frontend" module handles all of the user traffic coming from browsers, using the automatic scaling strategy. This is the default module for the website for the game, and serves all traffic for the main domain name. All apps have at least one module, and typically the default module uses automatic scaling. The example apps we've discussed so far have one module using this default configuration.

This multiplayer game has a mobile app. The mobile app communicates with the App Engine app via an API hosted in the "mobile frontend" module, with its own URL. Just like the web frontend, this API traffic comes from users, so we use automatic scaling for this module as well. Making it a separate module from the web traffic isolates it for the purposes of performance tuning and makes it easier to deploy changes to the web and mobile experiences separately. We may want to coordinate API support with mobile app store releases, or provision additional resident instances in anticipation of a scheduled mobile launch.

Both user-facing frontend modules use small instance classes and run code tailored to produce fast responses to user client requests. They communicate with the built-in App Engine services as usual, such as the datastore, memcache, and task queue services. We use two additional modules to provide custom services of our own.

The "battle simulation backend" service performs heavy-duty computation for updating the game world in response to major events. We configure this module to use a large instance class to take advantage of the faster CPU. We use the basic scaling strategy for this so we can provision more instances automatically, up to a fixed maximum number of instances. If we eventually discover that we need more battle simulation instances, we can evaluate the costs and benefits, and adjust the configuration accordingly. We might use the "pull queue" feature of the task queue service to send work to this backend, or we can call it directly from the frontends using an API of our own design. (For more information on task queues, see Chapter 16.)

The "world cache backend" maintains a copy of the data that describes the game world. This module is configured to use an instance class with a large amount of RAM and a fixed number of always-on resident instances. Of course, we must persist the game world to the datastore on a regular basis or risk losing data. So (in this hypothetical example) we use a *write-behind cache* that updates RAM first then periodically flushes to the datastore with minimal risk of loss. We use manual scaling because we want this special cache to stay resident as long as possible, and the amount of memory we need is proportional to the size of the world, not to the number of active users.

This example is simplified for illustration purposes; a real multiplayer game architecture might be more sophisticated. This provides a basic idea of how separate modules with distinct configurations allow you to optimize costs and performance.

Configuring Modules

You already know how to configure the default module using the *app.yaml* file. The file selects the runtime, specifies whether the code is threadsafe, defines handlers mapped to URL paths, and so forth. By default, the default module uses automatic scaling, and you can tune its parameters with the automatic_scaling options we discussed earlier.

To define a module other than the default module, create another file whose name ends in .yaml and isn't one of the other .yaml filenames recognized by App Engine. Give the module an ID using the module: parameter. It's typical to use the module ID for the filename as well, but it's not required. The module ID follows the same rules as the app ID: lowercase letters, numbers, hyphens, and the first character must be a letter.

Continuing the previous example, we can configure the mobile frontend module (mobile-fe) using a file named *mobile-fe.yaml*, like so:

```
module: mobile-fe
application: app-id
version: 1
runtime: python27
api_version: 1
threadsafe: true

instance_class: F2

automatic_scaling:
  min_idle_instances: 3

handlers:
# ...
```

The version parameter is specific to the given module, and does not have to be unique across all modules. The limit of 60 versions applies to the total count of versions across all modules.

The *app.yaml* file for the default module is just a module configuration file. App Engine knows it describes the default module because it does not contain a module ID parameter. You can also use the special module ID default to declare that a configuration file is for the default module.

Manual and Basic Scaling

To declare that the module uses a manual scaling strategy, include a manual_scaling section in the configuration (and do not include an automatic_scaling section). Our game's world data cache is scaled manually with five instances to start, so *world-cache.yaml* looks like this:

```
module: world-cache
application: app-id
version: 1
runtime: python27
api_version: 1
threadsafe: true

instance_class: B4_1G

manual_scaling:
  instances: 5
```

```
handlers:
# ...
```

The `instances` parameter sets the number of instances started when the configuration is deployed for the first time. You can start and stop instances after deployment by hand with the Cloud Console or programmatically with the modules API (described in "The Modules API" on page 121).

To declare that the module uses basic scaling, include a `basic_scaling` section. Our game's battle simulation infrastructure is only needed on demand, so *battle-sim.yaml* looks like this:

```
module: battle-sim
application: app-id
version: 1
runtime: python27
api_version: 1
threadsafe: true

instance_class: B8

basic_scaling:
  max_instances: 10
  idle_timeout: 5m

handlers:
# ...
```

With basic scaling, `max_instances` is the maximum number of instances to start in response to requests to the module. If a request arrives when all instances are busy and the number of active instances is less than the maximum, a new instance is started. `idle_timeout` is the amount of time an instance must be idle before it is shut down automatically, specified as a number and a unit (`m` for minutes).

Modules with manual or basic scaling use a different set of instance classes than modules with automatic scaling: B1, B2, B4, B4_1G, and B8. These are similar to the corresponding F* classes, with the addition of B8, which has 1 GB of memory and a 4.8 GHz CPU. If not specified, the default instance class for manual or basic scaling is B2.

If the module's configuration file does not specify the scaling strategy, or it includes an `automatic_scaling` section, then automatic scaling is used for the module.

Manual Scaling and Versions

You can create multiple versions of a module by changing the `version:` parameter in its configuration file, then deploying the module. Exactly one version is the default version for the module, and you can change the default version using the Cloud Console or the `appcfg.py` command. You can delete unused versions from the Cloud Console or the `appcfg.py` command as well.

With manual scaling, App Engine starts the requested number of instances when the module is deployed. If you have multiple versions of a manually scaled module, App Engine may be running the requested number of instances for *each* version of the module. Be sure to delete unused versions or shut down their instances to avoid burning through your quota or your budget.

This is different from automatic scaling and resident (minimum idle) instances: resident instances are only started and maintained for the default version. Manual scaling instances are started for all versions when they are deployed, and stay running until they are shut down via the Cloud Console, the `appcfg.py` command, or an API call.

Startup Requests

An instance does not run any code until it receives a request. This is reasonable for modules that respond to requests, such as a service that waits for an API call before doing any work. In many cases, you probably want the instance to start doing some work right away, either to kick off a long-running process or to prepare the instance for responding to future events.

When App Engine starts an instance in a module with manual or basic scaling, it issues a "start" request at the following URL path:

```
/_ah/start
```

You can map a request handler to this path in the `handlers:` section of the module's configuration. This handler is called on each instance that is started.

If the start handler returns, it must return an HTTP status code indicating success (200–299). A 404 status code is also considered "success," in case there is no handler mapped to the URL path. If the handler returns a server error, App Engine considers the instance startup to have failed and terminates the instance. It then starts a new instance, if needed.

An instance will not respond to other requests until the start handler has returned. If the module does not need to respond to requests, then you can put all of the module's work in the start handler. The start handler can even be a continuously running process: modules with manual scaling do not have a request deadline. If the module must do both background work and respond to requests, a better option is for the start handler to create a background thread, then exit immediately. We'll look at background threads in a moment.

Startup requests for modules with manual and basic scaling are similar to warmup requests for automatic scaling, but you set them up in different ways and use them for different purposes. (Refer back to "Warmup Requests" on page 98.)

Shutdown Hooks

There are two ways that application code can know when an instance is being shut down. One is to call the is_shutting_down() function from the google.appengine.api.runtime module periodically, and react accordingly if the method returns True:

```
import webapp2
from google.appengine.api import runtime

class MainHandler(webapp2.RequestHandler):
    def get(self):
        # Initialization.
        # ...

        while not runtime.is_shutting_down():
            # Do a bit of work...

        # Clean up.
        # ...

app = webapp2.WSGIApplication([('/_ah/start', MainHandler)])
```

Alternatively, the app can register a *shutdown hook* with the runtime environment. This hook is a Python function that App Engine calls in a new thread when it's about to shut down the instance.

If the function raises an exception, this exception will propagate to all active request handlers and threads. This makes it easy for the shutdown hook to interrupt all work in progress and coordinate cleanup efforts:

```
import webapp2
from google.appengine.api import runtime

class Shutdown(Exception):
    pass

def shutdown():
    # Clean up.
    # ...

    raise Shutdown()

class MainHandler(webapp2.RequestHandler):
    def get(self):
        # Set the shutdown hook.
```

```
runtime.set_shutdown_hook(shutdown)

# Initialization.
# ...

try:
    while True:
        # Do work...

except Shutdown:
    # Additional task-specific cleanup.
    # ...

app = webapp2.WSGIApplication([('/_ah/start', MainHandler)])
```

Once App Engine has decided to shut down an instance, the app has 30 seconds after the shutdown hook is called to finish what it is doing. At the end of the 30 seconds, the instance goes away.

Neither the shutdown hook nor the 30-second runway are guaranteed. Under rare circumstances, App Engine may need to kill an instance before the shutdown hook can be called or completed. Long-running processes should persist their state periodically and be able to recover from a sudden interruption.

 App Engine logs a request to the URL path /_ah/stop when it initiates shutdown on an instance. You can't map a request handler to this URL: it uses a built-in handler that invokes the shutdown hook. You can look for this request in the logs when you're troubleshooting issues with shutdown logic.

Background Threads

During a request handler, an app can invoke regular Python threads to perform concurrent work. Once the handler returns a response, App Engine assumes that any unfinished threads are no longer needed and terminates them. Regular threads cannot outlast the request handler. This isn't a problem for modules that do request handling with automatic scaling, as the request handler exits once it has a response and can use other means (such as task queues) to defer work. Nor is this a problem for a simple always-on instance with manual scaling, which can perform a large or continuously running job in its start handler and manage threads inside that process without terminating.

We need another solution for the case where a module with manual scaling needs to perform work in the background and also accept requests. Putting the background job in the start handler is insufficient because the instance can't accept requests until the start handler finishes. Instead, we need a way to initiate work from the start handler, then exit from the handler while the work continues in the background.

For this purpose, App Engine provides *background threads*, a special kind of thread that detaches from the request handler and continues running after the handler returns. Only instances with manual or basic scaling can use background threads. In Python, you use the `BackgroundThread` class from the `google.appengine.api.back ground_thread` module as you would the `threading.Thread` class from the Python standard library:

```
from google.appengine.api import background_thread

def work():
    # ...

# ...
        thread = background_thread.BackgroundThread(
            target=work)
        thread.start()
```

Log messages for background tasks appear in your logs under a virtual request for the URL `/_ah/background`. The virtual request information includes the ID of the instance on which it is running, and how much time has elapsed since it was started.

Modules and the Development Server

The development server can run multiple modules simultaneously on your local machine. Each module gets its own port number on `localhost`, chosen automatically from the available ports.

To start the development server with modules, run the `dev_appserver.py` command, and provide the path to the configuration file of each module you wish to run, including *app.yaml*:

```
dev_appserver.py app.yaml battle-sim.yaml mobile-fe.yaml world-cache.yaml
```

The development server prints the selected port numbers for each module to the console:

```
INFO ... Starting module "default" running at: http://localhost:8080
INFO ... Starting module "battle-sim" running at: http://localhost:8081
INFO ... Starting module "mobile-fe" running at: http://localhost:8082
INFO ... Starting module "world-cache" running at: http://localhost:8083
```

You can use these ports to send test traffic to modules directly. Traffic to the module ports is distributed to instances according to the scaling policy for the module.

The individual instances are also assigned ports. You can see the current state of the instances with statistics and links to all of them in the development server console at *http://localhost:8000*.

The development server simulates automatic scaling and manual scaling. For modules configured with basic scaling, the development server initializes the maximum number of instances, then issues the `/_ah/start` request for each instance when the instance receives its first request.

Unfortunately, there is no way to shut down a simulated instance in the development server. To test your shutdown hook, you must deploy the app to App Engine. When running on App Engine, you can shut down instances manually from the command line or the Cloud Console.

 When calling one module from another, you do not need to hard-code the `localhost` URLs into your app for testing. Instead, you can determine the URL for a module by calling a function. See "Addressing Modules with URLs" on page 115.

Deploying Modules

When we introduced deploying an application with the `appcfg.py update` command, we used the application root directory as its argument:

```
appcfg.py update myapp
```

When given the application root directory like this, the `appcfg.py update` command locates the *app.yaml* file in this directory, then deploys the app to the module described by that file. In previous examples, *app.yaml* described the default module with automatic scaling, so this did what we wanted. (This is the only way the filename *app.yaml* is special.)

The `appcfg.py update` command can also accept module configuration file names as arguments. When given a module configuration file, `appcfg.py update` deploys the app and all of its files to that module. This works with `app.yaml` or any other module configuration file:

```
appcfg.py update myapp/world-cache.yaml
```

You can list multiple module configuration files in one command to deploy them all in sequence:

```
appcfg.py update myapp/app.yaml myapp/mobile-fe.yaml \
            myapp/battle-sim.yaml myapp/world-cache.yaml
```

The `appcfg.py update` command assumes that the directory containing the configuration file is the application root directory for the purposes of the module, and it deploys all of the files it finds to the module. It's a good practice to use the same application files for all modules, and simply use different `handlers:` in each configuration file to control their individual behavior.

Alternatively, you can store each module's configuration file and code in a separate directory. As long as the application IDs are the same, they will all be deployed to the same application.

Deploying a module with manual or basic scaling causes all of its active instances to be stopped and started. If you know a module hasn't changed and you do not want its instances to be restarted when you deploy, be sure to exclude that module's configuration file from the `appcfg.py update` command.

So if the runtime environment is selected by a field in the module's configuration file, and each module can be deployed separately with different code, does that mean one app can use different runtime environments for different modules? Can you have one module implemented in Python and another module implemented in Java?

The answer is yes (!), with a proviso. You can write a module in Java and deploy it to an app that already has another module (possibly the default module) in Python, using the same application ID, different module IDs, and different runtime configurations. The proviso is that you can't easily test interactions between the two modules in a development server. The Python app and the Java app must run in separate development servers from their corresponding SDKs, and these development servers know nothing about each other. They can't share a simulated datastore or other data services, and they don't know each other's development URLs automatically. At the very least, you'd have to implement a layer that detects whether the app is in a development server (via the `SERVER_SOFTWARE` environment variable) and stub out the service calls.

This is still a useful scenario if you're willing to develop and test the modules separately, which is a reasonable thing to do anyway. And you can always deploy nondefault versions to App Engine for integration testing.

Addressing Modules with URLs

We've already seen how you can access a deployed application using its `appspot.com` URL, with the application ID as the leftmost subdomain:

```
http://app-id.appspot.com/
```

We now know that this URL accesses the *default version* of the *default module*. The default version is the version selected as the default in the Versions panel of the Cloud Console. The default module is the module whose configuration file omits the `module:` parameter or sets it to `default`, typically *app.yaml*.

If the app has multiple modules, each module gets its own domain name. This domain is formed by taking the appspot.com URL for the app and prefixing the module ID:

```
http://module-id.app-id.appspot.com/
```

This URL accesses the default version of the specified module. If the module has multiple instances, App Engine routes a web request for this URL to an instance selected by its load-balancing algorithm. With automatic scaling, and with basic scaling where the number of active instances is below the configured maximum, App Engine may start a new instance if all active instances are busy, though this doesn't have an immediate impact on where the current request is routed.

You may recall that it's possible to access a specific version of an app, with a URL like this:

```
http://version-id.app-id.appspot.com/
```

More specifically, this accesses a specific version of the default module. You've probably already guessed that this means there's a potential for version IDs on the default module and module IDs to conflict, and you're right. You can't use the same ID for a module and one of the versions of the default module.

You've also probably guessed that it's possible to access a specific version of a specific module, and you're right again:

```
http://version-id.module-id.app-id.appspot.com/
```

If a module with manual or basic scaling has multiple instances, you can address the instance directly with one more piece of the domain:

```
http://instance-id.module-id.app-id.appspot.com/
```

In this case, the instance ID must be a running instance of the default version for the module. You can also access an instance of a nondefault version of a module using the longest possible URL, containing all of the IDs:

```
http://instance-id.version-id.module-id.app-id.appspot.com/
```

Instance IDs are determined at runtime, so you need to call an API to figure out what they are. We'll see how in "The Modules API" on page 121.

Calling Modules from Other Modules

One of the most common uses of modules is to build backend services for other modules to access via endpoints. You can send a request from one module to another using the URL Fetch service, an App Engine service that manages outgoing HTTP requests. (See Chapter 13 for a complete introduction to this service.) The request can go to the module's URL, like any other:

```
from google.appengine.api import urlfetch

# ...
        module_url = 'http://module-id.app-id.appspot.com/api/list'
        result = urlfetch.fetch(module_url)
        if result.status_code == 200:
            # ...
```

Adding the module URL directly to the code like this is not a good practice. Better would be to calculate the module URL from environmental factors, including whether the app is running in the development server and what the current app's ID is. Helpfully, App Engine has an API for this:

```
from google.appengine.api import modules
from google.appengine.api import urlfetch

# ...
        module_url = 'http://{}/api/list'.format(
            modules.get_hostname(module='module-id'))

        result = urlfetch.fetch(module_url)
        if result.status_code == 200:
            # ...
```

The `get_hostname()` function in the `google.appengine.api.modules` module returns the appropriate module-specific domain name for the environment. In a development server, this is the `localhost` hostname with the appropriate port number added. On App Engine, this is calculated from the module ID and the current app ID. The `get_hostname()` function accepts optional `version` and `instance` parameters to select a specific version or instance, and you can omit any of `module`, `version`, or `instance` to select the module, version, and instance currently running the code (or the default version or instance when selecting a different module).

Module endpoints that are called by the app itself usually should not be called by outsiders that happen to know the URL. App Engine makes it easy to secure these endpoints so only calls from within the app and authenticated requests from the app's developers can access it. To set this up, configure the handler for the endpoint in the module's configuration file so that its `login:` property is `admin`:

```
module: module-id
# ...

handlers:
- url: /api/.*
  script: backend.app
  login: admin
```

We saw this administrator-only configuration in "Authorization with Google Accounts" on page 71. `login: admin` lets through URL Fetch requests coming from the app itself. We'll see this again later for other kinds of self-calling, such as in Chapter 16.

Module URLs and Secure Connections

Back in "Configuring Secure Connections" on page 67, we mentioned that `app spot.com` URLs with multiple parts need special treatment when using HTTPS. The same applies to all module-specific `appspot.com` URLs as well.

As a reminder, to access a module-specific URL with HTTPS, replace all of the dots (.) to the left of the app ID with `-dot-` (hyphen, the word "dot," hyphen), like so:

```
https://module-id-dot-app-id.appspot.com/
https://version-id-dot-module-id-dot-app-id.appspot.com/
```

Module URLs and Custom Domains

The `appspot.com` URLs are sufficient for internal calls. If you want to accept external requests directly to a specific module and you don't mind sharing your app ID with the world, you can advertise the `appspot.com` URL. There's nothing inherently wrong with exposing an app ID, but you might prefer to avoid it for aesthetic reasons.

If you set up a custom domain using the procedure discussed in "Domain Names" on page 62, you can use subdomains of your custom domain to access modules. For this to work, you must update the DNS record with your DNS hosting service so that the appropriate subdomains go to Google. You can make this a "wildcard subdomain," so all subdomains for your custom domain will work, and you don't have to update DNS records as you make changes to module names. Wildcard subdomains are required if you want to address individual instances directly, because instance IDs are determined dynamically.

With the appropriate DNS configuration in place, you can access a module using the module ID as a subdomain, like so:

```
http://module-id.example.com/
```

Similarly, you can access instances like so:

```
http://instance-id.module-id.example.com/
```

Subdomains of custom domains always use the default version for the module.

You cannot access modules via subdomains of a custom domain set up as a Google Apps domain. Unfortunately, at this time, this means that you cannot access modules with custom domains via HTTPS. If you need HTTPS, the only option is the `appspot.com` domain, using the `-dot-` notation.

Dispatching Requests to Modules

Sometimes you want requests to reach nondefault modules, but you don't want to expose URLs on subdomains. Instead, you want to map URL paths on the main domain to modules. For example, instead of using http://mobile-fe.example.com/ for your mobile REST API, you'd prefer to use http://www.example.com/api/

App Engine lets you do this using yet another configuration file, called *dispatch.yaml*. It looks like this:

```
dispatch:
- url: "*/static/*"
  module: default

- url: "*/api/*"
  module: mobile-fe

- url: "saucy-boomerang-123.appspot.com/test/*"
  module: test
```

By necessity, this file is very simple: each dispatch rule is a directive for Google's high-performance frontends to override its own decision about how to route a request. The file can contain up to 10 rules. Each rule consists of a url pattern, and the name of the module that should handle the request, where default is the name of the default module.

Unlike an *app.yaml* file, the URL pattern matches both the domain of the request and the URL path. The first slash (/) in the pattern always matches the boundary between the domain and the path, and so must be included. You can use a wildcard (*) character at the beginning, at the end, or both, to match zero or more characters. Fancier pattern matching is not supported.

Consider this url value:

```
- url: "*/api/*"
  module: mobile-fe
```

The beginning wildcard appears before the first slash, and so this rule applies to all domains, including the custom domain, the appspot.com domain, and all subdomains. The pattern after the first slash matches all URL paths that begin with /api/, followed by zero or more characters. All requests whose domain and path match this pattern are routed to the mobile-fe module.

If none of the rules in the *dispatch.yaml* file match the request, then the usual dispatch logic takes over.

As with other app-wide configuration files, the *dispatch.yaml* file is deployed with the rest of the application during appcfg.py update. You can also deploy just this file to the app by running appcfg.py update_dispatch.

Starting and Stopping Modules

When you deploy a module with manual scaling, App Engine ensures that the number of instances requested in the configuration file's `instances` parameter have started, starting new ones if necessary. From that point on, the number of instances in the module can be adjusted via the Cloud Console in the Instances panel, via the `appcfg.py` command, or programmatically by calling the modules API from the app.

Instances in a module with basic scaling can also be started and stopped in these ways. The main difference with basic scaling is that instances are also started and stopped in response to incoming requests and idle timeouts, respectively. Basic instances are stopped during a deployment so they can be restarted to pick up the new software.

To shut down instances from the Cloud Console, go to the Instances panel under Compute, App Engine, then select the appropriate module and version from the drop-down menus at the top. (The module drop-down only appears if multiple modules are deployed.) The panel includes performance graphs specific to the module and version, as well as a list of active instances. Click the Shutdown button to stop an instance.

There is no way to increase the number of instances in a module from the Cloud Console. The expectation with manual scaling is that the app will start instances as it needs them via the API. Or you can use the command-line tool.

From the command line, you can stop a module, and start a module. Stopping a module shuts down all of its instances, and starting a stopped module activates all of the instances configured for the module. The command takes the module's `.yaml` file as a parameter, or you can just set the `--application=…`, `--module=…`, and `--version=…` arguments directly:

```
appcfg.py stop_module_version world-cache.yaml
appcfg.py start_module_version world-cache.yaml

appcfg.py stop_module_version --application=saucy-boomerang-123 \
  --module=world-cache --version=alpha
```

Finally, you can use the modules API to stop and start modules, and also adjust the number of instances for a module with manual scaling without deploying a configuration change. We'll see how to do that in "The Modules API" on page 121.

Managing and Deleting Modules and Versions

When you deploy a module, App Engine checks the `version:` parameter in the configuration file and either creates a new version of the module with that ID if it does not exist, or replaces the version with that ID if it does.

When you deploy a module for the first time, the first version created becomes the default version. Otherwise, the default version doesn't change unless you use the Cloud Console or the `appcfg.py` command to change it. To change the default version from the Cloud Console, go to the Versions panel under Compute, App Engine. Click the checkbox next to the version you want to make the default, then click the "Make default" button.

Changing the default version for a module with manual or basic scaling changes the destination of requests to the module URL, and otherwise has no immediate effect on the module's instances. Each version's instances continue to run according to their scaling policies.

When you're working with automatic scaling, nondefault versions are mostly inconsequential, because versions that don't receive traffic don't consume resources. They either serve their purpose (as testing versions, for example), or they sit around waiting to be cleaned up when a developer notices that the app has hit its version count limit. With manual scaling, cleaning up old versions is much more important. Versions of modules with manual scaling keep their instances running until they are explicitly shut down or the version is deleted. It's worth keeping careful track of which versions have active instances that are not being used, and either shutting them down or deleting them as part of your deployment process.

To delete a version from the Cloud Console, go to the Versions panel as before. Click the checkboxes next to the versions to delete, then click the Delete button.

Notice that the default module does not have a checkbox next to it. This is a safety catch to prevent you from deleting the version that is serving the main traffic for the module. To delete the default version, you must first either make another version the default, or you must delete all of the other versions. Deleting all versions (by deleting all nondefault versions, then deleting the default version) deletes the module.

To delete a version from the command line, use the `appcfg.py delete_version` command, passing the app ID, module ID, and version ID as the `-A`, `-M`, and `-V` arguments, respectively. The `-M` argument can be omitted to delete a version from the default module, or you can specify `-M default`:

```
appcfg.py delete_version -A saucy-boomerang-123 -M world-cache -V alpha
```

This command will fail if you attempt to delete the default version and other versions exist. It won't try to pick a new default version automatically. You can delete the default version if it is the last version in a module.

The Modules API

App Engine gives you programmatic access to information about the modules and versions of the running app, as well as the identifiers of the module, version, and instance running the code. You can also adjust the number of instances for a module with manual scaling, and start and stop module versions just as you can from the command line. All of these functions are provided by the `google.appengine.api.modules` module.

We already looked at `get_hostname()`. This is essential for calculating the URL the app should use when calling one of its own modules via the URL Fetch service. This is the only method that will return `localhost` URLs when running in the development server.

You can get the IDs for the module, version, and instance running the current code using the `get_current_module_name()`, `get_current_version_name()`, and `get_current_instance_id()` functions. They take no arguments.

The `get_modules()` function returns a complete list of the app's module names, including `default` if it exists. (It is technically possible to deploy only named modules to an app, and therefore have no default module.)

The `get_versions()` function returns a list of version IDs. Without an argument, it returns the versions of the current module. When given a module name as its `module` argument, it returns the versions for that module, or raises an exception if the given module does not exist.

The related function `get_default_version()` returns the version ID of the default version. It too takes an optional module name argument, and uses the current module if this is omitted.

There are four methods you can use to manipulate the instances of modules with manual or basic scaling. You can use `get_num_instances()` and `set_num_instances(count)` to manipulate the number of instances for the module. These functions take optional `module` and `version` arguments that default to the module or version running the code. Deploying the module resets the number of instances to the number specified in the configuration file.

Finally, you can start and stop module versions with `start_version(module, version)` and `stop_version(module,version)`. The arguments to the `stop_version()` function are optional, and default to the current module and version. Calling `stop_version()` without arguments is a good way for a module to stop itself.

 Remember that stopping an instance will invoke its shutdown hook, if any, and wait 30 seconds for it to complete.

An Always-On Example

The following simple example illustrates how the start handler, background threads, and the shutdown hook work together on an always-on instance. The start handler registers the shutdown hook and kicks off the background thread, then returns. The background thread increments a global counter once per second. You can inspect the current value of the counter in a browser with a web request for the "/" URL path.

Here is the Python code. Let's call this file *counter.py*:

```python
import logging
import time
import webapp2

from google.appengine.api import runtime
from google.appengine.api import background_thread

GLOBAL_COUNTER = 1

class Shutdown(Exception):
    pass

def shutdown():
    logging.info('Shutdown hook called')
    raise Shutdown()

def counter_loop():
    global GLOBAL_COUNTER
    try:
        while GLOBAL_COUNTER < 600:
            GLOBAL_COUNTER += 1
            time.sleep(1)
        logging.info('Shutting down counter after 600 cycles')
    except Shutdown:
        logging.info('Counter loop saw shutdown')

class MainPage(webapp2.RequestHandler):
    def get(self):
        self.response.out.write('GLOBAL_COUNTER=%d' % GLOBAL_COUNTER)

class StartHandler(webapp2.RequestHandler):
    def get(self):
        runtime.set_shutdown_hook(shutdown)
        thread = background_thread.BackgroundThread(
            target=counter_loop)
        thread.start()

app = webapp2.WSGIApplication([('/', MainPage),
                               ('/_ah/start', StartHandler)], debug=True)
```

The configuration file for this module specifies manual scaling and one instance. We can put the configuration for the counter module in a file named *counter.yaml*:

```
module: counter
application: module-demo
version: 1
runtime: python27
api_version: 1
threadsafe: true

instance_class: B1
manual_scaling:
  instances: 1

handlers:
- url: .*
  script: counter.app
```

We can deploy this module with this command:

```
appcfg.py update counter.yaml
```

And access the interactive display with this URL (given the application and module IDs shown):

```
http://counter.module-demo.appspot.com/
```

If you want to try deploying this example, remember that with manual scaling, all of the requested instances are started as soon as you deploy. Instance running time consumes the "backend instance hours" quota, and apps without a budget set only get so many free hours a day. You'll want to keep close tabs on the running instance, and shut it down (or delete the module) when you're done experimenting.

You can reduce the risk of this example burning through your backend instance hours quota by changing it to use basic scaling. With basic scaling, the instance won't start until you load the interactive display. While the instance is running, the background thread will increment the counter once per second, up to 600 (the condition on the while loop). After 600 seconds, the instance will go idle, then shut down after the idle timeout you set in the configuration.

## CHAPTER 6

Datastore Entities

Most scalable web applications use separate systems for handling web requests and for storing data. The request handling system routes each request to one of many servers, and the server handles the request without knowledge of other requests going to other servers. Each request handler behaves as if it is *stateless*, acting solely on the content of the request to produce the response. But most web applications need to maintain state, whether it's remembering that a customer ordered a product, or just remembering that the user who made the current request is the same user who made an earlier request handled by another server. For this, request handlers must interact with a central database to fetch and update the latest information about the state of the application.

Just as the request handling system distributes web requests across many machines for scaling and robustness, so does the database. But unlike the request handlers, databases are by definition *stateful*, and this poses a variety of questions. Which server remembers which piece of data? How does the system route a data query to the server or servers that can answer the query? When a client updates data, how long does it take for all servers that know that data to get the latest version, and what does the system return for queries about that data in the meantime? What happens when two clients try to update the same data at the same time? What happens when a server goes down?

Google Cloud Platform offers several data storage services, and each service answers these questions differently. The most important service for scalable applications is Google Cloud Datastore, or as it is known to App Engine veterans, simply "the datastore." When App Engine was first launched in 2008, it included the datastore as its primary means of scalable data storage. The datastore has since gone through major revisions, and is now a prominent service in the Cloud Platform suite, accessible from

App Engine via the original API or from Compute Engine or elsewhere via a REST API.

As with App Engine's request handling, Cloud Datastore manages the scaling and maintenance of data storage automatically. Your application interacts with an abstract model that hides the details of managing and growing a pool of data servers. This model and the service behind it provide answers to the questions of scalable data storage specifically designed for web applications.

Cloud Datastore's abstraction for data is easy to understand, but it is not obvious how to best take advantage of its features. In particular, it is surprisingly different from the kind of database with which most of us are most familiar, the relational database (such as the one provided by Google Cloud SQL). It's different enough that we call it a "datastore" instead of a "database." (We're mincing words, but the distinction is important.)

Cloud Datastore is a robust, scalable data storage solution. Your app's data is stored in several locations by using a best-of-breed consensus protocol (similar to the "Paxos" protocol), making your app's access to this data resilient to most service failures and all planned downtime. When we discuss queries and transactions, we'll see how this affects how data is updated. For now, just know that it's a good thing.

We dedicate the next several chapters to this important subject.[1]

Entities, Keys, and Properties

Cloud Datastore is best understood as an object database. An object in the datastore is known as an *entity*.

An entity has a *key* that uniquely identifies the object across the entire system. If you have a key, you can fetch the entity for the key quickly. Keys can be stored as data in entities, such as to create a reference from one entity to another. A key has several parts, some of which we'll discuss here and some of which we'll cover later.

---

1 In 2011–2012, App Engine transitioned from an older datastore infrastructure, known as the "master/slave" (M/S) datastore, to the current one, known as the "high replication" datastore (HR datastore, or HRD). The two architectures differ in how data is updated, but the biggest difference is that the M/S datastore requires scheduled maintenance periods during which data cannot be updated, and is prone to unexpected failures. The HR datastore stays available during scheduled maintenance, and is far more resistant to system failure. All new App Engine applications use the HR datastore, and the M/S datastore is no longer an option. I only mention it because you'll read about it in older articles, and may see occasional announcements about maintenance of the M/S datastore. You may also see mentions of a datastore migration tool, which old apps still using the M/S datastore can use to switch to the new HR datastore. In this book, "the datastore" always refers to the HR datastore.

One part of the key is the project ID, which ensures that nothing else about the key can collide with the entities of any other project. It also ensures that no other app can access your app's data, and that your app cannot access data for other apps. This feature of keys is automatic, and doesn't appear in the API (or in any examples shown here).

An important part of the key is the *kind*. An entity's kind categorizes the entity for the purposes of queries, and for ensuring the uniqueness of the rest of the key. For example, a shopping cart application might represent each customer order with an entity of the kind "Order." The application specifies the kind when it creates the entity.

The key also contains an *entity ID*. This can be an arbitrary string specified by the app, or it can be an integer generated automatically by the datastore.[2] An entity has either a string ID or a numeric ID, but not both.

System-assigned numeric IDs are generally increasing, although they are not guaranteed to be monotonically increasing. If you want a strictly increasing ID, you must maintain this yourself in a transaction. (For more information on transactions, see Chapter 8.) If you purposefully do not want an increasing ID, such as to avoid exposing data sizes to users, you can either generate your own string ID, or allow the system to generate a numeric ID, then encrypt it before exposing it to users.

Consider a simple example where we store information about books in an online book catalog. We might represent each book with an entity in the datastore. The key for such an entity might use a kind of Book, and a system-assigned numeric ID, like so:

```
Book, 13579
```

Alternatively, we could use an externally defined identifier for each book, such as the ISBN, stored as a string ID on the key:

```
Book, "978-0-24680-321-0"
```

Once an entity has been created, its key cannot be changed. This applies to all parts of its key, including the kind and the ID.

The data for the entity is stored in one or more *properties*. Each property has a name and at least one value. Each value is of one of several supported data types, such as a string, an integer, a date-time, or a null value. We'll look at property value types in detail later in this chapter.

---

2 An entity ID specified by the app is sometimes known as the "key name" in older documentation, to distinguish it from the numeric ID. The newer terminology is simpler: every entity has an ID, and it's either a string provided by the app or a number provided by the datastore.

- A property can have multiple values, and each value can be of a different type. As you will see in "Multivalued Properties" on page 134, multivalued properties have unusual behavior, but are quite useful for modeling some kinds of data, and surprisingly efficient.

 It's tempting to compare these concepts with similar concepts in relational databases: kinds are tables, entities are rows, and properties are fields or columns. That's a useful comparison, but watch out for differences.

Unlike a table in a relational database, there is no relationship between an entity's kind and its properties. Two entities of the same kind can have different properties set or not set, and can each have a property of the same name but with values of different types. You can (and often will) enforce a data schema in your own code, and App Engine includes libraries to make this easy, but this is not required by the datastore.

Also, unlike relational databases, keys are not properties. You can perform queries on IDs just like properties, but you cannot change a string ID after the entity has been created.

A relational database cannot store multiple values in a single cell, while an App Engine property can have multiple values.

Introducing the Python Datastore API

In the Python API for the App Engine datastore, Python objects represent datastore entities. The class of the object corresponds to the entity's kind, where the name of the class is the name of the kind. You define kinds by creating classes that extend one of the provided base classes.

Each attribute of the object corresponds with a property of the entity. To create a new entity in the datastore, you call the class constructor, set attributes on the object, then call a method to save it. To update an existing entity, you call a method that returns the object for the entity (such as via a query), modify its attributes, and then save it.

Example 6-1 defines a class named Book to represent entities of the kind Book. It creates an object of this class by calling the class constructor, and then sets several property values. Finally, it calls the put() method to save the new entity to the datastore. The entity does not exist in the datastore until it is put() for the first time.

Example 6-1. Python code to create an entity of the kind Book

```python
from google.appengine.ext import ndb
import datetime

class Book(ndb.Expando):
    pass

# ...
        obj = Book()
        obj.title = 'The Grapes of Wrath'
        obj.author = 'John Steinbeck'
        obj.copyright_year = 1939
        obj.author_birthdate = datetime.datetime(1902, 2, 27)

        obj.put()
```

The Book class inherits from the class Expando in App Engine's ndb package. The Expando base class says Book objects can have any of their properties assigned any value. The entity "expands" to accommodate new properties as they are assigned to attributes of the object. Python does not require that an object's member variables be declared in a class definition, and this example takes advantage of this by using an empty class definition—the pass keyword indicates the empty definition—and assigning values to attributes of the object after it is created. The Expando base class knows to use the object's attributes as the values of the corresponding entity's properties.

The Expando class has a funny name because this isn't the way the API's designers expect us to create new classes in most cases. Instead, you're more likely to use the Model base class with a class definition that ensures each instance conforms to a structure, so a mistake in the code doesn't accidentally create entities with malformed properties. Here is how we might implement the Book class using Model:

```python
class Book(ndb.Model):
    title = ndb.StringProperty()
    author = ndb.StringProperty()
    copyright_year = ndb.IntegerProperty()
    author_birthdate = ndb.DateTimeProperty()
```

The Model version of Book specifies a structure for Book objects that is enforced while the object is being manipulated. It ensures that values assigned to an object's properties are of appropriate types, such as string values for title and author properties, and raises a runtime error if the app attempts to assign a value of the wrong type to a property. With Model as the base class, the object does not "expand" to accommodate other entities: an attempt to assign a value to a property not mentioned in the class definition raises a runtime error. Model and the various Property definitions also provide other features for managing the structure of your data, such as automatic values, required values, and the ability to add your own validation and serialization logic.

It's important to notice that these validation features are provided by the Model class and your application code, *not* the datastore. Even if part of your app uses a Model class to ensure a property's value meets certain conditions, another part of your app can still retrieve the entity without using the class and do whatever it likes to that value. The bad value won't raise an error until the app tries to load the changed entity into a new instance of the Model class. This is both a feature and a burden: your app can manage entities flexibly and enforce structure where needed, but it must also be careful when those structures need to change. Data modeling and the Model class are discussed in detail in Chapter 9.

The Book constructor accepts initial values for the object's properties as keyword arguments. The constructor code earlier could also be written like this:

```
obj = Book(title='The Grapes of Wrath',
           author='John Steinbeck',
           copyright_year=1939,
           author_birthdate=datetime.datetime(1902, 2, 27))
```

As written, this code does not set an ID for the new entity. Without an ID, the datastore generates a unique numeric ID when the object is saved for the first time. If you prefer to use an ID generated by the app, you call the constructor with the id parameter, as follows:

```
obj = Book(id='0143039431',
           title='The Grapes of Wrath',
           author='John Steinbeck',
           copyright_year=1939,
           author_birthdate=datetime.datetime(1902, 2, 27))
```

Because the Python API uses keyword arguments, object attributes, and object methods for purposes besides entity properties, there are several property names that are off-limits. For instance, you cannot use the Python API to set a property named id, because this could get confused with the id parameter for the object constructor. Names reserved by the Python API are enforced in the API, but *not* in the datastore itself.

The property names reserved by ndb are:

- id
- key
- namespace
- parent

The datastore itself reserves all property names beginning and ending with two underscores (such as __internal__). This particular rule also applies to kind names.

The Python API ignores all object attributes whose names begin with a single underscore (such as _counter). You can use such attributes to attach data and functionality to an object that should not be saved as properties for the entity.

The complete key of an entity, including the ID and kind, must be unique. (We'll discuss another part to keys that contributes to a key's uniqueness, called ancestors, in Chapter 8.) If you build a new object with a key that is already in use, and then try to save it, the save will replace the existing object. When you don't want to overwrite existing data, you can use a system-assigned ID in the key, or you can use a transaction to test for the existence of an entity with a given key and create it if it doesn't exist.

The API provides a shortcut for creating entities with app-assigned string IDs. The get_or_insert() class method takes a string ID and either returns an existing entity with that ID, or creates a new entity with that ID and returns it. The method also takes initial property values to use with the newly created entity. Property value arguments are ignored if an entity with the given ID already exists. Either way, the method is guaranteed to return an object that represents an entity in the datastore:

```
obj = Book.get_or_insert(
    key_name='0143039431'
    title='The Grapes of Wrath',
    author='John Steinbeck',
    copyright_year=1939,
    author_birthdate=datetime.datetime(1902, 2, 27))

# obj is a stored entity, either the previous entity with the
```

```
# key Book:'0143039431' (no changes to properties) or a new
# entity with that key and the provided property values.
```

Property Values

Each value data type supported by the datastore is represented by a primitive type in the language for the runtime or a class provided by the API. The data types and their language-specific equivalents are listed in Table 6-1. In this table, ndb is the Python package `google.appengine.ext.ndb`, and users is `google.appengine.api.users`.

Table 6-1. Datastore property value types and equivalent Python types

Data type	Python type
Unicode text string (up to 500 characters, indexed)	`unicode`
Long Unicode text string (not indexed)	`unicode` or `str`
Byte string (up to 500 bytes, indexed)	`str`
Long byte string (not indexed)	`str`
Boolean	`bool`
Integer (64-bit)	`int` or `long` (converted to 64-bit `long`)
Float (double precision)	`float`
Date-time	`datetime.datetime`
Null value	`None`
Entity key	`ndb.Key`
A Google account	`users.User`
A geographical point	`ndb.GeoPt`

Example 6-2 demonstrates the use of several of these data types.

Example 6-2. Code to set property values of various types

```
import datetime
import webapp2

from google.appengine.ext import ndb
from google.appengine.api import users
```

```
class Comment(ndb.Expando):
    pass

class CommentHandler(webapp2.RequestHandler):
    def post(self):
        c = Comment()
        c.commenter = users.get_current_user()  # returns a users.User object
        c.message = self.request.get('message')
        c.date = datetime.datetime.now()
        c.put()

        # Redirect to a result page...
```

 When you use Python's ndb.Expando, values that are converted to native datastore types when stored come back as the datastore types when you retrieve the entity. For example, an int value is stored as a long, and so appears as a long on the retrieved object. If you use ndb.Expando in your app, it's best to use the native datastore types, so the value types stay consistent.

The data modeling interfaces offer a way to store values in these alternative types and convert them back automatically when retrieving the entity. (For more information on data modeling, see Chapter 9.)

Strings, Text, and Bytes

The datastore has two distinct data types for storing strings of text: short strings and long strings. Short strings are indexed; that is, they can be the subject of queries, such as a search for every Person entity with a given value for a last_name property. Short string values must be less than 500 bytes in length. Long strings can be longer than 500 bytes, but are not indexed.

Text strings, short and long, are strings of characters from the Unicode character set. Internally, the datastore stores Unicode strings by using the UTF-8 encoding, which represents some characters using multiple bytes. This means that the 500-byte limit for short strings is not necessarily the same as 500 Unicode characters. The actual limit on the number of characters depends on which characters are in the string.

When using ndb.Expando and no Property declarations, fields are considered index-able by default. Setting a property to a str value longer than 500 bytes or a unicode value longer than 500 characters stores the propery as nonindexed automatically. For more control over this process, see Chapter 9.

Unset Versus the Null Value

One possible value of a property is the null value. In Python, the null value is represented by None.

A property with the null value is not the same as an unset property. Consider the following code:

```
class Entity(ndb.Expando):
    pass

# ...
        a = Entity()
        a.prop1 = 'abc'
        a.prop2 = None
        a.put()

        b = Entity()
        b.prop1 = 'def'
        b.put()
```

This creates two entities of the kind Entity. Both entities have a property named prop1. The first entity has a property named prop2; the second does not.

Of course, an unset property can be set later:

```
        b.prop2 = 123
        b.put()

        # b now has a property named "prop2."
```

Similarly, a set property can be made unset. In the API, you delete the property by deleting the attribute from the object, using the del keyword:

```
        del b.prop2
        b.put()

        # b no longer has a property named "prop2."
```

Multivalued Properties

As we mentioned earlier, a property can have multiple values. We'll discuss the more substantial aspects of multivalued properties when we talk about queries and data modeling. But for now, it's worth a brief mention.

A property can have one or more values. A property cannot have zero values; a property without a value is simply unset. Each value for a property can be of a different type, and can be the null value.

The datastore preserves the order of values as they are assigned. The API returns the values in the same order as they were set.

In Python, a property with multiple values is represented as a single Python `list` value:

```
e.prop = [1, 2, 'a', None, 'b']
```

 Because a property must have at least one value, it is an error to assign an empty list (`[]` in Python) to a property on an entity whose class is derived from the `ndb.Expando` class:

```
class Entity(ndb.Expando):
    pass

# ...
    e = Entity()
    e.prop = []  # ERROR
```

To be able to represent the empty list, you must declare the property type and specify that the property is `repeated`. In the following example, the property `prop` is declared as a `GenericProperty`, which does not enforce a type for the values in the list:

```
class Entity(ndb.Expando):
    prop = ndb.GenericProperty(repeated=True)

# ...
    e = Entity()
    e.prop = []  # OK
```

The `Property` declaration takes care of translating between "no property set" in the datastore and the empty list value in the code. Again, we'll see more about property declarations in Chapter 9.

Keys and Key Objects

The key for an entity is a value that can be retrieved, passed around, and stored like any other value. If you have the key for an entity, you can retrieve the entity from the datastore quickly, much more quickly than with a datastore query. Keys can be stored as property values, as an easy way for one entity to refer to another.

The API represents an entity key value as an instance of the `Key` class, in the `ndb` package. To get the key for an entity, you access the entity object's key attribute.[3] The `Key` instance provides access to its several parts by using accessor methods, including the kind, string ID (if any), and system-assigned ID (if the entity does not have a string ID).

---

3 If you are upgrading to `ndb` from the `ext.db` library, notice that the former `key()` method is now a key attribute. In general, keys are handled rather differently in `ndb` than in `ext.db`.

When you construct a new entity object and do not provide a string ID, the entity object has a key, but the key does not yet have an ID. The ID is populated when the entity object is saved to the datastore for the first time. You can get the key object prior to saving the object, but it will be incomplete:

```
e = Entity()
e.prop = 123

k = e.key  # key is incomplete, does not have an ID
kind = k.kind()  # 'Entity'

e.put()  # ID is assigned
k = e.key  # key is complete, has ID
id = k.id()  # the system-assigned ID
```

If the entity object was constructed with a string ID, the key is complete before the object is saved—although, if the entity has not been saved, the string ID is not guaranteed to be unique. (The entity class method get_or_insert(), mentioned earlier, always returns a saved entity, either one that was saved previously or a new one created by the call.)

If the key is incomplete, the id() method returns None. If the key is complete, id() returns either the string ID (as a str) or the numeric ID (long), whichever one it has. You can request the string ID or integer ID directly using string_id() or integerid(), respectively. These methods return None if the key is incomplete or if the ID is not of the requested type.

Once you have a complete key, you can assign it as a property value on another entity to create a reference:

```
e2 = Entity()
e2.ref = k
e2.put()
```

If you know the kind and ID of an entity in the datastore, you can construct the key for that entity without its object. The ndb.Key() constructor can take a kind name (str) and an ID (str or long). A complete explanation of this feature involves another feature we haven't mentioned yet (ancestor paths), but the following suffices for the examples you've seen so far:

```
e = Entity(id='alphabeta')
e.prop = 123
e.put()

# ...

k = ndb.Key('Entity', 'alphabeta')
```

Ancestor paths are related to how the datastore does transactions. (We'll get to them in Chapter 8.) For the entities we have created so far, the path is just the kind followed by the ID or name.

Keys can be converted to string representations for the purposes of passing around as textual data, such as in a web form or cookie. The string representation avoids characters considered special in HTML or URLs, so it is safe to use without escaping characters. The encoding of the value to a string is simple and easily reversed, so if you expose the string value to users, be sure to encrypt it, or make sure all key parts (such as kind names) are not secret. When accepting an encoded key string from a client, always validate the key before using it.

To get the URL-safe string representation of a key, call the `urlsafe()` method. To reconstruct a `Key` from such a string, pass it to the constructor's `urlsafe` named argument:

```
k_str = k.urlsafe()

# ...

k = ndb.Key(urlsafe=k_str)
```

Using Entities

Let's look briefly at how to retrieve entities from the datastore by using keys, how to inspect the contents of entities, and how to update and delete entities. The API methods for these features are straightforward.

Getting Entities Using Keys

Given a complete key for an entity, you can retrieve the entity from the datastore. Construct the `ndb.Key` object if you don't already have one, then call its `get()` method:

```
from google.appengine.ext import ndb

# ...
    k = ndb.Key('Entity', 'alphabeta')

    e = k.get()
```

If you know the kind and ID of the entity you are fetching, you can also use the `get_by_id()` class method on the appropriate entity class:

```
class Entity(ndb.Expando):
    pass

# ...
    e = Entity.get_by_id('alphabeta')
```

To fetch multiple entities in a batch, you can pass a list of Key objects to the ndb.get_multi() function. The method returns a list containing entity objects, with None values for keys that do not have a corresponding entity in the datastore:

```
entities = ndb.get_multi([k1, k2, k3])
```

Getting a batch of entities in this way performs a single service call to the datastore for the entire batch. This is faster than getting each entity in a separate call. ndb knows how to batch calls to the datastore service automatically, so you only need to use ndb.get_multi() when it is convenient for your code.

Of course, you won't always have the keys for the entities you want to fetch from the datastore. To retrieve entities that meet other criteria, you use datastore queries. (We'll discuss queries in Chapter 7.)

Inspecting Entity Objects

Entity objects have methods for inspecting various aspects of the entity.

The API has several features for inspecting entities worth mentioning here. You've already seen the key attribute of an entity object, which returns the ndb.Key.

Entity properties can be accessed and modified just like object attributes:

```
e.prop1 = 1
e.prop2 = 'two'

self.response.write('prop2 has the value ' + e.prop2)
```

You can use Python built-in functions for accessing object attributes to access entity properties. For instance, to test that an entity has a property with a given name, use the hasattr() built-in:

```
if hasattr(e, 'prop1'):
    # ...
```

To get or set a property whose name is defined in a string, use getattr() and setattr(), respectively:

```
# Set prop1, prop2, ..., prop9.
for n in range(1, 10):
    value = n * n
    setattr(e, 'prop' + str(n), value)

value = getattr(e, 'prop' + str(7))
```

We've seen that property values can be initialized with arguments passed to the entity class's constructor. As with all named arguments in Python, you can pass a mapping (dict) of keys and values to this constructor using the ** syntax:

```
props = {'name1': 'value1', 'name2': 'value2'}
e = Entity(**props)
```

The populate() method provides another way to set properties after the entity has been constructed. This method takes named arguments just like the constructor, and can also take a mapping using the ** syntax:

```
e.populate(name1='value1', name2='value2')

e.populate(**props)
```

You can get all of an entity's properties as a dict by calling the to_dict() method. By default, all properties are included. You can limit the mapping to a specific set of properties by passing a list of names as the include argument. Alternatively, you can exclude specific properties (and return all others) with the exclude argument. Here is an example using the default behavior:

```
e = Entity(name1='value1', name2='value2')

prop_dict = e.to_dict()
for name in prop_dict:
    # ... prop_dict[name] ...
```

Note that some Property declared types, such as JsonProperty, use mutable objects (such as dict values) to represent their values. to_dict() will return these values as direct references to those objects, not copies.

Saving Entities

Calling the put() method on an entity object saves the entity to the datastore. If the entity does not yet exist in the datastore, put() creates the entity. If the entity exists, put() updates the entity so that it matches the object:

```
e = Entity()
e.prop = 123

e.put()
```

When you update an entity, the app sends the complete contents of the entity to the datastore. The update is all or nothing: there is no way to send just the properties that have changed to the datastore. There is also no way to update a property on an entity without retrieving the complete entity, making the change, and then sending the new entity back.

You use the same API to create an entity as you do to update an entity. The datastore does not make a distinction between creates and updates. If you save an entity with a complete key (such as a key with a kind and a string ID) and an entity already exists with that key, the datastore replaces the existing entity with the new one.

If you want to test that an entity with a given key does not exist before you create it, you can do so using a transaction. You must use a transaction to ensure that another process doesn't create an entity with that key after you test for it and before you create it. For more information on transactions, see Chapter 8.

If you have several entity objects to save, you can save them all in one call using the put_multi() function in the ndb package:

```
ndb.put_multi([e1, e2, e3])
```

When the call to put() returns, the datastore entity records are up-to-date, and all future fetches of these entities in the current request handler and other handlers will see the new data. The specifics of how the datastore gets updated are discussed in detail in Chapter 8.

Deleting Entities

To delete an entity, you acquire or construct its ndb.Key, then call the delete() method:

```
e = ndb.Key('Entity', 'alphabeta').get()
# ...
e.key.delete()

# Deleting without first fetching the entity:
k = ndb.Key('Entity', 'alphabeta')
k.delete()
```

As with gets and puts, you can delete multiple keys in a single batch call with ndb.delete_multi():

```
ndb.delete_multi([e1, e2, e3])
```

Allocating System IDs

When you create a new entity without specifying an explicit string ID, the datastore assigns a numeric system ID to the entity. Your code can read this system ID from the entity's key after the entity has been created.

Sometimes you want the system to assign the ID, but you need to know what ID will be assigned before the entity is created. For example, say you are creating two entities, and the property of one entity must be set to the key of the other entity. One option is to save the first entity to the datastore, then read the key of the entity, set the property on the second entity, and then save the second entity:

```
class Entity(db.Expando):
    pass

# ...
        e1 = Entity()
        e1.put()

        e2 = Entity()
        e2.reference = e1.key()
        e2.put()
```

This requires two separate calls to the datastore in sequence, which takes valuable clock time. It also requires a period of time where the first entity is in the datastore but the second entity isn't.

We can't read the key of the first entity before we save it, because it is incomplete: reading e1.key before calling e1.put() would return an unusable value. We could use a string ID instead of a system ID, giving us a complete key, but it's often the case that we can't easily calculate a unique string ID, which is why we'd rather have a system-assigned ID.

To solve this problem, the datastore provides a method to allocate system IDs ahead of creating entities. You call the datastore to allocate an ID (or a range of IDs for multiple entities), then create the entity with an explicit ID. Notice that this is not the same as using a string ID: you give the entity the allocated numeric ID, and it knows the ID came from the system.

To allocate one or more system IDs, call the allocate_ids() class method of the entity class. The method takes a number of IDs to allocate (size) or a maximum ID value to allocate (max):

```
# Allocate 1 system ID for entities of kind "Entity".
ids = Entity.allocate_ids(size=1)

e1 = Entity(id=ids[0])
e2 = Entity()
e2.reference = e1.key

ndb.put_multi([e1, e2])
```

The allocate_ids() method acquires unused unique IDs given the rest of the key. In simple cases, the rest of the key is just the kind name, which is derived from the class whose allocate_ids() method you are calling. For keys with ancestory paths, you must also provide the parent argument, whose value is an ndb.Key. See Chapter 8 for information on keys with ancestor paths.

A batch put of two entities does not guarantee that both entities are saved together. If your app logic requires that either both entities are saved or neither are saved, you must use a transaction. For more information, see Chapter 8. (As you can probably tell by now, that's an important chapter.)

The Development Server and the Datastore

The development server simulates the datastore service on your local machine while you're testing your app. All datastore entities are saved to a local file. This file is associated with your app, and persists between runs of the development server, so your test data remains available until you delete it.

You can tell the development server to reset this data when it starts. From the command line, you pass the --clear_datastore argument to dev_appserver.py:

```
dev_appserver.py --clear_datastore appdir
```

## CHAPTER 7

Datastore Queries

Inevitably, an application that manages data must do more than store and retrieve that data one record at a time. It must also answer questions about that data: which records meet certain criteria, how records compare to one another, what a set of records represents in aggregate. Web applications in particular are expected not only to know the answers to questions about large amounts of data, but to provide them quickly in response to web requests.

Most database systems provide a mechanism for executing queries, and Cloud Datastore is no exception. But the datastore's technique differs significantly from that of traditional database systems. When the application asks a question, instead of rifling through the original records and performing calculations to determine the answer, Cloud Datastore simply finds the answer in a list of possible answers prepared in advance. The datastore can do this because it knows which questions are going to be asked.

This kind of list, or *index*, is common to many database technologies, and relational databases can be told to maintain a limited set of indexes to speed up some kinds of queries. But Cloud Datastore is different: it maintains an index for *every* query the application is going to perform. Because the datastore only needs to do a simple scan of an index for every query, the application gets results back quickly. And for large amounts of data, Cloud Datastore can spread the data and the indexes across many machines, and get results back from all of them without an expensive aggregate operation.

This indexing strategy has significant drawbacks. The datastore's built-in query engine is downright weak compared to some relational databases, and is not suited to sophisticated data processing applications that would prefer slow but powerful run-time queries to fast simple ones. But most web applications need fast results, and the dirty secret about those powerful query engines is that they can't perform at web speeds with large amounts of data distributed across many machines. Cloud Datastore uses a model suited to scalable web applications: calculate the answers to known questions when the data is written, so reading is fast.

In this chapter, we explain how queries and indexes work, how the developer tools help you configure indexes automatically, and how to manage indexes as your application evolves. We also discuss several powerful features of the query engine, including cursors and projection queries. By understanding indexes, you will have an intuition for how to design your application and your data to make the most of the scalable datastore.

Queries and Kinds

You've seen how to retrieve an entity from the datastore given its key. But in most cases, the application does not know the keys of the entities it needs; it has only a general idea that it needs entities that meet certain criteria. For example, a leaderboard for the game app would need to retrieve the 10 Player entities with the highest score property values.

To retrieve entities this way, the app performs a *query*. A query includes:

- The kind of the entities to query
- Zero or more *filters*, criteria that property values must meet for an entity to be returned by the query
- Zero or more *sort orders* that determine the order in which results are returned based on property values

A query based on property values can only return entities of a single kind. This is the primary purpose of kinds: to determine which entities are considered together as possible results for a query. In practice, kinds correspond to the intuitive notion that each entity of the same nominal kind represents the same kind of data. But unlike other database systems, it's up to the app to enforce this consistency if it is desired, and the app can diverge from it if it's useful.

It is also possible to perform a limited set of queries on entities regardless of kind. Kindless queries can use a filter on the ID or key name, or on ancestors. We'll discuss ancestors and kindless queries in Chapter 8.

Query Results and Keys

When retrieving results for an entity query, the datastore returns the full entity for each result to the application.

For large entities, this may mean more data is transmitted between the datastore and the app than is needed. It's possible to fetch only a subset of properties under certain circumstances (we'll see this in "Projection Queries" on page 186), but these are not full entities. Another option is to store frequently accessed properties on one entity, and less popular properties on a separate related entity. The first entity stores the key of the second entity as a property, so when the app needs the less popular data, it queries for the first entity, then follows the reference to the second entity.

The datastore can return just the keys for the entities that match your query instead of fetching the full entities. A keys-only query is useful for determining the entities that match query criteria separately from when the entities are used. Keys can be remembered in the memcache or in a datastore property, and vivified as full entities when needed. We'll look at the API for keys-only queries a bit later.

The Query API

Recall that the Python datastore API represents entities using objects of classes named after kinds. To review, here is code that creates three Player entities for an online role-playing game:

```python
from google.appengine.ext import ndb
import datetime

class Player(ndb.Model):
    name = ndb.StringProperty()
    level = ndb.IntegerProperty()
    score = ndb.IntegerProperty()
    charclass = ndb.StringProperty()
    create_date = ndb.DateTimeProperty(auto_now_add=True)

player1 = Player(name='wizard612',
                level=1,
                score=32,
                charclass='mage')
player1.put()

player2 = Player(name='druidjane',
                level=10,
                score=896,
                charclass='druid')
player2.put()

player3 = Player(name='TheHulk',
                level=7,
                score=500,
                charclass='warrior')
player3.put()
```

This example uses the `Model` base class and declared property types. Declared properties help to enforce a consistent layout, or *schema*, for your entities. As we start talking about queries, the importance of using a schema for entities of a kind will become apparent.

Here is a simple query for entities of the `Player` kind that have a `level` property greater than or equal to 5:

```
q = Player.query().filter(Player.level >= 5)

results = q.fetch(10)

for entity in results:
    # assert entity.level >= 5
    # ...
```

 When you create or update an entity with new data, the indexes that support queries about that data are also updated. For the type of queries discussed in this chapter, the call to `put()` may return before the indexes have been updated. If you perform such a query immediately after an update, the results may not reflect the change. The development server simulates this possibility with a delay:

```
player1.level = 6
player1.put()

# put() returns while the Player.level
# index update is still in progress.

q = Player.query().filter(Player.level >= 5)
results = q.fetch(10)

# results may not contain player1.
```

We'll discuss consistency guarantees and how to formulate queries transactionally in Chapter 8.

The API provides two ways to formulate queries, one using an object-oriented interface, and one based on a text-based query language called "GQL."

The Query Class

The first way to formulate a query is with an instance of the `Query` class. The `Query` object can be constructed in one of two ways, with equivalent results:

```
q = Player.query()

q = ndb.Query(kind=Player)
```

In both cases, q is assigned a new Query instance that represents all entities of the kind Player. The query is not executed right away; right now it's just a question waiting to be asked. Without filters or sort orders, the object represents a query for all objects of the given kind.

To apply a filter to the query, you call the filter() method on the Query object. This returns a new Query object, leaving the original object unchanged.[1] The argument to the filter() method is an expression that describes the filter, consisting of a property, an operator, and a value:

```
q = q.filter(Player.level > 5)
```

Yes, this looks a little weird, but it actually does what it looks like it does. The property is described using the attribute of the model class that functions as the property declaration (Player.level). With a little Python magic, applying the comparison operator and value to this attribute results in a filter expression that the filter() method understands. By referring to the class attribute directly in the code, ndb provides a bit of code safety, validating that you're using a real model class, a declared attribute, and the correct value type.

You specify multiple filters by calling the filter() method multiple times. An entity must meet all filter criteria in order to be a result for the query. That is, filters have a logical AND relationship with one another:

```
q = q.filter(Player.level > 5)
q = q.filter(Player.level < 20)
```

For convenience, the filter() method returns the Query object, so you can chain multiple calls to filter() in a single line:

```
q = q.filter(Player.level > 5).filter(Player.level < 20)
```

The filter() method supports the equality (==) operator and the four inequality operators (<, <=, >, and >=). The Query class also supports the != (not equal) and IN operators. These are not primitive datastore query operators: instead, the query library executes these operators by performing multiple datastore queries then aggregating the results.

To apply a sort order, you call the order() method. As with filter(), this returns a new Query object derived from the original. This method takes one argument, the property to sort by, in the form of a reference to the class attribute. By default, the sort will be in ascending order. To sort by the property in descending order, use the unary negation operator on the property:

---

1 In ndb, Query objects are immutable, and you use methods to derive new Query objects. This is unlike the old ext.db library, which mutated the Query object directly when methods like filter() were called.

```
q = q.order(Player.level)

q = q.order(-Player.score)
```

The datastore can sort query results by multiple properties. First, it sorts by the property and order from the first call to order(), then it sorts entities with equal values for the first property, using the second order, and so on. For example, the following sorts first by level ascending, then by score descending:

```
q = q.order(Player.level).order(-Player.score)
```

The query engine supports limiting the number of results returned, and skipping ahead a number of results. You specify the limit and offset when you retrieve the results, described later.

The property name used in an ndb filter or sort order expression refers to the property declaration stored as an attribute of the model class. When using the ndb.Expando base class, you can have properties on an entity that are not declared in this way. To refer to these properties in a filter or sort order expression, you can instantiate a temporary declaration using the ndb.GenericProperty() constructor:

```
class Document(ndb.Expando):
    pass

# ...
    q = Document.query()

    q = q.filter(ndb.GenericProperty('category')
                == 'biology')
```

AND and OR clauses

Setting multiple filters on a Query object is logically equivalent to combining each of the filters with a logical AND operator. You can state this more explicitly in the API using the ndb.AND() combination:

```
q = Player.query()
q = q.filter(Player.level > 5)
q = q.filter(Player.level < 20)

q = Player.query(ndb.AND(Player.level > 5,
                         Player.level < 20))
```

The ndb.AND() function takes two clauses. Either of these clauses can be another ndb.AND() expression.

This is mostly useful when combined with the ndb.OR() function, which forms a logical OR relationship between two clauses:

```
q = Player.query(ndb.OR(ndb.AND(Player.level > 5,
                                Player.level < 20),
                         ndb.AND(Player.charclass == 'mage'),
                                 Player.level > 3))
```

This query asks for `Player` entities that either have a level between 5 and 20, or are of a character class of `'mage'` and have a level greater than 3.

The datastore does not support logical OR natively. Instead, ndb normalizes the total logical expression into a form that can be expressed as multiple primitive queries that use only logical AND operators. It then makes multiple calls to the datastore and aggregates the results.

Notice that complex logical expressions may require many primitive datastore queries to perform. This can impact performance. Nevertheless, `ndb.OR()` is sometimes convenient.

GQL

ndb also supports a more succinct way to formulate queries: a text-based query language called *GQL*. This language is intended to resemble SQL, the query language of relational databases. It supports only the features of the datastore's query engine, and therefore lacks many features common to SQL. But it is expressive and concise enough to be useful for datastore queries.

Say we have entities of the kind `Player` representing players in an online role-playing game. The following GQL query retrieves all `Player` entities whose "level" property is an integer between 5 and 20, sorted by level in ascending order, then by score in descending order:

```
SELECT * FROM Player
      WHERE level >= 5
        AND level <= 20
    ORDER BY level ASC, score DESC
```

In Python code, you create the query object from a GQL statement using the `ndb.gql()` function:

```
q = ndb.gql("""SELECT * FROM Player
                 WHERE level > 5
                   AND level < 20
               ORDER BY level ASC, score DESC""")
```

Alternatively, you can call the `gql()` method on the model class, omitting the `SELECT * FROM Kind` from the string as this is implied by the use of the method:

```
q = Player.gql("""WHERE level > 5
                    AND level < 20
                  ORDER BY level ASC, score DESC""")
```

The first part of the SQL-like syntax in the preceding GQL query, SELECT * FROM Player, says that the datastore should return complete entities as results, and that it should only consider entities of the kind Player. This is the most common kind of query. Unlike a SQL database, the datastore cannot "join" properties from entities of multiple kinds into a single set of results. Only one kind can appear after the FROM.

Despite its similarity with SQL, GQL can only represent queries, and cannot perform updates, inserts, or deletes. In other words, every GQL query begins with SELECT.

The rest of the query syntax also resembles SQL, and translates directly to filters and sort orders. The WHERE clause, if present, represents one or more filter conditions, separated by AND. The ORDER BY clause, if present, represents one or more sort orders, separated by commas, applied from left to right.

Each condition in a WHERE clause consists of the name of a property, a comparison operator, and a value. You can also specify a condition that matches an entity's ID or key name by using the reserved name __key__ like a property name. (That's two underscores, the word "key," and two underscores.)

The datastore query engine supports five comparison operators for filters: =, <, <=, >, and >=. GQL also supports two additional operators: !=, meaning "not equal to," and IN, which tests that the value equals any in a set of values.

 With ndb, the equality operator is the Python equality operator: Player.level == 5. In GQL, the equality operator is a single = similar to SQL: SELECT * FROM Player WHERE level = 5.

For IN, the values are represented by a comma-delimited list of values surrounded by parentheses:

```
SELECT * FROM Player WHERE level IN (5, 6, 7)
```

Internally, GQL translates the != and IN operators into multiple datastore queries that have the same effect. If a query contains an IN clause, the query is evaluated once for each value in the clause, using an = filter. The results of all the queries are aggregated. The != operator performs the query once using a < filter and once using a >, then aggregates the results. Using these operators more than once in a GQL statement requires a query for each combination of the required queries, so be judicious in their use.

The WHERE clause is equivalent to one or more filters. It is not like SQL's WHERE clause, and does not support arbitrary logical expressions. In particular, GQL does not support testing the logical OR of two conditions.

The value on the righthand side of a condition can be a literal value that appears inside the query string. Seven of the datastore value types have string literal representations, as shown in Table 7-1.

Table 7-1. GQL value literals for datastore types

Type	Literal syntax	Examples
String	Single-quoted string; escape the quote by doubling it	`'Haven''t You Heard'`
Integer or float	Sign, digits; float uses decimal point	`-7 3.14`
Boolean	True or false keywords	`TRUE FALSE`

Date-time, date or time	Type, and value as numbers or a string
	
	`DATETIME(year, month, day, hour, minute, second)`
	
	`DATETIME('YYYY-MM-DD HH:MM:SS')`
	
	`DATE(year, month, day)`
	
	`DATE('YYYY-MM-DD')`
	
	`TIME(hour, minute, second)`
	
	`TIME('HH:MM:SS')`
		`DATETIME(1999, 12, 31, 23, 59, 59)`
		
		`DATETIME('1999-12-31 23:59:59')`
		
		`DATE(1999, 12, 31)`
		
		`DATE('1999-12-31')`
		
		`TIME(23, 59, 59)`
		
		`TIME('23:59:59')`

Entity key	Entity kind, and name or ID; can be a path
	`KEY('kind', 'name'/id)`
	
	`KEY('kind', 'name'/id, 'kind', 'name'/id, ...)`
		`KEY('Player', 1287)`

User object	`User('email-address')`	`User('edward@example.com')`
GeoPt object	`GEOPT(lat, long)`	`GEOPT(37.4219, -122.0846)`

The type of a filter's value is significant in a datastore query. If you use the wrong type for a value, such as by specifying a `'string_key'` when you meant to specify a `KEY(kind, key_name)`, your query may not return the results you intend, or may unexpectedly return no results.

A GQL query can specify a `LIMIT`, a maximum number of results to return. A query can also specify an `OFFSET`, a number of results to skip before returning the remaining results. The following example returns the third, fourth, and fifth results, and may return fewer if the query has fewer than five results:

```
SELECT * FROM Player LIMIT 3 OFFSET 2
```

GQL keywords, shown here in uppercase, are case insensitive. Kind and property names, however, are case sensitive.

As with SQL statements in code, it is not always safe to include query values directly in the query string, especially if those values come from outside sources. You don't want values to be accidentally (or maliciously) mistaken for GQL syntax characters. This is less of an issue for GQL than for SQL (since GQL statements can only perform queries and cannot modify data) but it's still good practice to isolate values from the query string.

To specify values separately from the query string, you use parameter substitution. With parameter substitution, the query string contains a placeholder with either a number or a name, and the actual value is passed to gql() as either a positional argument or a keyword argument. The number or name appears in the query string preceded by a colon (:1 or :argname):

```
q = ndb.gql("""SELECT * FROM Player
               WHERE level > :1
                 AND level < :2""",
            5, 20)

q = ndb.gql("""SELECT * FROM Player
               WHERE level > :min_level
                 AND level < :max_level""",
            min_level=5, max_level=20)
```

One advantage to parameter substitution is that each argument value is of the appropriate datastore type, so you don't need to bother with the string syntax for specifying typed values.

You can rebind new values to a GQL query by using parameter substitution after the query object has been instantiated using the bind() method. This means you can reuse the query multiple times for different values. This saves time because the query string only needs to be parsed once. The bind() method takes the new values as either positional arguments or keyword arguments, and returns a new query object with parameters bound.

You can save more time by caching parameterized query objects in global variables. This way, the query string is parsed only when a server loads the application for the first time, and the application reuses the object for all subsequent calls handled by that server:

```
_LEADERBOARD_QUERY = ndb.gql(
    """SELECT * FROM Player
```

```
      WHERE level > :min_level
        AND level < :max_level
    ORDER BY level ASC, score DESC""")

class LeaderboardHandler(webapp.RequestHandler):
    def get(self):
        q = _LEADERBOARD_QUERY.bind(min_level=5, max_level=20)
        # ...
```

 You can use GQL to perform queries from the Cloud Console. In the sidebar, expand Storage, Cloud Datastore, Query. Locate the dropdown menu that reads "Query by kind," then change it to "Query using GQL." Enter the GQL statement, then click the Run button to run it.

Note that to perform a query in the Console, the app must already have an index that corresponds to the query. We'll discuss indexes throughout this chapter.

Retrieving Results

Once you have a query object configured with filters, sort orders, and value bindings (in the case of GQL), you can execute the query, using one of several methods. The query is not executed until you call one of these methods, and you can call these methods repeatedly on the same query object to re-execute the query and get new results.

The `fetch()` method returns a number of results, up to a specified limit. `fetch()` returns a list of entity objects, which are instances of the kind class:

```
q = ndb.Player.query().order(-Player.score)

results = q.fetch(10)
```

When serving web requests, it's always good to limit the amount of data the datastore might return, so an unexpectedly large result set doesn't cause the request handler to exceed its deadline. The `fetch()` method requires an argument specifying the number of results to fetch (the `limit` argument).

The `fetch()` method also accepts an optional `offset` parameter. If provided, the method skips that many results, then returns subsequent results, up to the specified limit:

```
q = ndb.Player.query().order(-Player.score)

results = q.fetch(10, offset=20)
```

With GQL, the fetch result limit and offset are equivalent to the `LIMIT` and `OFFSET` that can be specified in the query string itself. The arguments to `fetch()` override those specified in the GQL statement. The limit argument to `fetch()` is required, so it always overrides a GQL `LIMIT` clause.

In order to perform a fetch with an offset, the datastore must find the first result for the query and then scan down the index to the offset. The amount of time this takes is proportional to the size of the offset, and may not be suitable for large offsets.

If you just want to retrieve results in batches, such as for a paginated display, there's a better way: query cursors. For information on cursors, see "Query Cursors" on page 182.

It's common for an app to perform a query expecting to get just one result, or nothing. You can do this with `fetch(1)`, and then test whether the list it returns is empty. For convenience, the query object also provides a `get()` method, which returns either the first result, or None if the query did not return any results:

```
q = ndb.Player.query().filter(Player.name == 'django97')

player = q.get()
if player:
    # ...
```

The `count()` method executes the query, then returns the number of results that would be returned instead of the results themselves. `count()` must perform the query to count the results in the index, and so takes time proportional to what it is counting. `count()` accepts a limit as a parameter, and providing one causes the method to return immediately once that many results have been counted:

```
q = ndb.Player.query().filter(Player.level > 10)
if q.count(100) == 100:
    # 100 or more players are above level 10.
```

To test whether a query would return a result, without retrieving any results:

```
if q.count(1) == 1:
    # The query has at least one result.
```

Query objects provide one other mechanism for retrieving results, and it's quite powerful. In the Python API, query objects are *iterable*. If you use the object in a context that accepts iterables, such as in a `for` loop, the object executes the query, then provides a Python standard iterator that returns each result one at a time, starting with the first result:

```
q = ndb.Player.query().order(-Player.score)
```

```
for player in q:
    # ...
```

As the app uses the iterator, the iterator fetches the results in small batches. The iterator will not stop until it reaches the last result. It's up to the app to stop requesting results from the iterator (to break from the for loop) when it has had enough.

Treating the query object as an iterable uses default options for the query. If you'd like to specify options but still use the iterable interface, call the iter() method. This method takes the same options as fetch(), but returns the batch-loading iterator instead of the complete list of results.

Unlike fetch(), the limit argument is optional for iter(). But it's useful! With the limit argument, results are fetched in batches with the iterator interface, but the query knows to stop fetching after reaching the limit:

```
for player in q.iter(limit=100):
    # ...
```

This is especially useful for passing the iterator to a template, which may not have a way to stop the iteration on its own.

You can adjust the size of the batches fetched by the iterator interface by passing the batch_size argument to the iter() method. The default is 20 results per batch.

Keys-Only Queries

Instead of returning complete entities, the datastore can return just the keys of the entities that match the query. This can be useful in cases when a component only needs to know which entities are results, and doesn't need the results themselves. The component can store the keys for later retrieval of the entities, or pass the keys to other components, or perform further operations on the key list before fetching entities.

You can query for keys by passing the keys_only=True argument to fetch() or iter():

```
q = ndb.Player.query()
for result_key in q.iter(keys_only=True):
    # ...
```

GQL also supports special syntax for keys-only queries, using SELECT __key__ (that's two underscores, the word "key," and two more underscores) in place of SELECT *:

```
q = ndb.gql('SELECT __key__ FROM Player')
for result_key in q:
    # ...
```

When performing a keys-only query, each result returned by the query object is a Key object instead of an instance of the model class.

Introducing Indexes

For every query an application performs, Cloud Datastore maintains an index, a single table of possible answers for the query. Specifically, it maintains an index for a set of queries that use the same filters and sort orders, possibly with different values for the filters. Consider the following simple query:

```
SELECT * FROM Player WHERE name = 'druidjane'
```

To perform this query, Cloud Datastore uses an index containing the keys of every Player entity and the value of each entity's name property, sorted by the name property values in ascending order. Such an index is illustrated in Figure 7-1.

Key	name ⬆
⋮	⋮
Player / 39278	dorac
Player / 13467	druidjane
Player / 98914	duncandonut
Player / 5256	duran89
⋮	⋮

Figure 7-1. An index of Player entity keys and "name" property values, sorted by name in ascending order, with the result for WHERE name = druidjane

To find all entities that meet the conditions of the query, Cloud Datastore finds the first row in the index that matches, then it scans down to the first row that doesn't match. It returns the entities mentioned on all rows in this range (not counting the nonmatching row), in the order they appear in the index. Because the index is sorted, all results for the query are guaranteed to be on consecutive rows in the table.

Cloud Datastore would use this same index to perform other queries with a similar structure but different values, such as the following query:

```
SELECT * FROM Player WHERE name = 'duran89'
```

This query mechanism is fast, even with a very large number of entities. Entities and indexes are distributed across multiple machines, and each machine scans its own index in parallel with the others. Each machine returns results to Cloud Datastore as it scans its own index, and Cloud Datastore delivers the final result set to the app, in order, as if all results were in one large index.

Another reason queries are fast has to do with how the datastore finds the first matching row. Because indexes are sorted, the datastore can use an efficient algorithm to find the first matching row. In the common case, finding the first row takes approximately the same amount of time regardless of the size of the index. In other words, the speed of a query is not affected by the size of the data set.

Cloud Datastore updates all relevant indexes when property values change. In this example, if an application retrieves a Player entity, changes the name, and then saves the entity with a call to the put() method, Cloud Datastore updates the appropriate row in the previous index. It also moves the row if necessary so the ordering of the index is preserved.

Similarly, if the application creates a new Player entity with a name property, or deletes a Player entity with a name property, Cloud Datastore updates the index. In contrast, if the application updates a Player but does not change the name property, or creates or deletes a Player that does not have a name property, Cloud Datastore does not update the name index because no update is needed.

Cloud Datastore maintains two indexes like the previous example for every property name and entity kind, one with the property values sorted in ascending order and one with values in descending order. Cloud Datastore also maintains an index of entities of each kind. These indexes satisfy some simple queries, and Cloud Datastore also uses them internally for bookkeeping purposes.

For other queries, you must tell Cloud Datastore which indexes to prepare. You do this using a configuration file named *index.yaml*, which gets uploaded along with your application's code.

It'd be a pain to write this file by hand, but thankfully you don't have to. While you're testing your application in the development web server from the SDK, when the app performs a datastore query, the server checks that the configuration file has an appropriate entry for the needed index. If it doesn't find one, it adds one. As long as the app performs each of its queries at least once during testing, the resulting configuration file will be complete.

The index configuration file must be complete, because when the app is running on App Engine, if the application performs a query for which there is no index, the query returns an error. You can tell the development web server to behave similarly if you want to test for these error conditions. (How to do this depends on which SDK you are using; see "Configuring Indexes" on page 189.)

Indexes require a bit of discipline to maintain. Although the development tools can help add index configuration, they cannot know when an index is unused and can be deleted from the file. Extra indexes consume storage space and slow down updates of properties mentioned in the index. And while the version of the app you're developing may not need a given index, the version of the app still running on App Engine may still need it. The App Engine SDK and the Cloud Console include tools for inspecting and maintaining indexes. We'll look at these tools in Chapter 20.

Before we discuss index configuration, let's look more closely at how indexes support queries. We just saw an example where the results for a simple query appear on consecutive rows in a simple index. In fact, this is how most queries work: the results for every query that would use an index appear on consecutive rows in the index. This is both surprisingly powerful in some ways and surprisingly limited in others, and it's worth understanding why.

Automatic Indexes and Simple Queries

As we mentioned, Cloud Datastore maintains two indexes for every single property of every entity kind, one with values in ascending order and one with values in descending order. Cloud Datastore builds these indexes automatically, regardless of whether they are mentioned in the index configuration file. These automatic indexes satisfy the following kinds of queries using consecutive rows:

- A simple query for all entities of a given kind, no filters or sort orders
- One filter on a property using the equality operator (=)
- Filters using greater-than, greater-than or equal to, less-than, or less-than or equal to operators (>, >=, <, <=) on a single property
- One sort order, ascending or descending, and no filters, or with filters only on the same property used with the sort order
- Filters or a sort order on the entity key
- Kindless queries with or without key filters

Let's look at each of these in action.

All Entities of a Kind

The simplest datastore query asks for every entity of a given kind, in any order. Stated in GQL, a query for all entities of the kind Player looks like this:

```
SELECT * FROM Player
```

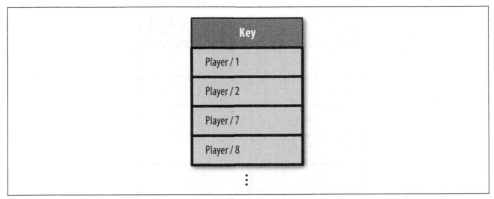

Figure 7-2. An index of all Player entity keys, with results for SELECT * FROM Player

Cloud Datastore maintains an index mapping kinds to entity keys. This index is sorted using a deterministic ordering for entity keys, so this query returns results in "key order." The kind of an entity cannot be changed after it is created, so this index is updated only when entities are created and deleted.

Because a query can only refer to one kind at a time, you can imagine this index as simply a list of entity keys for each kind. Figure 7-2 illustrates an example of this index.

When the query results are fetched, Cloud Datastore uses the entity keys in the index to find the corresponding entities, and returns the full entities to the application.

One Equality Filter

Consider the following query, which asks for every `Player` entity with a `level` property with a value of the integer 10:

```
SELECT * FROM Player WHERE level = 10
```

This query uses an index of `Player` entities with the `level` property, ascending—one of the automatic indexes. It uses an efficient algorithm to find the first row with a `level` equal to 10. Then it scans down the index until it finds the first row with a `level` not equal to 10. The consecutive rows from the first matching to the last matching represent all the `Player` entities with a `level` property equal to the integer 10. This is illustrated in Figure 7-3.

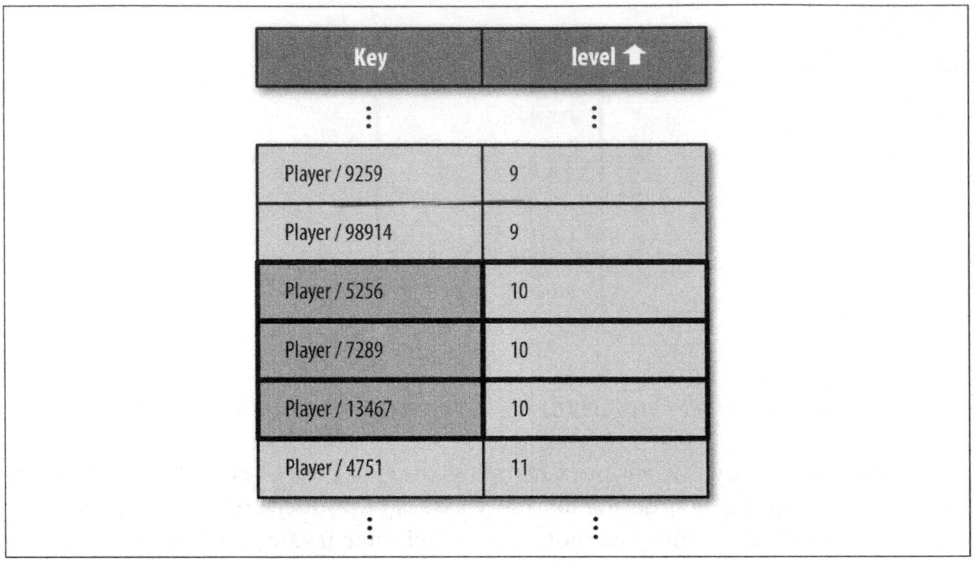

Figure 7-3. An index of the Player entity "level" properties, sorted by level then by key, with results for WHERE level = 10

Greater-Than and Less-Than Filters

The following query asks for every `Player` entity with a `score` property whose value is greater than the integer 500:

```
SELECT * FROM Player WHERE score > 500
```

This uses an index of `Player` entities with the `score` property, ascending, also an automatic index. As with the equality filter, it finds the first row in the index whose `score` is greater than 500. In the case of greater-than, because the table is sorted by `score` in ascending order, every row from this point to the bottom of the table is a result for the query. See Figure 7-4.

Similarly, consider a query that asks for every `Player` with a `score` less than 1,000:

```
SELECT * FROM Player WHERE score < 1000
```

Cloud Datastore uses the same index (`score`, ascending), and the same strategy: it finds the first row that matches the query, in this case the first row. Then it scans to the next row that doesn't match the query, the first row whose `score` is greater than or equal to `1000`. The results are represented by everything above that row.

Finally, consider a query for `score` values between 500 and 1,000:

```
SELECT * FROM Player WHERE score > 500 AND score < 1000
```

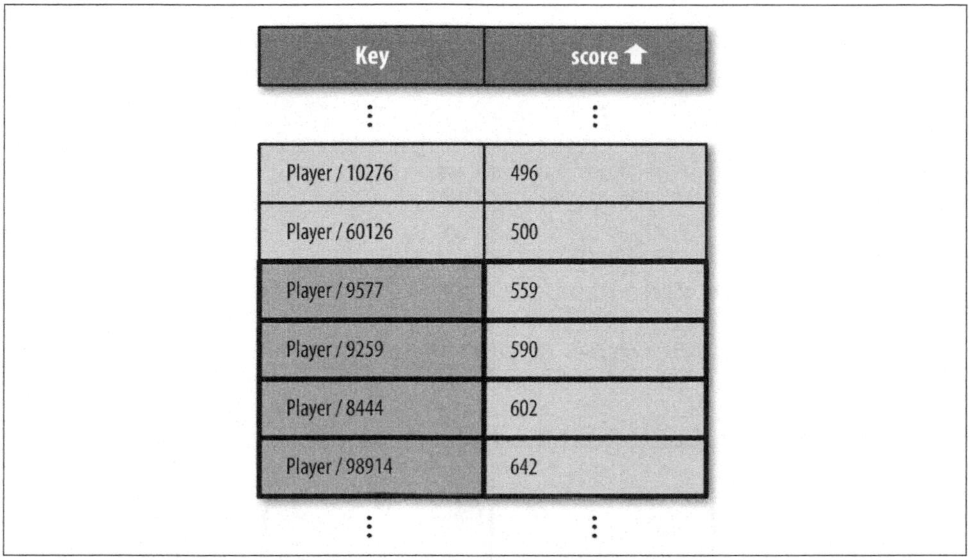

Key	score ⬆
⋮	⋮
Player / 10276	496
Player / 60126	500
Player / 9577	559
Player / 9259	590
Player / 8444	602
Player / 98914	642
⋮	⋮

Figure 7-4. An index of the Player entity "score" properties, sorted by score then by key, with results for WHERE score > 500

Once again, the same index and strategy prevail: Cloud Datastore scans from the top down, finding the first matching and next nonmatching rows, returning the entities represented by everything in between. This is shown in Figure 7-5.

If the values used with the filters do not represent a valid range, such as `score < 500 AND score > 1000`, the query planner notices this and doesn't bother performing a query, as it knows the query has no results.

One Sort Order

The following query asks for every `Player` entity, arranged in order by `level`, from lowest to highest:

```
SELECT * FROM Player ORDER BY level
```

As before, this uses an index of `Player` entities with `level` properties in ascending order. If both this query and the previous equality query were performed by the application, both queries would use the same index. This query uses the index to determine the order in which to return `Player` entities, starting at the top of the table and moving down until the application stops fetching results, or until the bottom of the table. Recall that every `Player` entity with a `level` property is mentioned in this table. See Figure 7-6.

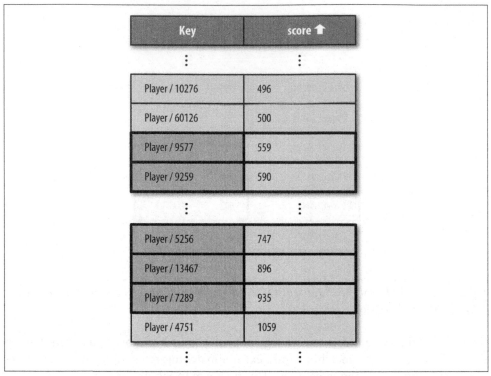

Key	score ⬆
⋮	⋮
Player / 10276	496
Player / 60126	500
Player / 9577	559
Player / 9259	590
⋮	⋮
Player / 5256	747
Player / 13467	896
Player / 7289	935
Player / 4751	1059
⋮	⋮

Figure 7-5. An index of the Player entity "score" properties, sorted by score, with results for WHERE score > 500 AND score < 1000

Key	level ⬆
Player / 39278	1
Player / 39320	1
Player / 40178	1
Player / 29911	2
Player / 84514	2
⋮	⋮

Figure 7-6. An index of the Player entity "level" properties sorted by level in ascending order, with results for ORDER BY level

The following query is similar to the previous one, but asks for the entities arranged by level from highest to lowest:

```
SELECT * FROM Player ORDER BY level DESC
```

This query cannot use the same index as before, because the results are in the wrong order. For this query, the results should start at the entity with the highest level, so the query needs an index where this result is in the first row. Cloud Datastore provides an automatic index for single properties in descending order for this purpose. See Figure 7-7.

Key	level ⬇
Player / 3359	12
Player / 4751	11
Player / 7243	11
Player / 5256	10
Player / 7289	10
⋮	⋮

Figure 7-7. An index of the Player entity "level" properties sorted by level in descending order, with results for ORDER BY level DESC

If a query with a sort order on a single property also includes filters on that property, and no other filters, Cloud Datastore still needs only the one automatic index to fulfill the query. In fact, you may have noticed that for these simple queries, the results are returned sorted by the property in ascending order, regardless of whether the query specifies the sort order explicitly. In these cases, the ascending sort order is redundant.

Queries on Keys

In addition to filters and sort orders on properties, you can also perform queries with filters and sort orders on entity keys. You can refer to an entity's key in a filter or sort order using the special name __key__.

An equality filter on the key isn't much use. Only one entity can have a given key, and if the key is known, it's faster to perform a key.get() than a query. But an inequality filter on the key can be useful for fetching ranges of keys. (If you're fetching entities in batches, consider using query cursors. See "Query Cursors" on page 182.)

Cloud Datastore provides automatic indexes of kinds and keys, sorted by key in ascending order. The query returns the results sorted in key order. This order isn't useful for display purposes, but it's deterministic. A query that sorts keys in descending order requires a custom index.

Cloud Datastore uses indexes for filters on keys in the same way as filters on properties, with a minor twist: a query using a key filter in addition to other filters can use an automatic index if a similar query without the key filter could use an automatic index. Automatic indexes for properties already include the keys, so such queries can just use the same indexes. And of course, if the query has no other filters beyond the key filter, it can use the automatic key index.

Kindless Queries

In addition to performing queries on entities of a given kind, the datastore lets you perform a limited set of queries on entities of all kinds. Kindless queries cannot use filters or sort orders on properties. They can, however, use equality and inequality filters on keys (IDs or names).

Kindless queries are mostly useful in combination with ancestors, which we'll discuss in Chapter 8. They can also be used to get every entity in the datastore. (If you're querying a large number of entities, you'll probably want to fetch the results in batches. See "Query Cursors" on page 182.)

Using the `Query` class, you perform a kindless query by omitting the model class argument from the constructor:

```
q = ndb.Query()

q = q.filter('__key__ >', last_key)
```

In GQL, you specify a kindless query by omitting the `FROM Kind` part of the statement:

```
q = ndb.gql('SELECT * WHERE __key__ > :1', last_key)
```

The results of a kindless query are returned in key order, ascending. Kindless queries use an automatic index.

The datastore maintains statistics about the apps data in a set of datastore entities. When the app performs a kindless query, these statistics entities are included in the results. The kind names for these entities all begin with the characters __Stat_ (two under-scores, the word "Stat," and another underscore). Your app will need to filter these out if they are not desired.

The `ndb` interface expects there to be an `ndb.Model` (or `ndb.Expando`) class defined or imported for each kind of each query result. When using kindless queries, you must define or import all possible kinds. To load classes for the datastore statistics entity kinds, import the `ndb.stats` module:

```
from google.appengine.ext.ndb import stats
```

For more information about datastore statistics, see "Accessing Metadata from the App" on page 249.

Custom Indexes and Complex Queries

All queries not covered by the automatic indexes must have corresponding indexes defined in the app's index configuration file. We'll refer to these as "custom indexes," in contrast with "automatic indexes." Cloud Datastore needs these hints because building every possible index for every combination of property and sort order would take a gargantuan amount of space and time, and an app isn't likely to need more than a fraction of those possibilities.

In particular, the following queries require custom indexes:

- A query with multiple sort orders
- A query with an inequality filter on a property and filters on other properties
- Projection queries

A query that uses just equality filters on properties does not need a custom index in most cases thanks to a specialized query algorithm for this case, which we'll look at in a moment. Also, filters on keys do not require custom indexes; they can operate on whatever indexes are used to fulfill the rest of the query.

Let's examine these queries and the indexes they require. We'll cover projection queries in "Projection Queries" on page 186.

Multiple Sort Orders

The automatic single-property indexes provide enough information for one sort order. When two entities have the same value for the sorted property, the entities appear in the index in adjacent rows, ordered by their entity keys. If you want to order these entities with other criteria, you need an index with more information.

The following query asks for all `Player` entities, sorted first by the `level` property in descending order, then, in the case of ties, sorted by the `score` property in descending order:

```
SELECT * FROM Player ORDER BY level DESC, score DESC
```

The index this query needs is straightforward: a table of `Player` entity keys, `level` values, and `score` values, sorted according to the query. This is not one of the indexes provided by the datastore automatically, so it is a custom index, and must be mentioned in the index configuration file. If you performed this query in the development web server, the server would add the following lines to the *index.yaml* file:

```
- kind: Player
  properties:
  - name: level
    direction: desc
  - name: score
    direction: desc
```

The order the properties appear in the configuration file matters. This is the order in which the rows are sorted: first by `level` descending, then by `score` descending.

This configuration creates the index shown in Figure 7-8. The results appear in the table, and are returned for the query in the desired order.

Key	level ⬇	score ⬇
Player / 3359	12	1366
Player / 7243	11	1280
Player / 4751	11	1059
Player / 7289	10	935
Player / 13467	10	896
⋮	⋮	⋮

Figure 7-8. An index of the Player entity "level" and "score" properties, sorted by level descending, then score descending, then by key ascending

Filters on Multiple Properties

Consider the following query, which asks for every `Player` with a `level` greater than the integer `10` and a `charclass` of the string `'mage'`:

```
SELECT * FROM Player WHERE charclass = 'mage' AND level > 10
```

To be able to scan to a contiguous set of results meeting both filter criteria, the index must contain columns of values for these properties. The entities must be sorted first by charclass, then by level.

The index configuration for this query would appear as follows in the *index.yaml* file:

```
- kind: Player
  properties:
  - name: charclass
    direction: asc
  - name: level
    direction: asc
```

This index is illustrated in Figure 7-9.

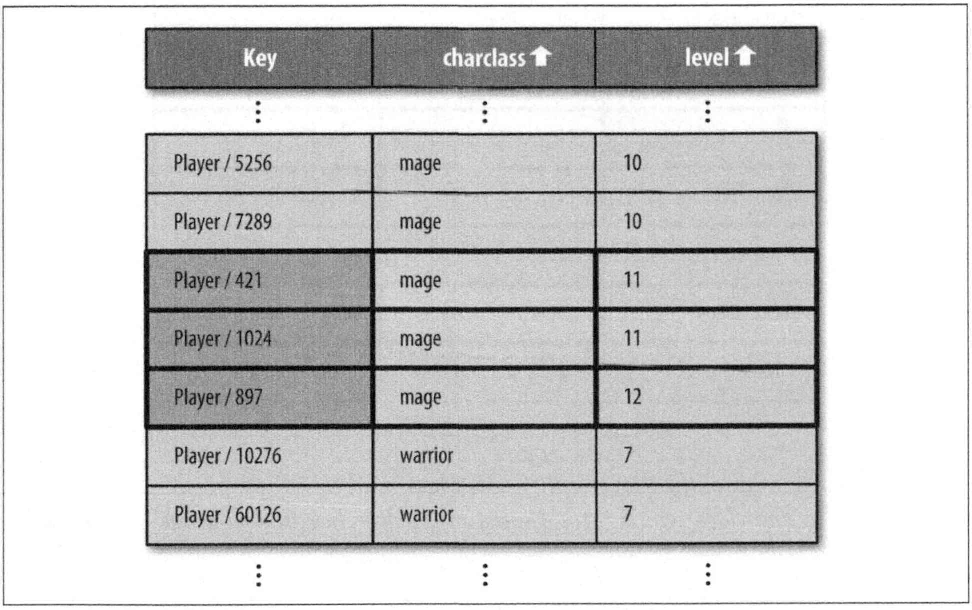

Key	charclass ⬆	level ⬆
⋮	⋮	⋮
Player / 5256	mage	10
Player / 7289	mage	10
Player / 421	mage	11
Player / 1024	mage	11
Player / 897	mage	12
Player / 10276	warrior	7
Player / 60126	warrior	7
⋮	⋮	⋮

Figure 7-9. An index of the Player entity "charclass" and "level" properties, sorted by charclass, then level, then key, with results for WHERE charclass = "mage" AND level > 10

The ordering sequence of these properties is important! Remember: the results for the query must all appear on adjacent rows in the index. If the index for this query were sorted first by level then by charclass, it would be possible for valid results to appear on nonadjacent rows. Figure 7-10 demonstrates this problem.

The index ordering requirement for combining inequality and equality filters has several implications that may seem unusual when compared to the query engines of other databases. Heck, they're downright weird. The first implication, illustrated previously, can be stated generally:

The First Rule of Inequality Filters: If a query uses inequality filters on one property and equality filters on one or more other properties, the index must be ordered first by the properties used in equality filters, then by the property used in the inequality filters.

This rule has a corollary regarding queries with both an inequality filter and sort orders. Consider the following possible query:

```
SELECT * FROM Player WHERE level > 10 ORDER BY score DESC
```

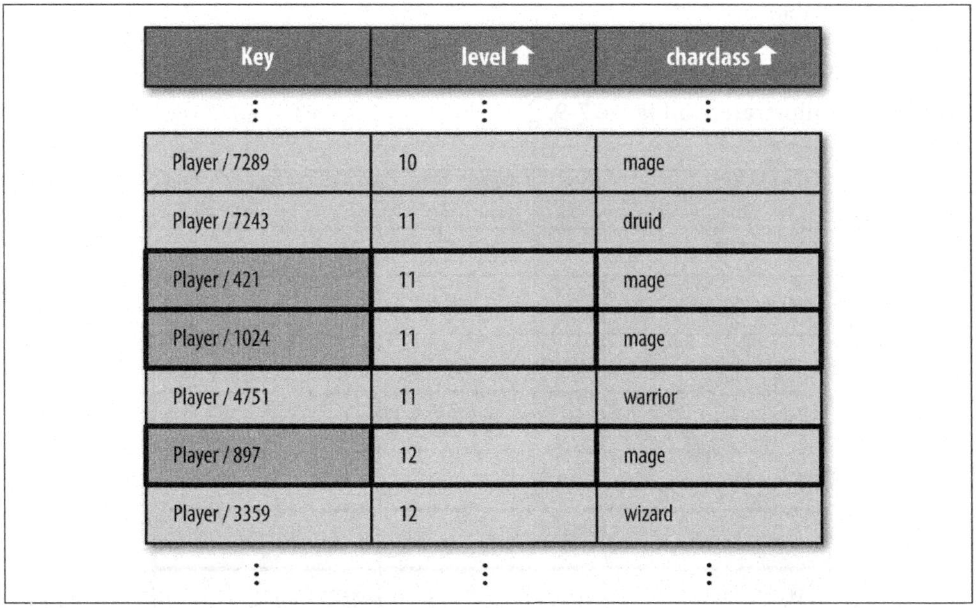

Key	level ⬆	charclass ⬆
⋮	⋮	⋮
Player / 7289	10	mage
Player / 7243	11	druid
Player / 421	11	mage
Player / 1024	11	mage
Player / 4751	11	warrior
Player / 897	12	mage
Player / 3359	12	wizard
⋮	⋮	⋮

Figure 7-10. An index of the Player entity "charclass" and "level" properties, sorted first by level then by charclass, which cannot satisfy WHERE charclass = "mage" AND level > 10 with consecutive rows

What would the index for this query look like? For starters, it would have a column for the level, so it can select the rows that match the filter. It would also have a column for the score, to determine the order of the results. But which column is ordered first?

The First Rule implies that level must be ordered first. But the query requested that the results be returned sorted by score, descending. If the index were sorted by score, then by level, the rows may not be adjacent.

To avoid confusion, Cloud Datastore requires that the correct sort order be stated explicitly in the query:

```
SELECT * FROM Player WHERE level > 10 ORDER BY level, score DESC
```

In general:

The Second Rule of Inequality Filters: If a query uses inequality filters on one property and sort orders of one or more other properties, the index must be ordered first by the property used in the inequality filters (in either direction), then by the other desired sort orders. To avoid confusion, the query must state all sort orders explicitly.

There's one last implication to consider with regard to inequality filters. The following possible query attempts to get all `Player` entities with a `level` less than 10 and a `score` less than 500:

```
SELECT * FROM Player WHERE level < 10 AND score < 500
```

Consider an index ordered first by `level`, then by `score`, as shown in Figure 7-11.

Key	level ⬆	score ⬆		Key	score ⬆	level ⬆
⋮	⋮	⋮		⋮	⋮	⋮
Player / 5052	8	498		Player / 5052	498	8
Player / 5176	8	500		Player / 8311	498	10
Player / 5844	9	499		Player / 5844	499	9
Player / 8311	10	498		Player / 5178	500	8
⋮	⋮	⋮		⋮	⋮	⋮

Figure 7-11. Neither possible index of the Player entity "level" and "score" properties can satisfy WHERE level < 10 AND score < 500 with consecutive rows

In fact, there is no possible index that could satisfy this query completely using consecutive rows. This is not a valid datastore query.

The Third Rule of Inequality Filters: A query cannot use inequality filters on more than one property.

A query *can* use multiple inequality filters on the same property, such as to test for a range of values.

Multiple Equality Filters

For queries using just equality filters, it's easy to imagine custom indexes that satisfy them. For instance:

```
SELECT * FROM Player WHERE charclass = 'mage' AND level = 10
```

A custom index containing these properties, ordered in any sequence and direction, would meet the query's requirements. But Cloud Datastore has another trick up its sleeve for this kind of query. For queries using just equality filters and no sort orders, instead of scanning a single table of all values, Cloud Datastore can scan the automatic single-property indexes for each property, and return the results as it finds them. Cloud Datastore can perform a "merge join" of the single-property indexes to satisfy this kind of query.

In other words, the datastore doesn't need a custom index to perform queries using just equality filters and no sort orders. If you add a suitable custom index to your configuration file, the datastore will use it. But a custom index is not required, and the development server's automatic index configuration feature will not add one if it doesn't exist.

Let's consider how the algorithm would perform the following query, using single-property indexes:

```
SELECT * FROM Kind WHERE a = 1 AND b = 2 AND c = 3
```

Recall that each of these tables contains a row for each entity with the property set, with fields for the entity's key and the property's value. The table is sorted first by the value, then by the key. The algorithm takes advantage of the fact that rows with the same value are consecutive, and within that consecutive block, rows are sorted by key.

To perform the query, the datastore uses the following steps:

1. The datastore checks the a index for the first row with a value of 1. The entity whose key is on this row is a candidate, but not yet a confirmed result.

2. It then checks the b index for the first row whose value is 2 *and* whose key is greater than or equal to the candidate's key. Other rows with a value of 2 may appear above this row in the b index, but the datastore knows those are not candidates because the first a scan determined the candidate with the smallest key.

3. If the datastore finds the candidate's key in the matching region of b, that key is still a candidate, and the datastore proceeds with a similar check in the index for c. If the datastore does not find the candidate in the b index but does find another larger key with a matching value, that key becomes the new candidate, and it proceeds to check for the new candidate in the c index. (It'll eventually go back to check a with the new candidate before deciding it is a result.) If it finds neither the candidate nor a matching row with a larger key, the query is complete.

4. If a candidate is found to match all criteria in all indexes, the candidate is returned as a result. The datastore starts the search for a new candidate, using the previous candidate's key as the minimum key.

Figure 7-12 illustrates this zigzag search across the single-property indexes, first with a failed candidate, then two successful candidates.

A key feature of this algorithm is that it finds results in the order in which they are to be returned: key order. The datastore does not need to compile a complete list of possible results for the query—possibly millions of entities—and sort them to determine which results ought to be first. Also, the datastore can stop scanning as soon as it has enough results to fulfill the query, which is always a limited number of entities.

Of course, this query could also use a custom index with all the filter properties in it. If you provide configuration for such an index, the query will use the custom index instead of doing the zigzag join. This can result in a query faster than the zigzag join, at the expense of added time to update the indexed entities.

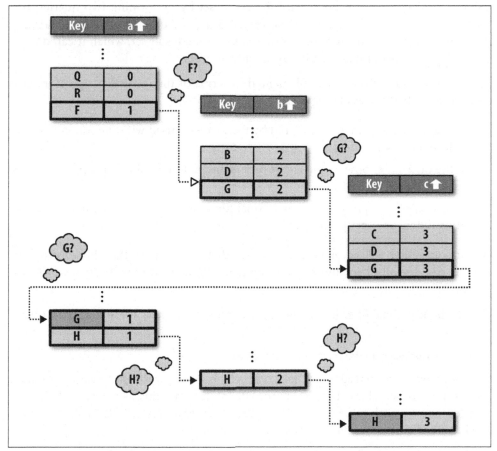

Figure 7-12. The merge join algorithm finding two entities WHERE a = 1 AND b = 2 AND c = 3

A zigzag-capable query using equality filters on properties can also use inequality filters on keys without needing a custom index. This is useful for fetching a large number of results in key ranges. (But if you're fetching batches, cursors might be more effective. See "Query Cursors" on page 182.)

Not-Equal and IN Filters

The query API supports two operators we haven't discussed yet: != (not-equal) and IN. These operators are not actually supported by the datastore itself. Instead, they are implemented by the datastore API as multiple queries in terms of the other operators.

The filter `prop != value` matches every entity whose property does not equal the value. The datastore API determines the result set by performing two queries: one using `prop < value` in place of the not-equal filter, and one using `prop > value` in place of the filter. It returns both sets of results as one result set, which it can do reasonably quickly because the results are already in order.

Because not-equal is actually implemented in terms of the inequality operators, it is subject to the three rules of inequality operators:

- The query's index must be ordered by the property used with the not-equal filter before other sort orders.
- If the query uses other explicit sort orders, the not-equal filter's property must be explicitly ordered first.
- And finally, any query using a not-equal filter cannot also use inequality or not-equal filters on other properties.

A not-equal filter will never return an entity that doesn't have the filtered property. This is true for all filters, but can be especially counterintuitive in the case of not-equal.

To use the not-equal filter in an `ndb` query expression, simply use Python's != operator:

```
q = Player.query().filter(Player.charclass != 'mage')
```

The filter `prop IN (value1, value2, value3)` matches every entity whose property equals any of the values. The datastore API implements this as a series of equality queries, one for each value to test. The more values that appear in the list, the longer the full set of queries will take to execute.

With `ndb`, you specify the IN operator using the `IN()` method of the property declaration:

```
q = Player.query().filter(Player.charclass.IN(['mage', 'druid', 'warrior']))
```

If a single query includes multiple IN filters on multiple properties, the datastore API must perform equality queries for every combination of values in all filters. `prop1 IN` (value1, value2, value3, value4) AND prop2 IN (value5, value6, value7) is equivalent to 12 queries using equality filters.

The != and IN operators are useful shortcuts. But because they actually perform multiple queries, they take longer to execute than the other operators. It's worth understanding their performance implications before using them.

Unset and Nonindexed Properties

As you've seen, an index contains columns of property values. Typically, an app creates entities of the same kind with the same set of properties: every Player in our game has a name, a character class, a level, and a score. If every entity of a kind has a given property, then an index for that kind and property has a row corresponding to each entity of the kind.

But the datastore neither requires nor enforces a common layout of properties across entities of a kind. It's quite possible for an entity to not have a property that other entities of the same kind have. For instance, a Player entity might be created without a character class, and go without until the user chooses one.

It is possible to set a property with a null value (None), but a property set to the null value is distinct from the property not being set at all. This is different from a tabular database, which requires a value (possibly null) for every cell in a row.

If an entity does not have a property used in an index, the entity does not appear in the index. Stated conversely, an entity must have *every* property mentioned in an index to appear in the index. If a Player does not have a charclass property, it does not appear in any index with a charclass column.

If an entity is not mentioned in an index, it cannot be returned as a result for a query that uses the index. Remember that queries use indexes for both filters and sort orders. A query that uses a property for any kind of filter or any sort order can never return an entity that doesn't have that property. The charclass-less Player can never be a result for a Player query that sorts results by charclass.

In "Strings, Text, and Bytes" on page 133, we mentioned that text and blob values are not indexed. Another way of saying this is that, for the purposes of indexes, a property with a text or blob value is treated as if it is unset. If an app performs a query by using a filter or sort order on a property that is always set to a text or blob value, that query will always return no results.

It is sometimes useful to store property values of other types, and exempt them from indexes. This saves space in index tables, and reduces the amount of time it takes to save the entity.

The only way to declare a property as unindexed is with the `ndb.Model` API. There is currently no other way to set a specific property as unindexed in this API. We'll look at this feature when we discuss the modeling API in Chapter 9.

If you need an entity to qualify as a result for a query, but it doesn't make sense in your data model to give the entity every property used in the query, use the null value to represent the "no value" case, and always set it. The Python modeling API makes it easy to ensure that properties always have values.

Sort Orders and Value Types

Cloud Datastore keeps the rows of an index sorted in an order that supports the corresponding query. Each type of property value has its own rules for comparing two values of the same type, and these rules are mostly intuitive: integers are sorted in numeric order, strings in Unicode order, and so forth.

Two entities can have values of different types for the same property, so Cloud Datastore also has rules for comparing such values, although these rules are not so intuitive. Values are ordered first by type, then within their type. For instance, all integers are sorted above all strings.

One effect of this that might be surprising is that all floats are sorted below all integers. The datastore treats floats and integers as separate value types, and so sorts them separately. If your app relies on the correct ordering of numbers, make sure all numbers are stored using the same type of value.

The datastore stores eight distinct types of values, not counting the nonindexed types (text and blob). The datastore supports several additional types by storing them as one of the eight types, then marshaling them between the internal representation and the value your app sees automatically. These additional types are sorted by their internal representation. For instance, a date-time value is actually stored as an integer, and will be sorted among other integer values in an index. (When comparing date-time values, this results in chronological order, which is what you would expect.)

Table 7-2 describes the eight indexable types supported by the datastore. The types are listed in their relative order, from first to last.

Table 7-2. How the datastore value types are sorted

Data type	Python type	Ordering
The null value	None	-
Integer and date-time	`long`, `datetime.datetime`	Numeric (date-time is chronological)
Boolean	`bool` (`True` or `False`)	False, then true

Data type	Python type	Ordering
Byte string	`str`	Byte order
Unicode string	`unicode`	Unicode character order
Floating-point number	`float`	Numeric
Geographical point	`ndb.GeoPt`	By latitude, then longitude (floating-point numbers)
A Google account	`users.User`	By email address, Unicode order
Entity key	`ndb.Key`	Kind (byte string), then ID (numeric) or name (byte string)

Queries and Multivalued Properties

In a typical database, a field in a record stores a single value. A record represents a data object, and each field represents a single, simple aspect of the object. If a data object can have more than one of a particular thing, each of those things is typically represented by a separate record of an appropriate kind, associated with the data object by using the object's key as a field value. Cloud Datastore supports both of these uses of fields: a property can contain a simple value or the key of another entity.

But Cloud Datastore can do something most other databases can't: it can store more than one value for a single property. With multivalued properties (MVPs), you can represent a data object with more than one of something without resorting to creating a separate entity for each of those things, if each thing could be represented by a simple value.

One of the most useful features of multivalued properties is how they match an equality filter in a query. The datastore query engine considers a multivalued property equal to a filter value if any of the property's values is equal to the filter value. This ability to test for membership means MVPs are useful for representing sets.

Multivalued properties maintain the order of values, and can have repeated items. The values can be of any datastore type, and a single property can have values of different types.

MVPs in Code

Consider the following example. The players of our online game can earn trophies for particular accomplishments. The app needs to display a list of all the trophies a player has won, and the app needs to display a list of all the players who have won a particular trophy. The app doesn't need to maintain any data about the trophies themselves;

it's sufficient to just store the name of the trophy. (This could also be a list of keys for trophy entities.)

One option is to store the list of trophy names as a single delimited string value for each `Player` entity. This makes it easy to get the list of trophies for a particular player, but impossible to get the list of players for a particular trophy. (A query filter can't match patterns within string values.)

Another option is to record each trophy win in a separate property named after the trophy. To get the list of players with a trophy, you just query for the existence of the corresponding property. However, getting the list of trophies for a given player would require either coding the names of all the trophies in the display logic, or iterating over all the `Player` entity's properties looking for trophy names.

With multivalued properties, we can store each trophy name as a separate value for the `trophies` property. To access a list of all trophies for a player, we simply access the property of the entity. To get a list of all players with a trophy, we use a query with an equality filter on the property.

In `ndb`, you can declare that a property is allowed to have multiple values by passing the `repeated=True` argument to the property declaration:

```
class Player(ndb.Model):
    # ...
    trophies = ndb.StringProperty(repeated=True)
```

The value of the property is a `list` whose elements are of the appropriate type:

```
p = ndb.Key(Player, user_id).get()
p.trophies = ['Lava Polo Champion',
              'World Building 2008, Bronze',
              'Glarcon Fighter, 2nd class']
p.put()

# ...

# List all trophies for a player.
p = ndb.Key(Player, user_id).get()
for trophy in p.trophies:
    # ...

# Query all players that have a trophy.
q = Player.gql("WHERE trophies = :1").bind('Lava Polo Champion')
for p in q:
    # ...
```

As with nonrepeated properties, the declaration enforces the type for all values in the list. To declare that a property can contain multiple values of various types, use `ndb.GenericProperty(repeated=True)`. Each member of the list must be of one of the supported datastore types.

With the `ndb.Expando` base class, you can leave the property undeclared, and simply assign a `list` value:

```
class Entity(ndb.Model):
    prop = ndb.GenericProperty(repeated=True)

e = Entity()
e.prop = ['value1', 123, users.get_current_user()]
```

Remember that `list` is not a datastore type; it is only the mechanism for manipulating multivalued properties. A list cannot contain another list.

Within the datastore, a property must have at least one value, otherwise the property does not exist (the property is unset). The property declaration knows how to translate between the empty list (`[]`) and the property being unset on an entity. If the property is undeclared (on an `ndb.Expando`), the model class doesn't know the difference between an empty list value and an unset property, so it behaves as if the property is unset. Take care to handle this case when using `ndb.Expando`, undeclared properties, and multiple values.

MVPs and Equality Filters

As you've seen, when a multivalued property is the subject of an equality filter in a query, the entity matches if any of the property's values are equal to the filter value:

```
e1 = Entity()
e1.prop = [3.14, 'a', 'b']
e1.put()

e2 = Entity()
e2.prop = ['a', 1, 6]
e2.put()

# Returns e1 but not e2:
q = Entity.gql('WHERE prop = 3.14')

# Returns e2 but not e1:
q = Entity.gql('WHERE prop = 6')

# Returns both e1 and e2:
q = Entity.gql("WHERE prop = 'a'")
```

Recall that a query with a single equality filter uses an index that contains the keys of every entity of the given kind with the given property and the property values. If an entity has a single value for the property, the index contains one row that represents the entity and the value. If an entity has multiple values for the property, the index contains one row for each value. The index for this example is shown in Figure 7-13.

This brings us to the first of several odd-looking queries that nonetheless make sense for multivalued properties. Because an equality filter is a membership test, it is possible for multiple equality filters to use the same property with different values and still return a result. An example in GQL:

```
SELECT * FROM Entity WHERE prop = 'a' AND prop = 'b'
```

Key	prop ⬆
e2	1
e2	6
e1	a
e2	a
e1	b
e1	3.14

Figure 7-13. An index of two entities with multiple values for the "prop" property, with results for WHERE prop = a

Cloud Datastore uses the "merge join" algorithm, described in "Multiple Equality Filters" on page 169 for multiple equality filters, to satisfy this query, using the `prop` single-property index. This query returns the `e1` entity because the entity key appears in two places in the index, once for each value requested by the filters.

The way multivalued properties appear in an index gives us another way of thinking about multivalued properties: an entity has one or more properties, each with a name and a single value, and an entity can have multiple properties with the same name. The API represents the values of multiple properties with the same name as a list of values associated with that name.

The datastore does not have a way to query for the exact set of values in a multivalued property. You can use multiple equality filters to test that each of several values belongs to the list, but there is no filter that ensures that those are the only values that belong to the list, or that each value appears only once.

MVPs and Inequality Filters

Just as an equality filter tests that any value of the property is equal to the filter value, an inequality filter tests that any value of the property meets the filter criterion:

```
e1 = Entity()
e1.prop = [1, 3, 5]
e1.put()
```

```
e2 = Entity()
e2.prop = [4, 6, 8]
e2.put()

# Returns e1 but not e2:
q = Entity.gql("WHERE prop < 2")

# Returns e2 but not e1:
q = Entity.gql("WHERE prop > 7")

# Returns both e1 and e2:
q = Entity.gql("WHERE prop > 3")
```

Figure 7-14 shows the index for this example, with the results of prop > 3 highlighted.

Key	prop ⬆
e1	1
e1	3
e2	4
e1	5
e2	6
e2	8

Figure 7-14. An index of two entities with multiple values for the "prop" property, with results for WHERE prop > 3

In the case of an inequality filter, it's possible for the index scan to match rows for a single entity multiple times. When this happens, the first occurrence of each key in the index determines the order of the results. If the index used for the query sorts the property in ascending order, the first occurrence is the smallest matching value. For descending, it's the largest. In this example, prop > 3 returns e2 before e1 because 4 appears before 5 in the index.

MVPs and Sort Orders

To summarize things we know about how multivalued properties are indexed:

- A multivalued property appears in an index with one row per value.
- All rows in an index are sorted by the values, possibly distributing property values for a single entity across the index.
- The first occurrence of an entity in an index scan determines its place in the result set for a query.

Together, these facts explain what happens when a query orders its results by a multivalued property. When results are sorted by a multivalued property in ascending order, the smallest value for the property determines its location in the results. When results are sorted in descending order, the largest value for the property determines its location.

This has a counterintuitive—but consistent—consequence:

```
e1 = Entity()
e1.prop = [1, 3, 5]
e1.put()

e2 = Entity()
e2.prop = [2, 3, 4]
e2.put()

# Returns e1, e2:
q = Entity.gql("ORDER BY prop ASC")

# Also returns e1, e2:
q = Entity.gql("ORDER BY prop DESC")
```

Because e1 has both the smallest value and the largest value, it appears first in the result set in ascending order *and* in descending order. See Figure 7-15.

Key	prop ⬆
e1	1
e2	2
e1	3
e2	3
e2	4
e1	5

Key	prop ⬇
e1	5
e2	4
e1	3
e2	3
e2	2
e1	1

Figure 7-15. Indexes of two entities with multiple values for the "prop" property, one ascending and one descending

MVPs and the Query Planner

The query planner tries to be smart by ignoring aspects of the query that are redundant or contradictory. For instance, a = 3 AND a = 4 would normally return no results, so the query planner catches those cases and doesn't bother doing work it doesn't need to do. However, most of these normalization techniques don't apply to multivalued properties. In this case, the query could be asking, "Does this MVP have a value that is equal to 3 and another value equal to 4?" The datastore remembers which properties are MVPs (even those that end up with one or zero values), and never takes a shortcut that would produce incorrect results.

But there is one exception. A query that has both an equality filter and a sort order on the same property will drop the sort order. If a query asks for a = 3 ORDER BY a DESC and a is a single-value property, the sort order has no effect because all values in the result are identical. For an MVP, however, a = 3 tests for membership, and two MVPs that meet that condition are not necessarily identical.

The datastore drops the sort order in this case anyway. To do otherwise would require too much index data and result in exploding indexes in cases that could otherwise survive. As always, the actual sort order is deterministic, but it won't be the requested order.

Exploding Indexes

There's one more thing to know about indexes when considering multivalued properties for your data model.

When an entity has multiple values for a property, each index that includes a column for the property must use multiple rows to represent the entity, one for each possible combination of values. In a single property index on the multivalued property, this is simply one row for each value, two columns each (the entity key and the property value).

In an index of multiple properties where the entity has multiple values for one of the indexed properties and a single value for each of the others, the index includes one row for each value of the multivalued property. Each row has a column for each indexed property, plus the key. The values for the single-value properties are repeated in each row.

Here's the kicker: if an entity has more than one property with multiple values, and more than one multivalued property appears in an index, the index must contain one row for each combination of values to represent the entity completely.

If you're not careful, the number of index rows that need to be updated when the entity changes could grow very large. It may be so large that the datastore cannot complete an update of the entity before it reaches its safety limits, and returns an error.

To help prevent "exploding indexes" from causing problems, Cloud Datastore limits the number of property values—that is, the number of rows times the number of columns—a single entity can occupy in an index. The limit is 5,000 property values, high enough for normal use, but low enough to prevent unusual index sizes from inhibiting updates.

If you do include a multivalued property in a custom index, be careful about the possibility of exploding indexes.

Query Cursors

A query often has more results than you want to process in a single action. A message board may have thousands of messages, but it isn't useful to show a user thousands of messages on one screen. It would be better to show the user a dozen messages at a time, and let the user decide when to look at more, such as by clicking a Next link, or scrolling to the bottom of the display.

A *query cursor* is like a bookmark in a list of query results. After fetching some results, you can ask the query API for the cursor that represents the spot immediately after the last result you fetched. When you perform the query again at a later time, you can include the cursor value, and the next result fetched will be the one at the spot where the cursor was generated.

Cursors are fast. Unlike with the "offset" fetch parameter, the datastore does not have to scan from the beginning of the results to find the cursor location. The time to fetch results starting from a cursor is proportional to the number of results fetched. This makes cursors ideal for paginated displays of items.

The following is code for a simple paginated display:

```python
import jinja2
import os
import webapp2

from google.appengine.datastore import datastore_query
from google.appengine.ext import ndb

template_env = jinja2.Environment(
    loader=jinja2.FileSystemLoader(os.getcwd()))

PAGE_SIZE = 10

class Message(ndb.Model):
    create_date = ndb.DateTimeProperty(auto_now_add=True)
    # ...

class ResultsPageHandler(webapp2.RequestHandler):
    def get(self):
        cursor_str = self.request.get('c', None)
        cursor = None
        if cursor_str:
            cursor = datastore_query.Cursor(urlsafe=cursor_str)

        query = Message.query().order(-Player.create_date)
        results, new_cursor, more = query.fetch_page(
            PAGE_SIZE, start_cursor=cursor)

        template = template_env.get_template('results.html')
        context = {
            'results': results,
        }
        if more:
            context['next_cursor'] = new_cursor.urlsafe()
        self.response.out.write(template.render(context))

app = webapp2.WSGIApplication([
    ('/results', ResultsPageHandler),
    # ...
    ],
    debug=True)
```

The *results.html* template is as follows (note the Next link in particular):

```
<html><body>

{% if results %}

  <p>Messages:</p>
  <ul>
  {% for result in results %}
    <li>{{ result.key.id() }}: {{ result.create_date }}</li>
  {% endfor %}
  </ul>

  {% if next_cursor %}
  <p><a href="/results?c={{ next_cursor }}">Next</a></p>
  {% endif %}

{% else %}
  <p>There are no messages.</p>
{% endif %}

</body></html>
```

This example displays all of the `Message` entities in the datastore, in reverse chrono-logical order, in pages of 10 messages per page. If there are more results after the last result displayed, the app shows a Next link back to the request handler with the `c` parameter set to the cursor pointing to the spot after the last-fetched result. When the user clicks the link, the query is run again, but this time with the cursor value. This causes the next set of results fetched to start where the previous page left off.

The `fetch_page()` method works just like the `fetch()` method, but it doesn't just return the list of results. Instead, it returns a tuple of three elements: the results, a cursor value that represents the end of the fetched results for the query, and a `bool` that is `True` if there are more results beyond the cursor. To fetch the next page of results, you call the `fetch_page()` method on an identical query, passing it the previous cursor value as the `start_cursor` argument.

The cursor value can be manipulated as a base64-encoded string that is safe to use as a URL query parameter. The cursor returned by `fetch_page()` is an instance of the `Cursor` class, from the `google.appengine.datastore.datastore_query` package. In this example, this value is converted to a URL-safe string via the `urlsafe()` method, then given to the web page template for use in a link. When the user clicks the link, the request handler sees the encoded value as a query parameter, then makes a new `Cursor`, passing the URL-safe value as the `urlsafe` argument to the constructor. The reconstructed `Cursor` is given to `fetch_page()`.

Note that, like the string form of datastore keys, the base64-encoded value of a cursor can be decoded to reveal the names of kinds and properties, so you may wish to further encrypt or hide the value if these are sensitive.

The `fetch_page()` method returns the new cursor with the results. You can also use the `start_cursor` argument with `fetch()`, `iter()`, `get()`, `count()`, though these methods do not return new cursors. You can also provide an `end_cursor` argument to any of these methods, after which point the methods will stop returning results. This highlights the "bookmark" nature of cursors: they represent locations in the result set.

> This example shows how to use cursors to set up a Next link in a paginated display. Setting up a Previous link is left as an exercise for the reader. Hint: the cursor used to display the current page, if any, is the one the next page needs for the link.

A cursor is only valid for the query used to generate the cursor value. All query parameters, including kinds, filters, sort orders, and whether or not the query is keys-only, must be identical to the query used to generate the cursor.

A cursor remains valid over time, even if results are added or removed above or below the cursor in the index. A structural change to the indexes used to satisfy the query invalidates cursors for that query. This includes adding or removing fields of a custom index, or switching between built-in indexes and custom indexes for a query. These only occur as a result of you updating your index configuration. Rare internal changes to datastore indexes may also invalidate cursors. Using a cursor that is invalid for a given query (for whatever reason) will raise an exception.

Because a cursor stays valid even after the data changes, you can use cursors to watch for changes in some circumstances. For example, consider a query for entities with creation timestamps, ordered by timestamp. A process traverses the results to the end, and then stores the cursor for the end of the list (with no results after it). When new entities are created with later timestamps, those entities are added to the index after the cursor. Running the query with the cursor pick ups the new results.

Conceptually, a cursor is a position in a list of results. Actually, a cursor is a position in the index (or path through multiple indexes) that represents the results for the query. This has a couple of implications.

You can't use a cursor on a query that uses not-equal (!=) or set membership (IN) queries. These queries are performed by multiple primitive queries behind the scenes, and therefore do not have all results in a single index (or index path).

A query with a cursor may result in a duplicate result if the query operates on a property with multiple values. Recall that an entity with multiple values for a property appears once for each value in the corresponding indexes. When a query gathers results, it ignores repeated results (which are consecutive in the index). Because a cursor represents a point in an index, it is possible for the same entity to appear both before and after the cursor. In this case, the query up to the cursor and the query after the cursor will both contain the entity in their results. It's a rare edge case—the entity would have to change after the cursor is created—but it's one to be aware of if you're using multivalued properties with queries and cursors.

Projection Queries

We've described the datastore as an object store. You create an entity with all of its properties. When you fetch an entity by key, the entire entity and all its properties come back. When you want to update a property of an entity, you must fetch the complete entity, make the change to the object locally, then save the entire object back to the datastore.

The types of queries we've seen so far reflect this reality as well. You can either fetch entire entities that match query criteria:

```
SELECT * FROM Kind WHERE ...
```

Or you can fetch just the keys:

```
SELECT __key__ FROM Kind WHERE ...
```

And really, an entity query is just a key query that fetches the entities for those keys. The query criteria drive a scan of an index (or indexes) containing property values and keys, and the keys are returned by the scan.

But sometimes you only need to know one or two properties of an entity, and it's wasteful to retrieve an entire entity just to get at those properties. For times like these, Cloud Datastore has another trick up its sleeve: *projection queries*. Projection queries let you request specific properties of entities, instead of full entities, under certain conditions:

```
SELECT prop1, prop2 FROM Kind WHERE ...
```

The entity objects that come back have only the requested properties (known as the "projected properties") and their keys set. Only the requested data is returned by the datastore service to the app.

The idea of projection queries is based on how indexes are used to resolve queries. While a normal query uses indexes of keys and property values to look up keys then fetch the corresponding entities, projection queries take the requested values directly from the indexes themselves.

Naturally, this trick requires that all of the projected properties be present in the index used to fulfill the query. For a projection query requesting only one property, the datastore can use the built-in index. For more than one, you must have a custom index with all of the projected properties in it. As with other complex queries, the development server adds index configuration for each combination of projected properties, kind, and other query criteria.

Projection queries tend to be faster than full queries, for several reasons. Result entities are not fetched in a separate step, as with normal queries. Instead, the result data comes directly from the index. Less data also means less communication with the datastore service. The entire procedure is to find the first row of the custom index and scan to the last row, returning the columns for the projected properties.

Several restrictions fall out of this trick, and they're fairly intuitive. Only indexed properties can be in a projection. Another way of saying this is, only entities with all the projected properties set to an indexable value can be a result for a projection query. A projection query needs a custom index even if the equivalent full-entity query does not.

There's another weird behavior we need to note here, and yes, once again it involves multivalued properties. As we saw earlier, if an entity contains multiple values for a property, an index containing that property contains a row for each value (and a row for each combination of values if you're indexing more than one multivalued property), repeating each of the single-valued properties in the index. Unlike an entity or key query, a projection query makes no attempt to de-duplicate the result list in this case. Instead, a projection on a multivalued property returns a separate result for each row in the index. Each result contains just the values of the properties on that row. Such a query returns one result for each combination of matching property values.

Each projection of more than one property requires its own custom index. If you have two queries with the same kind and filter structures but different projected properties, the queries require two custom indexes:

```
SELECT prop1, prop2 FROM Kind ...
SELECT prop1, prop3 FROM Kind ...
```

In this case, you can save space and time-to-update by using the same projection in both cases, and ignoring the unused properties:

```
SELECT prop1, prop2, prop3 FROM Kind ...
```

In ndb, you request a projection query by listing the properties for the projection when you fetch the results, as the projection argument:

```
q = MyModel.query()
results = q.fetch(10, projection=('prop1', 'prop2'))
```

You can also use the GQL syntax for projection queries with the ndb.gql() function:

```
q = ndb.gql('SELECT prop1, prop2 FROM MyModel')
results = q.fetch(10)
```

The results of a projection query are instances of the model class with only the projected properties set. The model class is aware that the result is from a projection query, and alters its behavior slightly to accommodate. Specifically, it will allow a property modeled as required=True to be unset if it isn't one of the projected properties. (We'll cover property modeling in Chapter 9.) Also, it won't allow the partial instance to be put() back to the datastore, even if you set all of its properties to make it complete.

As a sanity check, the query API will not let you project a property and use it in an equality filter in the same query. It also won't allow you to project the same property more than once.

As shown, a projection query will return one result for each row in the index it is scanning, which includes one or more rows for each entity that has all of the projected properties. For properties with common values, the results can be a bit repetitive:

```
class Player(ndb.Model):
    # ...
    charclass = ndb.StringProperty()
    level = ndb.IntegerProperty()

# ...
        q = Player.query(projection=('charclass', 'level'))
        for result in q:
            classlevel = (result.charclass, result.level)
            # ...
```

This might get results like this:

```
('mage', 1)
('mage', 1)
('mage', 1)
('mage', 2)
('mage', 2)
('mage', 3)
('warrior', 1)
('warrior', 1)
('warrior', 1)
```

Projection queries have a special feature for when you only want to know which distinct combinations of projected properties exist in the data, eliminating the duplicates. To request this, provide the distinct=True argument:

```
q = Player.query(projection=('charclass', 'level'),
                 distinct=True)
```

In this example, this would reduce the result set to one entry for each distinct combination of the charclass and level values:

```
('mage', 1)
('mage', 2)
('mage', 3)
('warrior', 1)
```

Distinct projection queries use only a minor modification to the index scanning algorithm. The rows are scanned in order as before, but a result is only emitted if it differs from the previous row. Only the projected properties are considered: two results are considered equivalent if all of the projected properties are equal between them, even if the nonprojected properties on the corresponding entities are not.

You can do a distinct projection query from GQL using the DISTINCT keyword, like so:

```
q = ndb.gql('SELECT DISTINCT charclass, level FROM Player')
```

Configuring Indexes

An application specifies the custom indexes it needs in a configuration file. Each index definition includes the kind, and the names and sort orders of the properties to include. A configuration file can contain zero or more index definitions.

Most of the time, you can leave the maintenance of this file to the development web server. The development server watches the queries the application makes, and if a query needs a custom index and that index is not defined in the configuration file, the server adds appropriate configuration automatically.

The development server will not remove index configuration. If you are sure your app no longer needs an index, you can edit the file manually and remove it. Note that removing index configuration does not automatically delete the index from App Engine. After you upload the new configuration and when you are sure no versions of the app are using the index, you must issue the `appcfg vacuum_indexes` command. (We'll cover this in more depth in Chapter 10.)

You can disable the automatic index configuration feature. Doing so causes the development server to behave like App Engine: if a query doesn't have an index and needs one, the query fails. How to do this is particular to the runtime environment, so we'll get to that in a moment.

Index configuration is global to all versions of your application. All versions of an app share the same datastore, including indexes. If you deploy a version of the app and the index configuration has changed, Cloud Datastore will use the new index configuration for all versions.

The index configuration file is named *index.yaml*, and is in the YAML format (similar to *app.yaml*). It appears in the application root directory.

The structure is a single YAML list named `indexes`, with one element per index. Each index definition has a `kind` element (the kind name, a string) and a `properties` element. If the index supports queries with ancestor filters, it has an `ancestor` element with a value of `yes`.

`properties` is a list, one element per column in the index, where each column has a `name` and an optional `direction` that is either `asc` (ascending order, the default) or `desc` (descending order). The order of the properties list is significant: the index is sorted by the first column first, then by the second column, and so on.

Here's an example of an *index.yaml* file, using indexes from earlier in this chapter:

```
indexes:
- kind: Player
  properties:
  - name: charclass
  - name: level
    direction: desc

- kind: Player
  properties:
  - name: level
    direction: desc
  - name: score
    direction: desc
```

By default, the development server adds index configuration to this file as needed. When it does, it does so beneath this line, adding it (and a descriptive comment) if it doesn't find it:

```
# AUTOGENERATED
```

You can move index configuration above this line to take manual control over it. This isn't strictly necessary, as the development server will never delete index configuration, not even that which was added automatically.

To disable automatic index configuration in the development server, start the server with the `--require_indexes` command-line option.

## CHAPTER 8

Datastore Transactions

With web applications, many users access and update data concurrently. Often, multiple users need to read or write to the same unit of data at the same time. This requires a data system that can give some assurances that simultaneous operations will not corrupt any user's view of the data. Most data systems guarantee that a single operation on a single unit of data maintains the integrity of that unit, typically by scheduling operations that act on the unit to be performed in a sequence, one at a time.

Many applications need similar data integrity guarantees when performing a set of multiple operations, possibly over multiple units of data. Such a set of operations is called a *transaction*. A data system that supports transactions guarantees that if a transaction succeeds, all the operations in the transaction are executed completely. If any step of the transaction fails, then none of its effects are applied to the data. The data remains in a consistent and predictable state before and after the transaction, even if other processes are attempting to modify the data concurrently.

For example, say you want to post a message to the bulletin board in the town square inviting other players to join your guild. The bulletin board maintains a count of how many messages have been posted to the board, so readers can see how many messages there are without reading every message object in the system. Posting a message requires three datastore operations:

1. Read the old message count
2. Update the message count with an incremented value
3. Create the new message object

Without transactions, these operations may succeed or fail independently. The count may be updated but the message object may not be created. Or, if you create the message object first, the object may be created, but the count not updated. In either case, the resulting count is inaccurate. By performing these operations in a single transaction, if any step fails, none of the effects are applied, and the application can try the entire transaction again.

Also consider what happens when two players attempt to post to the message board at the same time. To increment the message count, each player process must read the old value, and then update it with a new value calculated from the old one. Without transactions, these operations may be interleaved:

1. Process A reads the original count (say, 10).

2. Process B reads the count (also 10).

3. Process A adds 1 and updates the count with the new value (11).

4. Process B adds 1 to its value and updates the count (11).

Because Process B doesn't know that Process A updated the value, the final count is 1 less than it ought to be (12). With transactions, Process B knows right away that another process is updating the data and can do the right thing.

A scalable web application has several requirements that are at odds with transactions. For one, the application needs access to data to be fast, and to not be affected by how much data is in the system or how it is distributed across multiple servers. The longer it takes for a transaction to complete, the longer other processes have to wait to access the data reserved by the transaction. The combined effect on how many transactions can be completed in a period of time is called *throughput*. For web apps, high throughput is important.

A web app usually needs transactions to finish completely and consistently, so it knows that the effects of the transaction can be relied upon by other processes for further calculations. The transaction is complete when it is committed, replicated to multiple machines, and ready to be served to any process that asks for it. The promise that all processes can see the changes once a transaction is complete is known as *strong consistency*.

An alternative policy known as *eventual consistency* trades this promise for greater flexibility in how changes are applied. With strong consistency, if a process wants to read a value, but a change for that value has been committed to the datastore and not yet ready, the process waits until the save is complete, then reads the value. But if the process doesn't need the latest value, it can read the older value without waiting. Consistency is eventual because the impatient processes are not guaranteed to see the latest value, but will see it after the value is ready.

Cloud Datastore provides transactions with strong consistency and low overhead. It does this by limiting the scope of transactions: a single transaction can only read or write to entities that belong to a single *entity group*. Every entity belongs to an entity group, by default a group of its own. The app assigns an entity to a group when the entity is created, and the assignment is permanent.

By having the app arrange entities into groups, Cloud Datastore can treat each group independently when applying concurrent transactions. Two transactions that use different groups can occur simultaneously without harm. With a bit of thought, an app can ensure that entities are arranged to minimize the likelihood that two processes will need to access the same group, and thereby maximize throughput.

Entity groups also come into play with queries and indexes. If a query only needs results from a single entity group, the query can return strongly consistent results, as the group's local index data is updated transactionally with the group's entities. The query requests this behavior by identifying the group as part of the query, using a part of the key path, or *ancestor*. (We're finally going to explain what key paths are: they form entity groups by arranging keys in a hierarchy.)

Whereas ancestor queries are strongly consistent, queries across all entity groups are eventually consistent: global kind-based indexes are not guaranteed to be up-to-date by the time changes to entities are ready. This makes ancestor queries—and good entity group design in general—a powerful weapon in your datastore arsenal.

An app can request more flexible behaviors, with their corresponding trade-offs. *Cross-group transactions* (sometimes called "XG transactions") can act on up to five entity groups, in exchange for added latency and a greater risk of contention with other processes. An app can specify a *read policy* when reading data, which can request a faster eventually consistent read instead of a strongly consistent read that may have to wait on pending updates.

In this chapter, we discuss what happens when you update an entity group, how to create entities in entity groups, how to perform ancestor queries, and how to perform multiple operations on an entity group, using a transaction. We also discuss batch operations, how query indexes are built, and the consistency guarantees of Cloud Datastore.

Entities and Entity Groups

When you create, update, or delete a single entity, the change occurs in a transaction: either all your changes to the entity succeed, or none of them do. If you change two properties of an entity and save it, every request handler process that fetches the entity will see both changes. At no point during the save will a process see the new value for one property and the old value for the other. And if the update fails, the entity stays as it was before the save. In database terms, the act of updating an entity is *atomic*.

It is often useful to update multiple entities atomically, such that any process's view of the data is consistent across the entities. In the bulletin board example, the message count and each of the messages may be stored as separate entities, but the combined act of creating a new message entity and updating the count ought to be atomic. We need a way to combine multiple actions into a single transaction, so they all succeed or all fail.

To do this in a scalable way, Cloud Datastore must know in advance which entities may be involved in a single transaction. These entities are stored and updated together, so the datastore can keep them consistent and still access them quickly. You tell Cloud Datastore which entities may be involved in the same transaction by using entity groups.

Every entity belongs to an entity group, possibly a group containing just itself. An entity can only belong to one group. You assign an entity to a group when the entity is created. Group membership is permanent; an entity cannot be moved to another group once it has been created.

The datastore uses entity groups to determine what happens when two processes attempt to update data in the entity group at the same time. When this happens, the first update that completes "wins," and the other update is canceled. App Engine notifies the process whose update is canceled by raising an exception. In most cases, the process can just try the update again and succeed. But the app must decide for itself how to go about retrying, as important data may have changed between attempts.

This style of managing concurrent access is known as *optimistic concurrency control*. It's "optimistic" in the sense that the database tries to perform the operations without checking whether another process is working with the same data (such as with a "locking" mechanism), and only checks for collisions at the end, optimistic that the operations will succeed. The update is not guaranteed to succeed, and the app must reattempt the operations or take some other course of action if the data changes during the update.

Multiple processes vying for the opportunity to write to an entity group at the same time is known as *contention*. Two processes are contending for the write; the first to commit wins. A high rate of contention slows down your app, because it means many processes are getting their writes canceled and have to retry, possibly multiple times. In egregious cases, contention for a group may exclude a process to the point of the failure of that process. You can avoid high rates of contention with careful design of your entity groups.

Optimistic concurrency control is a good choice for web applications because reading data is fast—a typical reader never waits for updates—and almost always succeeds. If an update fails due to contention, it's usually easy to try again, or return an error message to the user. Most web applications have only a small number of users updating the same piece of data, so contention failures are rare.

 Updating an entity in a group can potentially cancel updates to *any* other entity in the group by another process. You should design your data model so that entity groups do not need to be updated by many users simultaneously.

Be especially careful if the number of simultaneous updates to a single group grows as your application gets more users. In this case, you usually want to spread the load across multiple entity groups, and increase the number of entity groups automatically as the user base grows. Scalable division of a data resource like this is known as *sharding*.

Also be aware that some data modeling tasks may not be practical on a large scale. Incrementing a value in a single datastore entity every time any user visits the site's home page is not likely to work well with a distributed strong consistency data system.

Keys, Paths, and Ancestors

To create an entity in a group with other entities, you associate it with the key of another entity from that group. One way to do this is to make the existing entity's key the *parent* of the new entity. The key of the parent becomes part of the key of the child. These parent–child relationships form a path of ancestors down to a *root* entity that does not have a parent. Every entity whose key begins with the same root is in the same group, including the root entity itself.

When you create an entity and do not specify a parent, the entity is created in a new group by itself. The new entity is the root of the new group.

We alluded to paths earlier when we discussed keys, so let's complete the picture. An entity's key consists of the path of ancestors in the entity's group, starting from the group's root. Each entity in the path is represented by the entity's kind followed by either the system-assigned numeric ID or the app-assigned string ID. The full path is a sequence of kind and ID pairs.

The following keys represent entities in the same group, because they all have the same root ancestor:

```
MessageBoard, "The_Archonville_Times"

MessageBoard, "The_Archonville_Times" / Message, "first!"

MessageBoard, "The_Archonville_Times" / Message, "pk_fest_aug_21"

MessageBoard, "The_Archonville_Times" / Message, "first!" / Message, "keep_clean"
```

With Python and ndb, there are two ways to make keys with ancestors. The first is to provide the `parent` argument to the `ndb.Key` constructor, whose value is another `ndb.Key`:

```
board_key = ndb.Key(MessageBoard, 'The_Archonville_Times')
board = board_key.get()

msg1_key = ndb.Key(Message, 'first!', parent=board_key)
msg1 = Message(key=msg1_key)
msg1.put()
```

Alternatively, the `ndb.Key` constructor can take positional arguments representing the kinds and IDs along the path:

```
msg2_key = ndb.Key(MessageBoard, 'The_Archonville_Times',
                   Message, 'pk_fest_aug_21')
msg2 = Message(key=msg2_key)
msg2.put()
```

The final kind in the ancestor path is the kind of the entity. In ndb, this must match the model class name. You can use the class object directly (as we've done here) or the string name of the class (`'Message'`).

As a shortcut, the model class constructor can accept a `parent` key and an `id` instead of a complete key:

```
msg3 = Message(parent=msg1.key(), id='keep_clean')
msg3.put()
```

GQL supports key literals with ancestors, as follows:

```
SELECT * FROM MessageAttachment
        WHERE message = KEY(MessageBoard, 'The_Archonville_Times',
                            Message, 'first!',
                            Message, 'keep_clean')
```

Notice that entities of different kinds can be in the same entity group. In the datastore, there is no relationship between kinds and entity groups. (You can enforce such a relationship in your app's code, if you like.)

Ancestors do not have to exist for a key to be valid. If you create an entity with a parent and then delete the parent, the key for the child is still valid and can still be assembled from its parts (such as with strings in the `ndb.Key` constructor). This is true even for a group's root entity: the root can be deleted and other entities in the group remain in the group.

You can even use a made-up key for an entity that doesn't exist as the parent for a new entity. Neither the kind nor the ID of an ancestor needs to represent an actual entity. Group membership is defined by the first key part in the ancestor path, regardless of whether that part corresponds to an entity. Here is Python code that creates two entities in the same group without a root entity:

```
root = ndb.Key('MessageBoard', 'The_Baskinville_Post')

msg1 = Message(parent=root)
msg1.put()

msg2 = Message(parent=root)
msg2.put()
```

After being saved with put(), the datastore assigns numeric IDs to these Message entities, and their complete keys resemble the following:

```
MessageBoard, "The_Baskinville_Post" / Message, 1

MessageBoard, "The_Baskinville_Post" / Message, 2
```

Ancestor Queries

The root ancestor in a key path determines group membership. Intermediate ancestors have no affect on group membership, which poses the question, what good are ancestor paths? One possible answer to that question: ancestor queries.

A datastore query can include a filter that limits the results to just those entities with a given ancestor. This can match any ancestor, not just the immediate parent. In other words, a query can match a sequence of key parts starting from the root.

Continuing the town square bulletin board example, where each MessageBoard is the root of an entity group containing things attached to the board, the following GQL query returns the 10 most recent Message entities attached to a specific board:

```
SELECT * FROM Message
        WHERE ANCESTOR IS KEY(MessageBoard,
                              'The_Archonville_Times')
        ORDER BY post_date DESC
        LIMIT 10
```

Most queries that use an ancestor filter need custom indexes. There is one unusual exception: a query does not need a custom index if the query also contains equality filters on properties (and no inequality filters or sort orders). In this exceptional case, the "merge join" algorithm can use a built-in index of keys along with the built-in property indexes. In cases where the query would need a custom index anyway, the query can match the ancestor to the keys in the custom index.

With ndb, you can set the ancestor for a query by passing an ndb.Key value as the ancestor parameter to the ndb.Query() constructor or the query() model class method:

```
q = Message.query(
    ancestor=ndb.Key(MessageBoard, 'The_Archonville_Times'))
```

```
q = q.order('-post_date')
# ...
```

As we mentioned in Chapter 7, the datastore supports queries over entities of all kinds. Kindless queries are limited to key filters and ancestor filters. Because ancestors can have children of disparate kinds, kindless queries are useful for getting every child of a given ancestor, regardless of kind:

```
SELECT * WHERE ANCESTOR IS KEY('MessageBoard', 'The_Archonville_Times')
```

A kindless ancestor query in Python:

```
q = ndb.Query(
    ancestor=ndb.Key('MessageBoard', 'The_Archonville_Times'))
```

 Although ancestor queries can be useful, don't get carried away building large ancestor trees. Remember that every entity with the same root belongs to the same entity group, and more simultaneous users that need to write to a group mean a greater likelihood of concurrency failures.

If you want to model hierarchical relationships between entities without the consequences of entity groups, consider using multivalued properties to store paths. For example, if there's an entity whose path in your hierarchy can be represented as /A/B/C/D, you can store this path as e.parents = ['/A', '/A/B', '/A/B/C']. Then you can perform a query similar to an ancestor query on this property: ... WHERE parents = '/A/B'.

What Can Happen in a Transaction

Entity groups ensure that the operations performed within a transaction see a consistent view of the entities in a group. For this to work, a single transaction must limit its operations to entities in a single group. The entity group determines the scope of the transaction.

Within a transaction, you can fetch, update, or delete an entity by using the entity's key. You can create a new entity that either is a root entity of a new group that becomes the subject of the transaction, or that has a member of the transaction's entity group as its parent. You can also create other entities in the same group.

You can perform queries over the entities of a single entity group in a transaction. A query in a transaction must have an ancestor filter that matches the transaction's entity group. The results of the query, including both the indexes that provide the results as well as the entities themselves, are guaranteed to be consistent with the rest of the transaction.

You do not need to declare the entity group for a transaction explicitly. You simply perform datastore actions on entities of the same group. If you attempt to perform actions that involve different entity groups within a transaction, the API raises an exception. The API also raises an exception if you attempt to perform a query in a transaction that does not have an ancestor filter.

Transactions have a maximum size. A single transaction can write up to 10 megabytes of data.

Transactional Reads

Sometimes it is useful to fetch entities in a transaction even if the transaction does not update any data. Reading multiple entities in a transaction ensures that the entities are consistent with one another. As with updates, entities fetched in a transaction must be members of the same entity group.

A transaction that only reads entities never fails due to contention. As with reading a single entity, a read-only transaction sees the data as it appears at the beginning of the transaction, even if other processes make changes after the transaction starts and before it completes.

The same is true for ancestor-only queries within a transaction. If the transaction does not create, update, or delete data from the entity group, it will not fail due to contention.

The datastore can do this because it remembers previous versions of entities, using timestamps associated with the entity groups. The datastore notes the current time at the beginning of every operation and transaction, and this determines which version of the data the operation or transaction sees. This is known as *multiversion concurrency control*, a form of optimistic concurrency control. This mechanism is internal to the datastore; the application cannot access previous versions of data, nor can it see the timestamps.

This timestamp mechanism has a minor implication for reading data within transactions. When you read an entity in a transaction, the datastore returns the version of the entity most recent to the beginning of the transaction. If you update an entity and then refetch the same entity within the same transaction, the datastore returns the entity as it appeared *before* the update. In most cases, you can just reuse the in-memory object you modified (which has your changes) instead of refetching the entity.

Eventually Consistent Reads

As described in the previous section, transactional reads are strongly consistent. When the app fetches an entity by key, the datastore ensures that all changes committed prior to the beginning of the current transaction are complete—and are therefore returned by the read—before continuing. Occasionally, this can involve a slight delay as the datastore catches up with a backlog of committed changes. In a transaction, a strongly consistent read can only read entities within the transaction's entity group.

Similarly, when the app performs an ancestor query in a transaction, the query uses the group's local indexes in a strongly consistent fashion. The results of the index scans are guaranteed to be consistent with the contents of the entities returned by the query.

You can opt out of this protection by specifying a *read policy* that requests eventual consistency. With an eventually consistent read of an entity, your app gets the current known state of the entity being read, regardless of whether there are still committed changes to be applied. With an eventually consistent ancestor query, the indexes used for the query are consistent with the time the indexes are read.

In other words, an eventual consistency read policy causes gets and queries to behave as if they are not a part of the current transaction. This may be faster in some cases, as the operations do not have to wait for committed changes to be written before returning a result.

Perhaps more importantly: an eventually consistent get operation can get an entity outside of the current transaction's entity group.

Transactions in Python

The Python API uses function objects to handle transactions. To perform multiple operations in a transaction, you define a function that executes the operations by using the @db.transactional() decorator. When you call your function outside of a transaction, the function starts a new transaction, and all datastore operations that occur within the function are expected to comply with the transaction's requirements:

```python
import datetime
from google.appengine.api import datastore_errors
from google.appengine.ext import ndb

class MessageBoard(ndb.Expando):
    pass

class Message(ndb.Expando):
    pass

@ndb.transactional()
def create_message_txn(board_name, message_name, message_title, message_text):
    board = ndb.Key('MessageBoard', board_name).get()
    if not board:
        board = MessageBoard(id=board_name)
        board.count = 0
```

```
        message = Message(id=message_name, parent=board.key)
        message.title = message_title
        message.text = message_text
        message.post_date = datetime.datetime.now()

        board.count += 1

        ndb.put_multi([board, message])

    # ...
        try:
            create_message_txn(
                board_name=board_name,
                message_name=message_title,
                message_title=message_title,
                message_text=message_text)

        except datastore_errors.TransactionFailedError, e:
            # Report an error to the user.
            # ...
```

All calls to the datastore to create, update, or delete entities within the transaction function take effect when the transaction is committed. Typically, you would update an entity by fetching or creating the model object, modifying it, then saving it, and continue to use the local object to represent the entity. In the rare case where the transaction function fetches an entity after saving it, the fetch will see the entity as it was *before* the update, because the update has not yet been committed.

If the transaction function raises an exception, the transaction is aborted, and the exception is reraised to the caller. If you need to abort the transaction but do not want the exception raised to the caller (just the function exited), raise the ndb.Rollback exception in the transaction function. This causes the function to abort the transaction, then return None.

If the transaction cannot be completed due to a concurrency failure, the function call is retried automatically. By default, it is retried three times. If all three of these retries fail, the function raises a datastore_errors.TransactionFailedError (from the google.appengine.api.datastore_errors module). You can configure the number of retries by providing the retries argument to the @ndb.transactional decorator:

```
@ndb.transactional(retries=10)
def create_message_txn(board_name, message_name, message_title, message_text):
    # ...
```

 Make sure your transaction function can be called multiple times safely without undesirable side effects. If this is not possible, you can set retries=0, but know that the transaction will fail on the first incident of contention.

The default behavior of @ndb.transactional functions is to start a new transaction if one isn't already started, and join the started transaction otherwise. This behavior is controlled by the propagation argument to the decorator, whose value is one of the following:

ndb.TransactionOptions.ALLOWED
> This is the default.

ndb.TransactionOptions.MANDATORY
> The function expects to be called during an already-started transaction, and throws datastore_errors.BadRequestError if called outside a transaction.

ndb.TransactionOptions.INDEPENDENT
> The function always starts a new transaction, pausing an already-started transaction, if any.

If a function should not be run in a transaction, you can isolate it by using the @ndb.non_transactional decorator. By default, calling a nontransactional function within a transaction pauses the transaction and does not start a new one, so datastore operations in the function do not participate in the transaction. If you specify allow_existing=False to the decorator, calling the nontransactional function during a transaction raises datastore_errors.BadRequestError.

Finally, if you have a function that should be called within a transaction by some callers and without a transaction by others, you can use the ndb.transaction() wrapper function. It takes the function to call as its first argument, and optional subsequent arguments like those you would pass to the @ndb.transactional decorator. It calls the function with no arguments, so if you want to call a function that accepts arguments, use a Python lambda expression:

```
def process_message_text(message_text):
    # ... datastore calls ...
    # result = ...

    return result

@ndb.transactional
def create_message_txn(board_name, message_name, message_title, message_text):
    # ...
    new_message_text = ndb.transaction(
        lambda: process_message_text(message_text))
```

As an added convenience, you can test whether the code is currently being executed within a transaction by calling ndb.in_transaction().

Within a transaction, reading entities and fetching results from an ancestor query uses a read policy of strong consistency. There's no reason (or ability) to use another read policy in this case: a transactional read either sees the latest committed state (as with strong consistency) or the transaction fails because the entity group has been updated since the transaction was started.

How Entities Are Updated

To fully understand how the datastore guarantees that your data stays consistent, it's worth discussing how transactions are performed behind the scenes. To do so, we must mention BigTable, Google's distributed data system that is the basis of the App Engine datastore. We won't go into the details of how entities, entity groups, and indexes are stored in BigTable, but we will refer to BigTable's own notion of atomic transactions in our explanation.

Figure 8-1 shows the phases of a successful transaction.

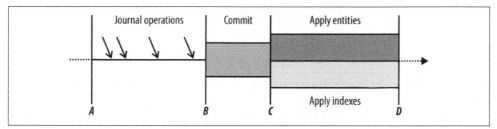

Figure 8-1. The timeline of a transaction: the operations, the commit phase, and the apply phase

The datastore uses a "journal" to keep track of changes that need to be applied to entities in an entity group. Each journal entry has a unique timestamp that indicates the order in which the changes were made. The datastore remembers the timestamp of the most recent change that has been committed, and guarantees that attempts to read the data will see all changes up to that point.

When an app begins a transaction for an entity group, the datastore makes a note of the current last-committed timestamp for the group (point A in Figure 8-1). As the app calls the datastore to update entities, the datastore writes the requested changes to the journal. Each change is marked as "uncommitted."

When the app finishes the transaction (point B), the datastore checks the group's last-committed timestamp again. If the timestamp hasn't changed since the transaction began, it marks all the transaction's changes as "committed" and then advances the group's timestamp. Otherwise, the timestamp was advanced by another request handler since the beginning of the transaction, so the datastore aborts the current transaction and reports a concurrency failure to the app.

Verifying the timestamp, committing the journal entries, and updating the timestamp all occur in an atomic BigTable operation. If another process attempts to commit a transaction to the same entity group while the first transaction's commit is in progress, the other process waits for the first commit to complete. This guarantees that if the first commit succeeds, the second process sees the updated timestamp and reports a concurrency failure. This is illustrated in Figure 8-2.

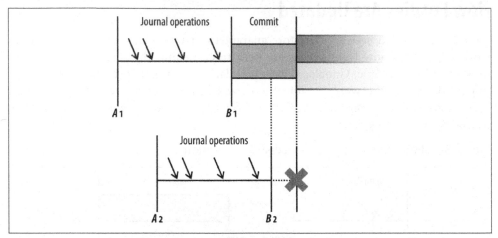

Figure 8-2. A timeline of two concurrent transactions; the first to commit "wins"

Once the journal entries have been committed (point C in Figure 8-1), the datastore applies each committed change to the appropriate entity and appropriate indexes, then marks the change as "applied." If there are multiple unapplied changes for an entity in the journal, they are applied in the order they were performed.

Here's the sneaky bit. If the apply phase fails for whatever reason (hard drive failure, power outage, meteorite), the committed transaction is still considered successful. If there are committed but unapplied changes the next time someone performs an operation on an entity in the entity group (within or without an explicit transaction), the datastore reruns the apply phase before performing the operation. This ensures that operations and transactions always see all changes that have been committed prior to the start of the operation or transaction. The datastore also uses background processes to roll forward unapplied operations, as well as purge old journal entries.

The roll-forward mechanism also ensures that subsequent operations can see all committed changes even if the apply phase is still in progress. At the beginning of an operation or transaction, the datastore notes the current time, then waits for all changes committed prior to that time to be applied before continuing.

Notice that the apply phase does not need to occur inside a BigTable transaction. Because of this, the datastore can spread multiple entities in the same group across multiple machines, and can allow an entity group to get arbitrarily large. Only the group's last-committed timestamp and journal need to be stored close enough together for a BigTable transaction. The datastore makes an effort to store entities of the same group "near" each other for performance reasons, but this does not limit the size or speed of entity groups.

When an app updates an entity outside of a transaction, the datastore performs the update with the same transactional mechanism, as if it were a transaction of just one operation. The datastore assumes that an update performed outside of a transaction is safe to perform at any time, and will retry the update automatically in the event of a concurrency failure. If several attempts fail, the datastore throws the concurrency exception. In contrast, an explicit transaction throws a concurrency exception on the first failure, because the datastore does not know if it is safe to commit the same changes. The app must retry the explicit transaction on its own. (The @ndb.transactional decorator knows how to rerun the function that performs the transaction, but this occurs as part of the application code.)

Cloud Datastore replicates all data to at least three places in each of at least two different data centers. The replication process uses a consensus algorithm based on "Paxos" to ensure that all sites agree that the change will be committed before proceeding. This level of replication ensures that your app's datastore remains available for both reads and writes during all planned outages—and most unplanned outages.

When an app calls the datastore to update data, the call does not return until the apply phase is complete. If an error occurs at any point in the process, the datastore call raises an exception in the application.

This is true even if the error occurs during the apply phase, after the commit phase is complete and the update is guaranteed to be applied before the next transaction. Because the application can't tell the difference between an error during the commit phase and an error during the apply phase, the application should react as if the update has not taken place.

In most cases, the app can simply retry the update. More care is needed if retrying the update relies on the previous attempt being unsuccessful, but these cases usually require testing the state of the data in a transaction, and the solution is simply to retry the entire transaction. If the transaction creates a new entity, one way to avoid creating a duplicate entity is to use a key name instead of a system-supplied numeric ID, precalculating and testing for the nonexistence of a global unique ID (GUID) if necessary.

Failures during the apply phase are very rare, and most errors represent a failure to commit. One of the most important principles in scalable app design is to be tolerant of the most rare kinds of faults.

How Entities Are Read

The timestamp mechanism explains what happens when two processes attempt to write to the same entity group at the same time. When one process commits, it updates the timestamp for the group. When the other process tries to commit, it notices the timestamp has changed, and aborts. The app can retry the transaction with fresh data, or give up.

The transaction is aborted only if the app attempted to update an entity during the transaction and another process has since committed changes. If the app only reads data in the transaction and does not make changes, the app simply sees the entities as they were at the beginning of the transaction. To support this, the datastore retains several old versions of each entity, marked with the timestamp of the most recently applied journal entry. Reading an entity in a transaction returns the version of the entity most recent to the timestamp at the beginning of the transaction.

Reading an entity outside of a transaction or with an eventual consistency read policy does not roll forward committed-but-unapplied changes. Instead, the read returns the entity as it appears as of the most recently applied changes. This is faster than waiting for pending changes to be applied, and usually not a concern for reads outside of transactions. But this means the entity may appear older or newer than other entities. If you need any consistency guarantees when reading multiple entities, use transactions and the strong consistency read policy.

Batch Updates

When you read, create, update, or delete an entity, the runtime environment makes a service call to the datastore. Each service call has some overhead, including serializing and deserializing parameters and transmitting them between machines in the data center. If you need to update multiple entities, you can save time by performing the updates together as a batch in one service call. (We introduced batch calls in Chapter 6.)

Here's a quick example of the Python batch API:

```python
# Creating multiple entities:
e1 = Message(id='m1', text='...')
e2 = Message(id='m2', text='...')
e3 = Message(id='m3', text='...')
message_keys = ndb.put_multi([e1, e2, e3])

# Getting multiple entities using keys:
message_keys = [ndb.Key('Message', 'm1'),
                ndb.Key('Message', 'm2'),
                ndb.Key('Message', 'm3')]
messages = ndb.get_multi(message_keys)
for message in messages:
```

```
    # ...

    # Deleting multiple entities:
    ndb.delete_multi(message_keys)
```

When the datastore receives a batch call, it bundles the keys or entities by their entity groups, which it can determine from the keys. Then it dispatches calls to the datastore machines responsible for each entity group. The datastore returns results to the app when it has received all results from all machines.

If the call includes changes for multiple entities in a single entity group, those changes are performed in a single transaction. There is no way to control this behavior, but there's no reason to do it any other way. It's faster to commit multiple changes to a group at once than to commit them individually, and no less likely to result in concurrency failures.

Outside of a transaction, a batch call can operate on multiple entity groups. In this case, each entity group involved in a batch update may fail to commit due to a concurrency failure. If a concurrency failure occurs for any update, the API raises the concurrency failure exception—even if updates to other groups were committed successfully.

Batch updates in disparate entity groups are performed in separate threads, possibly by separate datastore machines, executed in parallel to one another. This can make batch updates especially fast compared to performing each update one at a time.

Remember that if you use the batch API during a transaction, every entity or key in the batch must use the same entity group as the rest of the transaction.

How Indexes Are Updated

As we saw in Chapter 7, datastore queries are powered by indexes. The datastore updates these indexes as entities change, so results for queries can be determined without examining the entity properties directly. This includes an index of keys, an index for each kind and property, and custom indexes described by your app's configuration files that fulfill complex queries. When an entity is created, updated, or deleted, each relevant index is updated and sorted so subsequent queries match the new state of the data.

The datastore updates indexes after changes have been committed, during the apply phase. Changes are applied to indexes and entities in parallel. Updates of indexes are themselves performed in parallel, so the number of indexes to update doesn't necessarily affect how fast the update occurs.

As with entities, the datastore retains multiple versions of index data, labeled with timestamps. When you perform a query, the datastore notes the current time, then uses the index data that is most current up to that time. However, unless the query has an ancestor filter, the datastore has no way to know which entity groups are involved in the result set and so cannot wait for changes in progress to be applied.

This means that, for a brief period during an update, a query that doesn't have an ancestor filter (a nonancestor query, or global query) may return results that do not match the query criteria. While another process is updating an entity, the query may see the old version of its index but return the new version of the entity. And because changes to entities and changes to indexes are applied in parallel, it is possible for a query to see the new version of its index but return the old version of the entity.

Figure 8-3 illustrates one possibility of what nontransactional reads and queries may see while changes are being applied.

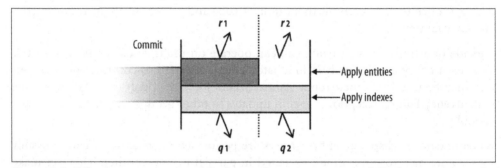

Figure 8-3. What nontransactional fetches and queries may see while changes are applied

Although fetches *r1* and *r2* both occur after the commit, because they do not occur within transactions, they see different data: *r1* fetches the entity as it is before the update, and *r2* fetches the entity as it is after the update has been applied. Queries *q1* and *q2* may use the same (preupdate) index data to produce a list of results, but they return different entity data depending on whether changes have been applied to the entities.

In rare cases, it's also possible for changes to indexes to be applied prior to changes to entities, and for the apply phase to fail and leave committed changes unapplied until the next transaction on the entity group. If you need stronger guarantees, fetch or query entities within transactions to ensure all committed changes are applied before the data is used.

A query with an ancestor filter knows its entity group, and can therefore offer the same strong consistency guarantees within transactions as fetches. But many useful queries span entity groups, and therefore cannot be performed in transactions. If it is important to your application that a result for a nontransactional query match the criteria exactly, verify the result in the application code before using it.

Cross-Group Transactions

Transactions and entity groups present a fundamental tension in designing data for the App Engine datastore. If all we cared about was data consistency, we'd put all our data in a single entity group, and every transaction would have a consistent and current view of the entire world—and would be battling with every other simultaneous transaction to commit a change. Conversely, if we wanted to avoid contention as much as possible, we'd keep every entity in its own group and never perform more than one operation in a transaction.

Entity groups are a middle ground. They allow us to define limited sets of data that demand strongly consistent transactional updates, and with some thought we can organize these boundaries so an increase in traffic does not result in an increase in simultaneous updates to a single group. For example, if a user only ever updates an entity group dedicated to that user, then an increase in users will never increase the number of users writing to a given group simultaneously.

But real-world data patterns are not always so clean. Most useful applications involve sharing data between users. At another extreme, it's possible all users can view and modify the same set of data. At that point, we need to make some sacrifices to operate at scale, using techniques like sharding and eventually consistent data structures updated by background tasks to spread the updates over time and space.

There are many common scenarios where it'd be convenient if we could just operate on a few entity groups in a transaction, when one group is too constraining but we don't need to update the world. Sometimes we need to operate on several disparate sets of data at once, but it'd make our data model too complex to try and manage them in groups. For these cases, App Engine has a feature: *cross-group transactions*.

A cross-group transaction (or an "XG transaction") is simply a transaction that's allowed to operate on up to five entity groups transactionally. The datastore uses a slightly different—and slightly slower—mechanism for this, so to use more than one group transactionally, you must declare that your transaction is of the cross-group variety. The cross-group mechanism is built on top of the existing single-group mechanism in BigTable. It manages the updates so all groups commit or fail completely.

The important idea here is that you do not need to say ahead of time which groups will be involved in a transaction. Any given cross-group transaction can pick any entity groups on which to operate, up to five.

As with a single group transaction, a cross-group transaction can read from, write to, and perform ancestor queries on any of the groups in the transaction. If any group in a given cross-group transaction is updated after the transaction is started but before it tries to commit, the entire transaction fails and must be retried. Whether failure due to contention is more likely with more groups depends entirely on the design of your app.

You declare a transaction as a cross-group transaction by setting the xg=True argument in the @ndb.transactional decorator for the transaction function. If a transactional function is XG, or calls a transactional function that is XG, the entire transaction becomes an XG transaction:

```
@ndb.transactional(xg=True):
def update_win_tallies(winning_player, losing_player):
    # ...
```

## CHAPTER 9

Data Modeling with ndb

Data modeling is the process of translating the data requirements of your application to the features of your data storage technology. While the application deals in players, towns, weapons, potions, and gold, the datastore knows only entities, entity groups, keys, properties, and indexes. The data model describes how the data is stored and how it is manipulated. Entities represent players and game objects, while properties describe the status of objects and the relationships between them. When an object changes location, the data is updated in a transaction, so the object cannot be in two places at once. When a player wants to know about the weapons in her inventory, the application performs a query for all weapon objects whose location is the player.

In the last few chapters, we've been using the Python class `ndb.Expando` to create and manipulate entities and their properties. As we've been doing it, this class illustrates the flexible nature of the datastore. The datastore itself does not impose or enforce a structure on entities or their properties, giving the application control over how individual entities represent data objects. This flexibility is also an essential feature for scalability: changing the structure of millions of records is a large task, and the proper strategy for doing this is specific to the task and the application.

But structure is needed. Every player has a number of health points, and a `Player` entity without a `health` property, or with a `health` property whose value is not an integer, is likely to confuse the battle system. The data ought to conform to a structure, or *schema*, to meet the expectations of the code. Because the datastore does not enforce this schema itself—the datastore is *schemaless*—it is up to the application to ensure that entities are created and updated properly.

App Engine includes a data modeling library for defining and enforcing data schemas in Python called ndb.[1] This library resides in the `google.appengine.ext.ndb` package. It includes several related classes for representing data objects, including `ndb.Model`, `ndb.Expando`, and `ndb.PolyModel`. To give structure to entities of a given kind, you create a subclass of one of these classes. The definition of the class specifies the properties for those objects, their allowed value types, and other requirements.

In this chapter, we'll introduce the `ndb` data modeling library and discuss how to use it to enforce a schema for the otherwise schemaless datastore. We'll also discuss how the library works and how to extend it. Finally, we'll look at the `ndb` library's powerful performance-related features for managing data caches.

Models and Properties

The `ndb.Model` superclass lets you specify a structure for every entity of a kind. This structure can include the names of the properties, the types of the values allowed for those properties, whether the property is required or optional, and a default value. Here is a definition of a Book class similar to the one we created in Chapter 6:

```python
from google.appengine.ext import ndb
import datetime

class Book(ndb.Model):
    title = ndb.StringProperty(required=True)
    author = ndb.StringProperty(required=True)
    copyright_year = ndb.IntegerProperty()
    author_birthdate = ndb.DateProperty()

obj = Book(title='The Grapes of Wrath',
           author='John Steinbeck')
obj.copyright_year = 1939
obj.author_birthdate = datetime.date(1902, 2, 27)

obj.put()
```

This Book class inherits from `ndb.Model`. In the class definition, we declare that all Book entities have four properties, and we declare their value types: `title` and `author` are strings, `copyright_year` is an integer, and `author_birthdate` is a date-time. If someone tries to assign a value of the wrong type to one of these properties, the assignment raises a `datastore_errors.BadValueError` (from the `google.appengine.api.datastore_errors` module).

---

[1] The ndb library is a successor to an older library called `ext.db`, which is still distributed with the App Engine SDK. While it carries on many of the ideas of `ext.db`, the ndb library is not backwards compatible. You can read a version of this chapter that covers `ext.db` for free on the website for this book (*http://www.dansanderson.com/appengine*).

We also declare that `title` and `author` are required properties. If someone tries to create a `Book` without these properties set as arguments to the `Book` constructor, the attempt will raise a `datastore_errors.BadValueError`. Both `copyright_year` and `author_birthdate` are optional, so we can leave them unset on construction, and assign values to the properties later. If these properties are not set by the time the object is saved, the resulting entity will have a value of `None` for these properties—and that's allowed by this model.

A property declaration ensures that the entity created from the object has a value for the property, possibly `None`. As we'll see in the next section, you can further specify what values are considered valid using arguments to the property declaration.

A model class that inherits from `ndb.Model` ignores all attributes that are not declared as properties when it comes time to save the object to the datastore. In the resulting entity, all declared properties are set, and no others.

This is the sole difference between `ndb.Model` and `ndb.Expando`. An `ndb.Model` class ignores undeclared properties. An `ndb.Expando` class saves all attributes of the object as properties of the corresponding entity. That is, a model using an `ndb.Expando` class "expands" to accommodate assignments to undeclared properties.

You can use property declarations with `ndb.Expando` just as with `ndb.Model`. The result is a data object that validates the values of the declared properties, and accepts any values for additional undeclared properties.

Properties with declarations are sometimes called *static properties*, while properties on an `ndb.Expando` without declarations are *dynamic properties*. These terms have a nice correspondence with the notions of static and dynamic typing in programming languages. Property declarations implement a sort of runtime validated static typing for model classes, on top of Python's own dynamic typing.

As we'll see, property declarations are even more powerful than static typing, because they can validate more than just the type of the value.

For both `ndb.Model` and `ndb.Expando`, object attributes whose names begin with an underscore (_) are always ignored. You can use these private attributes to attach transient data or functions to model objects.[2]

Beyond the model definition, `ndb.Model` and `ndb.Expando` have the same interface for saving, fetching, and deleting entities, and for performing queries and transactions. `ndb.Expando` is a subclass of `ndb.Model`.

---

2 It is possible to create an entity with a property whose name starts with an underscore. This convention only applies to object attributes in the modeling API.

Property Declarations

You declare a property for a model by assigning a property declaration object to an attribute of the model class. The name of the attribute is the name of the datastore property. The value is an object that describes the terms of the declaration. The ndb.StringProperty object assigned to the title class attribute says that an instance of the class, and therefore the entity it represents, can only have a string value for its title property. The required=True argument to the ndb.StringProperty constructor says that the object is not valid unless it has a value for the title property.

This can look a little confusing if you're expecting the class attribute to shine through as an attribute of an instance of the class, as it normally does in Python. Instead, the ndb.Model class hooks into the attribute assignment mechanism so it can use the property declaration to validate a value assigned to an attribute of the object. In Python terms, the model uses *property descriptors* to enhance the behavior of attribute assignment.

Property declarations act as intermediaries between the application and the datastore. They can ensure that only values that meet certain criteria are assigned to properties. They can assign default values when constructing an object. They can even convert values between a data type used by the application and one of the datastore's native value types, or otherwise customize how values are stored.

Property Value Types

ndb.StringProperty is an example of a property declaration class. There are several property declaration classes included with the Python SDK, one for each native datastore type. Each one ensures that the property can only be assigned a value of the corresponding type:

```
class Book(ndb.Model):
    title = ndb.StringProperty()

b = Book()

b.title = 99  # datastore_errors.BadValueError, title must be a string

b.title = 'The Grapes of Wrath'  # OK
```

Table 9-1 lists the datastore native value types and their corresponding property declaration classes.

Table 9-1. Datastore property value types and the corresponding property declaration classes

Data type	Python type	Property class
Unicode text string (up to 500 characters, indexed)	`unicode` or `str` (converted to `unicode` as ASCII)	`ndb.StringProperty`
Long Unicode text string (not indexed)	`unicode` or `str` (converted to `unicode` as ASCII)	`ndb.TextProperty`
Byte string (up to 500 bytes if indexed)	`str`	`ndb.BlobProperty`
Boolean	`bool`	`ndb.BooleanProperty`
Integer (64-bit)	`long` or `int` (converted to 64-bit `long`)	`ndb.IntegerProperty`
Float (double precision)	`float`	`ndb.FloatProperty`
Date-time	`datetime.datetime`	`ndb.DateTimeProperty`
	`datetime.date`	`ndb.DateProperty`
	`datetime.time`	`ndb.TimeProperty`
Entity key	`ndb.Key`	`ndb.KeyProperty`
A Google account	`users.User`	`ndb.UserProperty`

The `ndb` library includes several additional property declaration classes that perform special functions. We'll look at these later in this chapter.

There is one special property declaration class worth mentioning now: `ndb.GenericProperty`. This declaration accepts any type of value that can be stored directly to the datastore. (Refer back to Table 6-1.) This is useful for declaring properties whose values can be any of multiple types. (This class also comes in handy when forming query expressions based on undeclared properties and `ndb.Expando`, as we saw in Chapter 7.)

Property Validation

You can customize the behavior of a property declaration by passing arguments to the declaration's constructor. We've already seen one example: the `required` argument.

All property declaration classes support the `required` argument. If `True`, the property is required and must not be `None`. You must provide a value for each required property when creating a new object. If you attempt to store an entity without setting a required property, it raises `datastore_errors.BadValueError`:

```
class Book(ndb.Model):
    title = ndb.StringProperty(required=True)

b = Book()
b.put()  # datastore_errors.BadValueError, title is required

b = Book(title='The Grapes of Wrath')
b.put()  # OK

b = Book()
b.title = 'The Grapes of Wrath'
b.put()  # OK
```

The datastore makes a distinction between a property that is not set and a property that is set to the null value (`None`). Property declarations do not make this distinction, because all declared properties must be set (possibly to `None`). Unless you say otherwise, the default value for declared properties is `None`, so the `required` validator treats the `None` value as an unspecified property value.

You can change the default value with the `default` argument. When you create an object without a value for a property that has a default value, the constructor assigns the default value to the property.

A property that is required and has a default value uses the default if constructed without an explicit value. The value can never be `None`. For example:

```
class Book(ndb.Model):
    rating = ndb.IntegerProperty(default=1)

b = Book()  # b.rating == 1

b = Book(rating=5)  # b.rating == 5
```

You can declare that a property should contain only one of a fixed set of values by providing a list of possible values as the `choices` argument. If `None` is not one of the choices, this acts as a more restrictive form of `required`: the property must be set to one of the valid choices using a keyword argument to the constructor. For example:

```
_KEYS = ['C', 'C min', 'C 7',
         'C#', 'C# min', 'C# 7',
         # ...
        ]

class Song(ndb.Model):
    song_key = ndb.StringProperty(choices=_KEYS)
```

```
s = Song()

s.song_key = 'H min'  # datastore_errors.BadValueError

s.song_key = 'C# min'  # OK
```

All of these features validate the value assigned to a property, and raise a `data store_errors.BadValueError` if the value does not meet the appropriate conditions. For even greater control over value validation, you can define your own validation function and assign it to a property declaration as the validator argument. The function must take the property declaration object and the value as arguments, and either raise an exception if the value should not be allowed, or return the value to use:

```
def is_recent_year(prop, val):
    if val < 1923:
        raise datastore_errors.BadValueError
    return val

class Book(ndb.Model):
    copyright_year = ndb.IntegerProperty(validator=is_recent_year)

b = Book(copyright_year=1922)  # datastore_errors.BadValueError

b = Book(copyright_year=1924)  # OK
```

A validator function can return a different value than what was assigned to the property to act as a filter. However, the value must survive repeated calls to the validator. This is because values get revalidated each time the object is marshaled to the datastore. For example, a validator that returns `val.lower()` is fine, because passing the result through the validator again does not produce a new value. A validator that returns `'"' + val + '"'` would add quote marks around the string every time the object is saved, which isn't the desired effect.

Nonindexed Properties

In Chapter 7, we mentioned that you can set properties of an entity in such a way that they are available on the entity, but are considered unset for the purposes of indexes. In `ndb`, you establish a property as nonindexed using a property declaration. If the property declaration is given an `indexed` argument of `False`, entities created with that model class will set that property as nonindexed:

```
class Book(ndb.Model):
    first_sentence = ndb.StringProperty(indexed=False)

b = Book()
b.first_sentence = "On the Internet, popularity is swift and fleeting."
b.put()
```

```
# Count the number of Book entities with
# an indexed first_sentence property...
c = Book.all().order('first_sentence').count(1000)

# c = 0
```

Some property declarations are nonindexed by default, namely `TextProperty` and `BlobProperty`. In the case of `BlobProperty`, you can set `indexed=True`, as long as the value is no more than 500 bytes in length. (For a short indexed `TextProperty`, just use `StringProperty`.)

When using undeclared properties with an `ndb.Expando` model, all properties are considered indexed by default, unless the assigned value is a `unicode` longer than 500 characters or a `str` longer than 500 bytes (which cannot be indexed). As with `ndb.Model`, you can use property declarations in the class definition to override this default for specific properties. To change this default for all properties assigned to an `ndb.Expando` instance, set the `_default_indexed = False` class property:

```
class NonindexedEntity(ndb.Expando):
    _default_indexed = False

entity = NonindexedEntity()
entity.foo = 'bar'  # The foo property is stored as a nonindexed value.
entity.put()
```

Automatic Values

Several property declaration classes include features for setting values automatically.

The `ndb.DateProperty`, `ndb.DateTimeProperty`, and `ndb.TimeProperty` classes can populate the value automatically with the current date and time. To enable this behavior, you provide the `auto_now` or `auto_now_add` arguments to the property declaration.

If you set `auto_now=True`, the declaration class overwrites the property value with the current date and time when you save the object. This is useful when you want to keep track of the last time an object was saved:

```
class Book(ndb.Model):
    last_updated = ndb.DateTimeProperty(auto_now=True)

b = Book()
b.put()  # last_updated is set to the current time

# ...

b.put()  # last_updated is set to the current time again
```

If you set `auto_now_add=True`, the property is set to the current time only when the object is saved for the first time. Subsequent saves do not overwrite the value:

```
class Book(ndb.Model):
    create_time = ndb.DateTimeProperty(auto_now_add=True)

b = Book()
b.put()  # create_time is set to the current time

# ...

b.put()  # create_time stays the same
```

The ndb.UserProperty declaration class also includes an automatic value feature. If you provide the argument auto_current_user=True, the value is set to the user accessing the current request handler if the user is signed in. If you provide auto_current_user_add=True, the value is only set to the current user when the entity is saved for the first time, and left untouched thereafter. If the current user is not signed in, the value is set to None:

```
class BookReview(ndb.Model):
    created_by_user = ndb.UserProperty(auto_current_user_add=True)
    last_edited_by_user = ndb.UserProperty(auto_current_user=True)

br = BookReview()
br.put()  # created_by_user and last_edited_by_user set

# ...

br.put()  # last_edited_by_user set again
```

At first glance, it might seem reasonable to set a default for an ndb.UserProperty this way:

```
from google.appengine.api import users

class BookReview(ndb.Model):
    created_by_user = ndb.UserProperty(
        default=users.get_current_user())
    # WRONG
```

This would set the default value to be the user who is signed in *when the class is imported.* Subsequent requests handled by the instance of the application will use a previous user instead of the current user as the default.

To guard against this mistake, ndb.UserProperty does not accept the default argument. You can use only auto_current_user or auto_current_user_add to set an automatic value.

Repeated Properties

The ndb library includes support for multivalued properties, which it just calls "repeated" properties. You declare a multivalued property by specifying a property declaration with the `repeated=True` argument. Its value is a Python list, possibly empty, containing values of the corresponding type:

```
class Book(ndb.Model):
    tags = ndb.StringProperty(repeated=True)

b = Book()
b.tags = ['python', 'app engine', 'data']
```

The datastore does not distinguish between a multivalued property with no elements and no property at all. As such, an undeclared property on an `ndb.Expando` object can't store the empty list. If it did, when the entity is loaded back into an object, the property simply wouldn't be there, potentially confusing code that's expecting to find an empty list. To avoid confusion, `ndb.Expando` disallows assigning an empty list to an undeclared property.

When you declare a repeated property, the declaration takes care of translating between the absence of a property and the empty list representation in your code. A repeated property declaration makes it possible to keep an empty list value on a multivalued property. The declaration interprets the state of an entity that doesn't have the declared property as the property being set to the empty list, and maintains that distinction on the object. This also means that you cannot assign `None` to a declared list property—but this isn't of the expected type for the property anyway. (`None` can be one of the values in the list if it is allowed by the type of the declaration.)

The datastore *does* distinguish between a property with a single value and a multivalued property with a single value. An undeclared property on an `ndb.Expando` object can store a list with one element, and represent it as a list value the next time the entity is loaded.

A repeated property declaration cannot have a `default` value or `required=True`. If the declaration specifies a `validator` function, this function will be called once for each value in the list. This means the validator cannot act on the length of the list, only the individual values in the list.

 To declare a repeated property whose values can be of disparate types, use `ndb.GenericProperty(repeated=True)`.

Serialized Properties

The simple property types we've seen so far let you store basic values and index them for the purpose of queries. When you have a more sophisticated data value, such as a dictionary, and you don't need to index it, one way to store it on a property is to serialize it, then store the serialized blob as an `ndb.BlobProperty`. This has the disadvantage that your application code must manually serialize and deserialize the value when it is used and updated.

`ndb` has two property declaration classes that help with this common case: `ndb.JsonProperty` and `ndb.PickleProperty`. The `ndb.JsonProperty` class takes a Python data object that can be represented as a JSON data record, and converts it to and from the JSON format automatically. Similarly, `ndb.PickleProperty` does the same thing, but uses Python's `pickle` library to perform the serialization and deserialization. In both cases, the value is stored in the datastore as an unindexed blob value. To your application code, the value appears in its original form:

```python
class Player(ndb.Model):
    # ...
    theme = ndb.JsonProperty()

p = Player()
p.theme = {
    'background-color': '#000033',
    'color': 'white',
    'spirit_animal': 'phoenix'
}
p.put()

if p.theme['spirit_animal'] == 'cougar':
    # ...
    pass

p.theme['color'] = 'yellow'
p.put()
```

Both property declaration classes accept an optional `compressed` argument. If `True`, the value will be compressed as well as serialized when stored, and decompressed and deserialized when loaded. (`ndb.BlobProperty` also accepts the `compressed` argument.)

Remember that `ndb.JsonProperty` takes a data object, not a JSON string, as its value. If you need the JSON string form of the value, or you need to parse a JSON string into a data object, use the `json` module in the Python standard library.

Use `ndb.JsonProperty` when the object can be represented as JSON and you might need to access the serialized value from non-Python code. `ndb.PickleProperty` can accept a wider range of values, but uses a serialization format that is exclusive to Python.

Structured Properties

Using serialized property classes for storing data structures is easy enough, but the values cannot participate in queries (at least not meaningfully). When you need to store structured data across multiple properties that can participate in queries, ndb has yet another powerful feature: structured properties.

A structured property has a value that is an instance of an ndb.Model class. This value can have attributes, and these attributes are modeled using the same property declarations that you use to model an entity. When ndb stores the value, it converts the value into multiple properties, one for each inner property of the value. For example:

```
class NotificationPrefs(ndb.Model):
    news = ndb.BooleanProperty(default=False)
    messages = ndb.BooleanProperty(default=False)
    raids = ndb.BooleanProperty(default=False)
    last_updated = ndb.DateTimeProperty(auto_now=True, indexed=False)

class Player(ndb.Model):
    notifications = ndb.StructuredProperty(NotificationPrefs)

p = Player()
p.notifications = NotificationPrefs()
p.notifications.news = True
p.put()
```

In the preceding example, the Player model uses a structured property based on the NotificationPrefs class. To set this property, we construct a NotificationPrefs instance, and can access and set values on the instance as with any other instance variable (such as p.notification.news).

When the Player object is stored, ndb creates one entity of kind Player with four properties: notifications.news, notifications.messages, notifications.raids (all Boolean values), and notifications.last_updated (a datetime value). Because the Boolean values are described as indexable by the NotificationPrefs model, they are indexed by the datastore. notifications.last_updated has indexed=False and so is not indexed.

The indexed properties of the inner model can participate in queries, like so:

```
q = Player.query().filter(Player.notifications.news == True)

for player in q:
    # Send news notification...
```

Structured properties can be repeated (repeated=True). ndb simply repeats the inner properties as needed when storing the entity to the datastore. It stores enough information so that it can reassemble the inner structured values correctly when reading the entity. This poses a modest restriction: when a structured property's model has its own structured property, only one of the properties can be repeated.

If you like using model classes for declaring typed structures but do not need to index the inner properties, ndb also provides an `ndb.LocalStructuredProperty` property declaration class. Instead of storing inner properties as separate indexable properties of the entity, it serializes the structure and stores it as a blob value, much like `ndb.JsonProperty` or `ndb.PickleProperty`.

Computed Properties

It is often useful to have more than one view of an entity's property data, such as a normalized version of a value, or a summary of data on the entity. Within your application code, you might implement this calculation as a method or a property accessor on the model class:

```
class Player(ndb.Model):
    level = ndb.IntegerProperty()
    score = ndb.IntegerProperty()

    @property
    def score_per_level(self):
        if self.level == 0:
            return 0
        return float(self.score) / float(self.level)

p = Player(level=4, score=280)

# p.score_per_level == 70.0
```

Implemented this way, this calculated value is only available to your application code. It is not stored in the datastore, and therefore cannot be used in datastore queries.

With ndb, you can declare a *computed property* that calls a method to calculate the value of the property whenever the entity is stored. The `ndb.ComputedProperty` property declaration class takes a function as its argument. This function is passed the model instance as its only argument, and returns a value of one of the base datastore value types:

```
class Player(ndb.Model):
    level = ndb.IntegerProperty()
    score = ndb.IntegerProperty()
    score_per_level = ndb.ComputedProperty(lambda self: self._score_per_level())

    def _score_per_level(self):
        if self.level == 0:
            return 0
        return float(self.score) / float(self.level)

p = Player(level=4, score=280)
```

```
# Store the Player entity with level=4, score=280, score_per_level=70.
p.put()
```

The computed property value is calculated fresh every time it is accessed, as well as when the entity is stored.

Models and Schema Migration

Property declarations prevent the application from creating an invalid data object, or assigning an invalid value to a property. If the application always uses the same model classes to create and manipulate entities, then all entities in the datastore will be consistent with the rules you establish using property declarations.

In real life, it is possible for an entity that does not fit a model to exist in the datastore. When you change a model class—and you will change model classes in the lifetime of your application—you are making a change to your application code, not the datastore. Entities created from a previous version of a model stay the way they are.

If an existing entity does not comply with the validity requirements of a model class, you'll get a `datastore_errors.BadValueError` when you try to fetch the entity from the datastore. Fetching an entity gets the entity's data, then calls the model class constructor with its values. This executes each property's validation routines on the data.

Some model changes are "backward compatible" such that old entities can be loaded into the new model class and be considered valid. Whether it is sufficient to make a backward-compatible change without updating existing entities depends on your application. Changing the type of a property declaration or adding a required property are almost always incompatible changes. Adding an optional property will not cause a `datastore_errors.BadValueError` when an old entity is loaded, but if you have indexes on the new property, old entities will not appear in those indexes (and therefore won't be results for those queries) until the entities are loaded and then saved with the new property's default value.

The most straightforward way to migrate old entities to new schemas is to write a script that queries all of the entities and applies the changes. We'll discuss how to implement this kind of batch operation in a scalable way using task queues, in "Task Chaining" on page 352.

Modeling Relationships

You can model relationships between entities by storing entity keys as property values. In ndb, you use `ndb.KeyProperty` to declare that a property contains a datastore key value. You can optionally provide the `kind` argument to validate that all keys assigned to the property have the same kind. As with other property types, you can use the `repeated=True` argument to store multiple keys:[3]

```
class Author(ndb.Model):
    surname = ndb.StringProperty(required=True)
    # ...

class Book(ndb.Model):
    author_keys = ndb.KeyProperty(kind=Author, repeated=True)

a1 = Author(surname='Aniston')
a2 = Author(surname='Boggs')
a3 = Author(surname='Chavez')
ndb.put_multi([a1, a2, a3])

b = Book()
b.author_keys = [a1.key, a2.key, a3.key]
b.put()
```

The `kind` argument to the `ndb.KeyProperty` constructor takes either a model class or the kind name as a string. (This is generally true in several places in ndb that take a model class. Using a class instead of a string gives some added protection against typing errors.) You can use a string if you want an entity to store keys for its own kind.

A datastore key is just a value. Storing one does not require that an entity exists with that key. Because an entity's key does not change, a key reference to an existing entity will remain valid until the entity is deleted.

Key property values are queryable and orderable like any other value. In the data created in the preceding example, you can find every `Book` written by an `Author` with a query on entities of the kind `Book` and a filter on the `author_keys` property.

Storing a list of keys is one way to model a many-to-many relationship, like the relationship between books and authors. Another method is to store a separate entity to represent the relationship itself, with the keys of both parties. This method can be a bit more cumbersome, especially if relationships need to be updated in transactions. But it avoids having to extend existing entities when introducing new relationships. It also makes it easier to form queries about the relationships themselves.

Model Inheritance

In data modeling, it's often useful to derive new kinds of objects from other kinds. The game world may contain many different kinds of carryable objects, with shared

---

3 If you've used the older `ext.db` library, you may be familiar with its "reference properties" feature. This feature was dropped for ndb to make key handling easier to understand. Some use cases for reference properties are better met by ndb's structured properties feature.

properties and features common to all objects you can carry. Because you implement classes from the data model as Python classes, you'd expect to be able to use inheritance in the implementation to represent inheritance in the model. And you can, sort of.

If you define a class based on either ndb.Model or ndb.Expando, you can create other classes that inherit from that data class, like so:

```
class Carryable(ndb.Model):
    weight = ndb.IntegerProperty()
    location = ndb.KeyProperty(kind=Location)

class Bottle(Carryable):
    contents = ndb.StringProperty()
    amount = ndb.IntegerProperty()
    is_closed = ndb.BooleanProperty()
```

The subclass inherits the property declarations of the parent class. A `Bottle` has five property declarations: `weight`, `location`, `contents`, `amount`, and `is_closed`.

Objects based on the child class will be stored as entities whose kind is the name of the child class. The datastore has no notion of inheritance, and so by default will not treat `Bottle` entities as if they are `Carryable` entities. This is mostly significant for queries, and we have a solution for that in the next section.

If a child class declares a property already declared by a parent class, the child class declaration overrides the parent class. Take care when doing this that your code is using the correct value type for the child class.

A model class can inherit from multiple classes, using Python's own support for multiple inheritance:

```
class Pourable(ndb.Model):
    contents = ndb.StringProperty()
    amount = ndb.IntegerProperty()

class Bottle(Carryable, Pourable):
    is_closed = ndb.BooleanProperty()
```

The rules for inheriting property declarations correspond with the rules for class member variables in Python. When a property declaration is accessed, parent classes are searched in the order they are specified, left to right. For example, if `Pourable` had a `weight` property declared as an `ndb.FloatProperty` and `Carryable` declared `weight` as an `ndb.IntegerProperty`, `Bottle` would use the `weight` declaration from the leftmost class mentioned in its list of parents:

```
class Carryable(ndb.Model):
    location = ndb.KeyProperty(kind=Location)
    weight = ndb.IntegerProperty()
```

```
class Pourable(ndb.Model):
    contents = ndb.StringProperty()
    amount = ndb.IntegerProperty()
    weight = ndb.FloatProperty()

class Bottle(Pourable, Carryable):
    # Pourable.weight (float) wins over Carryable.weight (int)
    # ...

b = Bottle()
b.weight = 3.4    # OK

class Bottle(Carryable, Pourable):
    # Carryable.weight (int) wins over Pourable.weight (float)
    # ...

b = Bottle()
b.weight = 3.4    # datastore_errors.BadValueError: Expected integer
```

Parents that themselves share a common ancestor class form a "diamond inheritance" pattern. This is supported, and resolved in the usual way:

```
class GameObject(ndb.Model):
    name = ndb.StringProperty()
    location = ndb.KeyProperty(kind='Location')

class Carryable(GameObject):
    weight = ndb.IntegerProperty()

class Pourable(GameObject):
    contents = ndb.StringProperty()
    amount = ndb.IntegerProperty()

class Bottle(Carryable, Pourable):
    is_closed = ndb.BooleanProperty()
```

Queries and PolyModels

The datastore knows nothing of our modeling classes and inheritance. Instances of the Bottle class are stored as entities of the kind 'Bottle', with no inherent knowledge of the parent classes. It'd be nice to be able to perform a query for Carryable entities and get back Bottle entities and others. That is, it'd be nice if a query could treat Bottle entities as if they were instances of the parent classes, as Python does in our application code. We want polymorphism in our queries.

For this, the data modeling API provides a special base class: ndb.PolyModel. Model classes using this base class support polymorphic queries. Consider the Bottle class defined previously. Let's change the base class of GameObject to ndb.PolyModel, like so:

```
from google.appengine.ext.ndb import polymodel

class GameObject(polymodel.PolyModel):
    # ...
```

We can now perform queries for any kind in the hierarchy, and get the expected results:

```
location_key = ndb.Key('Location', 'babbling brook')

b = Bottle(location=location_key, weight=125)
b.put()

# ...

q = Carryable.query()
q = q.filter(GameObject.location == location_key)
q = q.filter(Carryable.weight > 100)

for obj in q:
    # obj is a carryable object that is at the babbling brook
    # and weighs more than 100 kilos.
    # ...
```

This query can return any Carryable, including Bottle entities. The query can use filters on any property of the specified class (such as weight from Carryable) or parent classes (such as location from GameObject).

Behind the scenes, polymodel.PolyModel does three clever things differently from its cousins:

- Objects of the class GameObject or any of its child classes are all stored as entities of the kind 'GameObject'.

- All such objects are given a property named class_ that represents the inheritance hierarchy starting from the root class. This is a multivalued property, where each value is the name of an ancestor class, in order.

- Queries for objects of any kind in the hierarchy are translated by the polymodel.PolyModel class into queries for the base class, with additional equality filters that compare the class being queried to the class property's values.

In short, polymodel.PolyModel stores information about the inheritance hierarchy on the entities, then uses it for queries to support polymorphism.

Each model class that inherits directly from `polymodel.PolyModel` is the root of a class hierarchy. All objects from the hierarchy are stored as entities whose kind is the name of the root class. As such, your data will be easier to maintain if you use many root classes to form many class hierarchies, as opposed to putting all classes in a single hierarchy. That way, the datastore viewer and bulk loading tools can still use the datastore's built-in notion of entity kinds to distinguish between kinds of objects.

Creating Your Own Property Classes

The property declaration classes serve several functions in your data model:

Value validation
> The model calls the class when a value is assigned to the property, and the class can raise an exception if the value does not meet its conditions.

Type conversion
> The model calls the class to convert from the value type used by the app (the *user value*) to one of the core datastore types for storage (the *base value*), and back again.

Automatic values
> The model calls the class to store the final value on the entity, giving it an opportunity to calculate the final value to be stored.

Every property declaration class inherits from the `ndb.Property` base class. This class implements features common to all property declarations, including support for the common constructor arguments (such as `required` and `indexed`). Declaration classes override methods and members to specialize the validation and type conversion routines.

When making your own property declaration classes, it's easiest to inherit from one of the built-in classes, such as `ndb.StringProperty`, instead of inheriting from `ndb.Property` directly. Choose the class whose type is most like the base value you wish to store in the datastore.

Validating Property Values

Here is a simple property declaration class. It accepts any `unicode` value, and stores it as a datastore short string (the default behavior for Python `unicode` values). Because it stores a short string, it inherits from `ndb.StringProperty`:

```
class PlayerNameProperty(ndb.StringProperty):
    def _validate(self, value):
        if not isinstance(value, unicode):
            raise datastore_errors.BadValueError(
```

```
                'Expected unicode, got {}'.format(value))
        return value
```

And here is how you would use the new property declaration:

```
class Player(ndb.Model):
    player_name = PlayerNameProperty()

p = Player()
p.player_name = u'Ned Nederlander'

p.player_name = 12345  # BadValueError: int is not unicode
p.player_name = 'Ned'  # BadValueError: str is not unicode
```

The `PlayerNameProperty` class overrides the default `_validate()` method, which takes the value to validate as its argument and either returns the value or raises an exception. Just like a custom `validator` function set by the declaration, the default validator can return a different value to act as a filter. The property class has other opportunities to perform value conversions, so this is best left to just perform validation.

Importantly, `_validate()` does *not* call the parent class's base method (`super`), and it must not call it even if the parent class is another property class with its own validator. The property API is "stackable." The `ndb.Property` base class invokes the validators for all classes in the inheritance chain automatically, starting with the closest class and working its way up to the base class. Each validator receives the result of the previous validator. This makes it easy to define new properties in terms of existing properties without worrying about the details of how the base property is implemented.

The `_validate()` method is not called if the property value is `None`. Any property that is not declared as `required` accepts a `None` value, and this value is not validated. As we'll see later, the property class can substitute a different value for `None` in a different method.

So far, this example doesn't do much beyond `ndb.StringProperty` other than require a `unicode` as the user value. This by itself can be useful to give the property type a class for future expansion. Let's add a requirement that player names be between 6 and 30 characters in length:

```
class PlayerNameProperty(ndb.StringProperty):
    def _validate(self, value):
        if not isinstance(value, unicode):
            raise datastore_errors.BadValueError(
                'Expected unicode, got {}'.format(value))
        if len(value) < 6 or len(value) > 30:
            raise datastore_errors.BadValueError(
                'Value must be between 6 and 30 characters.')
        return value
```

The new validation logic disallows strings with an inappropriate length:

```
p = Player()
p.player_name = 'Ned'    # BadValueError: length < 6
p.player_name = 'Ned Nederlander'    # OK

p = Player(player_name = 'Ned')  # BadValueError: length < 6
```

Marshaling Value Types

The datastore supports a fixed set of core value types for properties, listed in Table 6-1. A property declaration can support the use of other types of values in the attributes of model instances by marshaling between the desired type and one of the core datastore types. The value provided by and to the application code is called the *user value*, and the value sent to and received from the datastore is called the *base value*.

The _to_base_type() method takes a user value and returns a base value. The _from_base_type() method takes a base value and returns a user value. You can override these to customize their default behavior, which is to return the value unmodified.

Like the _validate() method, the property API stacks these methods. They must not call their parent methods themselves. When ndb needs to convert a user value to a base value, it calls the closest class's _to_base_type() with the user value, then passes the result of that to the parent method, and so on up to the base class. When it needs to convert a base value to a user value, it goes in the opposite direction: first it calls the base class's _from_base_type() method, then it passes the result to the next child class in line, and so on down to the bottommost child class.

Say we wanted to represent player name values within the application using a Player Name value class instead of a simple string. Each player name has a surname and an optional first name. We can store this value as a single property, using the property declaration to convert between the user value (PlayerName) and an appropriate base value (such as unicode):

```
class PlayerName(object):
    def __init__(self, first_name, surname):
        self.first_name = first_name
        self.surname = surname

    def is_valid(self):
        return (isinstance(self.first_name, unicode)
                and isinstance(self.surname, unicode)
                and len(self.surname) >= 6)

class PlayerNameProperty(ndb.StringProperty):
    def _validate(self, value):
```

```
            if not isinstance(value, PlayerName):
                raise datastore_errors.BadValueError(
                    'Expected PlayerName, got {}'.format(value))
            # Let the data class have a say in validity.
            if not value.is_valid():
                raise datastore_errors.BadValueError(
                    'Must be a valid PlayerName')
            # Disallow the serialization delimiter in the fields.
            if value.surname.find('|') != -1 or value.first_name.find('|') != -1:
                raise datastore_errors.BadValueError(
                    'PlayerName surname and first_name cannot contain a "|".')
            return value

    def _to_base_type(self, value):
        return '|'.join([value.surname, value.first_name])

    def _from_base_type(self, value):
        (surname, first_name) = value.split('|')
        return PlayerName(first_name=first_name, surname=surname)
```

And here's how you'd use it:

```
p = Player()
p.player_name = PlayerName(u'Ned', u'Nederlander')

p.player_name = PlayerName(u'Ned', u'Neder|lander')
    # BadValueError, surname contains serialization delimiter

p.player_name = PlayerName(u'Ned', u'Neder')
    # BadValueError, PlayerName.is_valid() == False, surname too short

p.player_name = PlayerName('Ned', u'Nederlander')
    # BadValueError, PlayerName.is_valid() == False, first_name is not unicode
```

Here, the application value type is a `PlayerName` instance, and the datastore value type is that value encoded as a Unicode string. The encoding format is the `surname` field, followed by a delimiter, followed by the `first_name` field. We disallow the delimiter character in the surname using the `_validate()` method. (Instead of disallowing it, we could also escape it in `_to_base_value()` and unescape it in `_from_base_value()`.)

In this example, `PlayerName(u'Ned', u'Nederlander')` is stored as this Unicode string:

```
Nederlander|Ned
```

The datastore value puts the surname first so that the datastore will sort `PlayerName` values first by surname, then by first name. In general, you choose a serialization format that has the desired ordering characteristics for your custom property type. The core type you choose also impacts how your values are ordered when mixed with other types, though if you're modeling consistently this isn't usually an issue.

If the conversion from the application type to the datastore type may fail, put a check for the conversion failure in the _validate() method. This way, the error is caught when the bad value is assigned, instead of when the object is saved.

Accepting Arguments

As we've seen in several of the built-in property declaration classes, it is useful to allow the user to customize the behavior of a property declaration on a per-use basis by providing arguments to the constructor.

Let's extend PlayerNameProperty with a require_first_name customization argument that defaults to False. When True, the _validate() method rejects PlayerName values that do not have a first_name:

```
class PlayerNameProperty(ndb.StringProperty):
    _attributes = ndb.Property._attributes + ['require_first_name']

    @utils.positional(1 + Property._positional)
    def __init__(self, name=None, require_first_name=False, **kwds):
        super(PlayerNameProperty, self).__init__(name=name, **kwds)
        self._require_first_name = require_first_name

    def _validate(self, value):
        # ...

        if self._require_first_name and not value.first_name:
            raise datastore_errors.BadValueError(
                'PlayerName must have a first_name')

        # ...
```

We made three changes:

- Set the _attributes class member variable (a list of strings) to ndb.Property._attributes extended with the new attribute

- Overrode the __init__() initializer to accept a require_first_name argument, call the parent initializer, then set the _require_first_name instance variable (shadowing the class member variable)

- Extended _validate() to test the instance variable and require that value.first_name be nonempty, if requested by the declaration

The _attributes class member variable is only used to generate a string representation of the property instance for debugging purposes. It doesn't affect how you use the argument, but it's a convenient way to extend internal error messages involving custom properties.

There is no magic in how we're collecting and storing the argument. We're overriding the initializer, adding a keyword argument, and storing it on the instance for later use. There is a small amount of crazy stuff here to comply with requirements internal to the `Property` class, specifically a `name` argument that must be the first positional argument to the initializer. The model class populates this with the property name (the class attribute) when setting up the declaration. Briefly:

- `@utils.positional(1 + Property._positional)` tells `Property`'s internal argument handling that `self` and `name` are positional arguments. Our custom argument is a keyword-only argument.
- `def __init__(self, name=None, …, **kwds):` preserves the `self` and `name` arguments as the first positional arguments, followed by our custom keyword arguments, then a `dict` to consume the remaining keyword arguments.
- `super(PlayerNameProperty, self).__init__(name=name, **kwds)` calls the parent class's initializer with the `name` in the first spot, followed by the keyword arguments we didn't reserve for ourselves. In typical Python 2.7 fashion, `Player NameProperty` is the name of the property class we are defining.

You'd use this feature as follows:

```
class Player(ndb.Model):
    player_name = PlayerNameProperty(require_first_name=True)

p = Player()
p.player_name = PlayerName(
    first_name=u'Ned', surname=u'Nederlander')
    # OK

p.player_name = PlayerName(u'', u'Madonna')
    # BadValueError: first_name is empty, but required by the declaration
```

Implementing Automatic Values

As we saw earlier, the `ndb.DateTimeProperty` has a special feature where if the user sets `auto_now=True`, the value is automatically updated to the current system time when the entity is saved. It does this in a hook called `_prepare_for_put()`. You can define this method in your property class to achieve a similar effect.

Why not put this in `_validate()` or `_to_base_value()`? This might work, depending on what you're trying to do. Keep in mind that these methods are not called if the value is `None` (or just isn't set). In the case of `auto_now`, it is important that the automatic value be set even if the app hasn't set a value for the property.

Continuing our `PlayerNameProperty` example, let's add an `auto_ned` parameter. If True, always use the name "Ned Nederlander" for the value, regardless of whether or how it was set by the application:

```
class PlayerNameProperty(ndb.StringProperty):
    _attributes = ndb.Property._attributes + ['require_first_name', 'auto_ned']

    def __init__(self, name=None,
                       require_first_name=False,
                       auto_ned=False,
                       **kwds):
        super(PlayerNameProperty, self).__init__(name=name, **kwds)
        self._require_first_name = require_first_name
        self._auto_ned = auto_ned

    # ...

    def _prepare_for_put(self, entity):
        if self._auto_ned:
            self._store_value(entity, PlayerName(u'Ned', u'Nederlander'))
```

ndb calls the `_prepare_for_put()` method of each declared property prior to storing the entity in the datastore. This is another stacking API, and must not call the parent class. The method takes the entire entity (not just the property) as its argument, and is allowed to examine the entity and update the property value.

To update the value, we call the property class's own `self._store_value(entity, value)` method. The `value` in this case is a user value. ndb will pass this value through `_to_base_value()` as needed. Alternatively, you can pass a base value by wrapping it in `ndb._BaseValue(val)`. This tells ndb that it doesn't need converting. In this case, we create a `PlayerName` user value, and let `_to_base_value()` do its thing.

Here's how you'd use this silly new option:

```
class Player(ndb.Model):
    player_name = PlayerNameProperty(auto_ned=True)

p = Player()
p.player_name = PlayerName(u'', u'Madonna')

p.put()  # p.player_name is now PlayerName(u'Ned', u'Nederlander')
```

That gets us behavior similar to `ndb.DateTimeProperty`'s `auto_now`. What if we want something like `auto_now_add`, which only sets the value if the value is not set? We can use `self._has_value(entity)` to test whether a value is present. Here is an implementation of an `auto_ned_add` feature for `PlayerNameProperty`:

```
class PlayerNameProperty(ndb.StringProperty):
    _attributes = ndb.Property._attributes + ['require_first_name',
        'auto_ned', 'auto_ned_add']
```

```python
def __init__(self, name=None,
             require_first_name=False,
             auto_ned=False,
             auto_ned_add=False,
             **kwds):
    super(PlayerNameProperty, self).__init__(name=name, **kwds)
    self._require_first_name = require_first_name
    self._auto_ned = auto_ned
    self._auto_ned_add = auto_ned_add

# ...

def _prepare_for_put(self, entity):
    if (self._auto_ned or
        (self._auto_ned_add and not self._has_value(entity))):
        self._store_value(entity, PlayerName(u'Ned', u'Nederlander'))
```

And here is how to use it:

```python
class Player(ndb.Model):
    player_name = PlayerNameProperty(auto_ned_add=True)

p = Player()
p.put()  # p.player_name is PlayerName(u'Ned', u'Nederlander')

p = Player()
p.player_name = PlayerName(u'', u'Madonna')
p.put()  # p.player_name is PlayerName(u'', u'Madonna')
```

Automatic Batching

Calling the datastore service each time your application reads or writes an entity takes a significant amount of time. Especially when making synchronous calls, where your app code waits for the call to succeed before proceeding, calling the datastore efficiently can make a big difference to your application's performance. (See Chapter 17 for more information about calling services asynchronously.) The ndb library knows how to batch calls to the datastore automatically, and does so invisibly to your app.

We've already seen how to initiate a batch call from the application code. Consider this example:

```python
class Entity(ndb.Model):
    pass

e1 = Entity()
e1.put()

e2 = Entity()
e2.put()
```

```
e3 = Entity()
e3.put()
```

You could paraphrase this to use an explicit batch call to `ndb.put_multi()`, like so:

```
class Entity(ndb.Model):
    pass

e1 = Entity()
e2 = Entity()
e3 = Entity()

ndb.put_multi([e1, e2, e3])
```

The batch call makes one remote procedure call to store all three entities, which is more efficient than making a remote procedure call for each entity.

Brilliantly, ndb knows better than to make three RPCs in the first example. ndb keeps track of how your application code manipulates datastore data and will optimize calls to the datastore as batch calls automatically whenever it can. It even knows how to do this with more complex calling patterns, such as code that interleaves gets and puts of overlapping data. The library preserves all transactional guarantees, and is generally more careful with calls that participate in a transaction.

In other words, thanks to ndb, the first example is generally equivalent to the second example with regards to how the datastore is called. Your code can simply call ndb when it is convenient and obvious to do so, and ndb will make it as fast as possible.

Automatic Caching

Another major technique for optimizing datastore calls is to use a *cache:* keep the data in memory, and prefer to read from memory than from the datastore. ndb uses two separate strategies for caching datastore data: an *in-context cache* and the *distributed memcache.*

The in-context cache is a temporary cache that lives in RAM, and lasts as long as the request handler is running, from request to response. Each request handler gets its own in-context cache. (It does not persist on the instance, and is not shared between handlers.) Like automatic batching, the in-context cache is something you might build yourself to save on calls to the datastore if ndb weren't doing it for you. For example:

```
def add_props(id):
    entity = ndb.Key('Entity', id).get()
    return entity.prop1 + entity.prop2

def mult_props(id):
    entity = ndb.Key('Entity', id).get()
    return entity.prop1 * entity.prop2
```

```
sum = add_props('foo')
product = mult_props('foo')
```

Here we have two call paths that want to operate on the same entity. These call paths don't know anything about each other, and probably shouldn't: they're easily understood as separate functions that, internally, access the datastore and perform some calculation. Without ndb's help, calling each path would result in two calls to the datastore to read the same data twice. You could try to fix this yourself with a little in-memory cache of your own:

```
# (This is unnecessary with ndb.)
CACHE = {}
def get_entity(id):
    if id not in CACHE:
        CACHE[id] = ndb.Key('Entity', id).get()
    return CACHE[id]

def add_props(id):
    entity = get_entity(id)
    return entity.prop1 + entity.prop2

def mult_props(id):
    entity = get_entity(id)
    return entity.prop1 * entity.prop2

sum = add_props('foo')
product = mult_props('foo')
```

If you trace through these calls, you'll see that `ndb.Key('Entity', 'foo').get()` is only called once, and the second access uses `CACHE`. This puts undue burden on your code to perform a basic bookkeeping task.

By default, ndb will handle the first example like the second example, using its in-context cache for the second call to `get()` with the same key. This is usually what you want, at least for short-lived request handlers. It assumes that the request handler prefers to see the same version of an entity when the entity is requested twice, even if another process has updated the entity between the calls. Once again, ndb is smart enough to do the right thing when updating data or performing transactions. It's a free performance benefit when the benefit makes sense, and you don't have to contort your code in weird ways to get it.

In addition to the in-context cache, ndb uses App Engine's distributed memcache service for further performance benefits across multiple request handlers. We'll discuss this service in more detail in Chapter 12. For common cases where you would normally store a datastore entity in memcache by its key to avoid a call to the datastore, it's best to rely on ndb's built-in automatic support for doing just that. ndb has robust logic for determining when to read from memcache and when to invalidate the cached data and go straight to the datastore. And again, ndb is careful when it comes to transactions.

Setting the Cache Policy for a Kind

You don't always want to use a cache. Especially with memcache, your code may need more direct control over when the app goes to the datastore for fresh data versus reading from the cache, which may have stale data. You can tell ndb to not use either the in-context cache, memcache, or both under certain circumstances.

Most often, you'll want to set this *cache policy* based on the kind of the data. The easiest way to do this is to set special class variables on the ndb.Model subclass for the kind. For example:

```
class Entity(ndb.Model):
    _use_cache = False
    _use_memcache = False

e1 = ndb.Key('Entity', 'foo').get()  # calls the datastore

# ...

e2 = ndb.Key('Entity', 'foo').get()  # calls the datastore
```

If cls._use_cache is False, ndb never uses the in-context cache for entities of this kind. If cls._use_memcache is False, ndb never uses memcache automatically for entities of this kind. As in this example, if both are False, ndb goes straight to the datastore when asked to do so.

Putting memcache in front of the datastore means that when a datastore entity changes, there is a period of time where memcache may have old data, and therefore request handlers reading that data from memcache will not see the change. When ndb stores an entity in memcache, it sets an upper bound for this period of time, sometimes called a *timeout*, an *expiration time*, or the *time-to-live* (TTL). After that period has elapsed (or possibly sooner), memcache evicts the value. The next process to use ndb to read the entity will call the datastore, and update memcache with the latest data.

To adjust the memcache timeout for entities of a kind, set the cls._memcache_time out class member, as a number of seconds:

```
class Entity(ndb.Model):
    _memcache_timeout = 20 * 60   # 20 minutes
```

ndb does attempt to invalidate memcache values when the corresponding datastore entity is updated or deleted. However, this is not guaranteed. The memcache does not participate in datastore transactions, and so the datastore update may succeed while the memcache update may fail. The timeout ensures that memcache will eventually forget its stale data.

 Even short cache timeouts can be useful. If an entity is read once per second, a timeout of two minutes replaces 99.16% of datastore calls with memcache calls. The data that is read will be at most two minutes old.

In addition to disabling the in-context cache or memcache (or both) for a kind, you can also disable the datastore. Why would you do that? With one or both caches enabled and the datastore disabled, ndb becomes a great way to cache structured data. Caches are not persistent storage, but they are useful to avoid repeating calculations or expensive network operations, just as they are useful to avoid unnecessary trips to the datastore. To disable datastore storage for a kind, use the `cls._use_datastore` class member.

More Complex Cache Policies

You can set a cache policy based on more complex criteria than just the kind of an entity. To do so, you define a function that takes the `ndb.Key` of an entity being manipulated and returns `True` if caching is allowed for that entity, or `False` if not. You install this cache policy using a method on the *context object*, which you obtain from the function `ndb.get_context()`:

```
def never_cache_test_data(key):
    id = key.string_id()
    return not id or not id.startswith('test_')

ctx = ndb.get_context()
ctx.set_memcache_policy(never_cache_test_data)
```

This example sets a global cache policy for memcache that says any entity (of any kind) that has a string ID that begins with `test_` should never be stored in memcache. This policy applies to all uses of ndb by this request handler, and only applies to the use of memcache, not the in-context cache or the datastore.

As written, this example overrides the default global policy for memcache, which is to test the `_use_memcache` member variable of the kind model class. If a model class sets `_use_memcache`, it will be ignored. Your global cache policy function can fall back to this behavior by calling `ndb.Context.default_memcache_policy()`:

```
def never_cache_test_data(key):
    id = key.string_id()
    if id.startswith('test_'):
        return False
    return ndb.Context.default_memcache_policy(key)
```

```
ctx = ndb.get_context()
ctx.set_memcache_policy(never_cache_test_data)
```

The equivalent functions for the in-context cache are `ctx.set_cache_policy()` to set the policy, and `ndb.Context.default_cache_policy()` to fall back on the default global policy. For the datastore, these are `ctx.set_datastore_policy()` and `ndb.Context.default_datastore_policy()`, respectively.

You can also set a global policy for the memcache timeout. The policy function takes a key and returns the timeout as a number of seconds. To register this policy, pass the function to `ctx.set_memcache_timeout_policy()`.

Ignoring Caches per Call

Finally, there's an easy way to tell ndb to ignore one of the caches on a per-call basis. Methods that call the datastore accept `use_cache`, `use_memcache`, `use_datastore`, and `memcache_timeout` keyword arguments. Set these to override the established cache policy for the purposes of the call:

```
entity = ndb.Key('Entity', 'foo').get(use_memcache=False)
```

Remember that the default cache policies use all three of the datastore, in-context cache, and memcache. If you don't want one or more of these in some cases, you must establish an alternative cache policy using one of these techniques.

## CHAPTER 10

Datastore Administration

Your data is the heart of your application, so you'll want to take good care of it. You'll want to watch it, and understand how it grows and how it affects your app's behavior. You'll want to help it evolve as your app's functionality changes. You may even want up-to-date information about data types and sizes. And you'll want to poke at it, and prod it into shape using tools not necessarily built into your app.

App Engine provides a variety of administrative tools for learning about, testing, protecting, and fixing your datastore data. In this chapter, we look at a few of these tools, and their associated best practices.

Inspecting the Datastore

The first thing you might want to do with your app's datastore is see what's in it. Your app provides a natural barrier between you and how your data is stored physically in the datastore, so many data troubleshooting sessions start with pulling back the covers and seeing what's there.

In the Storage section of the Cloud Console is a set of panels for Cloud Datastore (Figure 10-1). This is your main view of your project's datastore entities. The Dashboard summarizes how your storage space is used, including space for entities and their properties, as well as space for built-in and custom (composite) indexes. Select a kind from the drop-down menu to see a breakdown by named property.

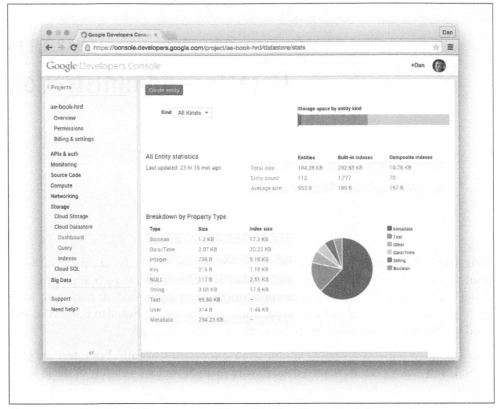

Figure 10-1. The Cloud Datastore Dashboard in the Cloud Console

In the Query panel, you can browse entities by kind. You can also apply query filters to this view by clicking the Filters button. The panel knows the names of all of the indexed properties of entities of the given kind, making it easy to compose queries on existing properties.

From any of these panels, you can click the Create Entity button to create a new entity. You can pick from a list of existing kinds, and property names and types known to be used with existing entities will appear automatically. You can also create an entity of a new kind, and add and remove arbitrary properties. Currently, only simple keys (without ancestors) are supported for entities created via the Console.

When browsing entities in the Query panel, you can click on the key of an entity to view its properties in more detail. You can also edit the properties in this view, within the limitations of the Console's property editor.

The property value types supported by the Console for property editing and query filters include the following:

A date and time

You enter a date and time into the form field using the format YYYY-MM-DD HH:MM:SS, such as 2014-12-31 23:59:59. As with storing datetime values in general, there is no time zone component.

A string

Note that string values in the form field have leading and trailing spaces truncated, and there is no way to specify a value with leading or trailing spaces.

A number

The datastore treats integers and floating-point values as distinct types. In these panels, a number value containing a decimal point (5.0) is interpreted as a floating-point value. Without the point (5), it's an integer.

A Boolean value

Here, the panel helps you out and displays a drop-down menu for the value (either true or false).

A Google user

The value is the current email address of the corresponding account, whether an account for that address exists or not.

A datastore key

A key value is a sequence of kind/ID pairs, with single quotes around kinds and string IDs, wrapped in a Key(…) specifier. For example: Key('MessageBoard', 'The_Archonville_Times', 'Message', 12345)

Currently, the Console does not support null values and geographical point values in the property editor and query composer. It also doesn't support multivalued properties. You also cannot create or edit blob values (unindexed binary values) with this interface.

The datastore panels are useful for inspecting entities and troubleshooting data issues, and may be sufficient for administrative purposes with simple data structures. However, you will probably want to build a custom administrative panel for browsing app-specific data structures and performing common administrative tasks.

 Applying filters in the Query panel performs a datastore query just as your application does. These filters are subject to the same restrictions, and use the same indexes as the app. If a set of filters requires a custom index (such as inequality filters on two distinct properties), that index must already be in the app's deployed index configuration to support querying with those filters from the Console. See Chapter 7.

Managing Indexes

When you upload the datastore index configuration for an app, the datastore begins building indexes that appear in the configuration but do not yet exist. This process is *not* instantaneous, and may take many minutes for new indexes that contain many rows. The datastore needs time to crawl all the entities to build the new indexes.

You can check on the build status of new indexes using the Cloud Console, in the Indexes section. An index being built appears with a status of "Building." When it is ready, the status changes to "Serving." Figure 10-2 shows a simple example of the Indexes section.

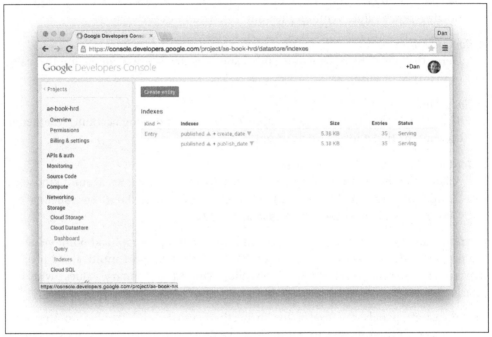

Figure 10-2. The Cloud Datastore Indexes panel in the Cloud Console

If an index's build status is "Error," the index build failed. It's possible that the failure was due to a transient error. To clear this condition, you must first remove the index from your configuration and then upload the new configuration. It is also possible for an index build to fail due to an entity reaching its index property value limit. In these cases, you can delete the entities that are causing the problem. Once that is done, you can add the index configuration back and upload it again.

If your application performs a query while the index for the query is building, the query will fail. You can avoid this by uploading the index configuration, waiting until the index is built, and then making the app that uses that query available. The most convenient way to do this depends on whether you upload the new application in a new version:

- If you are uploading the new application with the version identifier that is currently the "default" version, upload the index configuration alone using the `appcfg.py update_indexes` command. When the indexes are built, upload the app.

- If you are uploading the application as a new version, or as a version that isn't the default and that nobody is actively using, you can safely upload the application and index configuration together (`appcfg.py update`). Wait until the indexes are built before making the new version the default.

If you upload index configuration that does not mention an index that has already been built, the datastore does not delete the unused index, as it might still be in use by an older version of the app. You must tell App Engine to purge unused indexes. To do this, run the AppCfg command with the `vacuum_indexes` option. For instance:

```
appcfg.py vacuum_indexes app-dir
```

App Engine will purge all custom indexes not mentioned in the index configuration uploaded most recently. This reclaims the storage space used by those indexes.

 As we saw earlier, the development server tries to be helpful by creating new index configuration entries for queries that need them as you're testing your app. The development server will *never* delete an index configuration. As your app's queries change, this can result in unnecessary indexes being left in the file. You'll want to look through this file periodically, and confirm that each custom index is needed. Remove the unused index configuration, upload the file, and then vacuum indexes.

Accessing Metadata from the App

There are several ways to get information about the state of your datastore from within the application itself. The information visible in the Datastore Dashboard panel of the Cloud Console is also readable and queryable from entities in your app's datastore. Similarly, the facilities that allow the Query panel to determine the current kinds and property names are available to your app in the form of APIs and queryable metadata. You can also use APIs to get additional information about entity groups, index build status, and query planning.

We won't describe every metadata feature here. Instead, we'll look at a few representative examples. You can find the complete details in the official App Engine documentation.

Querying Statistics

App Engine gathers statistics about the contents of the datastore periodically, usually about once a day. It stores these statistics in datastore entities in your application. The Datastore Dashboard panel of the Cloud Console gets its information from these entities. Your app can also fetch and query these entities to access the statistics.

In Python, each statistic has an ndb data model class, in the `google.appengine.ext.ndb.stats` module. You use these model classes to perform queries, like you would any other query. The actual kind name differs from the model class name.

Here's an example in Python that queries storage statistics for each entity kind:

```python
import logging
from google.appengine.ext.ndb import stats

# ...
        kind_stats = stats.KindStat.query()
        for kind_stat in kind_stats:
            logging.info(
                'Stats for kind %s: %d entities, '
                'total %d bytes (%d entity bytes)',
                kind_stat.kind_name, kind_stat.count,
                kind_stat.bytes, kind_stat.entity_bytes)
```

Here's another example that reports the properties per kind taking up more than a terabyte of space:

```python
import logging
from google.appengine.ext.ndb import stats

# ...
        q = stats.KindPropertyNameStat.query()
        q = q.filter('bytes >', 1024 ** 4)
        for kind_prop in q:
            logging.info(
                'Large property detected: %s:%s total size %d',
                kind_prop.kind_name, kind_prop.property_name,
                kind_prop.bytes)
```

Every statistic entity has a `count` property, a `bytes` property, and a `timestamp` property. `count` and `bytes` represent the total count and total size of the unit represented by the entity. The statistic for a kind has a `bytes` property equal to the total amount of storage used by entities of the kind for properties and indexes. The `timestamp` property is the last time the statistic entity was updated. Statistic entity kinds have additional properties specific to the kind.

The `__Stat_Total__` kind (represented in Python by the `GlobalStat` class) represents the grand total for the entire app. The `count` and `bytes` properties represent the number of all entities, and the total size of all entities and indexes. These numbers are broken down further in several properties: `entity_bytes` is the storage for just the entities (not indexes), `builtin_index_bytes` and `builtin_index_count` are the total size and number of indexed properties in just the built-in indexes, and `composite_index_bytes` and `composite_index_count` are the same for just custom (composite) indexes. There is only one `__Stat_Total__` entity for the app.

The `__Stat_Kind__` kind (`KindStat`) represents statistics for each datastore kind individually, as existed at the time the statistics were last updated. There is one of these statistic entities for each kind. The `kind_name` property is set to the kind name, so you can query for a specific kind's statistics, or you can iterate over all kinds to determine which kinds there are. These entities have the same statistic properties as `__Stat_Total__`.

The `__Stat_PropertyName_Kind__` kind (`KindPropertyNameStat`) represents each named property of each kind. The `property_name` and `kind_name` properties identify the property and kind for the statistic. The statistic properties are `count`, `bytes`, `entity_bytes`, `builtin_index_bytes`, and `builtin_index_count`.

For a complete list of the statistics entity kinds, see the official App Engine website.

Querying Metadata

The datastore always knows which namespaces, kinds, and property names are in use by an application. Unlike statistics, this metadata is available immediately. Querying this metadata can be slower than querying a normal entity, but the results reflect the current state of the data.

Each namespace has an entity of the kind `__namespace__`. Each kind is a `__kind__`, and each property name (regardless of kind) is a `__property__`. These entities have no properties: all information is stored in the key name. For example, a `__kind__` entity uses the kind name as its key name. (The full key is `__kind__` / `KindName`.) A `__property__` entity has both the kind name and the property name encoded in its key name.

This information is derived entirely from the built-in indexes. As such, only indexed properties have corresponding `__property__` entities.

These all have `ndb` model classes defined in the `google.appengine.ext.ndb.metadata` module. They are named `Namespace`, `Kind`, and `Property`. The classes include Python property methods for accessing names, as if they were datastore properties. The module also provides several convenience functions for common queries.

Here's a simple example in Python that lists all the kinds for which there is an entity, using a convenience function to get the list of kind names:

```
import logging
from google.appengine.ext.ndb import metadata

# ...
    kinds = metadata.get_kinds()
    for k in kinds:
        logging.info('Found a datastore kind: %s', k)
```

Index Status and Queries

The Datastore Indexes panel of the Cloud Console reports on the indexes configured for the app, and the serving status of each. The app can get this same information by using the datastore API. A Python app can also ask the datastore which index was used to resolve a query, after the query has been executed.

You ask for the state of indexes by calling the `get_indexes()` function of the `google.appengine.ext.ndb` module. This function returns a list of tuples, each representing an index. Each tuple contains an index object, and a state value. The index object has the methods `kind()`, `has_ancestor()`, and `properties()`, representing the latest uploaded index configuration. The state value is one of several constants representing the index build states: `datastore.Index.BUILDING`, `data store.Index.SERVING`, `datastore.Index.DELETING`, or `datastore.Index.ERROR` (from the `google.appengine.api.datastore` module):

```
from google.appengine.api import datastore
from google.appengine.ext import ndb

# ...
    for index in ndb.get_indexes():
        if index.state != datastore.Index.SERVING:
            kind = index.definition.kind
            ancestor_str = ' (ancestor)' if index.definition.ancestor else ''

            index_props = []
            for prop in index.definition.properties:
                dir_str = ('ASC'
                            if prop.direction == datastore.Index.ASCENDING
                            else 'DESC')
                index_props.append(prop.name + ' ' + dir_str)
            index_property_spec = ', '.join(index_props)

            index_spec = '%s%s %s' % (kind, ancestor_str,
                                        index_property_spec)

            logging.info('Index is not serving: %s', index_spec)
```

An ndb query object has an `index_list()` method that returns a list of index objects representing the indexes used to resolve the query. You must execute the query before calling this method, so it knows which indexes were involved in performing the query.

Entity Group Versions

In Chapter 8, we described the datastore as using multiversioned optimistic concurrency control, with the entity group as the unit of transactionality. Each time any entity in an entity group is updated, the datastore creates a new version of the entity group. If any process reads an entity in the entity group before the new version is fully stored, the process simply sees the earlier version.

Each of these versions gets an ID number, and this number increases strictly and monotonically. You can use the metadata API to get the entity group version number for an entity.

This is the get_entity_group_version() function in the goo gle.appengine.ext.ndb.metadata module. It takes an ndb.Key instance as an argument, and returns an integer, or None if the given entity group doesn't exist:

```
from google.appengine.ext import ndb
from google.appengine.ext.ndb import metadata

class MyKind(ndb.Expando):
    pass

# ...
        # Write to an entity group, and get its version number.
        parent = MyKind()
        parent.put()
        version = metadata.get_entity_group_version(parent.key)

        # Update the entity group by creating a child entity.
        child = MyKind(parent=parent)
        child.put()

        # The version number of the entire group has been incremented.
        version2 = metadata.get_entity_group_version(parent.key)
```

Remote Controls

One of the nice features of a relational database running in a typical hosting environment is the ability to connect directly to the database to perform queries and updates on a SQL command line or to run small administrative scripts. App Engine has a facility for doing something similar, and it works for more than just the datastore: you can call any live service on behalf of your application using tools running on your computer. The tools do this using a remote proxy API.

The proxy API is a request handler that you install in your app. It is restricted to administrators. You run a client tool that authenticates as an administrator, connects to the request handler, and issues service calls over the connection. The proxy performs the calls and returns the results.

App Engine includes versions of the proxy handler in the Python libraries. The client library and related tools are also implemented in Python.

The remote shell tool opens a Python command prompt, with the App Engine Python service libraries modified to use the remote API. You type Python statements as they would appear in app code, and all calls to App Engine services are routed to the live app automatically. This is especially useful in conjunction with Python apps, where you can import your app's own data models and request handler modules, and do interactive testing or data manipulation. You can also write your own tools in Python using the remote API, for repeated tasks.

 The remote API is clever and useful, but it's also slow: every service call is going over the network from your local computer to the app, then back. It is not suitable for running large jobs over arbitrary amounts of data. For large data transformation jobs, you're better off building something that runs within the app, using task queues.

Let's take a look at how to set up the proxy, how to use the remote Python shell, and how to write a Python tool that calls the API.

Setting Up the Remote API

The remote API request handler is included in the runtime environment. To set it up, you activate a built-in in *app.yaml*, like so:

```
builtins:
- remote_api: on
```

This establishes a web service endpoint at the URL `/_ah/remote_api/`. Only clients authenticated using application administrator accounts can use this endpoint.

You can test this URL in a browser using the development server. Visit the URL (such as *http://localhost:8080/_ah/remote_api*), and make sure it redirects to the fake authentication form. Check the box to sign in as an administrator, and click Submit. You should see this message:

```
This request did not contain a necessary header.
```

The remote API expects an HTTP header identifying the remote API protocol version to use, which the browser does not provide. But this is sufficient to test that the handler is configured correctly.

Using the Remote Shell Tool

With the remote API handler installed, you can use a tool included with the Python SDK to manipulate a live application's services from an interactive Python shell. You interact with the shell by using Python statements and the Python service APIs. This tool uses the remote API handler.

To start a shell session, run the `remote_api_shell.py` command. As with the other Python SDK commands, this command may already be in your command path:

```
remote_api_shell.py app-id
```

The tool prompts for your developer account email address and password. (Only registered developers for the app can run this tool, or any of the remote API tools.)

By default, the tool connects to the application via the domain name `app-id.appspot.com`, and assumes the remote API handler is installed with the URL path `/_ah/remote_api`. To use a different URL path, provide the path as an argument after the application ID:

```
remote_api_shell.py app-id /admin/util/remote_api
```

To use a different domain name, such as to use a specific application version, or to test the tool with the development server, give the domain name with the `-s …` argument:

```
remote_api_shell.py -s dev.app-id.appspot.com app-id
```

The shell can use any service API that is supported by the remote API handler. This includes URL Fetch, memcache, Images, Mail, Google Accounts, and of course the datastore. (As of this writing, XMPP is not supported by the remote API handler.) Several of the API modules are imported by default for easy access.

The tool does not add the current working directory to the module load path by default, nor does it know about your application directory. You may need to adjust the load path (`sys.path`) to import your app's classes, such as your data models.

Here is an example of a short shell session:

```
% remote_api_shell.py clock
Email: juliet@example.com
Password:
App Engine remote_api shell
Python 2.7.6 (v2.7.6:3a1db0d2747e, Nov 10 2013, 00:42:54)
[GCC 4.2.1 (Apple Inc. build 5666) (dot 3)] on darwin
The db, users, urlfetch, and memcache modules are imported.
clock> import os.path
clock> import sys
clock> sys.path.append(os.path.realpath('.'))
clock> import models
clock> books = models.Book.query().fetch(6)
```

```
clock> books
[<models.Book object at 0x7a2c30>, <models.Book object at 0x7a2bf0>,
<models.Book object at 0x7a2cd0>, <models.Book object at 0x7a2cb0>,
<models.Book object at 0x7a2d30>, <models.Book object at 0x7a2c90>]
clock> books[0].title
u'The Grapes of Wrath'
clock> from google.appengine.api import mail
clock> mail.send_mail('juliet@example.com', 'test@example.com',
'Test email', 'This is a test message.')
clock>
```

To exit the shell, press Ctrl-D.

Using the Remote API from a Script

You can call the remote API directly from your own Python scripts by using a library from the Python SDK. This configures the Python API to use the remote API handler for your application for all service calls, so you can use the service APIs as you would from a request handler directly in your scripts.

Here's a simple example script that prompts for a developer account email address and password, then accesses the datastore of a live application:

```python
#!/usr/bin/python

import getpass
import sys

# Add the Python SDK to the package path.
# Adjust these paths accordingly.
sys.path.append('~/google_appengine')
sys.path.append('~/google_appengine/lib/yaml/lib')

from google.appengine.ext.remote_api import remote_api_stub

import models

# Your app ID and remote API URL path go here.
APP_ID = 'app_id'
REMOTE_API_PATH = '/_ah/remote_api'

def auth_func():
    email_address = raw_input('Email address: ')
    password = getpass.getpass('Password: ')
    return email_address, password

def initialize_remote_api(app_id=APP_ID,
                          path=REMOTE_API_PATH):
    remote_api_stub.ConfigureRemoteApi(
        app_id,
        path,
        auth_func)
```

```
    remote_api_stub.MaybeInvokeAuthentication()

def main(args):
    initialize_remote_api()

    books = models.Book.query().fetch(10)
    for book in books:
        print book.title

    return 0

if __name__ == '__main__':
    sys.exit(main(sys.argv[1:]))
```

The ConfigureRemoteApi() function (yes, it has a TitleCase name) sets up the remote API access. It takes as arguments the application ID, the remote API handler URL path, and a callable that returns a tuple containing the email address and password to use when connecting. In this example, we define a function that prompts for the email address and password, and pass the function to ConfigureRemoteApi().

The function also accepts an optional fourth argument specifying an alternative domain name for the connection. By default, it uses app-id.appspot.com, where app-id is the application ID in the first argument.

The MaybeInvokeAuthentication() function sends an empty request to verify that the email address and password are correct, and raises an exception if they are not. (Without this, the script would wait until the first remote call to verify the authentication.)

Remember that every call to an App Engine library that performs a service call does so over the network via an HTTP request to the application. This is inevitably slower than running within the live application. It also consumes application resources like web requests do, including bandwidth and request counts, which are not normally consumed by service calls in the live app.

On the plus side, because your code runs on your local computer, it is not constrained by the App Engine runtime sandbox or the 30-second request deadline. You can run long jobs and interactive applications on your computer without restriction, using any Python modules you like—at the expense of consuming app resources to marshal service calls over HTTP.

## CHAPTER 11

Using Google Cloud SQL with App Engine

A sizable portion of this book is dedicated to Google Cloud Datastore, a schemaless persistent object store designed for applications that scale to arbitrary sizes. Those automatic scaling capabilities come at the expense of features common to relational databases such as MySQL, PostgreSQL, and Oracle Database. While many common tasks of web application programming are well suited, or even better suited, for a scalable datastore, some cases call for a real relational database, with normalized entries, real-time join queries, and enforced and migratable data schemas. And sometimes you just want to run third-party software that expects you to have a SQL database on hand.

For those cases, there's Google Cloud SQL. A feature of Google Cloud Platform, Cloud SQL gives you a straight-up no-nonsense MySQL relational database, designed for ease of use from Cloud Platform runtime environments like App Engine. Your database lives on a Cloud SQL *instance,* a virtual machine of a particular size that runs for as long as you need the database to be available. Your app code connects to the instance to execute SQL statements and queries using a standard database interface. You can also configure an IP address for the instance and connect to it with any MySQL client.

Naturally, Cloud SQL is the opposite of Cloud Datastore when it comes to scaling. Each SQL instance has a large but limited capacity for concurrent connections, CPU, and data. If you need more capacity than a single instance can provide, it's up to you to start new instances, divide traffic, and shard or replicate data. Cloud SQL includes special support (currently in a beta release) for *read replicas,* special instances in a read-only mode that copy all of the updates from a master instance. You manage Cloud SQL instances just like you would a fleet of MySQL machines, with all of the flexibility and overhead that comes with it. Cloud SQL offers many instance types, and for many applications you can upgrade a single instance quite far before you have to worry about scaling.

In this chapter, we'll give a brief overview of how to get started with Cloud SQL, and how to develop App Engine applications that use it. We won't cover every feature of MySQL, as there is plenty of documentation online and many excellent books on the subject. For information on advanced subjects like read replicas, see the official documentation (*https://cloud.google.com/sql/*).

Choosing a Cloud SQL Instance

With Cloud SQL, as with all of Google Cloud Platform, you only pay for the resources you use. Cloud SQL's billable resources include instance hours, storage, I/O operations to storage, and outbound network bandwidth. Network traffic between App Engine and Cloud SQL is free. Every instance gets a free externally visible IPv6 address, and inbound network traffic is also free of charge. You can pay a little more for an IPv4 address for the instance if you have a client on a network that doesn't issue global IPv6 addresses.

Like App Engine instances, Cloud SQL instances are available in multiple sizes: D0, D1, D2, D4, D8, D16, and D32. The instance tiers mainly differ in RAM, ranging from 0.125 gigabytes for a D0 to 16 gigabytes for a D32, and the maximum number of concurrent connections, from 250 to 4,000.

Storage is billed per gigabyte used per month, and you only pay for the disk space used by MySQL over time. This includes storage for system tables and logs, as well as your app's table schemas and rows. You don't need to specify (or pay for) a maximum size. An instance of any tier can grow its data up to 250 gigabytes by default, and you can raise this limit to 500 gigabytes by purchasing a Google Cloud support package at the "silver" level.

There are two billing plans for Cloud SQL: per use billing, and package billing. With per use billing, you are billed for each hour an instance runs, with a minimum of one hour each time you enable an instance, rounded to the nearest hour. You can start and stop the instance as needed, and the database persists when the instance is stopped, with storage billed at the usual storage rate. This is useful for single user sessions or applications that only need the database during a fixed window of time, where the instance does not need to run continuously.

If you intend to keep the instance running over a sustained period of multiple days, such as to keep it available for a web application, you can claim a substantial discount by selecting package billing. With package billing, you are billed for each day that the instance exists. You can keep the instance running continuously for no additional charge. The package price also includes an amount of storage and I/O, and you aren't charged for these resources until usage exceeds the bundled amount.

As with App Engine instances, the rate differs by instance tier, with D0 being the least expensive. You can change an instance's tier at any time. Doing so results in only a few seconds of downtime.

As usual, prices change frequently enough that we won't bother to list specific numbers here. See the official documentation (*https://cloud.google.com/sql/pricing*) for the latest pricing information.

When you first sign up for Cloud SQL, or other Cloud Platform services such as Compute Engine, you may be eligible for a free trial of the Platform. The free trial gives you a starting budget of free resources so you can try out Cloud SQL without charge. This is a one-time trial budget for you to spend on these services. (This is different from App Engine's free quotas, which refresh daily.) Go to the Cloud Platform website (*https://cloud.google.com/*) and look for the Free Trial button to get started.

Installing MySQL Locally

While developing and maintaining an app that uses Cloud SQL, you will use a MySQL administrative client to connect to the Cloud SQL instance from your local machine. In addition, you will probably want to run a MySQL server locally to test your application without connecting to Cloud SQL. You can download and install MySQL Community Edition from Oracle's website to get both the client and the server tools for Windows, Mac OS X, or Linux. MySQL Community Edition is free.

To download MySQL, visit the MySQL Community Downloads page (*http://dev.mysql.com/downloads/*). Be sure to get the version of MySQL that matches Cloud SQL. Currently, this is version 5.5.

Linux users can install MySQL using `apt-get` like so:

```
sudo apt-get install mysql-server mysql-client
```

Once you have MySQL server installed, the server is running locally and can accept local connections. If the installation process did not prompt you to set a password for the root account, set one using the `mysqladmin` command, where `new-password` is the password you wish to set:

```
mysqladmin -u root password "new-password"
```

Try connecting to the server using the `mysql` command:

```
mysql -u root -p
```

Enter the password when prompted. When successful, you see a `mysql>` prompt. You can enter SQL statements at this prompt to create and modify databases. The `root` account has full access, and can also create new accounts and grant privileges.

See the MySQL documentation (*http://dev.mysql.com/doc/refman/5.5/en/*) for more information about setting up the local server.

 While you're at the MySQL website, you might also want to get MySQL Workbench, a visual client for designing and managing databases. You can download MySQL Workbench Community Edition for free.

Installing the MySQLdb Library

App Engine's Python runtime environment supports the MySQLdb library, an implementation of the Python DB API for MySQL, for connecting to Cloud SQL instances. You can request this library from the runtime environment using the `libraries:` section in your *app.yaml* file:

```
libraries:
- name: MySQLdb
  version: latest
```

This library is not distributed with the App Engine SDK, so you must install it locally for development and testing. This can a bit of a challenge: MySQLdb uses extensions written in C to interface with the official MySQL libraries, and so building MySQLdb from its original sources requires that you have a C compiler and appropriate libraries installed. You can download prebuilt versions of MySQLdb from unofficial repositories, as long as you're careful to get the correct version.

For Windows, visit this website (*http://www.codegood.com/archives/129*) to get an unofficial build of MySQLdb for Python 2.7, available in 32-bit and 64-bit varieties.

For Linux, you can install the prebuilt package for your distribution. For example, on Ubuntu and others, this command installs the correct library and its dependencies:

```
sudo apt-get install python-mysqldb
```

For Mac OS X, one way to install MySQLdb is with `pip`. You must have Apple's Xcode tools installed so that `pip` can use the C compiler. Xcode is a free download from the Mac App Store. The `pip` command is as follows:

```
sudo pip install MySQL-python
```

With the library installed via `pip`, you must also add the MySQL client library to the dynamic library load path. Put this in your *.bashrc* file (if you use `bash`):

```
export DYLD_LIBRARY_PATH=/usr/local/mysql/lib:$DYLD_LIBRARY_PATH
```

As an alternative on Mac OS X, you can use a package manager such as MacPorts (*http://www.macports.org/*). MacPorts builds the software from sources, and manages dependencies automatically. You can install MacPorts using the instructions on the MacPorts website (*https://www.macports.org/*).

With MacPorts installed, use the `port install` command to install the `py-mysql` package:

```
sudo port install py-mysql
```

Using MacPorts requires that you use the MacPorts version of the Python 2.7 interpreter. You can find this at */opt/local/bin/python2.7*. Be sure to use this interpreter when running `dev_appserver.py`:

```
/opt/local/bin/python2.7 ~/google-cloud-sdk/bin/dev_appserver.py myproject
```

On all platforms, you can verify that MySQLdb is installed by importing it from the Python prompt:

```
% python
Python 2.7.9 (default, Dec 13 2014, 15:13:49)
[GCC 4.2.1 Compatible Apple LLVM 6.0 (clang-600.0.56)] on darwin
Type "help", "copyright", "credits" or "license" for more information.
>>> import MySQLdb
>>>
```

For more information, see the MySQLdb v1 Github repository (*https://github.com/farcepest/MySQLdb1*) and an article about installation by the author (*http://mysql-python.blogspot.com/2012/11/is-mysqldb-hard-to-install.html*).

Creating a Cloud SQL Instance

Open a browser and visit the Cloud Console (*https://console.developers.google.com/*). Create a new project, or select an existing project, in the usual way. In the sidebar navigation, expand Storage, then select Cloud SQL. If this is your first Cloud SQL instance, you see a "Create an instance" button. Click it.

The form for creating a new Cloud SQL instance appears short and simple, asking for an instance ID, region, and tier. Click "Show advanced options..." to see the full list of capabilities. A portion of the full screen is shown in Figure 11-1.

The instance ID is a unique name for the Cloud SQL instance. It always begins with the project ID that "owns" the instance, followed by a colon and the name that you specify.

The region is the major geographical region where the instance lives. When using Cloud SQL with App Engine, this must be set to United States. In the future, when App Engine is available in other regions, the SQL instance and the App Engine app must be hosted in the same region.

The tier is the tier for this instance. The database version selects a version of MySQL to use; version 5.5 is fine. Below that, you can select the billing plan for this instance, either the per use plan or the package plan. Adjusting the tier changes the pricing information displayed in this section.

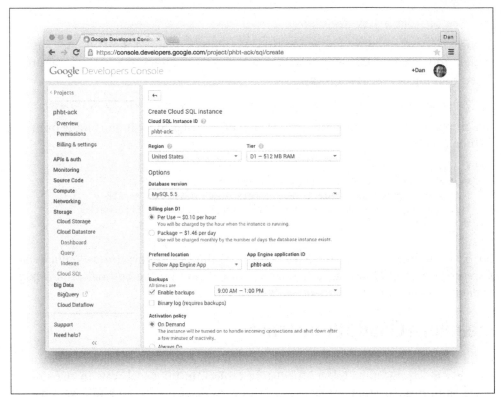

Figure 11-1. The "Create Cloud SQL instance" form with advanced options shown (excerpt)

The "Preferred location" is more specific than the region. For an App Engine app, you want to set this to Follow App Engine App to minimize the latency between the app and the database. Set the App Engine app ID (the project ID) to tell it to follow this app. You can adjust this if you have more than one distinct app using the same database instance, and you want the database to follow a specific app that isn't in this project.

Cloud SQL can do automatic daily backups of the database. This increases storage costs, but is likely to be less expensive than backing up to an external repository (which consumes outgoing bandwidth). If you want backups, make sure "Enable backups" is checked, and adjust the time range if needed. You can optionally store a MySQL binary log in addition to backups. The binary log contains every change event to the database, which is useful for restoring changes that were made since the last backup.

The "Activation policy" determines how the instance responds to usage. If you set this to On Demand, it will attempt to limit the instance running time by activating the instance for traffic then shutting it down after a few minutes without a connection. You can pair this with a per use billing plan and allow Cloud SQL to activate the instance as needed. The "Always On" option activates the instance as soon as you create it, and leaves it running even when idle. You might as well choose this option if you've selected package billing and expect the database to be used at least once a day. The "Never" option leaves the instance disabled, and only activates it in response to administrative commands.

If you intend to connect to this database with an external client and that client's network does not support IPv6, select "Assign an IPv4 address to my Cloud SQL instance." With an IPv4 address assigned, you are charged a small amount of money every hour the instance is idle.

Advanced options let you adjust the filesystem replication method, authorize specific IP ranges for clients, and set MySQL server flags for the instance. We'll adjust the external authorization settings in the next section.

Set the options as you like them, then click Save. When the instance has been created, it appears with a status of either "Runnable" or "Running," depending on how you set the activation policy.

Connecting to an Instance from Your Computer

Your new instance is ready to accept connections from your App Engine app. In theory, you could use code deployed to App Engine to connect to the database and create tables. More likely, you'll want to do this with an administrative client or another tool running on your local computer. To connect to an instance using something other than App Engine, you must configure the instance to allow incoming connections from a specific IP address or address range.

Before doing anything else, set a root password for the instance. In the Cloud Console, locate and select the Cloud SQL instance. Select the Access Control tab. Under Set Root Password, enter a password, then click Set. You will use this password when connecting with the root account.

Next, you need to authorize incoming connections from your computer to the instance. You can configure the instance to accept connections from specific IP addresses or network ranges, using either IPv6 addresses or IPv4 addresses. You can only connect to the instance via its IPv6 address if your network has assigned a public IPv6 address to your computer. If your computer does not have an IPv6 address, you must request an IPv4 address for the instance, then authorize your computer's IPv4 address to connect to it. There is an hourly charge to reserve an IPv4 address, but only if you leave it idle.

The easiest way to determine whether your computer has an IPv6 address is to visit the What's My Web IP website (*http://whatsmywebip.appspot.com*) using your browser. If this displays an IPv6 address, such as `fba2:2c26:f4e4:8000:abcd:1234:b5ef:7051`, then your computer connected to the site with an IPv6 address. You can confirm that this is your address using your computer's Network settings panel, or by running the `ipconfig` command on Windows or the `ifconfig` command on Mac OS X or Linux.

If this displays an IPv4 address, such as `216.123.55.120`, then your computer connected to the site with an IPv4 address. Even if your network assigned an IPv6 address to your computer, that address is only used locally and won't be used to make the final connection to the Cloud SQL instance. You must request an IPv4 address for the instance in order to connect to it from your computer's network.

If you need an IPv4 address, click Request an IP Address. An address is assigned to the instance and displayed.

To authorize your network to connect to the instance, click the Add Authorized Network button. Copy and paste your computer's address into the form field, then click Add.

Finally, use the `mysql` command to connect to the instance. You can find the instance's IPv6 address on the Overview tab, or use the IPv4 address you requested. Specify the address as the `--host=…` parameter:

```
# Using the IPv6 address of the instance:
mysql --host=2001:4860:4864:1:9e4a:e5a2:abcd:ef01 --user=root --password

# Or with an IPv4 address:
mysql --host=173.194.225.123 --user=root --password
```

When using an IPv6 address, you may get a message such as this:

```
ERROR 2013 (HY000): Lost connection to MySQL server at
'reading initial communication packet', system error: 22
```

If you do, try authorizing a wider portion of your network's address space. For example, if your computer's address is `fba2:2c26:f4e4:8000:abcd:1234:b5ef:7051`, take the first four groups, then add `::/64`, like this: `fba2:2c26:f4e4:8000::/64`. Authorize that network, then try the `mysql` command again with the instance's IPv6 address.

A successful connection results in a `mysql>` prompt. You can enter SQL commands at this prompt. For example, the `show databases;` command lists the databases currently on the instance. MySQL always starts with several databases it uses for maintenance and configuration:

```
mysql> SHOW DATABASES;
+--------------------+
| Database           |
+--------------------+
| information_schema |
| mysql              |
| performance_schema |
+--------------------+
3 rows in set (0.07 sec)
```

Type quit to terminate the connection and close the client.

If you requested an IPv4 address and do not intend to connect remotely on a regular basis, you can remove the IP address to save on costs. Click Remove next to the IP address in the Access Control tab. Removing the address abandons it, and you may not get the same address the next time you request one.

If your network assigns IP addresses dynamically or you change networks, you may need to authorize a new address the next time you connect.

 Cloud SQL supports secure connections over SSL. You can set up SSL certificates from the Access Control tab for the instance. This is only needed if you want external clients to connect with SSL. Traffic between App Engine and Cloud SQL is always secure.

Setting Up a Database

Your Cloud SQL instance begins life with MySQL's initial databases, but no database for your app to use. The next step is to create a database for the app, then create one or more accounts with passwords and appropriate privileges to access the new database.

We'll continue using the mysql command-line client, but you might also use MySQL Workbench or some other tool to create the database and users. Remember that you will need to replicate these steps for your local server as well as the Cloud SQL instance, and possibly create more than one database with the same tables so you can use one for testing and another for the live app. Some web application frameworks have features to automate and replicate databases and tables for this purpose.

Set up a new connection with the mysql command as in the previous section, repeating the network authorization step if necessary. Use the root account and password. At the mysql> prompt, create a new database:

```
CREATE DATABASE mmorpg;
```

(As is traditional with SQL, we will capitalize SQL keywords, but you can type these in lowercase. Names and values are case sensitive. And don't forget the semicolon.)

You must enter another command to tell the MySQL client to use the new database for subsequent commands in this session. For subsequent sessions, you can give the database name as an argument to the `mysql` command, or just type this as the first SQL command in the session:

```
USE mmorpg;
```

The `root` account you are currently using has maximum privileges across the Cloud SQL instance, including the powers to create and delete entire databases. It's a good practice to use a separate account with limited privileges when connecting from your app. If a coding error in the app accidentally allows an attacker to run arbitrary SQL commands (a *SQL injection* attack), you can limit the damage to just the privileges granted to the app's account. Most apps need permission to `DELETE` rows from a table, but few apps need to be able to `DROP` databases, `GRANT` privileges to other accounts, or `SHUTDOWN` the server.

Some web application frameworks automate the management of tables, and need an account with wider privileges to create and delete tables than would normally be used by the app while handling user requests. If your framework allows it, you can create a separate account specifically for these management tools, and use a more limited account within the app itself.

To create a user, enter the `CREATE USER` command. The following command creates a user named `app` with the password `p4$$w0rd`:

```
CREATE USER 'app' IDENTIFIED BY 'p4$$w0rd';
```

You can change the password for this account later (as `root`) with the `SET PASSWORD` command:

```
SET PASSWORD FOR 'app' = PASSWORD('new-p4$$w0rd');
```

App Engine does not need a password to connect to a Cloud SQL instance, even when the account has a password set. You only need the password for connecting to the Cloud SQL instance from outside of App Engine. Your app code does need a password when connecting to your local development database if the local account has a password.

A new account starts with no privileges. To grant the `app` account the ability to `SELECT`, `INSERT`, `UPDATE`, and `DELETE` rows in all tables in the `mmorpg` database:

```
GRANT SELECT, INSERT, UPDATE, DELETE ON mmorpg.* TO 'app';
```

For accounts that need to create and drop tables, the `CREATE`, `DROP`, and `ALTER` privileges are also needed. `GRANT ALL ON mmorpg.*` will give the account complete access to the database. See the documentation on the GRANT statement (*http://dev.mysql.com/doc/refman/5.5/en/grant.html*) for more information about privileges.

We won't go into detail about how to create tables here. For now, here is a simple example of creating a table with a few columns in the mmorpg database:

```
CREATE TABLE guild (id VARCHAR(20) PRIMARY KEY, title VARCHAR(50),
                    created_date DATETIME, min_level INT);
```

You can test the app account by disconnecting (type quit) then reconnecting using the app username and password:

```
mysql --host=... --user=app -p
```

Use the mmorpg database, then list the tables:

```
USE mmorpg;
SHOW TABLES;
```

The list of tables includes the guild table we created:

```
mysql> show tables;
+------------------+
| Tables_in_mmorpg |
+------------------+
| guild            |
+------------------+
1 row in set (0.07 sec)
```

Still using the app account, try inserting a row:

```
INSERT INTO guild VALUES ('superawesomes', 'The Super Awesomes', NOW(), 7);
```

Select the rows of the table to see the newly added row:

```
SELECT * FROM guild;
```

Connecting to the Database from App Engine

It's time to try connecting to the database from App Engine code. With Python and MySQLdb, you use the Cloud SQL instance as you would any other database. The only difference is the initial connection: App Engine provides a named socket based on the name you provided when you created the instance. You use this name as part of an argument to the MySQLdb.connect() function.

Unlike the App Engine services and Cloud Datastore, the App Engine development server does not attempt to emulate the presence of Cloud SQL on your local computer. You must add code to your app that detects whether it is running in the development server and react accordingly. It's up to you whether you want the development server to connect to your local MySQL database, to a Cloud SQL instance or database reserved for testing, or to the Cloud SQL instance and database used by the live app. It's a good idea to use some kind of test database that is separate from the live database for your regular development, regardless of whether it lives on a separate Cloud SQL instance or your local machine.

What follows is a simple example that reads and displays the guild table, and prompts the user to add a row. We'll use a minimum of features to highlight the MySQLdb connection code. In a real app, you might use a framework to manage the SQL statements and form handling.

A file named *main.py* contains all of the code for connecting to the database, reading and displaying all rows in the table, and inserting a new row based on submitted form data:

```python
import jinja2
import logging
import MySQLdb
import os
import re
import webapp2

INSTANCE_NAME = 'saucy-boomerang-123:mydb'
DATABASE = 'mmorpg'
DB_USER = 'app'
DB_PASSWORD = 'p4$$w0rd'

template_env = jinja2.Environment(
    loader=jinja2.FileSystemLoader(os.getcwd()))

def get_db():
    if os.environ.get('SERVER_SOFTWARE', '').startswith('Development'):
        # This is a development server.
        db = MySQLdb.connect(host='127.0.0.1', port=3306,
                            db=DATABASE, user=DB_USER, passwd=DB_PASSWORD)
    else:
        # This is on App Engine.  A password is not needed.
        db = MySQLdb.connect(unix_socket='/cloudsql/' + INSTANCE_NAME,
                            db=DATABASE, user=DB_USER)
    return db

class MainPage(webapp2.RequestHandler):
    def get(self):
        guilds = []

        db = get_db()
        try:
            cursor = db.cursor()
            cursor.execute('SELECT id, title, created_date, '
                        'min_level FROM guild;')
            for (id, title, created_date, min_level) in cursor.fetchall():
                guilds.append({
                    'id': id,
```

```
                        'title': title,
                        'created_date': created_date,
                        'min_level': min_level
                    })
            finally:
                db.close()

            template = template_env.get_template('home.html')
            context = {
                'guilds': guilds,
            }
            self.response.out.write(template.render(context))

    def post(self):
        title = self.request.get('title').strip()
        min_level_str = self.request.get('min_level').strip()

        db = get_db()
        try:
            assert len(title) > 0
            min_level = int(min_level_str)

            key = re.sub(r'\W', '_', title.lower())

            cursor = db.cursor()
            cursor.execute('INSERT INTO guild VALUES (%s, %s, NOW(), %s);',
                        (key, title, min_level))
            db.commit()
        except (AssertionError, ValueError), e:
            logging.info('Invalid value from user: title=%r min_level=%r',
                        title, min_level_str)
        finally:
            db.close()

        self.redirect('/')

app = webapp2.WSGIApplication([('/', MainPage)], debug=True)
```

The file *home.html* contains the Jinja2 template for the list and form:

```
<!doctype html>
<html>
  <head>
    <title>Guild List</title>
  </head>
  <body>
    {% if guilds %}
    <p>Guilds:</p>
    <ul>
      {% for guild in guilds %}
      <li>
        {{ guild.title }},
        minimum level: {{ guild.min_level }},
```

```
      created {{ guild.created_date }}
    </li>
    {% endfor %}
  </ul>
  {% else %}
  <p>There are no guilds.</p>
  {% endif %}

  <p>Create a guild:</p>
  <form action="/" method="post">
    <label for="title">Title:</label>
    <input type="text" id="title" name="title" /><br />
    <label for="min_level">Minimum level:</label>
    <input type="text" id="min_level" name="min_level" /><br />
    <input type="submit" name="Create Guild" />
  </form>
  </body>
</html>
```

The *app.yaml* for the app routes all requests to the app:

```
application: myapp
version: 1
runtime: python27
api_version: 1
threadsafe: true

handlers:
- url: .*
  script: main.app

libraries:
- name: MySQLdb
  version: latest
- name: jinja2
  version: "2.6"
- name: markupsafe
  version: "0.15"
```

In this example, we define the function get_db() to prepare the database connection based on whether the app is running in a development server or on App Engine. We test for this using the SERVER_SOFTWARE environment variable, which is set by both the development server and App Engine:

```
if os.environ.get('SERVER_SOFTWARE', '').startswith('Development'):
    # This is a development server.
    # ...
else:
    # This is on App Engine.
    # ...
```

The MySQLdb.connect() function makes the connection. To connect to the local MySQL instance from the development server, we simply provide the localhost address `127.0.0.1`, the appropriate port number (`3306` by default), the name of the database, and the user and password we created earlier:

```
db = MySQLdb.connect(host='127.0.0.1', port=3306,
                     db=DATABASE, user=DB_USER, passwd=DB_PASSWORD)
```

When running on App Engine, we connect to the Cloud SQL instance. Instead of a host and port, we provide the path to a Unix socket that App Engine uses to locate the instance. The socket path is `/cloudsql/` followed by the name of the instance, including the project ID and a colon. For example, if the project ID is `saucy-boomerang-123` and we created an instance named `mydb`, the complete socket path is `/cloudsql/saucy-boomerang-123:mydb`.

Provide this path to the `MySQLdb.connect()` function as the `unix_socket` argument. Do not provide a password in this case: doing so will convince the library to try to connect to `localhost`, and you'll get a permissions error in your application logs. App Engine does not need a password when connecting to the instance, as it is specially authorized to do so. You still need to provide a username, which determines the database privileges for the app:

```
db = MySQLdb.connect(unix_socket='/cloudsql/' + INSTANCE_NAME,
                     db=DATABASE, user=DB_USER)
```

When you are done with the connection, be sure to call `db.close()` to free it:

```
try:
    # ...
finally:
    db.close()
```

You prepare a "cursor" object by calling the `db.cursor()` function, then execute a SQL statement by passing it to the `cursor.execute()` method. For statements that return results, you can fetch the results with a method such as `cursor.fetchall()`:

```
cursor = db.cursor()
cursor.execute('SELECT id, title, created_date, '
               'min_level FROM guild;')
for (id, title, created_date, min_level) in cursor.fetchall():
    # ...
```

When using values derived from an external source, such as data submitted by the user via a form, use parameter substitution: use a formatting placeholder such as `%s` in the SQL string for each value, then provide a tuple of values as the second argument to `cursor.execute()`:

```
cursor.execute('INSERT INTO guild VALUES (%s, %s, NOW(), %s);',
               (key, title, min_level))
```

Do not use a Python string formatting operator here! The value tuple must be the second argument to `cursor.execute()` for parameter substitution to be effective.

Parameter substitution prevents the data from being misconstrued as SQL statement syntax. This is especially important because it prevents *SQL injection attacks* from malicious users. (See "xkcd: Exploits of a Mom," by Randall Munroe (*http://xkcd.com/327/*).)

The MySQLdb calling code conforms to the Python DB standard. For more information about this API, see PEP 249: Python Database API Specification v2.0 (*https://www.python.org/dev/peps/pep-0249/*).

Backup and Restore

If you opted for backups when you created the instance, Cloud SQL performs regular backups of your database automatically. You can enable and disable backups at a later time from the Cloud Console by editing the instance configuration. You can also adjust the time of day during which backups occur.

To restore from a recent backup via the Cloud Console, select your Cloud SQL instance, then scroll down to Backups. Recent backups are listed by timestamp. Find the backup you want to restore, then click Restore.

Backups are intended for convenient and automatic recovery of the Cloud SQL instance. If you want to copy data out of Cloud Platform for archival storage or offline processing, you must export the data. (We'll cover this in the next section.)

Exporting and Importing Data

The Cloud Console provides a convenient way to import and export data from your database. The format for this data is a text file containing SQL statements, equivalent to using the `mysqldump` command.

Exports and imports use Google Cloud Storage for the data file. This can save you the cost of external bandwidth if you intend to manipulate the data file further using Google Cloud Platform, such as with a batch job running on App Engine or Compute Engine.

Each Cloud Storage object has a name (like a filename) and belongs to a *bucket* (like a directory). The path to a Cloud Storage object consists of `gs://`, the bucket name, a slash, and the object name:

```
gs://bucket-name/object-name
```

Bucket names must be unique across all of Cloud Storage, much like usernames. Cloud Storage reserves bucket names that look like domain names (containing dots) for the owners of the domains, so if you have verified ownership of your domain using Google Webmaster Tools (*https://www.google.com/webmasters/tools*), you can use your domain name as your bucket name. Otherwise, you can register any bucket name that hasn't already been registered by someone else.

You must create a Cloud Storage bucket before you can export Cloud SQL data. To create the bucket, go to the Cloud Console, then navigate to Storage, Cloud Storage, "Storage browser." Click "Create bucket" (or "Add bucket"), then enter a name for the bucket and click the Create button.

To export one or more databases from Cloud Console, navigate to the Cloud SQL instance, then click the Export... button. In the dialog, enter a Cloud Storage path using the bucket you just created, followed by a filename. A file of that name must not already exist in the bucket. Optionally, click "Show advanced options..." then enter the names of the databases to export. By default, all databases are exported. Click OK. The export takes a few moments to complete.

To access the exported data, return to the Storage browser, then select the bucket. The bucket contains the exported file you requested, as well as a log file. You can select these files in the Cloud Console to download them via your browser.

Importing data via the Cloud Console is similar. Go to the Storage browser, select the bucket, then click the "Upload files" button. Follow the prompts to select the data file on your local computer and upload it to the bucket. Next, navigate to the Cloud SQL instance, then click Import.... Enter the Cloud Storage path to the file you uploaded, then click OK. The import process reads the data file and executes the SQL statements inside it.

The file generated by an export includes SQL statements to drop tables before recreating them. Importing such a file effectively resets the tables to the state they were in at the time of export. It does not merge old data with new, nor does it result in duplicate rows.

 Because exported data is a file of SQL statements, you can save space and bandwidth by compressing the file. To export data compressed using the gzip file format, specify a file path that ends in .gz. To import a gzip-compressed file, make sure the path ends in .gz.

The gcloud sql Commands

All of the administrative features for Cloud SQL instances that you see in the Cloud Console are also available from the command line. The gcloud sql family of commands can create, delete, restart, and clone instances, as well as import and export data. These commands are an alternative to the Cloud Console for some interactive actions, and can also be used in scripts for automation.

Make sure `gcloud` is configured to use your project, you are signed in, and you have the `sql` component installed:

```
gcloud config set project project-id
gcloud auth login
gcloud components update sql
```

To list the current Cloud SQL instances for the project:

```
gcloud sql instances list
```

To get detailed information about the instance in YAML format:

```
gcloud sql instances describe instance-name
```

To get a list of automatic backups for the instance, each identified by a timestamp:

```
gcloud sql backups list --instance instance-name
```

To restore a backup from this list:

```
gcloud sql instances restore-backup --instance instance-name --due-time timestamp
```

You can initiate exports and imports from the command line as well. As with doing this from the Cloud Console, exports and imports use Cloud Storage for storing or reading data. To initiate an export of all databases on the instance to a given Cloud Storage path:

```
gcloud sql instances export instance-name gs://bucket-name/object-name
```

You can narrow the export to specific databases or tables using the `--database` and `--table` flags.

The command to import a file from Cloud Storage is similar:

```
gcloud sql instances import instance-name gs://bucket-name/object-name
```

Naturally, you can upload and download files to and from Cloud Storage from the command line as well. For this, you use the `gsutil` command. Make sure you have this command installed:

```
gcloud components update gsutil
```

To download a file from Cloud Storage:

```
gsutil cp gs://bucket-name/object-name .
```

Just like the `cp` command, `gsutil cp` takes a path to the file to copy, and a destination path. If the destination path is a directory path (like . for the current directory), the file is copied using its original filename.

To upload a file to Cloud Storage, use the `gsutil cp` command with a `gs://` path as the second argument:

```
gsutil cp filename.gz gs://bucket-name/object-name
```

The Cloud SDK command-line interface has many features for fetching SQL status and configuration as structured data, as well as for waiting for initiating operations asynchronously and waiting for operations to complete. You can use the `gcloud help` command to browse information on these features. For example, to learn about creating Cloud SQL instances from the command line:

```
gcloud help sql instances create
```

## CHAPTER 12

The Memory Cache

Durable data storage requires a storage medium that retains data through power loss and system restarts. Today's medium of choice is the hard drive, a storage device composed of circular platters coated with magnetic material on which data is encoded. The platters spin at a constant rate while a sensor moves along the radius, reading and writing bits on the platters as they travel past. Reading or writing a specific piece of data requires a *disk seek* to position the sensor at the proper radius and wait for the platter to rotate until the desired data is underneath. All things considered, hard drives are astonishingly fast, but for web applications, disk seeks can be costly. Fetching an entity from the datastore by key can take time on the order of tens of milliseconds.

Most high-performance web applications mitigate this cost with a *memory cache*. A memory cache uses a volatile storage medium, usually the RAM of the cache machines, for very fast read and write access to values. A *distributed memory cache* provides scalable, consistent temporary storage for distributed systems, so many processes on many machines can access the same data. Because memory is volatile—it gets erased during an outage—the cache is not useful for long-term storage, or even short-term primary storage for important data. But it's excellent as a secondary system for fast access to data also kept elsewhere, such as the datastore. It's also sufficient as global high-speed memory for some uses.

The App Engine distributed memory cache service, known as *memcache* in honor of the original memcached system that it resembles, stores key-value pairs. You can set a value with a key, and get the value given the key. A value can be up to a megabyte in size. A key is up to 250 bytes, and the API accepts larger keys and uses a hash algorithm to convert them to 250 bytes.

The memcache does not support transactions like the datastore does, but it does provide several atomic operations. Setting a single value in the cache is atomic: the key either gets the new value or retains the old one (or remains unset). You can tell memcache to set a value only if it hasn't changed since it was last fetched, a technique known as "compare and set" in the API. The App Engine memcache also includes the ability to increment and decrement numeric values as an atomic operation.

A common way to use the memcache with the datastore is to cache datastore entities by their keys. When you want to fetch an entity by key, you first check the memcache for a value with that key, and use it if found (known as a *cache hit*). If it's not in the memcache (a *cache miss*), you fetch it from the datastore, then put it in the memcache so future attempts to access it will find it there. At the expense of a small amount of overhead during the first fetch, subsequent fetches become much faster.

If the entity changes in the datastore, you can attempt to update the memcache when the entity is updated in the datastore, so subsequent requests can continue to go to the cache but see fresh data. This mostly works, but it has two minor problems. For one, it is possible that the memcache update will fail even if the datastore update succeeds, leaving old data in the cache. Also, if two processes update the same datastore entity, then update the memcache, the datastore will have correct data (thanks to datastore transactions), but the memcache update will have the value of whichever update occurs last. Because of this possibility, it's somewhat better to just delete the memcache key when the datastore changes, and let the next read attempt populate the cache with a current value. Naturally, the delete could also fail.

Because there is no way to update both the datastore and the memcache in a single transaction, there is no way to avoid the possibility that the cache may contain old data. To minimize the duration that the memcache will have a stale value, you can give the value an expiration time when you set it. When the expiration time elapses, the cache unsets the key, and a subsequent read results in a cache miss and triggers a fresh fetch from the datastore.

Of course, this caching pattern works for more than just datastore entities. You can use it for datastore queries, web service calls made with URL Fetch, expensive calculations, or any other data that can be replaced with a slow operation, where the benefits of fast access outweigh the possibility of staleness.

This is so often the case with web applications that a best practice is to cache aggressively. Look through your application for opportunities to make this trade-off, and implement caching whenever the same value is needed an arbitrary number of times, especially if that number increases with traffic. Site content such as an article on a news website often falls into this category. Caching speeds up requests and saves CPU time.

The APIs for the memcache service are straightforward. Let's look at each of the memcache features.

Calling Memcache from Python

The Python API for the memcache service is provided by the `google.appengine.api.memcache` package. The API comes in two flavors: a set of simple functions (such as `set()` and `get`), and a `Client` class whose methods are equivalent to the corresponding functions.

This API is intended to be compatible with the Python memcached library, which existing code or third-party libraries might use. When a feature of this library does not apply to App Engine, the method or argument for the feature is supported, but does nothing. We won't discuss the compatibility aspects here, but see the official documentation for more information.

The `Client` class supports one feature that the simple functions do not: compare-and-set. This mechanism needs to store state between calls, and does so on the `Client` instance. This class is not threadsafe, so be sure to create a new `Client` instance for each request handler, and don't store it in a global variable.

Here's a simple example that fetches a web feed by using the URL Fetch service (via App Engine's version of the `urllib2` library), stores it in the memcache, and uses the cached value until it expires five minutes (300 seconds) later. The key is the feed URL, and the value is the raw data returned by URL Fetch:

```python
import urllib2
from google.appengine.api import memcache

def get_feed(feed_url):
    feed_data = memcache.get(feed_url)
    if not feed_data:
        feed_data = urllib2.urlopen(feed_url).read()
        memcache.set(feed_url, feed_data, time=300)
    return feed_data
```

Keys and Values

The memcache service stores key-value pairs. To store a value, you provide both a key and a value. To get a value, you provide its key, and memcache returns the value.

Both the key and the value can be data of any type that can be serialized. The Python API serializes both the key and the value using the `pickle` module in the standard library.

The key can be of any size. App Engine converts the key data to 250 bytes by using a hash algorithm, which makes for a number of possible unique keys larger than a 1 followed by 600 zeroes. You generally don't have to think about the size of the key.

The value can be up to 1 megabyte in its serialized form. In practice, this means that pretty much anything that can fit in a datastore entity can also be a memcache value.

Setting Values

The simplest way to store a value in memcache is to set it. If no value exists for the given key, setting the value will create a new value in memcache for the key. If there is already a value for the key, it will be replaced with the new value.

In Python, you call either the set() function, or the equivalent method on a Client instance. The method returns True on success. It only returns False if there was an issue reaching the memcache service. Because memcache may evict (delete) values at any time, it is typical to ignore this return value:

```
success = memcache.set(key, value)

# Or:
memcache_client = memcache.Client()
success = memcache_client.set(key, value)

if not success:
    # There was a problem accessing memcache...
```

Setting Values That Expire

By default, a memcache value stays in the memcache until it is deleted by the app with a service call, or until it is evicted by the memcache service. The memcache service will evict a value if it runs out of space, or if a machine holding a value goes down or is turned down for maintenance.

When you set a value, you can specify an optional expiration time. If provided, the memcache service will make an effort to evict the value when the expiration time is reached. The timing may not be exact, but it'll be close. Setting an expiration time encourages a cache-backed process to refresh its data periodically, without the app having to track the age of a cached value and forcibly delete it.

To set an expiration for a value in Python, you include a time argument to set(). Its value is either a number of seconds in the future relative to the current time up to one month (2,592,000 seconds), or it is an absolute date and time as a Unix epoch date:

```
success = memcache.set(key, value, time=300)
```

A value's expiration date is updated every time the value is updated. If you replace a value with an expiration date, the new value does not inherit the old date. There is no way to query a key for "time until expiration."

Adding and Replacing Values

There are two subtle variations on setting a value: adding and replacing.

When you add a value with a given key, the value is created in memcache only if the key is not already set. If the key is set, adding the value will do nothing. This operation is atomic, so you can use the add operation to avoid a race condition between two request handlers doing related work.

Similarly, when you replace a value with a given key, the value is updated in memcache only if the key is set. If the key is not set, the replace operation does nothing, and the key remains unset. Replacing a value is useful if the absence of the value is meaningful to another process, such as to inspire a refresh after an expiration date. Note that, as with replacing values with set, the replaced value will need its own expiration date if the previous value had one, and there is no way to preserve the previous expiration after a replacement.

In Python, you invoke these variants using separate functions: add() and replace(). As with set(), these functions have equivalent methods on the Client class. Both of these methods accept the time argument for setting an expiration date on the added or replaced value. The return value is True on success—and unlike set(), the add or replace may fail due to the existence or absence of the key, so this might be useful to know:

```
success = memcache.add(key, value)
if not success:
    # The key is already set, or there was a problem accessing
    # memcache...

success = memcache.replace(key, value)
if not success:
    # The key is not set, or there was a problem accessing memcache...
```

If the memcache service is unavailable or there is an error accessing the service, attempts to set, add, or replace values report failure as if the put failed due to the set policy.

Getting Values

You can get a value out of the memcache by using its key.

In Python, you call the get() function (or method). If the key is not set, it returns None:

```
value = memcache.get(key)
if value is None:
    # The key was not set...
```

If the memcache service is unavailable, the memcache API behaves as if keys do not exist. Attempts to get values will behave as cache misses.

Deleting Values

An app can force an eviction of a value by deleting its key. The deletion is immediate, and atomic.

In Python, you pass the key to the `delete()` function or method. This returns one of three values: `memcache.DELETE_SUCCESSFUL` if the key existed and was deleted successfully, `memcache.DELETE_ITEM_MISSING` if there was no value with the given key, or `memcache.DELETE_NETWORK_FAILURE` if the delete could not be completed due to a service failure. These constants are defined such that if you don't care about the distinction between a successful delete and a missing key, you can use the result as a conditional expression. (`DELETE_NETWORK_FAILURE` is 0.)

```
success = memcache.delete(key)
if not success:
    # There was a problem accessing memcache...
```

Locking a Deleted Key

When you delete a value, you can tell memcache to lock the key for a period of time. During this time, attempts to add the key will fail as if the key is set, while attempts to get the value will return nothing. This is sometimes useful to give mechanisms that rely on an add-only policy some breathing room, so an immediate reading of the key doesn't cause confusion.

Only the add operation is affected by a delete lock. The set operation will always succeed, and will cancel the delete lock. The replace operation will fail during the lock period as long as the key is not set; it otherwise ignores the lock.

To lock the key when deleting in Python, you specify the optional `seconds` argument. Its value is either a number of seconds in the future up to a month, or an absolute Unix epoch date-time. The default is 0, which says not to use a lock:

```
success = memcache.delete(key, seconds=20)
```

Atomic Increment and Decrement

Memcache includes special support for incrementing and decrementing numeric values as atomic operations. This allows for multiple processes to contribute to a shared value in the cache without interfering with each other. With just the get and set operations we've seen so far, this would be difficult: incrementing a value would involve reading then setting the value with separate operations, and two concurrent processes might interleave these operations and produce an incorrect result. The atomic increment operation does not have this problem.

When considering using memcache for counting, remember that memcache is nondurable storage. Your process must be resilient to the counter value being evicted at any time. But there are many forms this resilience can take. For instance, the app can periodically save the counter value to the datastore, and detect and recover if the increment fails due to the key being unset. In other cases, the counter may be helpful but not strictly necessary, and the work can proceed without it. In practice, unexpected cache evictions are rare, but it's best to code defensively.

You can use the increment and decrement operations on any unsigned integer value. Memcache integers are 64 bits in size. Incrementing beyond the maximum 64-bit integer causes the value to wrap around to 0, and decrementing has the same behavior in reverse. If the value being incremented is not an integer, nothing changes.

When you call the increment operation, you can specify an optional initial value. Normally, the increment does nothing if the key is not set. If you specify an initial value and the key being incremented is not set, the key is set to the initial value, and the initial value is returned as the result of the operation.

The Python API provides two functions: incr() and decr(). Given a key as its sole argument, the functions will increment or decrement the corresponding integer value by 1, respectively. You can specify a different amount of change with the optional delta argument, which must be a nonnegative integer. In addition, you can specify an initial_value, which sets the value if the key is unset. Without an initial value, incrementing or decrementing an unset key has no effect. The function returns the new value, or None if the increment does not occur:

```python
# Increment by 1, if key is set. v = v + 1
result = memcache.incr(key)
if result is None:
    # The key is not set, or another error occurred...

# Increment by 9, or initialize to 0 if not set.
result = memcache.incr(key, delta=9, initial_value=0)

# Decrement by 3, if key is set. v = v - 3
result = memcache.decr(key, delta=3)
```

Compare and Set

While memcache does not support general-purpose transactions across multiple values, it does have a feature that provides a modest amount of transactionality for single values. The "compare and set" primitive operation sets a value if and only if it has not been updated since the last time the caller read the value. If the value was updated by another process, the caller's update does not occur, and the operation reports this condition. The caller can retry its calculation for another chance at a consistent update.

This is a simpler version of the optimistic concurrency control we saw with datastore transactions, with some important differences. "Compare and set" can only operate on one memcache value at a time. Because the value is retained in fast nondurable storage, there is no replication delay. Read and write operations occur simply in the order they arrive at the service.

The API for this feature consists of two methods: a different get operation that returns both the value and a unique identifier (the compare-and-set ID, or CAS ID) for the value that is meaningful to the memcache, and the compare-and-set operation that sends the previous CAS ID with the updated value. The CAS ID for a key in memcache changes whenever the key is updated, even if it is updated to the same value as it had before the update. The memcache service uses the provided CAS ID to decide whether the compare-and-set operation should succeed.

In Python, the CAS IDs of retrieved values are kept internal to the Client instance you use to interact with the service. You call a slightly different method for getting values, gets(), which knows to ask for and remember the CAS ID for the key. To update with "compare and set," you call the cas() method on a key previously retrieved using gets(). Arguments for these methods are similar to get() and set(). There are no function-style equivalents to these Client methods because the methods store the CAS IDs for keys in the client instance:

```
memcache_client = memcache.Client()

# Attempt to append a string to a memcache value.
retries = 3
while retries > 0:
    retries -= 1
    value = memcache_client.gets(key) or ''
    value += 'MORE DATA!\n'
    if memcache_client.cas(key, value):
        break
```

The Client instance keeps track of all CAS IDs returned by calls to the gets() method. You can reset the client's CAS ID store by calling the cas_reset() method.

Batching Calls to Memcache

The memcache service includes batching versions of its API methods, so you can combine operations in a single remote procedure call. As with the datastore's batch API, this can save time in cases where the app needs to perform the same operation on multiple independent values. And as with the datastore, batching is not transactional: some operations may succeed while others fail. The total size of the batch call parameters can be up to 32 megabytes, as can the total size of the return values.

The Python API includes separate batch functions for each operation, both as stand-alone functions and as `Client` methods. The names of the batch methods all end with `_multi`.

`set_multi()` sets multiple values. It takes a mapping of keys and values as its first argument, and an optional expiration `time` argument that applies to all values set. The method returns a list of keys *not* set. An empty list indicates that all values were set successfully:

```
value_dict = {}
for result in results:
    value_dict[key_for_result(result)] = result

keys_not_set = memcache.set_multi(value_dict)
if keys_not_set:
    # Keys in keys_not_set were not set...
```

`add_multi()` and `replace_multi()` behave similarly. They take a mapping argument and the optional `time` argument, and return a list of keys not set. As with `add()` and `replace()`, these methods may fail to set keys because they are already set, or are not set, respectively.

`get_multi()` takes a list of keys, and returns a mapping of keys to values for all keys that are set in memcache. If a provided key is not set, it is omitted from the result mapping:

```
value_dict = memcache.get_multi(keys)
for key in keys:
    if key not in value_dict:
        # key is unset...
    else:
        value = value_dict[key]
        # ...
```

`delete_multi()` takes a list of keys, and an optional `seconds` argument to lock all the keys from adds for a period of time. The method returns `True` if all keys were deleted successfully or are already unset, or `False` if any of the keys could not be deleted. Unlike `delete()`, `delete_multi()` does not distinguish between a successful delete and an unset key:

```
success = memcache.delete_multi(keys)
```

Batch increments and decrements are handled by a single method, `offset_multi()`. This method takes a mapping of keys to delta values, where positive delta values are increments and negative delta values are decrements. You can also provide a single `initial_value` argument, which applies to all keys in the mapping. The return value is a mapping of keys to updated values. If a key could not be incremented, its value in the result mapping is None:

```
increments = {}
for key in keys:
    increments[key] = increment_for_key(key)

value_dict = memcache.offset_multi(increments, initial_value=0)
```

To get multiple values for later use with "compare and set," you call the get_multi() method with an additional argument: for_cas=True. This returns a mapping of results just as it would without this argument, but it also stores the CAS IDs in the Client:

```
memcache_client = memcache.Client()

value_dict = memcache_client.get_multi(keys, for_cas=True)
```

To batch "compare and set" multiple values, you call the cas_multi() method with a mapping of keys and their new values. As with the other methods that update values, this method returns a list of keys not set successfully, with an empty list indicating success for all keys. If a key was not updated because it was updated since it was last retrieved, the key appears in the result list:

```
keys_not_set = memcache_client.cas_multi(value_dict)
```

Each Python batch function takes an optional key_prefix argument, a bytestring value. If provided, this prefix is prepended to every key sent to the service, and removed from every key returned by the service. This is useful as an inexpensive way to partition values. Note that key prefixes are distinct from namespaces:

```
prefix = 'alphabeta:'

value_dict = {'key1': 'value1',
              'key2': 'value2',
              'key3': 'value3'}
# Set 'alphabeta:key1', 'alphabeta:key2', 'alphabeta:key3'.
memcache.set_multi(value_dict, key_prefix=prefix)

keys = ['key1', 'key2', 'key3']
value_dict = memcache.get_multi(keys, key_prefix=prefix)
# value_dict['key1'] == 'value1'
# ('alphabeta:' does not appear in the value_dict keys.)
```

Memcache Administration

With the memcache service playing such an important role in the health and well-being of your application, it's important to understand how your app is using it under real-world conditions. App Engine provides a Memcache viewer in the Cloud Console (Compute, App Engine, Memcache), which shows you up-to-date statistics about your app's memcache data, and lets you browse, query, edit, and create values. You can also delete the entire contents of the cache from this panel, a drastic but sometimes necessary act.

The viewer displays the number of hits (successful attempts to get a value), the number of misses (attempts to get a value using a key that was unset), and the ratio of these numbers. The raw numbers are roughly over the lifetime of the app, but it's the ratio that's the more useful number: the higher the hit ratio, the more time is being saved by using a cached value instead of performing a slower query or calculation.

Also shown is the total number of items and the total size of all items. These numbers mostly serve as vague insight into the overall content of the cache. They don't apply to any fixed limits or billable quotas, and there's no need to worry if these numbers are large. Understanding the average item size might be useful if you're troubleshooting why small items used less frequently than very large items are getting evicted.

A particularly interesting statistic is the "oldest item age." This is a bit of a misnomer: it's actually the amount of time since the last access of the least recently accessed item, not the full age of that item. Under moderate load, this value approximates the amount of time a value can go without being accessed before it is evicted from the cache to make room for hotter items. You can think of it as a lower bound on the usefulness of the cache. Note that more popular cache items live longer than less popular ones, so this age refers to the least popular item in the cache.

You can use the Memcache panel to query, create, and modify a value in the memcache, if you have the key. The API lets you use any serializable data type for keys, and the Memcache panel can't support all possible types, so this feature is only good for some key types. String keys are supported for Python. Similarly, updating values from the panel is limited to several data types, including bytestrings, Unicode text strings, Booleans, and integers.

Lastly, the Memcache panel has a big scary button to flush the cache, evicting (deleting) all of its values. Hopefully you've engineered your app to not depend on a value being available in the cache, and clicking this button would only inconvenience the app while it reloads values from primary storage or other computation. But for an app of significant size under moderate traffic with a heavy reliance on the cache, flushing the cache can be disruptive. You may need this button to clear out data inconsistencies caused by a bug after deploying a fix (for example), but you may want to schedule the flush during a period of low traffic.

The Python development server includes a version of the Memcache viewer in the development server console, so you can inspect statistics, query specific (string) keys, and flush the contents of the simulated memcache service. With your development server running, visit the development server console, then select Memcache Viewer from the sidebar.

Cache Statistics

The memcache statistics shown in the Cloud Console are also available to your app through a simple API.

In Python, you fetch memcache statistics with the `get_stats()` method. This method returns a dictionary containing the statistics:

```python
import logging

stats = memcache.get_stats()

logging.info('Memcache statistics:')
for stat in stats.iteritems():
    logging.info('%s = %d' % stat)
```

Available statistics include the following:

hits
> The number of cache hits counted

misses
> The number of cache misses counted

items
> The number of items currently in the cache

bytes
> The total size of items currently in the cache

byte_hits
> The total number of bytes returned in response to cache hits, including keys and values

oldest_item_age
> The amount of time since the last access of the least recently accessed item in the cache, in milliseconds

Flushing the Memcache

You can delete every item in the memcache for your app, using a single API call. Just like the button in the Cloud Console, this action is all or nothing: there is no way to flush a subset of keys, beyond deleting known keys individually or in a batch call.

If your app makes heavy use of memcache to front-load datastore entities, keep in mind that flushing the cache may cause a spike in datastore traffic and slower request handlers as your app reloads the cache.

To flush the cache in Python, you call the `flush_all()` function. It returns `True` on success:

```
memcache.flush_all()
```

## CHAPTER 13

Fetching URLs and Web Resources

An App Engine application can connect to other sites on the Internet to retrieve data and communicate with web services. It does this not by opening a connection to the remote host from the application server, but through a scalable service called the URL Fetch service. This takes the burden of maintaining connections away from the app servers, and ensures that resource fetching performs well regardless of how many request handlers are fetching resources simultaneously. As with other parts of the App Engine infrastructure, the URL Fetch service is used by other Google applications to fetch web pages.

The URL Fetch service supports fetching URLs using the HTTP protocol as well as using HTTP with SSL (HTTPS). Other methods sometimes associated with URLs (such as FTP) are not supported.

Because the URL Fetch service is based on Google infrastructure, the service inherits a few restrictions that were put in place in the original design of the underlying HTTP proxy. The service supports the five most common HTTP actions (GET, POST, PUT, HEAD, and DELETE) but does not allow for others or for using a non-standard action. Also, it can only connect to TCP ports in several allowed ranges: 80–90, 440–450, and 1024–65535. By default, it uses port 80 for HTTP, and port 443 for HTTPS. The proxy uses HTTP 1.1 to connect to the remote host.

The outgoing request can contain URL parameters, a request body, and HTTP headers. A few headers cannot be modified for security reasons, which mostly means that an app cannot issue a malformed request, such as a request whose `Content-Length` header does not accurately reflect the actual content length of the request body. In these cases, the service uses the correct values, or does not include the header.

Request and response sizes are limited, but generous. A request can be up to 5 megabytes in size (including headers), and a response can be up to 32 megabytes in size.

The service waits for a response up to a time limit, or "deadline." The default fetch deadline is 5 seconds, but you can increase this on a per-request basis. The maximum deadline is 60 seconds during a user request, or 10 minutes during a task queue or scheduled task or from a backend. That is, the fetch deadline can be up to the request handler's own deadline, except for backends (which have none).

The Python runtime environment offers implementations of standard libraries used for fetching URLs that call the URL Fetch service behind the scenes. These are the `urllib`, `httplib`, and `urllib2` modules. These implementations give you a reasonable degree of portability and interoperability with other libraries.

Naturally, the standard interfaces do not give you complete access to the service's features. When using the standard libraries, the service uses the following default behaviors:

- If the remote host doesn't respond within 5 seconds, the request is canceled and a service exception is raised.
- The service follows HTTP redirects up to five times before returning the response to the application.
- Responses from remote hosts that exceed 32 megabytes in size are truncated to 32 megabytes. The application is not told whether the response is truncated.
- HTTP over SSL (HTTPS) URLs will use SSL to make the connection, but the service will not validate the server's security certificate. (The App Engine team has said certificate validation will become the default for the standard libraries in a future release, so check the App Engine website.)

All of these behaviors can be customized when calling the service APIs directly. You can increase the fetch response deadline, disable the automatic following of redirects, cause an exception to be thrown for responses that exceed the maximum size, and enable validation of certificates for HTTPS connections.

The development server simulates the URL Fetch service by making HTTP connections directly from your computer. If the remote host might behave differently when your app connects from your computer rather than from Google's proxy servers, be sure to test your URL Fetch calls on App Engine.

In this chapter, we introduce the standard-library and direct interfaces to the URL Fetch service. We also examine several features of the service, and how to use them from the direct APIs.

Fetching resources from remote hosts can take quite a bit of time. Like several other services, the URL Fetch service offers a way to call the service asynchronously, so your application can issue fetch requests and do other things while remote servers take their time to respond. See Chapter 17 for more information.

Fetching URLs

You call the URL Fetch service by using the `google.appengine.api.urlfetch` module, or you can use Python standard libraries such as `urllib2`.

The Python runtime environment overrides portions of the `urllib`, `urllib2`, and `httplib` modules in the Python standard library so that HTTP and HTTPS connections made with these modules use the URL Fetch service. This allows existing software that depends on these libraries to function on App Engine, as long as the requests function within certain limitations. `urllib2` has rich extensible support for features of remote web servers such as HTTP authentication and cookies. We won't go into the details of this module here, but Example 13-1 shows a brief example using the module's `urlopen()` convenience function.

Example 13-1. A simple example of using the urllib2 module to access the URL Fetch service

```
import urllib2
from google.appengine.api import urlfetch

# ...
        try:
            newsfeed = urllib2.urlopen('http://ae-book.appspot.com/blog/atom.xml/')
            newsfeed_xml = newsfeed.read()
        except urllib2.URLError, e:
            # Handle urllib2 error...

        except urlfetch.Error, e:
            # Handle urlfetch error...
```

In this example, we catch both exceptions raised by `urllib2` and exceptions raised from the URL Fetch Python API, `google.appengine.api.urlfetch`. The service may throw one of its own exceptions for conditions that `urllib2` doesn't catch, such as a request exceeding its deadline.

Because the service follows redirect responses by default (up to five times) when using `urllib2`, a `urllib2` redirect handler will not see all redirects, only the final response.

If you use the service API directly, you can customize these behaviors. Example 13-2 shows a similar example using the urlfetch module, with several options changed.

Example 13-2. Customizing URL Fetch behaviors, using the urlfetch module

```
from google.appengine.api import urlfetch

# ...
    try:
        newsfeed = urlfetch.fetch('http://ae-book.appspot.com/blog/atom.xml/',
                                  allow_truncated=False,
                                  follow_redirects=False,
                                  deadline=10)
        newsfeed_xml = newsfeed.content
    except urlfetch.Error, e:
        # Handle urlfetch error...
```

We'll consider the direct URL Fetch API for the rest of this chapter.

Outgoing HTTP Requests

An HTTP request can consist of a URL, an HTTP method, request headers, and a payload. Only the URL and HTTP method are required, and the API assumes you mean the HTTP GET method if you only provide a URL.

You fetch a URL using HTTP GET by passing the URL to the fetch() function in the google.appengine.api.urlfetch module:

```
from google.appengine.api import urlfetch

# ...
    response = urlfetch.fetch('http://www.example.com/feed.xml')
```

The URL

The URL consists of a scheme, a domain, an optional port, and a path. For example:

```
https://www.example.com:8081/private/feed.xml
```

In this example, https is the scheme, www.example.com is the domain, 8081 is the port, and /private/feed.xml is the path.

The URL Fetch service supports the http and https schemes. Other schemes, such as ftp, are not supported.

If no port is specified, the service will use the default port for the scheme: port 80 for HTTP, and port 443 for HTTPS. If you specify a port, it must be within 80–90, 440–450, or 1024–65535.

As a safety measure against accidental request loops in an application, the URL Fetch service will refuse to fetch the URL that maps to the request handler doing the fetching. An app can make connections to other URLs of its own, so request loops are still possible, but this restriction provides a simple sanity check.

As just shown, the API takes the URL as a string passed to the `fetch()` function as its first positional argument.

The HTTP Method and Payload

The HTTP method describes the general nature of the request, as codified by the HTTP standard. For example, the GET method asks for the data associated with the resource identified by the URL (such as a document or database record). The server is expected to verify that the request is allowed, then return the data in the response, without making changes to the resource. The POST method asks the server to modify records or perform an action, and the client usually includes a payload of data with the request.

The URL Fetch service can send requests using the GET, POST, PUT, HEAD, and DELETE methods. No other methods are supported.

You set the method by providing the `method` keyword argument to the `fetch()` function. The possible values are provided as constants by the `urlfetch` method. If the argument is omitted, it defaults to `urlfetch.GET`. To provide a payload, you set the `payload` keyword argument:

```
profile_data = profile.get_field_data()
response = urlfetch.fetch('http://www.example.com/profile/126542',
                          method=urlfetch.POST,
                          payload=new_profile_data)
```

Request Headers

Requests can include headers, a set of key-value pairs distinct from the payload that describe the client, the request, and the expected response. App Engine sets several headers automatically, such as `Content-Length`. Your app can provide additional headers that may be expected by the server.

The `fetch()` function accepts additional headers as the `headers` keyword argument. Its value is a mapping of header names to values:

```
response = urlfetch.fetch('http://www.example.com/article/roof_on_fire',
                          headers={'Accept-Charset': 'utf-8'},
                          payload=new_profile_data)
```

Some headers cannot be set directly by the application. This is primarily to discourage request forgery or invalid requests that could be used as an attack on some servers. Disallowed headers include `Content-Length` (which is set by App Engine automatically to the actual size of the request), `Host`, `Vary`, `Via`, `X-Forwarded-For`, and `X-ProxyUser-IP`.

The `User-Agent` header, which most servers use to identify the software of the client, can be set by the app. However, App Engine will append a string to this value identifying the request as coming from App Engine. This string includes your application ID. This is usually enough to allow an app to coax a server into serving content intended for a specific type of client (such as a specific brand or version of web browser), but it won't be a complete impersonation of such a client.

HTTP over SSL (HTTPS)

When the scheme of a URL is `https`, the URL Fetch service uses HTTP over SSL to connect to the remote server, encrypting both the request and the response.

The SSL protocol also allows the client to verify the identity of the remote host, to ensure it is talking directly to the host and traffic is not being intercepted by a malicious host (a "man in the middle" attack). This protocol involves security certificates and a process for clients to validate certificates.

By default, the URL Fetch service does *not* validate SSL certificates. With validation disabled, traffic is still encrypted, but the remote host's certificates are not validated before sending the request data. You can tell the URL Fetch service to enable validation of security certificates.

To enable certificate validation in Python, you provide the `validate_certificate=True` argument to `fetch()`:

```
response = urlfetch.fetch('https://secure.example.com/profile/126542',
                          validate_certificate=True)
```

The standard libraries use the default behavior and do not validate certificates. If you need to validate certificates, you must use the `urlfetch` API.

Request and Response Sizes

The request can be up to 5 megabytes in size, including the headers and payload. The response can be up to 32 megabytes in size.

The URL Fetch service can do one of two things if the remote host returns a response larger than 32 megabytes: it can truncate the response (delete everything after the first 32 megabytes), or it can raise an exception in your app. You control this behavior with an option.

The `fetch()` function accepts an `allow_truncated=True` keyword argument. The default is `False`, which tells the service to raise a `urlfetch.ResponseTooLargeError` if the response is too large:

```
response = urlfetch.fetch('http://www.example.com/firehose.dat',
                          allow_truncated=True)
```

The standard libraries tell the URL Fetch service to allow truncation. This ensures that the standard libraries won't raise an unfamiliar exception when third-party code fetches a URL, at the expense of returning unexpectedly truncated data when responses are too large.

Request Deadlines

The URL Fetch service issues a request, waits for the remote host to respond, and then makes the response available to the app. But the service won't wait on the remote host forever. By default, the service will wait 5 seconds before terminating the connection and raising an exception with your app.

You can adjust the amount of time the service will wait (the "deadline") as an option to the fetch call. You can set a deadline up to 60 seconds for fetches made during user requests, and up to 10 minutes (600 seconds) for requests made during tasks. That is, you can wait up to the maximum amount of time your request handler can run. Typically, you'll want to set a fetch deadline shorter than your request handler's deadline, so it can react to a failed fetch.

To set the fetch deadline, provide the `deadline` keyword argument, whose value is a number of seconds. If a fetch exceeds its deadline, the service raises a `urlfetch.Dead lineExceededError`:

```
response = urlfetch.fetch('http://www.example.com/users/ackermann',
                          deadline=30)
```

Handling Redirects

You can tell the service to follow redirects automatically, if HTTP redirect requests are returned by the remote server. The server will follow up to five redirects, then return the last response to the app (regardless of whether the last response is a redirect or not).

`urlfetch.fetch()` accepts a `follow_redirects=True` keyword argument. The default is `False`, which means to return the first response even if it's a redirect. When using the `urllib2`, redirects are followed automatically, up to five times:

```
response = urlfetch.fetch('http://www.example.com/bounce',
                          follow_redirects=True)
```

When following redirects, the service does not retain or use cookies set in the responses of the intermediate steps. If you need requests to honor cookies during a redirect chain, you must disable the automatic redirect feature, and process redirects manually in your application code.

Response Objects

The `fetch()` function returns an object with response data available on several named properties. (The class name for response objects is `_URLFetchResult`, which implies that only the `fetch()` function should be constructing these objects—or relying on the class name.)

The response fields are as follows:

`content`
>   The response body. A Python `str`.

`status_code`
>   The HTTP status code. An `int`.

`headers`
>   The response headers, as a mapping of names to values.

`final_url`
>   The URL that corresponds to the response data. If automatic redirects were enabled and the server issued one or more redirects, this is the URL of the final destination, which may differ from the request URL. A Python `str`.

`content_was_truncated`
>   `True` if truncation was enabled and the response data was larger than 32 megabytes.

## CHAPTER 14

Sending and Receiving Email Messages

While today's Internet offers many modes of communication, one of the oldest modes is still one of the most popular: email. For web applications, email is the primary mechanism for representing and validating identity, and managing access to application-specific accounts. Email is how your app reaches out to your users when they are not on your website and signed in.

An App Engine app can send email messages by calling the Mail service API. An app might send email to notify users of system events or the actions of other users (such as to send social networking invitations), confirm user actions (such as to confirm an order), follow up on long-term user actions (such as to send a shipping notice for an order), or send system notifications to administrators. The app can send email on behalf of itself or the app's administrators. The app can also send email on behalf of the currently signed-in user, during the request handler.

Sending email messages is similar to initiating HTTP requests: the app calls a service by using an API, and the service takes care of making remote connections and managing the appropriate protocols. Unlike the URL Fetch service, the Mail service does not return a response immediately. Instead, messages are enqueued for delivery, and errors are reported via "bounce" email messages to the sender address.

An app can also receive email messages sent to specific addresses. This might allow an app to provide an email interface to the application, or to moderate or monitor email discussions. The app can reply to the email immediately, or set up work that causes a reply to be sent later.

Receiving email messages is also similar to receiving HTTP requests. In fact, this uses the same mechanism: request handlers. When a service receives an email message intended for your app, the Mail service sends an HTTP request to the app using a specified URL with the message in the HTTP payload. The app processes incoming messages, using request handlers mapped to the specified URLs. The service ignores the response for the request; if the app needs to reply to the user, it can send a message using the API.

Figure 14-1 illustrates the flow of incoming email messages.

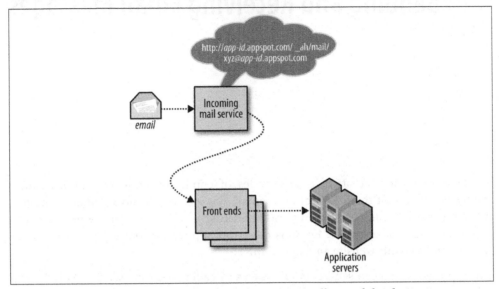

Figure 14-1. Architecture of incoming email messages, calling web hooks in response to incoming message events

Each app has its own set of incoming email addresses, based on its application ID. For email, the app can receive messages at addresses of these forms:

```
app-id@appspotmail.com

anything@app-id.appspotmail.com
```

App Engine does not support receiving email at an address on an app's custom domain name. However, you can use an email address on your custom domain as a "From" address by setting it up as a Google account, and then making that account a "developer" of the app in the Cloud Console. You can further configure automatic forwarding of replies to that address by using Gmail.

In this chapter, we discuss the APIs for sending and receiving email messages, and language-specific tools for creating and processing those messages.

Sending Email Messages

To send an email message, you call the API of the Mail service. The outgoing message has a sender address ("From"), one or more recipients ("To," "Cc," or "Bcc"), a subject, a message body, and optional file attachments.

An email message can contain a limited set of message headers, which are understood by mail servers and clients. The headers an app can set are restricted to prevent the service from being abused to send forged messages. (See the official documentation for the current list of allowed headers.) The Mail service attaches additional headers to the message, such as the date and time the message is sent.

You can specify a multipart message body, such as to include both plain text and HTML versions of the message, and to include attachments. The total size of the message, including all headers and attachments, cannot exceed 10 megabytes.

The call to the Mail service is asynchronous. When your application calls the Mail service to send a message, the message is enqueued for delivery, and the service call returns. If there is a problem delivering the message, such as if the remote mail server cannot be contacted or the remote server says the address is invalid, an error message is sent via email to the sender address. The app is not notified of the failure by the service directly. If the app must be notified of a message send failure, you can use an incoming email address for the app as the sender address. The app will have to parse the message sent by the remote server for an error.

When running on App Engine, outgoing email counts toward your outgoing bandwidth quota, as well as the quota for the total number of email recipients. You can increase these quotas by adjusting your billing settings. Email messages sent to the application administrators use a separate limit (Admins Emailed in the Quotas display of the Cloud Console) to allow for apps that send maintenance reports and alerts to administrators but do not need to send email to arbitrary recipients.

App Engine gives special treatment to the limit on email recipients to prevent abuse of the system, such as sending junk or scam email (which is against the terms of service and an all-around lousy thing to do). New apps are only allowed a small number of email recipients per month under the free plan. When you activate billing for an app for the first time, this limit is not raised until the first charge to your billing account succeeds. This is intended to discourage abusers from activating billing with invalid payment details just to temporarily raise the recipient limit.

If your app relies on sending email to many users (such as for registration confirmation), be sure to activate billing and test your email features two weeks in advance of launching your website.

Sending Email from the Development Server

When your app runs in the development server, sending a message causes the server to print information about the message to the logs, and no message is sent. In the development server, you can configure the server to actually send email messages by using either Sendmail (if it's set up on your machine) or an SMTP server.

To configure the Python development server to use Sendmail to send email, give the server the --enable_sendmail flag:

```
dev_appserver.py --enable_sendmail appdir
```

To configure the Python development server to use an SMTP server to send email, use the --smtp_host=... (with optional --smtp_port=...), --smtp_user=..., and --smtp_password=... arguments:

```
dev_appserver.py \
    --smtp_host=smtp.example.com \
    --smtp_user=exmail \
    --smtp_password="t3!!t43w0r!d" \
    appdir
```

Sender Addresses

The sender ("From") address on an outgoing email message must be one of the allowed addresses:

- The Google Account address of one of the application administrators
- The address of the user currently signed in to the app with Google Accounts (during the request handler that is sending the message)
- A valid incoming email address for the application

Replies to messages sent by the app go to the sender address, as do error messages sent by the outgoing mail server (such as "Could not connect to remote host") or the remote mail server (such as "User not found").

You can use an application developer's Google account address as the sender address. To add accounts as application administrators, go to the Developers section of the Cloud Console. If you do not want to use the account of a specific developer as the sender address, you can create a new Google account for a general-purpose address, then add it as a developer for the app: in the Console, select Permissions, then invite the user account. Be sure to select the Viewer role, so if someone gets the account's password, that person cannot make changes to the app. You can use Gmail to monitor the account for replies, and you can set up automatic email forwarding in Gmail to relay replies to specific administrators or a mailing list (or Google Group) automatically.

A Google account can use a Gmail address or a Google Apps domain address. If your app has a custom domain, you can create a new Google account with an address on the domain (such as `support@example.com`), give the account Viewer permissions for the app, and use the address for outgoing mail.

If you don't have a Google Apps domain, you can create a Gmail account using the application ID, and add `app-id@gmail.com` as a developer. Note that if you create the Gmail account before you register the application ID, you must be signed in using the Gmail account when you register the application ID. App Engine won't let you register an app ID that matches a Gmail account name unless you are signed in with that account.

You can use the email address of a user as the sender address if and only if the address is of a registered Google Account, the user is signed in, and the user initiated the request whose handler is sending the email. That is, you can send email on behalf of the "current" user. This is useful if the email is triggered by the user's action and if replies to the message ought to go to the user's email address. The Google Accounts API does not expose the user's human-readable name, so you won't be able to provide that unless you get it from the user yourself.

As we mentioned earlier, an application can receive email messages at addresses of the form `app-id@appspotmail.com` or `anything@app-id.appspotmail.com`, where `app-id` is your application ID and `anything` can be any string that's valid on the left side of the email address (it can't contain an @ symbol). You can use an incoming email address as the sender of an email message to have replies routed to a request handler.

The "anything" lets you create custom sender addresses on the fly. For example, a customer support app could start an email conversation with a unique ID and include the ID in the email address (`support+ID@app-id.appspotmail.com`), and save replies for that conversation in the datastore so the entire thread can be viewed by customer service personnel.

Note that the sender address will also receive error ("bounce") messages. If you use an incoming mail address as the sender, you could have the app process error messages to remove invalid email addresses automatically. Note that different remote email servers may use different formatting for error messages.

Any email address can also have a human-friendly name, such as `"The Example Team <admin@example.com>"`. How you do this is specific to the interface; we'll look at the interfaces in a moment.

You can include a separate "Reply-to" address in addition to the sender ("From") address. Most mail readers and servers will use this address instead of the sender address for replies and error messages. The "Reply-to" address must meet the same requirements as the sender address.

The development server does not check that the sender address meets these conditions because it doesn't know who the app's developers are. Be sure to test features that send email while running on App Engine.

Recipients

An outgoing email message can use any address for a recipient, and can have multiple recipients.

A recipient can be a primary recipient (the "To" field), a secondary or "carbon-copied" recipient (the "Cc" field), or a "blind carbon-copied" recipient ("Bcc"). The "To" and "Cc" recipients are included in the content of the message, so a reply intended for all recipients can be sent to the visible addresses. The "Bcc" recipients receive the message, but their addresses are not included in the content of the message, and so are not included in replies.

The "Bcc" recipient type is especially useful if you want a single message to go to multiple recipients, but you do not want any recipient to know who received the message. You can use this technique to send an email newsletter to users without exposing the users' email addresses. A common technique for newsletters is to use the sender address as the sole "To" recipient, and make everyone else a "Bcc" recipient.

The number of recipients for an email message counts toward an email recipient quota. This quota is initially small to prevent unsolicited email advertisers from abusing the system. You can raise this quota by allocating part of your budget toward email recipients.

 When you enable billing in your app for the first time, the email recipients quota will not increase from the free level until your first payment is processed. This is one of several measures to prevent spammers from abusing the service.

Attachments

An app can attach files to an email message. One good use of attachments is to include images for rich HTML email messages.

For security reasons (mostly having to do with insecure email clients), some file types are not allowed as email attachments. A file's type is determined by its filename extension. For example, files that represent executable programs (such as *.exe*, *.bat*, or *.sh*) are not allowed. Some file archive types like *.zip* are allowed, but the archive cannot contain files that are executable programs.

The MIME content type of each attachment is derived from the filename extension. If a filename extension is not recognized, the content type is set to `application/octet-stream`.

See the official documentation for the complete list of disallowed attachment types, as well as a list of mappings from extensions to MIME content types.

 If you want to deliver files to users that are not allowed as attachments, one option is to send a link to a request handler that delivers the file through the browser. The link can be personalized with a temporary unique ID, or restricted using Google Accounts authentication.

Sending Email

The API includes two ways of preparing and sending messages. One way is to call a function with the fields of the message as keyword arguments. Another is to prepare the message in an object, then call a method on the object to send the message. The Mail service API is provided by the `google.appengine.api.mail` package.

The `send_mail()` method takes the fields of the message as parameters:

```
from google.appengine.api import mail
from google.appengine.api import users

message_body = '''
Welcome to Example!  Your account has been created.
You can edit your user profile by clicking the
following link:

http://www.example.com/profile/

Let us know if you have any questions.

The Example Team
'''

# (admin@example.com is a Google Account that has
# been added as a developer for the app.)
mail.send_mail(
    sender='The Example Team <admin@example.com>',
    to=users.get_current_user().email(),
    subject='Welcome to Example.com!',
    body=message_body)
```

Alternatively, you can prepare the message using an `EmailMessage` object, then call its `send()` method. The `EmailMessage` constructor accepts the same arguments as the `send_mail()` function:

```
message = mail.EmailMessage(
    sender='The Example Team <admin@example.com>',
    to=users.get_current_user().email(),
    subject='Welcome to Example.com!',
    body=message_body)

message.send()
```

You can also set the fields of an `EmailMessage` using attributes of the object. This allows you to reuse the same object to send multiple messages with modified values.

The possible fields of a message are listed in Table 14-1.

Table 14-1. Fields of an email message in the Python interface

Field	Value	Required?
sender	The sender's email address. A string.	Required
to	A "To" recipient address as a string, or multiple "To" recipient addresses as a list of strings.	Required
subject	The subject of the message. A string.	Required
body	The plain-text body of the message. A string.	Required
cc	A "Cc" recipient address as a string, or multiple "Cc" recipient addresses as a list of strings.	Optional
bcc	A "Bcc" recipient address as a string, or multiple "Bcc" recipient addresses as a list of strings. "Bcc" recipients receive the message, but are not included in the content of the message.	Optional
reply_to	An alternative address to which clients should send replies instead of the sender address. A string.	Optional
html	An alternative HTML representation of the body of the message, displayed instead of body by HTML-capable email readers. A string.	Optional
attach ments	File attachments for the message. A list of tuples, one per attachment, each containing the filename and the file data.	Optional
headers	A `dict` of additional message headers. See the official documentation for a list of allowed headers.	Optional

The value of an email address field (sender, to, cc, bcc, reply_to) can be a plain email address:

```
'juliet@example.com'
```

It can also be an address with a human-readable name, in the standard format (RFC 822):

```
'Juliet <juliet@example.com>'
```

When you call the send() method or the send_mail() function, the API checks the message to make sure it is valid. This includes testing the email addresses for validity, and making sure the message has all the required fields. You can call functions to perform these checks separately. The is_email_valid(address) function returns True if it considers an email address valid. The is_initialized() method of an EmailAddress object returns True if the object has all the fields necessary for sending.

The API includes a shortcut method that sends an email message to all administrators (developers) for the application. The send_mail_to_admins() function accepts the same arguments as send_mail(), but without the recipient fields. There is also an AdminEmailMessage class that is similar to the EmailMessage class, but with recipients set to be the app administrators automatically. When calling this function, the message size is limited to 16 kilobytes. (This is a safety limit that ensures delivery of important administrative messages.)

Example 14-1 shows a larger example using EmailMessage, with both plain-text and HTML parts, and an attachment.

Example 14-1. An example of sending an email message in Python, using several features

```python
from google.appengine.api import mail

def send_registration_key(user_addr, software_key_data):
    message_body = '''
Thank you for purchasing The Example App, the best
example on the market!  Your registration key is attached
to this email.

To install your key, download the attachment, then select
"Register..." from the Help menu.  Select the key file, then
click "Register".

You can download the app at any time from:
  http://www.example.com/downloads/

Thanks again!

The Example Team
```

```
'''

html_message_body = '''
<p>Thank you for purchasing The Example App, the best
example on the market!  Your registration key is attached
to this email.</p>

<p>To install your key, download the attachment, then select
<b>Register...</b> from the <b>Help</b> menu.  Select the key file, then
click <b>Register</b>.</p>

<p>You can download the app at any time from:</p>

<p>
  <a href="http://www.example.com/downloads/">
    http://www.example.com/downloads/
  </a>
</p>

<p>Thanks again!</p>

<p>The Example Team<br />
<img src="http://www.example.com/images/logo_email.gif" /></p>
'''

message = mail.EmailMessage(
    sender='The Example Team <admin@example.com>',
    to=user_addr,
    subject='Your Example Registration Key',
    body=message_body,
    html=html_message_body,
    attachments=[('example_key.txt', software_key_data)])

message.send()
```

Receiving Email Messages

To receive incoming email messages, you must first enable the feature in your app's configuration. Incoming email is disabled by default, so unwanted messages are ignored and do not try to contact your app or incur costs.

To enable inbound services, you add a section to the app's configuration file. In Python, you add a section similar to the following in the *app.yaml* file:

```
inbound_services:
- mail
```

Once your app is deployed, you can confirm that the incoming mail service is enabled from the Cloud Console, under Application Settings. If your app does not appear to be receiving HTTP requests for incoming email messages, check the Console and update the configuration if necessary.

With the `mail` inbound service enabled in configuration, an application can receive email messages at any of several addresses. An incoming mail message is routed to the app in the form of an HTTP request.

Email sent to addresses of the following forms are routed to the default version of the app:

app-id@appspotmail.com

anything@*app-id*.appspotmail.com

The HTTP request uses the POST action, and is sent to the following URL path:

/_ah/mail/*to-address*

The recipient email address of the message is included at the end of the URL path, so the app can distinguish between different values of "anything."

The body content of the HTTP POST request is the complete MIME email message, including the mail headers and body. It can be parsed by any library capable of parsing MIME email messages.

The development server console (*http://localhost:8000/*) includes a feature for simulating incoming email by submitting a web form. The development server cannot receive actual email messages.

 If the app has the incoming mail service enabled but does not have a request handler for the appropriate URL, or if the request handler returns an HTTP response code other than 200 for the request, the message gets "bounced" and the sender receives an error email message.

To configure your app to receive email, you map the incoming email URL path to a script handler in the *app.yaml* file:

```
handlers:
- url: /_ah/mail/.+
  script: handle_email.application
```

The app address used for the message is included in the URL path, so you can set up separate handlers for different addresses directly in the configuration:

```
handlers:
- url: /_ah/mail/support%40.*app-id\.appspotmail\.com
  script: support_contact.application
- url: /_ah/mail/.+
  script: handle_email.application
```

Email addresses are URL-encoded in the final URL, so this pattern uses %40 to represent an @ symbol. Also notice you must include a .* before the application ID when using this technique, so the pattern works for messages sent to version-specific addresses (such as `support@dev.app-id.appspotmail.com`).

The Python SDK includes a class for parsing the POST content into a convenient object, called `InboundEmailMessage` (in the `google.appengine.api.mail` package). It takes the multipart MIME data (the POST body) as an argument to its constructor. Here's an example using the webapp framework:

```python
from google.appengine.api import mail
from google.appengine.ext import webapp2

class IncomingMailHandler(webapp2.RequestHandler):
    def post(self):
        message = mail.InboundEmailMessage(self.request.body)
        sender = message.sender
        recipients = message.to
        body = list(message.bodies(content_type='text/plain'))[0]
        # ...

application = webapp2.WSGIApplication([('/_ah/mail/.+', IncomingMailHandler)],
                                      debug=True)
```

The `InboundEmailMessage` object includes attributes for the fields of the message, similar to `EmailMessage`. `sender` is the sender's email address, possibly with a displayable name in the standard format (Mr. Sender *<sender@example.com>*). `to` is a list of primary recipient addresses, and `cc` is a list of secondary recipients. (There is no `bcc` on an incoming message, because blind-carbon-copied recipients are not included in the message content.) `subject` is the message's subject.

The `InboundEmailMessage` object may have more than one message body: an HTML body and a plain-text body. You can iterate over the MIME multipart parts of the types `text/html` and `text/plain`, using the `bodies()` method. Without arguments, this method returns an iterator that returns the HTML parts first, and then the plain-text parts. You can limit the parts returned to just the HTML or plain-text parts by setting the `content_type` parameter. For example, to get just the plain-text bodies:

```python
for text_body in message.bodies(content_type='text/plain'):
    # ...
```

In the example earlier, we extracted the first plain-text body by passing the iterator to the `list()` type, then indexing its first argument (which assumes one exists):

```python
text = list(message.bodies(content_type='text/plain'))[0]
```

If the incoming message has file attachments, then these are accessible on the `attachments` attribute. As with using `EmailMessage` for sending, this attribute is a list of tuples whose first element is the filename and whose second element is the data byte string. `InboundEmailMessage` allows all file types for incoming attachments, and does not require that the filename accurately represent the file type. *Be careful* when using files sent to the app by users, as they may not be what they say they are, and have not been scanned for viruses.

The Python SDK includes a convenient webapp handler base class for processing incoming email, called InboundMailHandler in the google.appen gine.ext.webapp.mail_handlers package. You use the handler by creating a subclass that overrides the receive() method, then installing it like any other handler. When the handler receives an email message, the receive() method is called with an InboundEmailMessage object as its argument:

```
from google.appengine.ext.webapp import mail_handlers

class MyMailHandler(mail_handlers.InboundMailHandler):
    def receive(self, message):
        # ...

application = webapp2.WSGIApplication([('/_ah/mail/.+', MyMailHandler)],
                                      debug=True)
```

## CHAPTER 15

Sending and Receiving Instant Messages with XMPP

So far, we've seen two mechanisms an app can use to communicate with the outside world. The first and most prominent of these is HTTP: an app can receive and respond to HTTP requests, and can send HTTP requests to other hosts and receive responses with the URL Fetch service. The second is email: an app can send email messages by using the Mail service, and can receive messages via a proxy that calls a request handler for each incoming email message.

In this chapter, we introduce a third method of communication: XMPP, also known as "instant messages," or simply "chat." An app can participate in a chat dialogue with a user of any XMPP-compatible chat service. The XMPP service is useful for chat interfaces, such as a chat-based query engine, or a customer service proxy. App Engine does not act as an XMPP service itself. Instead, it connects to Google's own XMPP infrastructure to participate as a chat user.

Sending and receiving XMPP messages works similarly to email messages. To send a message, an app calls the XMPP service API. To receive a message, the app declares that it accepts such messages in its configuration, and then handles HTTP requests sent by the XMPP service to special-purpose URLs. Figure 15-1 illustrates the flow of incoming XMPP messages.

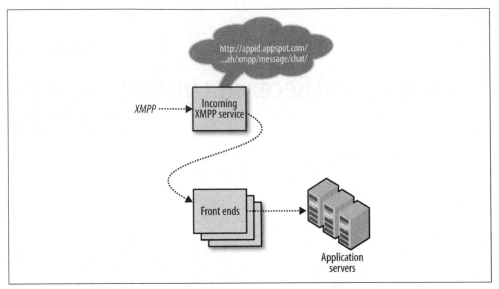

Figure 15-1. Architecture of incoming XMPP messages, calling web hooks in response to incoming message events

Each participant in an XMPP communication has an address similar to an email address, known as a *JID*. (JID is short for "Jabber ID," named after the Jabber project, where XMPP originated.) A JID consists of a username, an "at" symbol (@), and the domain name of the XMPP server. A JID can also have an optional "resource" string, which is used to identify specific clients connected to the service with the username. A message sent to the ID without the resource goes to all connected clients:

```
username @ domain / resource
```

To send a message, a chat participant sends an XMPP message to its own XMPP server. The participant's chat service contacts the recipient service's host by using the domain name of the JID and a standard port, then delivers the message. If the remote service accepts messages for the JID and someone is connected to the service with a chat client for that JID, the service delivers the message to the client.

As with email, each app has its own set of JIDs, based on its application ID. For XMPP chat, the app can receive messages at addresses of these forms:

```
app-id@appspot.com
```

```
anything@app-id.appspotchat.com
```

(Notice the differences in the domain names from the options available for incoming email.)

App Engine does not support XMPP addresses on a custom domain. This is one of only a few cases where exposing your application ID to users cannot be avoided.

Let's take a look at the features and API of the XMPP service.

Inviting a User to Chat

Before a user of an XMPP-compatible instant messaging service will see any messages your app sends, the service needs to know that the user is expecting your messages. This can happen in two ways: either the user explicitly adds your app's JID to her contact list, or she accepts an invitation to chat sent by the app.

An app can send an invitation to chat by calling the XMPP service API. For apps, it's polite to get the user's permission to do this first, so the complete workflow looks something like this:

1. The user visits the website, and activates the chat-based feature of the service, providing a JID.
2. The app sends an invitation to chat to the user's JID.
3. The user accepts the invitation in her chat client.
4. The user and app exchange chat messages.

The alternative where the user adds the app's JID to her contact list is usually equivalent to sending an invitation to the app. App Engine accepts all such invitations automatically, even if the app does not accept chat messages.

An accepted invitation entitles both parties to know the other party's *presence* status, whether the party is connected and accepting messages. This includes the ability to know when an invitation is accepted. (For more information, see "Managing Presence" on page 324.)

In the development server, inviting a user to chat emits a log message, but otherwise does nothing.

To invite a user to chat, you call the send_invite() function in the google.appengine.api.xmpp module. It takes the recipient JID as its first argument, and an optional sender JID (from_jid) as its second argument. By default, it uses app-id@appspot.com as the sender JID:

```
from google.appengine.api import xmpp

jid = 'juliet@example.com'

xmpp.send_invite(jid)  # from app-id@appspot.com

xmpp.send_invite(jid, from_jid='support@app-id.appspotchat.com')
```

Sending Chat Messages

An XMPP message includes a sender address, one or more recipient addresses, a message type, and a message body.

The sender address must be one of the app's incoming XMPP addresses. These are of the form `app-id@appspot.com` or `anything@app-id.appspotchat.com`, where `app-id` is your application ID and `anything` can be any string that's valid on the left side of a JID (it can't contain an @ symbol). Unlike incoming email addresses, it's not as convenient to use the "anything" form for creating IDs on the fly, because the recipient needs to accept an invitation from that ID before receiving messages. But it can still be useful for sessions that begin with an invitation, or addresses that represent specific purposes or users of the app (`support@app-id.appspotchat.com`).

If the version of the app that is sending an XMPP message is not the default version, App Engine modifies the sender address to a version-specific address, so replies go directly to the correct version: either `anything@version.app-id.appspotchat.com` or `app-id@version.app-id.appspotchat.com`.

App Engine adds a "resource" to the end of the sender JID (after the domain name) that looks like this: `/bot`. This is mostly just to comply with the best practice of sending messages using JIDs with resources. It isn't noticed by chat users, and is not needed when a user wishes to send a message to the app. You'll see it in log messages.

The message type can be any of the types in the XMPP standard, including chat, error, groupchat, headline, and normal. An app can only receive messages of the types chat, normal, and error, and so cannot participate in group chats. For straightforward communication between an app and a chat user, you usually want to send chat messages. For an app and a custom client, you can do what you like.

Messages are sent asynchronously. The service call returns immediately, and reports success only if the XMPP service enqueued the message successfully. You can configure the app to receive error messages, such as to be notified if a sent message was not received because the user went offline. (See "Handling Error Messages" on page 323.)

When an app is running in the development server, sending an XMPP chat message or invitation causes the server to print the message to the console. The development server does not contact the XMPP service or send messages.

To send a chat message in Python, you call the send_message() function in the goo
gle.appengine.api.xmpp module. The function takes a JID or list of JIDs, the body
of the message, and an optional sender JID (from_jid). It returns a success code, or a
list of success codes, one for each recipient JID:

```
result = xmpp.send_message(
    'juliet@example.com',
    'Your dog has reached level 12!')

if result != xmpp.NO_ERROR:
    # ...
```

By default, this sends a message of the "chat" type. You can send a message of a different type by setting the message_type parameter. Acceptable values include:

- xmpp.MESSAGE_TYPE_CHAT (the default)

- xmpp.MESSAGE_TYPE_ERROR

- xmpp.MESSAGE_TYPE_GROUPCHAT

- xmpp.MESSAGE_TYPE_HEADLINE

- xmpp.MESSAGE_TYPE_NORMAL

Complete XMPP messages are sent over the network as XML data. By default,
send_message() treats the text of the message as plain text, and knows to escape
XML characters. Instead of a text message, you can send an XML stanza. This is
included verbatim (assuming the stanza is well formed) in the XMPP message, so you
can send structured data to XMPP clients. To tell send_message() that the content is
an XML stanza so it doesn't escape XML characters, provide the raw_xml=True
parameter.

The send_message() function returns a status code for each recipient JID, as a single
value if called with a single JID, or as a list of codes if called with a list of JIDs. The
possible status values are:

- xmpp.NO_ERROR

- xmpp.INVALID_JID

- xmpp.OTHER_ERROR

Receiving Chat Messages

As with email, to receive incoming XMPP messages, you must first enable the feature by adding the XMPP inbound services to your app's *app.yaml* configuration file:

```
inbound_services:
- xmpp_message
```

This is the same configuration list as the `mail` inbound service. If you're enabling both email and XMPP, you provide one list of inbound services with all the items.

Deploy your app, and confirm that incoming XMPP is enabled using the Cloud Console, under Application Settings. If your app does not appear to be receiving HTTP requests for incoming XMPP messages, check the Console and update the configuration if necessary.

The `xmpp_message` inbound service routes incoming XMPP messages of the types chat and normal to your app.

An app receives XMPP messages at several addresses. Messages sent to addresses of these forms are routed to the default version of the app:

> `app-id@appspot.com`

> `anything@app-id.appspotchat.com`

Messages sent to addresses of this form are routed to the specified version of the app, useful for testing:

> `anything@version.app-id.appspotmail.com`

Each message is delivered to the app as an HTTP POST request to a fixed URL path. Chat messages (both chat and normal) become POST requests to this URL path:

> `/_ah/xmpp/message/chat/`

(Unlike incoming email, the sender JID is not included in these URL paths.)

The body content of the HTTP POST request is a MIME multipart message, with a part for each field of the message:

`from`
> The sender's JID

`to`
> The app JID to which this message was sent

`body`
> The message body content (with characters as they were originally typed)

`stanza`
> The full XML stanza of the message, including the previous fields (with XML special characters escaped); useful for communicating with a custom client using XML

The API includes classes for parsing the request data into objects. (See the sections that follow.)

The development server console (*http://localhost:8000/*) includes a feature for simulating incoming XMPP messages by submitting a web form. The development server cannot receive actual XMPP messages.

 When using the development server console to simulate an incoming XMPP message, you must use a valid JID for the app in the "To:" field, with the application ID that appears in the app's configuration. Using any other "To:" address in the development server is an error.

To handle the incoming messages, you map the URL path to a script handler in the *app.yaml* file, as usual:

```
handlers:
- url: /_ah/xmpp/message/chat/
  script: handle_xmpp.application
  login: admin
```

As with all web hook URLs in App Engine, this URL handler can be restricted to `admin` to prevent anything other than the XMPP service from activating the request handler.

The Python library provides a `Message` class that can contain an incoming chat message. You can parse the incoming message into a `Message` object by passing a mapping of the POST parameters to its constructor. With the webapp2 framework, this is a simple matter of passing the parsed POST data (a mapping of the POST parameter names to values) in directly:

```
from google.appengine.api import xmpp
from google.appengine.ext import webapp2

class IncomingXMPPHandler(webapp2.RequestHandler):
    def post(self):
        message = xmpp.Message(self.request.POST)

        message.reply('I got your message! '
                      'It had %d characters.' % len(message.body))

application = webapp2.WSGIApplication([('/_ah/xmpp/message/chat/',
                                        IncomingXMPPHandler)],
                                      debug=True)
```

The `Message` object has attributes for each message field: sender, to, and body. (The attribute for the "from" field is named `sender` because `from` is a Python keyword.) It also includes a convenience method for replying to the message, `reply()`, which takes the body of the reply as its first argument.

Handling Commands over Chat

The `Message` class includes methods for parsing chat-style commands of this form:

```
/commandname args
```

If the chat message body is of this form, the `command` attribute of the `Message` is the command name (without the slash), and the `arg` attribute is everything that follows. If the message is not of this form, `command` is `None`.

webapp includes a request handler base class that makes it easy to implement chat interfaces that perform user-issued commands. Here's an example that responds to the commands /stats and /score username, and ignores all other messages:

```python
from google.appengine.api import xmpp
from google.appengine.ext import webapp2
from google.appengine.ext.webapp import xmpp_handlers

def get_stats():
    # ...

def get_score_for_user(username):
    # ...

class UnknownUserError(Exception):
    pass

class ScoreBotHandler(xmpp_handlers.CommandHandler):
    def stats_command(self, message):
        stats = get_stats()
        if stats:
            message.reply('The latest stats: %s' % stats)
        else:
            message.reply('Stats are not available right now.')

    def score_command(self, message):
        try:
            score = get_score_for_user(message.arg)
            message.reply('Score for user %s: %d' % (message.arg, score))
        except UnknownUserError, e:
            message.reply('Unknown user %s' % message.arg)

application = webapp2.WSGIApplication(
    [('/_ah/xmpp/message/chat/', ScoreBotHandler)],
    debug=True)
```

The `CommandHandler` base class, provided by the `google.appen` `gine.ext.webapp.xmpp_handlers` package, parses the incoming message for a command. If the message contains such a command, the handler attempts to call a method named after the command. For example, consider a scenario where the app receives this chat message:

```
/score druidjane
```

The handler will call the `score_command()` method with a message where `message.arg` is `'druidjane'`.

If there is no method for the parsed command, the handler will call the `unhandled_command()` method, whose default implementation replies to the message with "Unknown command." You can override this method to customize its behavior.

The base handler calls the command method with the `Message` object as an argument. The method can use the `command` and `arg` properties to read the parsed command.

If the incoming message does not start with a `/commandname`-style command, the base handler calls the `text_message()` method with the `Message` as its argument. The default implementation does nothing, and you can override it to specify behavior in this case.

This package also contains a simpler handler class named `BaseHandler`, with several useful features. It parses incoming messages, and logs and ignores malformed messages. If a message is valid, it calls its `message_received()` method, which you override with the intended behavior. The class also overrides `webapp.RequestHandler`'s `handle_exception()` method to send an XMPP reply with a generic error message when an uncaught exception occurs, so the user isn't left to wonder whether the message was received. (`CommandHandler` extends `BaseHandler`, and so also has these features.)

Handling Error Messages

When an app calls the XMPP service to send a message, the message is queued for delivery and sent asynchronously with the call. The call will only return with an error if the message the app is sending is malformed. If the app wants to know about an error during delivery of the message (such as the inability to connect to a remote server), or an error returned by the remote XMPP server (such as a nonexistent user), it can listen for error messages.

Error messages are just another type of chat message, but the XMPP service separates incoming error messages into a separate inbound service. To enable this service, add the `xmpp_error` inbound service to the app's *app.yaml* configuration file:

```
inbound_services:
- xmpp_message
- xmpp_error
```

Error messages arrive as POST requests at this URL path:

```
/_ah/xmpp/error/
```

You handle an error message just as you would a chat message: create a request handler, map it to the URL path, and parse the POST request for more information.

The SDK's library doesn't provide any assistance parsing incoming error messages. While XMPP error messages are similar in structure to chat messages (with a type of error), minor differences are not recognized by the message parsers provided. You can examine the XML data structure in the POST message body, which conforms to the XMPP message standard. (See the XMPP specification (*http://xmpp.org/*) for details.)

Managing Presence

After the user accepts an app's invitation to chat, both parties are able to see whether the other party is available to receive chat messages. In XMPP RFC 3921 (*http://xmpp.org/rfcs/rfc3921.html*), this is known as *presence*. The process of asking for and granting permission to see presence is called *subscription*. For privacy reasons, one user must be successfully subscribed to the other before she can send messages, see presence information, or otherwise know the user exists.

When a user accepts an app's invitation to chat (subscription request), the user's client sends a "subscribed" message to the app, to confirm that the app is now subscribed. If, later, the user revokes this permission, the client sends an "unsubscribed" message. While the app is subscribed to a user, the user's client will send all changes in presence to the app as another kind of message.

Conversely, a user can also send "subscribe" and "unsubscribe" messages to the app. It's the app's responsibility to maintain a list of subscribed users to use when sending presence updates.

If you'd like to receive these new message types (and be billed for the bandwidth), you must enable these as separate inbound services. Subscription information (invitation responses and subscription requests) use the xmpp_subscribe service, and presence updates use the xmpp_presence service.

Here's the configuration for *app.yaml* that enables all four XMPP inbound message types:

```
inbound_services:
- xmpp_message
- xmpp_error
```

```
- xmpp_subscribe
- xmpp_presence
```

 If you want to know when a user accepts or revokes your app's chat invitation, but otherwise do not need to see the user's presence updates, you can enable the `xmpp_subscribe` service without the `xmpp_presence` service. This can save on costs associated with the incoming bandwidth of changes in the user's presence, which can be frequent.

As with chat messages, you can simulate incoming subscription and presence messages in the development server by using the development server console. Outgoing subscription and presence messages in the development server are logged to the console, but not actually sent.

Managing Subscriptions

An app subscribes to a user when it sends an invitation to chat, with the `send_invite()` function. An app cannot send an explicit "unsubscribe" message, only "subscribe."

When the user accepts the invitation, her chat client sends a `subscribed` message to the app. If the user later revokes the invitation, the client sends an `unsubscribed` message.

These messages arrive via the `xmpp_subscribe` inbound service as POST requests on the following URL paths:

```
/_ah/xmpp/subscription/subscribed/
/_ah/xmpp/subscription/unsubscribed/
```

A user can send an explicit subscription request (invitation to chat) to the app by sending a `subscribe` message. Similarly, the user can explicitly unsubscribe from presence updates by sending an `unsubscribe` message. These arrive at the following URL paths:

```
/_ah/xmpp/subscription/subscribe/
/_ah/xmpp/subscription/unsubscribe/
```

The subscription process typically happens just once in the lifetime of the relationship between two chat users. After the users are successfully subscribed, they remain subscribed until one party explicitly unsubscribes from the other (`unsubscribe`), or one party revokes the other party's invitation (`unsubscribed`).

If you intend for your app to have visible changes in presence, the app must maintain a roster of subscribers based on `subscribe` and `unsubscribe` messages, and send updates only to subscribed users.

Incoming subscription-related requests include form-style fields in the POST data, with the following fields:

`from`
> The sender's JID

`to`
> The app JID to which this message was sent

`stanza`
> The full XML stanza of the subscription message, including the previous fields

Because the POST data for these requests does not contain a body field, you cannot use the SDK's `Message` class to parse the data. You access these fields simply as POST form fields in the request.

The app gets the subscription command from the URL path.

Here is an outline for a request handler that processes subscription-related messages, using Python and webapp2:

```python
import webapp2
from google.appengine.api import xmpp

def truncate_jid(jid):
    # Remove the "resource" portion of a JID.
    if jid:
        i = jid.find('/')
        if i != -1:
            jid = jid[:i]
    return jid

class SubscriptionHandler(webapp2.RequestHandler):
    def post(self, command):
        user_jid = truncate_jid(self.request.POST.get('from'))

        if command == 'subscribed':
            # User accepted a chat invitation.
            # ...

        if command == 'unsubscribed':
            # User revoked a chat invitation.
            # ...

        if command == 'subscribe':
            # User wants presence updates from the app.
            # ...

        if command == 'unsubscribed':
            # User no longer wants presence updates from the app.
            # ...
```

```
application = webapp2.WSGIApplication(
    [('/_ah/xmpp/subscription/(.*)/', SubscriptionHandler)],
    debug=True)
```

As mentioned earlier, an app sends a subscription request ('subscribe') to a user by calling the xmpp.send_invite(jid) function. There is no way to send an 'unsubscribe' message from an app. If the app no longer cares about a user's presence messages, the only choice is to ignore the incoming presence updates from that user.

Managing Presence Updates

While an app is subscribed to a user, the user sends changes in presence to the app. If the app is configured to receive inbound presence messages via the xmpp_presence service, these messages arrive as POST requests on one of these URL paths:

```
/_ah/xmpp/presence/available/
/_ah/xmpp/presence/unavailable/
```

Chat clients typically send an available message when connecting, and an unavailable message when disconnecting (or going "invisible").

A presence message can also contain additional status information: the *presence show* ("show me as") value and a *status message*. Most chat clients represent the show value as a colored dot or icon, and may display the status message as well. And of course, most chat clients allow the user to change the show value and the message. The possible show values, along with how they typically appear in chat clients, are as follows:

chat
> The user is available to chat. Green, "available."

away
> The user is away from her computer temporarily and not available to chat. Yellow, "away." A typical chat client switches to this presence show value automatically when the user is away from the keyboard.

dnd
> "Do not disturb": the user may be at her computer, but does not want to receive chat messages. Red, "busy."

xa
> "Extended away": the user is not available to chat and is away for an extended period. Red.

In XMPP, availability and the presence show value are distinct concepts. For a user to appear as "busy," the user must be available. For example, a red-colored "busy" user is available, with a show value of "dnd." Chat clients represent unavailable users either with a grey icon or by showing the user in another list.

An incoming presence update request includes form-style fields in the POST data, with the following fields:

from
> The sender's JID

to
> The app JID to which this message was sent

show
> One of several standard presence show values; if omitted, this implies the "chat" presence

status
> A custom status message; only present if the user has a custom status message set, or is changing her status message

stanza
> The full XML stanza of the subscription message, including the previous fields

An app can notify users of its own presence by sending a presence message. If the app's presence changes, it should attempt to send a presence message to every user known to be subscribed to the app. To support this, the app should listen for "subscribe" and "unsubscribe" messages, and keep a list of subscribed users, as described in "Managing Subscriptions" on page 325.

An app should also send a presence message to a user if it receives a *presence probe* message from that user. (See "Probing for Presence" on page 330.)

As with chat and subscription messages, the development server can simulate incoming presence messages. However, it cannot include presence show and status strings in these updates.

Here is an outline for a request handler for processing incoming presence updates, using webapp2:

```
import webapp2
from google.appengine.api import xmpp

def truncate_jid(jid):
    # Remove the "resource" portion of a JID.
    if jid:
        i = jid.find('/')
        if i != -1:
            jid = jid[:i]
    return jid
```

```
class PresenceHandler(webapp2.RequestHandler):
    def post(self, command):
        user_jid = truncate_jid(self.request.POST.get('from'))

        if command == 'available':
            # The user is available.

            show = self.request.POST.get('show')
            status_message = self.request.POST.get('status')
            # ...

        elif command == 'unavailable':
            # The user is unavailable (disconnected).
            # ...

application = webapp2.WSGIApplication(
    [('/_ah/xmpp/presence/(.*)/', PresenceHandler)],
    debug=True)
```

To send a presence update to a single user in Python, you need to call the
`xmpp.send_presence()` method:

```
xmpp.send_presence(user_jid,
                   status="Doing fine.",
                   presence_type=xmpp.PRESENCE_TYPE_AVAILABLE,
                   presence_show=xmpp.PRESENCE_SHOW_CHAT)
```

The `send_presence()` function takes the `jid`, a `status` message (up to 1 kilobyte),
the `presence_type`, and the `presence_show` as arguments. `presence_type` is
either `xmpp.PRESENCE_TYPE_AVAILABLE` or `xmpp.PRESENCE_TYPE_UNAVAILABLE`.
`presence_show` is one of the standard presence show values, which are also available
as library constants: `xmpp.PRESENCE_SHOW_CHAT`, `xmpp.PRESENCE_SHOW_AWAY`,
`xmpp.PRESENCE_SHOW_DND`, and `xmpp.PRESENCE_SHOW_XA`.

When the app wishes to broadcast a change in presence, it must
call `send_presence()` once for each user currently subscribed to
the app. Unlike `send_message()`, you can't pass a list of JIDs to
`send_presence()` to send many updates in one API call. A best
practice is to use task queues to query your data for subscribed
users and send presence updates in batches. (See Chapter 16 for
more information on task queues.)

Probing for Presence

Chat services broadcast presence updates to subscribed users as a user's presence changes. But this is only useful while the subscribed users are online. When a user comes online after a period of being disconnected (such as if her computer was turned off or not on the Internet), the user's client must *probe* the users in her contact list to get updated presence information.

When a user sends a probe to an app, it comes in via the `xmpp_presence` inbound service, as a POST request to this URL path:

    /_ah/xmpp/presence/probe/

The POST data contains the following fields:

`from`
> The sender's JID

`to`
> The app JID to which this message was sent

`stanza`
> The full XML stanza of the subscription message, including the previous fields

If your app receives this message, it should respond immediately by sending a presence update just to that user.

An app can send a presence probe message to a user. If the app is subscribed to the user, the user will send a presence message to the app in the usual way.

In the development server, outgoing probe messages are logged to the console, and not actually sent. There is currently no way to simulate an incoming probe message in the development console.

Here's how you would extend the `PresenceHandler` in the previous Python example to respond to presence probes:

```python
class PresenceHandler(webapp2.RequestHandler):
    def post(self, command):
        user_jid = truncate_jid(self.request.POST.get('from'))

        if command == 'available':
            # ...
        elif command == 'unavailable':
            # ...

        elif command == 'probe':
            # The user is requesting the app's presence information.
            xmpp.send_presence(
                user_jid,
```

```
presence_type=xmpp.PRESENCE_TYPE_AVAILABLE,
presence_show=xmpp.PRESENCE_SHOW_CHAT)
```

To send a presence probe to a user, you call xmpp.send_presence() with a presence_type of xmpp.PRESENCE_TYPE_PROBE:

```
xmpp.send_presence(jid, presence_type=xmpp.PRESENCE_TYPE_PROBE)
```

The reply comes back as a presence update message.

## CHAPTER 16

Task Queues and Scheduled Tasks

The App Engine architecture is well suited for handling web requests, small amounts of work that run in a stateless environment with the intent of returning a response to the user as fast as possible. But many web applications have other kinds of work that need to get done, work that doesn't fit in the fast response model. Instead of doing the work while the user waits, it's often acceptable to record what work needs to get done, respond to the user right away, then do the work later, within seconds or minutes. The ability to make this trade-off is especially useful with scalable web applications that use a read-optimized datastore, because updating an element of data may require several related but time-consuming updates, and it may not be essential for those updates to happen right away.

Consider a simple example. You're the leader of your guild, and you're scheduling a raid on the Lair of the Basilisk for next Thursday. When you post the invitation, two things need to happen: the raid is recorded on the guild calendar, and an invitation is sent to each member of the guild by email. If the app tries to do all of this in a single request handler, you might be staring at the browser's spinning wheel for a while as the app calls the Mail API for each member of the guild. For a particularly large guild, the request handler might not even finish within 60 seconds, you'll see a server error, and only some members will see the invitation. How do we fix this?

What we need is a way to do work outside of a user-facing request handler. By "outside," we mean code that is run separately from the code that evaluates a request from a user and returns a response to the user. This work can run in parallel to the user-facing request handler, or after the request handler has returned a response, or completely independently of user requests. We also need a way to request that this work be done.

App Engine has two major mechanisms for initiating this kind of work: *task queues* and *scheduled tasks*. A *task* is simply a request that a unit of work be performed separately from the code requesting the task. Any application code can call the task queue service to request a task, and the task queue manages the process of driving the task to completion. Scheduled tasks are tasks that are invoked on a schedule that you define in a configuration file, separately from any application code or queue (although a scheduled task is welcome to add other tasks to a queue, as is any other task running on App Engine).

In the terminology of task queues, a *producer* is a process that requests that work be done. The producer *enqueues* a task that represents the work onto a queue. A *consumer* is a process, separate from the producer, that *leases* tasks on the queue that it intends to perform. If the consumer performs a task successfully, it deletes the task from the queue so no other consumer tries to perform it. If the consumer fails to delete the task, the queue assumes the task was not completed successfully, and after an amount of time, the lease expires and becomes available again to other consumers. A consumer may also explicitly revoke the lease if it can't perform the task.

Task queues are a general category for two mechanisms for driving work to completion: *push queues* and *pull queues*. With push queues, App Engine is the consumer: it executes tasks on the queues at configurable rates, and retries tasks that return a failure code. With pull queues, you provide the consumer mechanism that leases task records off of a queue, does the work they represent, and then deletes them from the queue. Your custom mechanism can run on App Engine, or it can run on your own infrastructure and pull tasks, using a REST API.

To perform a task on a push queue, App Engine does what it does best: it invokes a request handler! You can configure a URL path in your app per queue, or specify a specific URL path when you enqueue a task. To implement the task, you simply implement a request handler for requests sent to that URL. Naturally, you can secure these URLs against outside requests, so only tasks can trigger that logic. This is why we've been making a distinction between "user-facing" request handlers and other handlers. All code on App Engine runs in a request handler, and typically code for handling user requests is distinct from code for performing tasks.

Scheduled tasks also run on App Engine, and also use request handlers. You configure a schedule of URL paths and times, and App Engine calls your application at those URL paths at the requested times. Scheduled tasks are not retried to completion, but you can achieve this effect by having a scheduled task enqueue a task on a queue.

All of these mechanisms support a major design goal for App Engine applications: do as much work outside of user-facing requests as possible, so user-facing requests are as fast as possible. Task queues allow your code to request that work be done separately from the current unit of work. Scheduled tasks initiate computation on a predefined schedule, independently of other code. The results of this work can be stored in the datastore, memcache, and Cloud Storage, so user-facing request handlers can retrieve and serve it quickly, without doing the work itself.

Enqueueing a task is fast, about three times faster than writing to the datastore. This makes tasks useful for pretty much anything whose success or failure doesn't need to be reported to the user in the response to the user request that initiates the work. For example, an app can write a value to the memcache, then enqueue a task to persist that value to the datastore. This saves time during the user request, and allows the task to do bookkeeping or make other time-consuming updates based on the change (assuming it meets the application's needs that the bookkeeping happens later than the initial update).

App Engine invokes a request handler for a push queue task or scheduled task in the same environment as it does a handler for a user request, with a few minor differences. Most notably, a task handler can run continuously for up to 10 minutes, instead of 60 seconds for user-facing request handlers. In some cases, it can be better to implement task handlers with short running times, then split a batch of work over multiple tasks, so the tasks can be executed in parallel in multiple threads or on multiple instances. But 10 minutes of headroom let you simplify your code for work that can or must take its time on an instance.

Figure 16-1 illustrates how task queues and scheduled tasks take advantage of the request handler infrastructure.

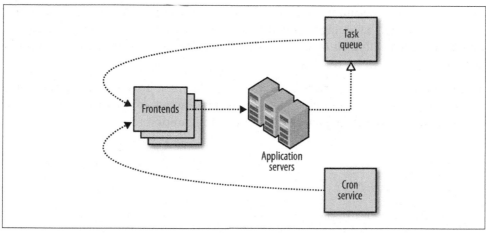

Figure 16-1. Architecture of push queues and scheduled tasks ("cron")

The development server maintains push and pull queues, and can run push queues in the background and simulate their timing and throttling behaviors. Of course, it won't be as fast as running on App Engine, but it's enough to test the behavior. You can use the development server console to inspect the configured queues, check their contents, and delete individual tasks or all tasks on a queue ("Purge Queue"). With push queues, you can also force a task to run from the console.

Basilisk raid invitations are now easy. When you submit the raid event creation form, a single request handler stores the event information in the datastore, initiates a task, then returns a success code. Later, possibly mere seconds later, App Engine pops the task off the task queue and calls the "send email" handler. This task can run for up to 10 minutes, so it can just iterate over all of the guild members and send an email for each one. If there are so many members that 10 minutes isn't enough, the handler can enqueue another task, storing a datastore query cursor with the task data to mark where it left off. Everyone shows up, and the raid is a smashing success.

Task queues are an important part of App Engine, with several powerful features for structuring your work and optimizing your application's behavior. Not the least of these features is how task queues integrate with the App Engine datastore transactions. In this chapter, we describe the concepts of task queues and scheduled tasks, and how to use them in applications. We take a brief look at pull queues and consider how they are useful. We cover using tasks and datastore transactions to achieve special effects, especially eventually consistent data operations and task chaining. And finally, we review the queue-related features of the Cloud Console.

Configuring Task Queues

Every app has one default push queue with default settings. You can use a configuration file to change the settings of the default push queue, create new named push and pull queues each with their own settings, and set global parameters for task queues in general.

To configure task queues, create a file named *queue.yaml*. This is a YAML file (same as *app.yaml*). Here is an example file that updates the rate of the default queue, and defines a new named push queue with its own configuration:

```
queue:
- name: default
  rate: 10/s
- name: attack_effects
  rate: 100/s
  bucket_size: 20
```

(We'll see what these settings do in a moment.)

Task queues contain durable data, and this storage counts toward your billable storage quota, just like data in the datastore. You can set a total limit for the amount of task queue data to store with configuration. In *queue.yaml*, this setting is named `total_storage_limit`:

```
total_storage_limit: 200M

queue:
# ...
```

Its value is a number followed by a unit of storage measurement, such as M for megabytes, G for gigabytes, or T for terabytes.

The default mode for a queue is to be a push queue. To declare a queue a pull queue, you set the mode of the queue to pull:

```
queue:
- name: process_images
  mode: pull
```

We'll mention additional configuration options when we discuss push queues and pull queues in more detail.

Task queue configuration is uploaded when you deploy your application. You can upload new task queue configuration separately from the rest of your app with the AppCfg tool's update_queues command:

```
appcfg.py update_queues appdir
```

 Task queue configuration is distinct from application configuration (*app.yaml*), and is kept in a separate file. Unlike application configuration, task queue configuration modifies the behavior of task queues for the entire application. All application versions use the same task queue configuration.

Enqueuing a Task

Your app adds a task to a queue (it *enqueues* the task) by calling the task queue service API with appropriate arguments. Some arguments are specific to push queues or pull queues, but the main API is the same for both.

An application enqueues tasks by using the API provided by the google.appengine.api.labs.taskqueue module. The simplest way to enqueue a task is to call the add() function. Without arguments, the add() function enqueues a task to the default queue by using the default options for that queue:

```
from google.appengine.api import taskqueue

# ...
        taskqueue.add()
```

The default queue is a push queue, so App Engine will process this task by invoking a request handler at a URL path. The default URL path for the default queue is:

```
/_ah/queue/default
```

You map the URL to a request handler that performs the task in the *app.yaml* file. You can restrict the URL so that it can only be called by task queues and by the app's developers (for testing), using `login: admin`, like so:

```
handlers:
- url: /_ah/queue/default
  script: default_task.app
  login: admin
```

With this configuration, the no-argument call to the `add()` function enqueues the task on the default queue with the default URL and no arguments. When the task queue processes this task, it issues an HTTP POST request with default arguments to the URL path /_ah/queue/default, which invokes the *default_task.app* request handler.

The `add()` function returns immediately after the task is enqueued. The actual execution of the task happens separately from the rest of the code that called `add()`.

You can pass arguments to the `add()` function to specify aspects of the task or the queue. The Python API offers an object-oriented alternative with the `Task` and `Queue` classes. For example, here are several ways to add a task to a queue named `reward_players`:

```
# Add a task to the reward_players queue, using the add() function.
taskqueue.add(queue_name='reward_players')

# Construct a Task, and add it to the reward_players queue,
# using its add() method.
t = taskqueue.Task()
t.add(queue_name='reward_players')

# Construct a Queue for the reward_players queue, then add
# a Task to it.
t = taskqueue.Task()
q = taskqueue.Queue('reward_players')
q.add(t)
```

As shown, the `queue_name` argument to the `add()` function, the `Task` object's `add()` method, or the `Queue` constructor, specifies the queue name. This corresponds with the `name` queue configuration parameter in *queue.yaml*. If the queue name is anything other than `'default'`, the queue must appear in the configuration file with the `name` parameter for the queue to exist.

You set parameters of the task itself by passing keyword arguments to either the `add()` function or the `Task` constructor. We'll introduce these parameters in a moment.

You can add multiple tasks to a single queue in a single service call (a batch call). You must use the Queue object's add() method for this. To make a batch call, pass an iterable of Task objects as the first argument to add():

```
# ...
    tasks = []
    for e in elems:
        tasks.append(Task(params=e.params))

    queue = Queue('process_elems')
    queue.add(tasks)
```

 Tasks are routed and handled by the app like any other request. If you want a task queue task (or cron job) to be processed by a module other than the default module, use a *dispatch.yaml* file to route requests for a URL path to the module, then assign that URL to the tasks. (Refer back to Chapter 5.)

Task Parameters

A task record on a queue carries two kinds of parameters: parameters that are passed on to the code or system performing the task, and parameters that affect how the task is managed on the queue. You set these parameters when you enqueue the task. After the task is enqueued, the parameters can't be changed, although you can delete and re-create a task, as needed.

The following sections describe task parameters common to both push queues and pull queues. We'll look at mode-specific options later.

Payloads

A task's *payload* is a set of data intended for the system performing the task. You don't need a payload if the task handler already knows what to do, but it's useful to write task handling code in a general way, and parameterize its behavior with a payload.

For example, you could have a task that performs a transformation on a datastore entity, such as to update its property layout to a new schema. The task handler would take the ID of an entity to transform, and perform one transformation. You'd then have a process (possibly also managed with task queues) that traverses all the entities that need transformation with a datastore query, and creates a task for each entity, using the task handler and a payload.

For convenience, the task API has two ways to set a payload: as a byte string, or as a set of named parameters with byte string values. When you set a payload as a set of parameters, the data is formatted like a web form (application/x-www-form-urlencoded), so the task handler can parse the payload into parameters, using typical web request handling code. Payloads and parameters are mutually exclusive: you set one or the other, not both.

To set a payload, you specify either the payload argument as a str, or the params argument as a mapping of names to values. A parameter value may be a string, or a list of strings:

```
taskqueue.add(payload=img_data)

taskqueue.add(params={'entity_key': str(e.key()), 'version': '7'})

t = taskqueue.Task(payload=img_data)
q = taskqueue.Queue()
q.add(t)
```

Task Names

Every task has a unique name. By default, App Engine will generate a unique name for a task when it is added to a queue. You can also set the task name in the app. A task name can be up to 500 characters, and can contain letters, numbers, underscores, and hyphens.

If an app sets the name for a task and another task already exists for that name on a given queue, the API will raise an exception when the app adds the task to the queue. Task names prevent the app from enqueuing the same task more than once on the same queue. App Engine remembers in-use task names for a period of time after the task completes, on the order of days. (The remembered names are called *tombstones* or *tombstoned tasks*.)

This is especially useful when enqueuing a task from within a push task handler. Consider the datastore entity transformation example again. A master task performs a datastore query, then creates a transformation task for each entity in the results, like so:

```
class MasterTaskHandler(webapp2.RequestHandler):
    def post(self):
        for entity in models.MyEntity.all():
            taskqueue.add(queue_name='upgrade',
                          params={'entity_key': str(entity.key()),
                                  'version': '7'})
```

If there is a datastore error while the master task is fetching results, the datastore raises an exception, which bubbles up to webapp, and the request handler returns an HTTP 500 server error. The push queue sees the error, then retries the master task from the beginning. If the first run of the master task successfully enqueued some tasks for entities to the 'upgrade' queue, those entities will be added to the queue again, wasting work.

The master task handler can guard against this by using a task name for each task that uniquely represents the work. In the preceding example, a good task name might be the entity's key concatenated with the upgrade version (the two parameters to the task):

```
import re
import webapp2

from google.appengine.api import taskqueue

class MasterTaskHandler(webapp2.RequestHandler):
    def post(self):
        for entity in models.MyEntity.all():
            try:
                task_name = str(entity.key()) + 'v7'
                task_name = re.sub('[^a-zA-Z0-9_-]', '_', task_name)
                taskqueue.add(queue_name='upgrade',
                              name=task_name,
                              params={'entity_key': str(entity.key()),
                                      'version': '7'})
            except taskqueue.DuplicateTaskNameError, e:
                pass
```

As seen here, you set the task name with the `name` parameter. An attempt to add a task with a name already in use raises a `DuplicateTaskNameError`. (In this example, we catch and ignore the exception because we can be confident that the task is enqueued and will be completed.)

 Take care when using datastore keys, query cursors, and other values as parts of task names that the resulting name meets the requirements of task names. A task name can contain letters, numbers, underscores, and hyphens. Base64-encoded values (such as string-ified datastore keys) use this alphabet, but may use equal-sign (=) characters for padding. The preceding examples use a regular expression to substitute characters outside of this alphabet with underscores.

Countdowns and ETAs

By default, a task is made available to run immediately. A push queue can execute an available task whenever it is ready (subject to its rate limiting configuration, which we'll see later). The consumer of a pull queue sees only available tasks when it requests a lease.

You can delay the availability of a task when you add it, so it doesn't become available until a later time. You specify this as either a number of seconds into the future from the time of the enqueue operation (a countdown), or an explicit date and time in the future (an earliest time of availability, or ETA). Delaying the availability of a task can be a useful way to slow down a complex multistage process, such as to avoid hitting a remote server too often.

In task configuration, these are the countdown and eta options, respectively. A count down is a number of seconds. An eta is a Unix epoch date-time in the future:

```
# Execute no earlier than 5 seconds from now.
taskqueue.add(params={'url': next_url}, countdown=5)

# Execute no earlier than December 31, 2012, midnight UTC.
taskqueue.add(params={'url': next_url}, eta=1356940800)
```

 Countdowns and ETAs specify the earliest time the task will be available, not the exact time the task will be performed. Do not rely on ETAs as exact timers.

Push Queues

Push queues are queues of tasks that are performed automatically by App Engine at a configurable rate. App Engine performs a task by invoking a request handler of your app. It forms an HTTP request based on the contents of the task record, and issues the request to a URL path associated with the task. App Engine uses the HTTP status code of the response to decide whether the task was completed successfully and should be deleted from the queue. Unsuccessful tasks are retried again later.

Because tasks on push queues are just requests to your app, they use the same infrastructure as any other request handler. You implement tasks by implementing request handlers mapped to URLs, using your web application framework of choice. Tasks are executed in threads of instances, and use the same automatic scaling mechanism as user requests. A queue with multiple tasks will distribute the tasks to multiple instances to be performed in parallel, based on the availability of instances and the processing rate of the queue.

You can control aspects of the HTTP request for a task by setting task options. You can also configure aspects of how push queues process tasks, and how tasks are retried.

Task Requests

You can set various aspects of the HTTP request issued for a task using task options, including the URL, the HTTP method, and request headers. The payload for the task also becomes part of the request, depending on the method.

By default, the URL path for a task is based on the queue name, in this format:

```
/_ah/queue/queue_name
```

You can override the URL path for an individual task. This is the `url` option to `task queue.Task()` or `taskqueue.add()`:

```
taskqueue.add(url='/admin/tasks/persist_scores')
```

 If there is no request handler mapped to the URL for a task (or the task's queue, if no custom URL is specified), the invocation of the task will return a 404 status code. This is interpreted by the push queue as task failure, and the task is added back to the queue to be retried. You can delete these tasks by flushing the queue in the Cloud Console, or by pushing a software version that supplies a successful handler for the task URL.

By default, the HTTP request uses the POST method. You can change this with the `method` option, with one of these string values: `'GET'`, `'POST'`, `'PUT'`, `'PULL'`, `'HEAD'`, or `'DELETE'`.

You can set HTTP headers on the task's request. To do so, provide a `headers` argument, whose value is a mapping of header names to header string values. Alternatively, you can set multiple headers in one call with the `headers()` builder method, which takes a mapping (`dict`).

Task queues have special behavior with regard to app versions. If the version of the app that enqueued a task was the default version, then the task uses the default version of the app when it executes—even if the default version has changed since the task was enqueued. If the version of the app that enqueued the task was not the default version at the time, then the task uses that version specifically when it executes. This allows you to test nondefault versions that use tasks before making them the default. You can set a specific version for a task by using the `target` option.

App Engine adds the following headers to the request automatically when invoking the request handler, so the handler can identify the task record:

X-AppEngine-QueueName
:   The name of the queue issuing the task request

X-AppEngine-TaskName
:   The name of the task, either assigned by the app or assigned by the system

X-AppEngine-TaskRetryCount
:   The number of times this task has been retried

X-AppEngine-TaskETA
:   The time this task became available, as the number of microseconds since January 1, 1970; this is set when the app specifies a countdown or an ETA, or if the task was retried with a delay

Incoming requests from outside App Engine are not allowed to set these headers, so a request handler can test for these headers to confirm the request is from a task queue.

Task requests are considered to be from an administrator user for the purposes of the URL access control in *app.yaml*. You can restrict task URLs to be administrator-only, and then only task queues (and actual app administrators) can issue requests to the URL.

The body of a response from a task's request handler is ignored. If the task needs to store or communicate information, it must do so by using the appropriate services or by logging messages.

A call to a task handler appears in the request log, just like a user-initiated web request. You can monitor and analyze the performance of tasks just as you would user requests.

Processing Rates and Token Buckets

The processing rate for a queue is controlled using a "token bucket" algorithm. In this algorithm, a queue has a number of "tokens," and it spends a token for each task it executes. Tokens are replenished at a steady rate up to a maximum number of tokens (the "bucket size"). Both the replenishment rate and the bucket size are configurable for a queue.

If a queue contains a task and has a token, it usually executes the task immediately. If a queue has many tasks and many available tokens, it executes as many tasks as it can afford, immediately and in parallel. If there are tasks remaining, the queue must wait until a token is replenished before executing the next task. The token bucket algorithm gives a queue the flexibility to handle bursts of new tasks, while still remaining within acceptable limits. The larger the bucket, the more tasks an idle queue will execute immediately when the tasks are enqueued all at once.

I say it *usually* executes the tasks immediately because App Engine may adjust the method and rate of how it executes tasks based on the performance of the system. In general, task queue schedules are approximate, and may vary as App Engine balances resources.

A queue does not wait for one task to finish before executing the next task. Instead, it initiates the next task as soon as a token is available, in parallel with any currently running tasks. Tasks are not strictly ordered, but App Engine makes an effort to perform tasks in the order they are enqueued. Tasks must not rely on being executed serially or in a specific order.

Each task queue has a name and processing rate (token replenishment rate and bucket size). Every app has a queue named `default` that processes 5 tasks per second, with a bucket size of 5. If you don't specify a queue name when enqueueing a task, the task is added to the default queue. You can adjust the rate and bucket size of the default queue, and can set the rate to 0 to turn it off. Tasks enqueued to a paused queue remain on the queue until you upload the new configuration with a positive rate.

Task queues and token buckets help you control how tasks are executed so you can plan for maximizing throughput, making the most efficient use of system resources to execute tasks in parallel. Tasks inevitably share resources, even if the resource is just the pool of warmed-up application servers. Executing a bunch of tasks simultaneously may not be the fastest way to complete all the tasks, because App Engine may need to start up new instances of the application to handle the sudden load. If multiple tasks operate on the same entity groups in the datastore, it may be faster to perform only a few tasks at a time and let datastore retries sort out contention, instead of relying on task retries to drive in all the changes. Limiting the execution rate with token buckets can actually result in faster completion of multiple tasks.

Queue processing rates are configured using the *queue.yaml* configuration file. You specify the rate of bucket replenishment using the `rate` option for a queue. Its value is a number, a slash (/), and a unit of time (`s` for seconds), such as `20/s` for 20 tokens per second.

You specify the size of the token bucket with the `bucket_size` option. Its value is a number:

```
queue:
- name: fast_queue
  rate: 20/s
  bucket_size: 10
```

In addition to the rate and bucket size, you can set a maximum number of tasks from the queue that can be executed at the same time, with the `max_concurrent_requests` option. Its value is the number of tasks. If this many task requests are in progress, the queue will wait to issue another task even if there are tokens in the bucket. This allows for large bucket sizes but still prevents bursts of new tasks from flooding instances. It also accommodates tasks that take a variable amount of time, so slow tasks don't take over your instances.

Together, these options control the flow of tasks from the push queue into the request queue for the application. If a given queue is processing tasks too quickly, you can upload a new temporary configuration for the queue that tells it to run at a slower rate, and the change will take effect immediately. You can experiment with different rates and token bucket sizes to improve task throughput.

Retrying Push Tasks

To ensure that tasks get completed in a way that is robust against system failure, a task queue will retry a task until it is satisfied the task is complete.

A push queue retries a task if the request handler it invokes returns an HTTP response with a status code other than a "success" code (in the range 200–299). It retries the task by putting it back on the queue with a countdown, so it'll wait a bit before trying again in the hopes that the error condition will subside. You can configure the retry behavior for every queue in a task by using the queue configuration, and you can override this configuration on a per-task basis with task options.

Under very rare circumstances, such as after a system failure, a task may be retried even if it completed successfully. This is a design trade-off that favors fast task creation over built-in, once-only fault tolerance. A task that can be repeated without changing the end result is called *idempotent*. Whether a task's code must be strictly idempotent depends on what the task is doing and how important it is that the calculation it is performing be accurate. For instance, a task that deletes a datastore entity can be retried because the second delete fails harmlessly.

Because a task on a push queue is retried when its handler returns anything other than a successful HTTP status code, a buggy handler that always returns an error for a given input will be retried indefinitely, or until the retry limit is reached if a retry limit was specified.

If a task needs to abort without retrying, it must return a success code.

There are five parameters that control how push queues retry a given task. We'll define these parameters first. Then we'll see how to set defaults for these parameters in queue configuration, and how to override them for a specific task.

The `task_retry_limit` is the maximum number of times a failing task is retried before it is deleted from the queue. If you do not specify a retry limit, the task is retried indefinitely, or until you flush the cache or delete the task by some other means. A retry limit is a good guard against perpetual failure (such as a bug in a task), and in some cases it makes sense to abort a task in transient but long-lasting failure conditions. Be sure to set it high enough so that tasks can accommodate brief transient failures, which are to be expected in large distributed systems.

The `task_age_limit` calls for automatic deletion of an incomplete task after a period of time on the queue. If not specified, the task lives until it succeeds, hits its retry limit, or is deleted by other means. Its value is a number followed by a unit of time: s for seconds, m for minutes, h for hours, d for days. For example, 3d is three days.

When a task fails, it is added back to the queue with a countdown. The duration of this countdown doubles each time the task is retried, a method called *exponential backoff*. (The queue is "backing off" the failing task by trying it less frequently with each failure.) Three settings control the backoff behavior. min_backoff_seconds is the minimum countdown, the countdown of the first retry. max_backoff_seconds is the maximum; retries will increase the countdown up to this amount. These values are an amount of time, as a number of seconds. Finally, the max_doublings setting lets you set the number of times the countdown doubles. After that many retries, the countdown stays constant for each subsequent retry.

To set any of these retry options as the default for all tasks added to a queue, you add them to the queue configuration file, in a retry_parameters subsection of the queue's configuration. Here's an example of retry configuration in *queue.yaml*:

```
queue:
- name: respawn_health
  rate: 2/s
  retry_parameters:
    task_retry_limit: 10
    max_doublings: 3
```

To override these settings for a task, you set the retry_options argument to task queue.Task() or taskqueue.add() with an instance of the TaskRetryOptions() class. The class's constructor takes the retry options as keyword arguments, and validates them:

```
t = taskqueue.Task(
    retry_options=taskqueue.TaskRetryOptions(
        task_retry_limit=10,
        max_doublings=3))
q = taskqueue.Queue('respawn_health')
q.add(t)
```

Pull Queues

In our initial definition of a task queue, we said that a queue has a producer and a consumer. With push queues, the producer is application code running in an App Engine request handler, and the consumer is the App Engine push queue mechanism, which calls request handlers to do the actual work of the task. With pull queues, you provide the consumer logic. The consumer calls the pull queue to lease one or more tasks, and the queue ensures that a task is leased to only one consumer at a time. Typically, the consumer deletes the task from the queue after performing the corresponding work, so no other consumer sees it. If the consumer fails to delete it, eventually the lease expires and the pull queue makes the task available to consumers again.

A pull queue is useful when you want to customize the consumer logic. For example, the push queue driver consumes one task at a time, executing a separate request handler for each task. With a pull queue, a custom consumer can lease multiple related tasks at once, and perform them together as a batch. This might be faster or more productive than doing it one at a time. For example, each task might represent an update to an entity group in the datastore. If a pull queue consumer sees multiple updates in the queue, it can lease them all in a batch, and make a single transactional update to the entity group for all of them. This is likely to be faster than multiple push queue tasks each trying to make their own transactional update to the same data.

You can build pull queue consumers on App Engine, using request handlers (such as a scheduled task that processes the queue periodically), or using a long-running process on a backend that polls for new tasks on a recurring basis. You can also build a consumer that runs on a remote system, using the task queue web service REST API. With a remote consumer, your app can enqueue tasks that trigger behavior in separate systems. The REST API also allows you to build remote producers that add tasks to pull queues. (A remote producer can't add to push queues directly, but a local consumer running on App Engine could periodically convert remotely added tasks to push queue tasks.)

To create a pull queue, you add it to the queue configuration file. A pull queue must have a name, and must have its mode set to `pull`. In *queue.yaml*:

```
queue:
- name: update_leaderboard
  mode: pull
```

Enqueuing Tasks to Pull Queues

You enqueue a task on a pull queue similarly to how you enqueue a task on a push queue, using a named queue whose mode is `pull`. As with push queues, a task on a pull queue can have a payload, a task name, and a countdown or ETA.

A task added to a pull queue must have a `method` set to `PULL`. This tells the queue that the task is only compatible with the queue when it is in the pull queue mode. This is the `method='PULL'` argument:

```
taskqueue.add(queue_name='update_leaderboard', method='PULL')
```

Leasing and Deleting Tasks

A pull queue consumer running on App Engine can use the task queue service API to lease and delete tasks.

A lease is a guarantee that the consumer that acquired the lease has exclusive access to a task for a period of time. During that time, the consumer can do whatever work corresponds with that task record. The consumer is expected to delete the task at the end.

To lease tasks from a pull queue, you call a method of the queue specifying the duration of the lease and the maximum number of tasks. The service reserves up to that many tasks currently available on the queue for the requested amount of time, then returns identifiers for each of the successfully leased tasks. You can use these identifiers to delete the tasks, or update leases.

You construct the `Queue` object for the named pull queue, then call the `lease_tasks()` method. Its arguments are the lease duration as a number of seconds, and the maximum number of tasks to return. The method returns a list of `Task` objects, possibly empty if the queue has no available tasks:

```
# Lease 5 tasks from update_leaderboard for up to 20 seconds.
queue = Queue('update_leaderboard')
tasks = queue.lease_tasks(20, 5)

for task in tasks:
    # Read task.payload and do the corresponding work...
```

Once the consumer has executed the work for a task successfully, it must delete the task to prevent it from being re-leased to another consumer. You call the `delete_task()` method of the `Queue`, passing it a `Task` object or a list of `Task` objects to delete:

```
# ...
queue.delete_task(tasks)
```

 Each of the examples shown here leases a batch of tasks, does the work for all the tasks, and then deletes them all with another batch call. When using this pattern, make sure the lease duration is long enough to accommodate all the work in the batch. Even if you delete each task as it finishes, the last task must wait for all of the others.

If the consumer needs more time, you can renew the lease without relinquishing it to another consumer. The `Queue` method `modify_task_lease()` takes the `Task` and a number of seconds for the new lease.

Retrying Pull Queue Tasks

When a lease duration on a task expires, the task becomes available on the pull queue. When another consumer leases tasks from the queue, it may obtain a lease on the task and start the work again. This is the pull queue equivalent of a "retry": if the first consumer failed to delete the task before the lease expired, then the task is assumed to have failed and needs to be tried again.

You can set a limit to the number of times a task is retried. This can be a default for all tasks added to a queue, in the queue configuration. You can also set this for an individual task, overriding the queue default. If the lease for a task is allowed to expire as many times as the limit for the task, the task is deleted automatically.

To configure a retry limit for a queue in *queue.yaml*, you extend the queue's configuration with a `retry_parameters` section, including a `task_retry_limit` value:

```
queue:
- name: update_leaderboard
  retry_parameters:
    task_retry_limit: 10
```

To set the limit for an individual task, you provide the `retry_options` argument with a `TaskRetryOptions` instance as its value, passing the limit to the constructor:

```
t = taskqueue.Task(
    retry_options=taskqueue.TaskRetryOptions(
        task_retry_limit=10))
q = taskqueue.Queue('update_leaderboard')
q.add(t)
```

Transactional Task Enqueueing

Task queues are an essential reliability mechanism for App Engine applications. If a call to enqueue a task is successful, and the task can be completed, the task is guaranteed to be completed, even given the possibility of transient service failure. It is common to pair the reliability of task queues with the durability of the datastore: tasks can take datastore values, act on them, and then update the datastore.

To complete this picture, the task queue service includes an extremely useful feature: the ability to enqueue a task as part of a datastore transaction. A task enqueued within a transaction is only enqueued if the transaction succeeds. If the transaction fails, the task is not enqueued.

This opens up a world of possibilities for the datastore. Specifically, it enables easy transactions that operate across an arbitrary number of entity groups, with eventual consistency.

Consider the message board example from Chapter 8. To maintain an accurate count of every message in each conversation, we have to update the count each time a message is posted. To do this with strong consistency, the count and the message have to be updated in the same transaction, which means they have to be in the same entity group—and therefore every message in the thread has to be in the same entity group. This might be acceptable for a count of messages per conversation, as it's unlikely that many users will be posting to the same conversation simultaneously, and even so, the delay for resolving concurrency failures might not be noticed.

But what if we want a count of every message on the website? Putting every message in a single entity group would be impractical, as it would effectively serialize all updates to the entire site. We need a way to update the count reliably without keeping everything in one entity group.

Transactional task enqueueing lets us update the count reliably without concern for entity groups. To post a message, we use a transaction to create the message entity and enqueue a task that will update the count. If the transaction fails, the task is not enqueued, so the count remains accurate. The task is performed outside of the transaction, so the count does not need to be in the same entity group as the message, but transactional enqueueing and task retries ensure that the count is updated, but only under the proper circumstances.

Of course, this comes with a trade-off: it must be acceptable for the count to be inaccurate between the time the message entity is created and the time the count is updated. In other words, we must trade strong consistency for *eventual consistency*. Transactional task enqueueing gives us a simple way to implement eventually consistent global transactions.

You might think that eventual consistency is suitable for the global message count, because who cares if the message count is accurate? But eventual consistency is useful for important data as well. Say the user Alicandria posts a quest with a bounty of 10,000 gold, and a guild of 20 players completes the quest, claiming the bounty. Because any player can trade gold with any other player, it is impractical to put all players in the same entity group. A typical person-to-person exchange can use a cross-group transaction, but this can only involve up to five entity groups. So to distribute the bounty, we use transactional task enqueueing: the app deducts 10,000 gold pieces from Alicandria's inventory, then enqueues a task to give 500 gold pieces to each member of the guild, all in a transaction. We use task names and memcache locks to ensure the system doesn't accidentally create new gold pieces if it retries the task. Also, because the guild might get angry if they don't get their money quickly, we configure the gold transfer queue to execute at a fast rate and with a large token bucket.

You can enqueue up to five tasks transactionally. In a typical case, it's sufficient to start a master task within the transaction, then trigger additional tasks as needed, and let the queue-retry mechanism drive the completion of the work.

Only the task enqueuing action joins the datastore transaction. The task itself is executed outside of the transaction, either in its own request handler (push queues) or elsewhere (pull queues). Indeed, by definition, the task is not enqueued until the transaction is committed, so the task itself has no way to contribute further actions to the transaction.

The API for transactional task enqueuing is simple, and typically just means calling the task queue API during an active transaction.

Recall from Chapter 8 that we perform a transaction in Python and ndb by calling a function that has the decorator @ndb.transactional. Every datastore call made between the start and end of the function participates in a single transaction, unless the call opts out of the current transaction (by joining or creating another transaction).

The add() function, the add() convenience method of a Task, and the add() method of a Queue all take an optional transactional=True argument. If provided, the task will be enqueued as part of the current transaction. If there is no current transaction, it raises a taskqueue.BadTransactionStateError. If the argument is not provided (or its value is False), the task is enqueued immediately, regardless of whether the transaction commits or aborts.

Here's an example of transferring gold from one player to many other players in a single transaction:

```python
from google.appengine.api import taskqueue
from google.appengine.ext import ndb


@ndb.transactional
def pay_quest_bounty(quest_master_key, guild_member_keys, amount):
    quest_master = quest_master_key.get()
    assert quest_master is not None

    quest_master.gold -= amount
    quest_master.put()
    taskqueue.add(url='/actions/payment/bounty',
                  params={'user_key': guild_member_keys,  # repeated element
                          'total_amount': str(amount)},
                  transactional=True)
```

The deduction and the task enqueue occur in the same transaction, so there's no risk of the deduction happening without enqueueing the task (gold disappears), nor is there a risk of the task getting enqueued without the deduction succeeding (gold is created). Assuming the bounty task is implemented correctly (and properly handles edge cases like a guild member's account being deleted), the transaction will complete with eventual consistency.

Task Chaining

A single task performed by a push queue can run for up to 10 minutes. There's a lot you can get done in 10 minutes, but the fact that there's a limit at all raises a red flag: a single task does not scale. If a job uses a single task and the amount of work it has to do scales with a growing factor of your app, the moment the amount of work exceeds 10 minutes, the task breaks.

One option is to use a master task, a task whose job is to figure out what work needs to be done, and then create an arbitrary number of tasks to do fixed-size units of the work. For example, the master task could fetch a feed URL from a remote host, and then create a task for each entry in the feed to process it. This goes a long way to doing more work within the 10-minute limit, and is useful to parallelize the units of work to complete the total job more quickly. But it's still a fixed capacity, limited to the number of child tasks the master task can create in 10 minutes.

For jobs of arbitrary size, another useful pattern is a *task chain*. The idea is straightforward: complete the job with an arbitrary number of tasks, where each task is responsible for creating the subsequent task, in addition to doing a fixed amount of work. Each task must be capable of performing its own amount of work in a fixed amount of time, as well as determining what the next unit of work ought to be.

Task chains are especially useful when combined with datastore query cursors, which meet these exact requirements. A task that ought to update every entity of a kind (possibly those that match other query criteria) can use the following steps:

1. Start a query for entities of the kind. If the task payload includes a cursor, set the query to start at the cursor location.

2. Read and process a fixed number of entities from the query results.

3. Take the cursor after the last query result. If there are any results after the cursor, create a new task with the new cursor as its payload.

4. Return a success code.

This produces the simple task chain shown in Figure 16-2. Each new task starts just as the previous task finishes.

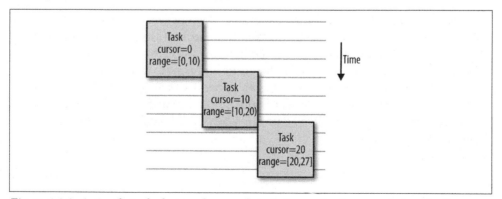

Figure 16-2. A simple task chain, where each task does a fixed amount of work, then creates the next task

If the work for the next task can be determined before performing the work for the current task, and the next task does not depend upon the completion of the current task, we can improve the performance of this job by creating the next task before we begin the work. In the case of iterating over every result of a query, we can get the next cursor immediately after performing the query:

1. Start a query for entities of the kind. If the task payload includes a cursor, set the query to start at the cursor location.

2. Read a fixed number of entities from the query results.

3. Take the cursor after the last query result. If there are any results after the cursor, create a new task with the new cursor as its payload.

4. Process the results from the query.

5. Return a success code.

This technique compresses the timeline so the work of each task is performed concurrently. App Engine will perform the tasks up to the capacity of the queue, and will utilize instances based on your app's performance settings, so you can create tasks aggressively and throttle their execution to your taste. Figure 16-3 shows the timeline of the compressed behavior.

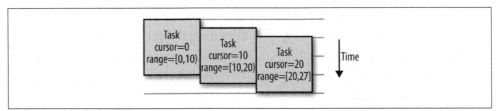

Figure 16-3. An improved task chain, where each task creates the next task before doing its own work

The last step of each task is to return a success code. This tells the push queue that the task was successful and can be deleted from the queue. If the task does not return a success code, such as due to a transient service error throwing an uncaught exception, the push queue puts the task back on the queue and tries it again. As we've described it so far, this is a problem for our task chain, because retrying one task will create another task for the next unit of work, and so on down the rest of the chain. We might end up with something like Figure 16-4, with a ton—potentially an exponential amount—of wasted work.

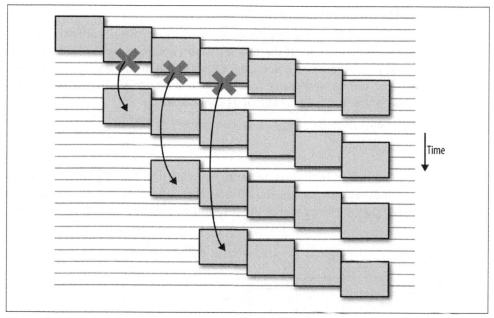

Figure 16-4. A transient error in a naive task chain explodes into many chains of wasted work, as links in the chain are retried

You might think the solution is to go back to the previous version of the task, where the work is performed before the next task is enqueued. This would reduce the likelihood that a transient service error occurs after the next link in the chain is created, but this doesn't eliminate the possibility. Even with no lines of code following the task enqueue operation in the handler, a failure on the app instance might still cause an error condition, and a fork in the chain.

The real solution is to use task names. As we saw earlier, every task has a unique name, either specified by the app or by the system. A given task name can only be used once (within a reasonably long period of time, on the order of days). When a named task finishes, it leaves behind a "tombstone" record to prevent the name from being reused right away.

A task name can be any string that identifies the next unit of work, and that the current task can calculate. In the datastore traversal example, we already have such a value: the query cursor. We can prepend a *nonce value* that identifies the job, to distinguish the query cursor for this job from a similar cursor of a job we might run later.

Our resilient task routine is as follows:

1. Start a query for entities of the kind. If the task payload includes a cursor, set the query to start at the cursor location.

2. Read a fixed number of entities from the query results.

3. Take the cursor after the last query result. If there are any results after the cursor, prepare to create a new task. If the task payload contains a nonce value for the job, use it, otherwise generate a new one. Generate the next task name based on the nonce value and the new query cursor. Create a new task with the task name, and the nonce value and the new cursor as its payload.

4. Process the results from the query.

5. Return a success code.

Transient errors no longer bother us, resulting in a pattern like Figure 16-5. Tasks that fail due to transient errors are retried and may cause their units of work to complete later, but they no longer cause the rest of the chain to be re-created for each failure.

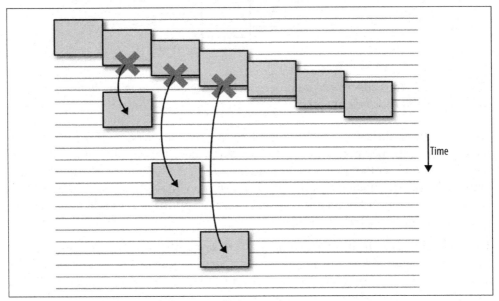

Figure 16-5. Named tasks prevent an exploding chain during a transient error

We close this discussion of task chains with an example implementation:

```
import datetime
import re
import time
import urllib
import webapp2

from google.appengine.api import taskqueue
from google.appengine.ext import ndb
```

```
TASK_SIZE = 10

class Quest(ndb.Model):
    # ...
    end_timestamp = ndb.IntegerProperty()
    end_datetime = ndb.DateTimeProperty()

class UpgradeQuestEntitiesTaskHandler(webapp2.RequestHandler):
    def post(self):
        cursor_str = self.request.get('cursor', None)
        cursor = None
        if cursor_str:
            cursor = ndb.Cursor(urlsafe=cursor_str)
        query = Quest.query(start_cursor=cursor)

        (results, new_cursor, more) = query.fetch_page(TASK_SIZE)

        if more:
            job_id = self.request.get('job_id')
            task_name = job_id + '_' + new_cursor
            task_name = re.sub('[^a-zA-Z0-9_-]', '_', task_name)
            taskqueue.add(
                name=task_name,
                url='/admin/jobs/upgradequests/task',
                params={
                    'job_id': job_id,
                    'cursor': new_cursor})

        # Do the work.
        for quest in results:
            # Upgrade end_timestamp to end_datetime.
            quest.end_datetime = datetime.fromtimestamp(quest.end_timestamp)
        ndb.put_multi(results)

class StartUpgradeQuestEntitiesJob(webapp2.RequestHandler):
    def get(self):
        started_job_id = self.request.get('job_id', None)
        if started_job_id is not None:
            self.response.out.write(
                '<p>Job started: %s</p>' % started_job_id)
        self.response.out.write("""
<form action="/admin/jobs/upgradequests/start" method="POST">
  <input type="submit" value="Start New Upgrade Quest Entities Job" />
</form>
""")

    def post(self):
        job_id = ('UpgradeQuestEntities_%s' % int(time.time()))
        taskqueue.add(
            name=job_id,
            url='/admin/jobs/upgradequests/task',
            params={'job_id': job_id})
```

```
        self.redirect('/admin/jobs/upgradequests/start?'
            + urllib.urlencode({'job_id': job_id}))

application = webapp2.WSGIApplication([
    ('/admin/jobs/upgradequests/task', UpgradeQuestEntitiesTaskHandler),
    ('/admin/jobs/upgradequests/start', StartUpgradeQuestEntitiesJob)],
    debug=True)
```

Task Queue Administration

The Cloud Console provides a great deal of information about the current status of your task queues and their contents. The Task Queues panel lists all the queues you have configured, with their rate configurations and current running status. You can click on any queue to get more information about individual tasks, such as their calling parameters and how many times they have been retried. You can also delete tasks or force tasks to run, pause and restart the queue, or purge all tasks.

The features of this panel are intuitive, so we'll just add one comment on a common use of the panel: finding and deleting stuck tasks. If a queue has a task that is failing and being retried repeatedly, the Oldest Task column may have a suspiciously old date. Select the queue, then browse for a task with a large number in the Retries column. You can trace this back to logs from an individual attempt by copying the URL from the Method/URL column, then going to the Logs panel to do a search for that path. You may need to force a run of the task by clicking the Run Now button to get a recent entry to show up in the logs.

How you fix the problem depends on how important the data in the task record is. If the task is failing because of an error in the code that can be fixed, you can leave the task in the queue, fix the bug in the code, and then deploy new code to the target version of the task. When the task is retried, it'll use the new code, and proceed to completion. If the task is failing because the task record is incompatible with a recent change to the code, you can try to rescue the task record with a code change, or just delete the task record. It's often easier to delete old task records and re-create the activity they represent than to figure out how to usher them to completion.

Deferring Work

The task queue library includes a handy utility that makes it easy to throw work into a task without writing a custom task handler. The utility uses a prepackaged general-purpose task handler to process deferred work.

To defer work, you create a Python function or other callable object that performs the work to be executed outside of the current request handler, then pass that callable object to the defer() function from the google.appengine.ext.deferred package.

The defer() function takes the object to call within the task and arguments to pass to the callable object.

To use this feature, you must set up the deferred work task handler. This is a built-in for *app.yaml*:

```
builtins:
- deferred: on
```

Here's a simple example that spans two Python modules, one containing the deferred function, and one containing the request handler that defers it. First, here's the function, to appear in a module named *invitation.py*:

```
from google.appengine.api import mail
import logging

_INVITATION_MESSAGE_BODY = '''
You have been invited to join our community...
'''

def send_invitation(recipient):
    mail.send_mail('support@example.com',
                   recipient,
                   'You\'re invited!',
                   _INVITATION_MESSAGE_BODY)
    logging.info('Sent invitation to %s' % recipient)
```

And here's the request handler script:

```
from google.appengine.ext import webapp2
from google.appengine.ext import deferred
import invitation

class SendInvitationHandler(webapp2.RequestHandler):
    def get(self):
        # recipient = ...
        deferred.defer(invitation.send_invitation, recipient)

        # ...

application = webapp2.WSGIApplication([
    ('/sendinvite', SendInvitationHandler),
    ], debug=True)
```

The defer() function enqueues a task on the default queue that calls the given callable object with the given arguments. The arguments are serialized and deserialized using Python's pickle module; all argument values must be pickle-able.

Most Python callable objects can be used with defer(), including functions and classes defined at the top level of a module, methods of objects, class methods, instances of classes that implement __call__(), and built-in functions and methods. defer() does not work with lambda functions, nested functions, nested classes, or instances of nested classes. The task handler must be able to access the callable object by name, possibly via a serializable object, because it does not preserve the scope of the call to defer().

You also can't use a function or class in the same module as the request handler class from which you call defer(). This is because pickle believes the module of the request handler class to be __main__ while it is running, and so it doesn't save the correct package name. This is why the previous example keeps the deferred function in a separate module.

You can control the parameters of the task, such as the delay, by passing additional arguments to defer(). These are the same arguments you would pass to Task(), but with the argument names prepended with an underscore so they are not confused with arguments for the callable:

```
deferred.defer(invitation.send_invitation,
               'juliet@example.com',
               _countdown=86400)
```

To call the callable, the task handler determines the module location of the callable from the description saved by the defer() function, imports the required module, re-creates any required objects from their serialized forms, then calls the callable. If the module containing the callable imports other modules, those imports will occur during the task. If the deferred callable requires any additional setup, such as changes to the module import path, make sure this happens in the callable's module, or within the callable itself.

The task handler determines the success or failure of the task based on exceptions raised by the callable. If the callable raises a special exception called deferred.PermanentTaskFailure, the task handler logs the error, but returns a success code to the task queue so the task is not retried. If the callable raises any other exception, the exception is propagated to the Python runtime and the handler returns an error code, which causes the task queue to retry the task. If the callable does not raise an exception, the task is considered successful.

The deferred library is careful to raise deferred.PermanentTaskFailure for errors it knows will prevent the task from ever succeeding. Such errors log messages, then return success to flush the task from the queue.

Scheduled Tasks

Applications do work in response to external stimuli: user requests, incoming email and XMPP messages, HTTP requests sent by a script on your computer. And while task queues can be used to trigger events across a period of time, a task must be enqueued by application code before anything happens.

Sometimes you want an application to do something "on its own." For instance, an app may need to send nightly email reports of the day's activity, or fetch news headlines from a news service. For this purpose, App Engine lets you specify a schedule of tasks to perform on a regular basis. In the App Engine API, scheduled tasks are also known as "cron jobs," named after a similar feature in the Unix operating system.

A scheduled task consists of a URL path to call and a description of the recurring times of the day, week, or month at which to call it. It can also include a textual description of the task, which is displayed in the Cloud Console and other reports of the schedule.

To execute a scheduled task, App Engine calls the URL path by using an empty GET request. A scheduled task cannot be configured with parameters, headers, or a different HTTP method. If you need something more complicated, you can do it in the code for the request handler mapped to the scheduled task's URL path.

As with task queue handlers, you can secure the URL path by restricting it to application developers in the frontend configuration. The system can call such URL paths to execute scheduled tasks.

The HTTP request includes the header X-AppEngine-Cron: true to differentiate it from other App Engine–initiated requests. Only App Engine can set this header. If an external request tries to set it, App Engine removes it before it reaches your app. You can use the header to protect against outside requests triggering the job. Scheduled task requests are also treated like requests from an administrator user (similarly to push queue tasks), so you can guard task URLs by using a login requirement in *app.yaml*.

Just like tasks in push queues, scheduled tasks have a request deadline of 10 minutes, so you can do a significant amount of computation and service calls in a single request handler. Depending on how quickly the task needs to be completed, you may still wish to break work into small pieces and use task queues to execute them on multiple instances in parallel.

Unlike push queues, scheduled tasks that fail are not retried. If a failed schedule task should be retried immediately, the scheduled task should put the work onto a push queue.

The development server does not execute scheduled tasks automatically. If you need to test a scheduled task, you can visit the task URL path while signed in as an administrator. The development server console includes a Cron Jobs section that lists the URL paths in the configuration file for easy access.

If you have enabled billing for your application, your app can have up to 100 task schedules. At the free billing tier, an app can have up to 20 task schedules.

Configuring Scheduled Tasks

The schedule is a configuration file named *cron.yaml*. It contains a value named `cron`, which is a list of task schedules. Each task schedule has a `description`, a `url`, and a `schedule`. You can also specify a `timezone` for the schedule:

```
cron:
- description: Send nightly reports.
  url: /cron/reports
  schedule: every day 23:59
  timezone: America/Los_Angeles
- description: Refresh news.
  url: /cron/getnews
  schedule: every 1 hours
```

As with other service configuration files, the scheduled task configuration file applies to the entire app, and is uploaded along with the application. You can also upload it separately:

```
appcfg.py update_cron app-dir
```

You can validate your task schedule and get a human-readable description of it by using `appcfg.py cron_info app-dir`. The report includes the exact days and times of the next few runs, so you can make sure that the schedule is what you want.

These are the possible fields for each scheduled task:

description
> A textual description of the scheduled task, displayed in the Cloud Console

url
> The URL path of the request handler to call for this task

schedule
> The schedule on which to execute this task

timezone
> The time zone for the schedule, as a standard "zoneinfo" time zone descriptor (such as `America/Los_Angeles`); if omitted, the schedule times are interpreted as UTC time

target
> The ID of the app version to use for the task; if omitted, App Engine calls the version that is the default at the time the task executes

If you choose a time zone identifier where Daylight Saving Time (DST) is used and have a task scheduled during the DST hour, your task will be skipped when DST advances forward an hour, and run twice when DST retreats back an hour. Unless this is desired, pick a time zone that does not use DST, or do not schedule tasks during the DST hour. (The default time zone UTC does not use DST.)

Specifying Schedules

The value for the schedule element uses a simplified English-like format for describing the recurrence of the task. It accepts simple recurrences, such as:

```
every 30 minutes
every 3 hours
```

The minimum interval is every 1 minutes. The parser's English isn't that good: it doesn't understand every 1 minute or every minute. It does understand every day, as an exception.

The interval every day accepts an optional time of day, as a 24-hour hh:mm time. This runs every day at 11:59 p.m.:

```
every day 23:59
```

You can have a task recur weekly using the name of a weekday, as in every tuesday, and can also include a time: every tuesday 23:59. In another English parsing foible, day names must use all lowercase letters. You can abbreviate day names using just the first three letters, such as every tue 23:59.

You can have a task recur monthly or on several days of a given month by specifying a comma-delimited list of ordinals (such as 2nd, or first,third) and a comma-delimited list of weekday names (monday,wednesday,friday or sat,sun). You can also include a time of day, as earlier. This occurs on the second and fourth Sunday of each month:

```
2nd,4th sunday
```

You can have a task recur yearly by including the word "of" and a comma-delimited list of lowercase month names (january,july, or oct,nov,dec). This schedule executes at 6 p.m. on six specific days of the year:

```
3rd,4th tue,wed,thu of march 18:00
```

You can specify recurrences to occur between two times of the day. This executes the task every 15 minutes between 3 a.m. and 5 a.m. every day:

```
every 15 mins from 03:00 to 05:00
```

By default, when a schedule uses a time interval without an explicit start time, App Engine will wait for the previous task to complete before restarting the timer. If a task runs every 15 minutes and the task takes 5 minutes to complete, each task's start time begins 20 minutes apart. If you'd prefer the next task to start at a specific interval from the previous start time regardless of the time taken to complete the previous task (or whether the previous task has finished), use the synchronized keyword:

```
every 15 mins synchronized
```

## CHAPTER 17

Optimizing Service Calls

Handlers for user-facing requests spend most of their time calling App Engine services, such as the datastore or memcache. As such, making user-facing requests fast requires understanding how your application calls services, and applying techniques to optimize the heaviest uses of calls.

We've seen three optimization techniques already, but they're worth reviewing:

- Store heavily used results of datastore queries, URL fetches, and large computations in memcache. This exchanges expensive operations (even simple datastore gets) for fast calls to the memcache in the vast majority of cases, at the expense of a potentially stale view of the data in rare cases.

- Defer work outside of the user-facing request by using task queues. When the work to prepare results for users occurs outside of the user-facing request, it's easy to see how user-facing requests are dominated by requests to the datastore or memcache.

- Use the datastore and memcache batch APIs when operating on many independent elements (when batch size limitations are not an issue). Every call to the service has remote procedure call overhead, so combining calls into batches saves overhead. It also reduces clock time spent on the call, because the services can perform the operations on the elements in parallel.

Another important optimization technique is to call services *asynchronously*. When you call a service asynchronously, the call returns immediately. Your request handler code can continue executing while the service does the requested work. When your code needs the result, it calls a method that waits for the service call to finish (if it hasn't finished already), and then returns the result. With asynchronous calls, you can get services and your app code doing multiple things at the same time, so the user response is ready sooner.

App Engine supports asynchronous service APIs to the datastore, memcache, and URL Fetch services. Support for asynchronous calls is also currently supported in a few other places.

All of these optimization techniques require understanding your application's needs and recognizing where the benefits of the technique justify the added code complexity. App Engine includes a tool called AppStats to help you understand how your app calls services and where you may be able to optimize the call patterns. AppStats hooks into your application logic to collect timing data for service calls, and reports this data visually in a web-based interface.

In this chapter, we demonstrate how to call services using the asynchronous APIs. We also walk through the process of setting up and using AppStats, and see how it can help us understand our application's performance.

Calling Services Asynchronously

Consider the following call to the URL Fetch service, shown here in Python:

```python
from google.appengine.api import urlfetch

# ...
        response = urlfetch.fetch('http://store.example.com/products/molasses')
        process_data(response)
```

When execution of the request handler reaches this line, a sequence of events takes place. The app issues a remote procedure call to the URL Fetch service. The service prepares the request, then opens a connection with the remote host and sends it. The remote host does whatever it needs to do to prepare a response, invoking handler logic, making local connections to database servers, performing queries, and formatting results. The response travels back over the network, and the URL Fetch service concludes its business and returns the response data to the app. Execution of the request handler continues with the next line.

From the point when it makes the service call to the point it receives the response data, the app is idle. If the app has multithreading enabled in its configuration, the handler's instance can use the spare CPU to handle other requests. But no further progress is made on this request handler.

In the preceding case, that's the best the request handler can do: it needs the response in order to proceed to the next line of execution. But consider this amended example:

```python
        ingred1 = urlfetch.fetch('http://store.example.com/products/molasses')
        ingred2 = urlfetch.fetch('http://store.example.com/products/sugar')
        ingred3 = urlfetch.fetch('http://store.example.com/products/flour')

        combine(ingred1, ingred2, ingred3)
```

Here, the request handler issues the first request, then waits for the first response before issuing the second request. It waits again for the second response before issuing the third. The total running time of just these three lines is equal to the sum of the execution times of each call, and during that time the request handler is doing nothing but waiting. Most importantly, the code does not need the data in the first response in order to issue the second or third request. In fact, it doesn't need any of the responses until the fourth line.

These calls to the URL Fetch service are *synchronous*: each call waits for the requested action to be complete before proceeding. With synchronous calls, your code has complete results before it proceeds, which is sometimes necessary, but sometimes not. Our second example would benefit from service calls that are *asynchronous*, where the handler can do other things while the service prepares its results.

When your app makes an asynchronous service call, the call returns immediately. Its return value is not the result of the call (which is still in progress). Instead, the call returns a special kind of object called a *future*, which represents the call and provides access to the results when you need them later. A future is an I.O.U., a promise to return the result at a later time. Your app is free to perform additional work while the service does its job. When the app needs the promised result, it calls a method on the future. This call either returns the result if it's ready, or waits for the result.

A synchronous call can be thought of as an asynchronous call that waits on the future immediately. In fact, this is precisely how the App Engine synchronous APIs are implemented.

Here is the asynchronous version of the second example:

```
ingred1_rpc = urlfetch.make_fetch_call(
    urlfetch.create_rpc(), 'http://store.example.com/products/molasses')
ingred2_rpc = urlfetch.make_fetch_call(
    urlfetch.create_rpc(), 'http://store.example.com/products/sugar')
ingred3_rpc = urlfetch.make_fetch_call(
    urlfetch.create_rpc(), 'http://store.example.com/products/flour')

combine(
    ingred1_rpc.get_result(),
    ingred2_rpc.get_result(),
    ingred3_rpc.get_result())
```

The make_fetch_call() function calls each issue their request to the service, then return immediately. The requests execute in parallel. The total clock time of this code, including the get_result() calls, is equal to the longest of the three service calls, not the sum. This is a potentially dramatic speed increase for our code.

Figure 17-1 illustrates the difference between a synchronous and an asynchronous call, using the Python URL Fetch API as an example.

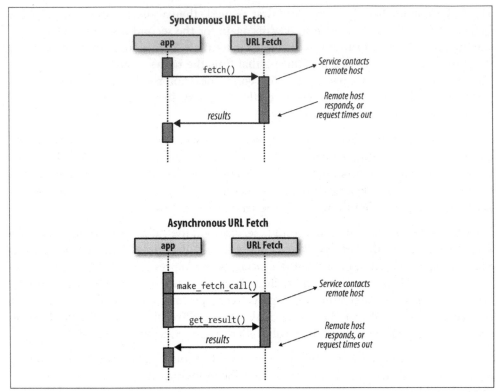

Figure 17-1. Sequence diagrams of a synchronous URL fetch and an asynchronous URL fetch

The preceding example was trivial: we could determine an obvious optimization just from looking at the code, and the change was not complicated. In a real app, reordering your code and data dependencies to best exploit asynchronous calls can add complexity. Like most optimization, it's an investment to gain performance.

The service APIs have their own particular ways of making asynchronous calls. Let's take a look at what's available.

Asynchronous Calls in Python

The Python runtime environment has documented asynchronous calls for the datastore, memcache, and URL Fetch services, as well as the App Engine Blobstore. The calling syntax varies slightly between the URL Fetch service and the other services, but the general idea is the same.

All asynchronous calls in Python return an RPC (remote procedure call) object. You can call the `get_result()` method of this object to wait for results (if necessary), and either raise exceptions to report service errors, or return the result.

More specifically, the RPC object advances through four states during its lifetime:

1. Created: the object has been created, but has not been associated with a call
2. In progress: the service call has been initiated and associated with the object
3. Ready: the call has completed, either with results or with an error
4. Checked: the status of the call has been reported to the application, such as by having raised an exception to represent an error

When you call a service's asynchronous function, the service returns an RPC object in the "in progress" state. Calling the RPC object's `get_result()` method advances it through the "ready" state to the "checked" state. Calling `get_result()` on an RPC object in the "checked" state will return the result (if any) again, but will not reraise exceptions.

You can advance the RPC object through the last two states manually by using methods. The `wait()` method waits for the fetch to finish ("in progress" to "ready"). The `check_result()` method verifies and reports the final status ("ready" to "checked"). Calling any of these methods advances the object to the appropriate state, performing the tasks along the way. If the starting state for the method has already passed, such as calling `wait()` when in the "ready" state, the method does nothing.

Figure 17-2 illustrates the RPC object states and transitions.

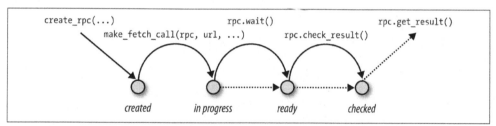

Figure 17-2. The RPC object states and transitions, using URL Fetch as an example

Datastore

The Python datastore API in the `google.appengine.ext.ndb` package has asynchronous equivalents for the major functions. The arguments are the same. Instead of returning a result, the asynchronous functions return an RPC object, whose `get_result()` method returns the expected result. Table 17-1 lists each function and its asynchronous equivalent.

Table 17-1. Python functions in ndb and their asynchronous equivalents

Synchronous	Asynchronous
key.get()	key.get_async()
key.delete()	key.delete_async()
query.count()	query.count_async()
query.fetch()	query.fetch_async()
query.fetch_page()	query.fetch_page_async()
query.get()	query.get_async()
query.map()	query.map_async()
ndb.Model.allocate_ids()	ndb.Model.allocate_ids_async()
ndb.Model.get_by_id()	ndb.Model.get_by_id_async()
ndb.Model.get_or_insert()	ndb.Model.get_or_insert_async()
model.put()	model.put_async()
ndb.delete_multi()	ndb.delete_multi_async()
ndb.get_multi()	ndb.get_multi_async()
ndb.put_multi()	ndb.put_multi_async()
ndb.transaction()	ndb.transaction_async()

A brief example:

```
from google.appengine.ext import ndb

# ...
        k1 = ndb.Key('MyKind', 1)
        k2 = ndb.Key('MyKind', 2)
        k3 = ndb.Key('MyKind', 3)
        keys = [k1, k2, k3]

        get_rpcs = {}
        for key in keys:
            get_rpcs[key] = key.get_async()
            # ...
```

```
      # ...
      v1 = get_rpcs[k1].get_result()
```

A transaction function can contain asynchronous function calls. When the transaction function exits, any asynchronous calls made within the function that are not in the "checked" state are resolved before the transaction commits.

Queries can also be performed asynchronously. Normally, a Query object doesn't make a service call until results are fetched. If you use the object as an iterable, the first few results are fetched immediately, and subsequent results are prefetched asynchronously, as needed. You can start the asynchronous prefetching process early by calling the iter() method. iter() returns an iterable of results just like the object. The only difference is the asynchronous prefetching process is started before the first use of the iterable:

```
from google.appengine.ext import ndb

class Player(ndb.Expando):
    pass

# ...
        # Prepare the query (no service calls).
        query = Player.query().order('-score')

        # Call the service asynchronously to start prefetching results.
        results_iter = query.iter()

        # ...

        for player in results_iter:
            # ...
```

In contrast, the fetch() method initiates synchronous service calls to perform the query and retrieve the requested number of result entities.

Memcache

The Python memcache API includes asynchronous versions of a set of the Client methods. All of the memcache's functionality is available with asynchronous calls, although only a subset of the calling syntax is supported. In particular, only methods of the Client class have asynchronous versions, not the package functions. For most methods, only the batch versions have asynchronous equivalents, but of course you can always call a batch method with a single element. Table 17-2 lists the methods.

Table 17-2. Python methods of api.memcache.Client and their asynchronous equivalents

Synchronous	Asynchronous
client.get_multi()	client.get_multi_async()
client.set_multi()	client.set_multi_async()
client.add_multi()	client.add_multi_async()
client.replace_multi()	client.replace_multi_async()
client.cas_multi()	client.cas_multi_async()
client.incr()	client.incr_async()
client.decr()	client.decr_async()
client.offset_multi()	client.offset_multi_async()
client.flush_all()	client.flush_all_async()
client.get_stats()	client.get_stats_async()

An example:

```
from google.appengine.api import memcache

# ...
        client = memcache.Client()

        add_rpc = client.add_multi_async(mapping)
        # ...

        if add_rpc.get_result().get(k, None) is None:
            # ...
```

Blobstore

The Python Blobstore API has asynchronous versions of the major functions. Table 17-3 lists the functions.[1]

---

1 See the book's website (*http://www.dansanderson.com/appengine*) for a free bonus chapter about the Blobstore service.

Table 17-3. Python functions in ext.blobstore and their asynchronous equivalents

Synchronous	Asynchronous
blobstore.create_upload_url()	blobstore.create_upload_url_async()
blobstore.delete()	blobstore.delete_async()
blobstore.fetch_data()	blobstore.fetch_data_async()
blobstore.create_gs_key()	blobstore.create_gs_key_async()

The `BlobInfo` methods do no have asynchronous equivalents. To delete a Blobstore value asynchronously, use the `blobstore` function.

In this example, we call the Blobstore service asynchronously to create an upload URL, then pass the RPC object to the template engine rendering the page. This allows us to finish other work and fire up the template engine while the service call is in progress. The template itself blocks on the RPC object to get the result when it is needed at the last possible moment:

```
import jinja2
from google.appengine.ext import blobstore

template_env = jinja2.Environment(
    loader=jinja2.FileSystemLoader(os.getcwd()))

# ...
        template = template_env.get_template('form.html')
        context = {
            'upload_url_rpc': blobstore.create_upload_url_async('/formhandler'),
            'orig_data': load_orig_data(),
        }
        self.response.out.write(template.render(context))
```

The template calls the `get_result()` method of the RPC object to get the value it needs:

```
<!-- ... -->

    <form action="{{ upload_url_rpc.get_result() }}" method="post">
      <!-- ... -->
    </form>
```

URL Fetch

The Python URL Fetch asynchronous API uses a slightly different syntax from the others. The asynchronous equivalent of `urlfetch.fetch(...)` is `urlfetch.make_fetch_call(urlfetch.create_rpc(), ...)`. Like the `_async()` methods, it returns an RPC object. Unlike the others, you must create the RPC object first, and pass it in as the first argument. The function updates the RPC object, then returns it. The remaining arguments are equivalent to `urlfetch.fetch()`.

 This style of passing an RPC object to a service call predates the _async-style methods in the other APIs. It appears inconsistently throughout the Python service APIs, so you might notice some other modules have it. The `ext.blobstore` module has a `create_rpc()` method, and many methods accept an `rpc` keyword argument. The `api.memcache` module also has a `create_rpc()` method, although only the _async methods of the `Client` class support it.

Asynchronous calling of the URL Fetch service is only available using the `urlfetch` API. The Python standard library `urllib2` always calls the service synchronously.

Using callbacks

To make the most of the parallel execution of asynchronous calls, a request handler should initiate the call as soon as possible in the handler's lifetime. This can be as straightforward as calling asynchronous methods early in a routine, then calling the `get_results()` method at the point in the routine where the results are needed. If your handler uses multiple diverse components to perform tasks, and each component may require the results of asynchronous calls, you could have the main routine ask each component to initiate its service calls, then allow the components to get their own results as control reaches the appropriate points in the code.

The Python RPC object offers another way to organize the code that handles the results of fetches: callbacks. A callback is a function associated with the RPC object that is called at some point after the RPC is complete, when the app calls the `wait()`, `check_results()`, or `get_results()` method. Specifically, the callback is invoked when the object goes from the "in progress" state to the "ready" state. Because the RPC never reverts states, the callback is only called once, even if the app accesses results multiple times.

You can set a callback by setting the `callback` attribute of the RPC object. (Be sure to do this before calling `wait()`, `check_results()`, or `get_results()`.)

```python
rpc = ndb_key.get_async()
rpc.callback = some_func

# ...

# Wait for the call to finish, then calls some_func.
rpc.wait()
```

In the URL Fetch API, and other APIs that let you create an RPC object explicitly, you can also pass the callback function value as the `callback` keyword argument to `create_rpc()`.

The callback function is called without arguments. This is odd, because a common use for a callback function is to process the results of the service call, so the function needs access to the RPC object. There are several ways to give the callback function access to the object.

One way is to use a *bound method*, a feature of Python that lets you refer to a method of an instance of a class as a callable object. Define a class with a method that processes the results of the call, using an RPC object stored as a member of the class. Create an instance of the class, then create the RPC object, assigning the bound method as the callback. Example 17-1 demonstrates this technique.

Example 17-1. Using an object method as a callback to access the RPC object

```
from google.appengine.api import urlfetch

# ...
class CatalogUpdater(object):
    def prepare_urlfetch_rpc(self):
        self.rpc = urlfetch.make_fetch_call(
            urlfetch.create_rpc(),
            'http://api.example.com/catalog_feed')
        self.rpc.callback = self.process_results
        return self.rpc

    def process_results(self):
        try:
            results = self.rpc.get_result()
            # Process results.content...

        except urlfetch.Error, e:
            # Handle urlfetch errors...

class MainHandler(webapp.RequestHandler):
    def get(self):
        rpcs = []

        catalog_updater = CatalogUpdater(self.response)
        rpcs.append(catalog_updater.prepare_urlfetch_rpc())

        # ...

        for rpc in rpcs:
            rpc.wait()
```

Another way to give the callback access to the RPC object is to use a *nested function* (sometimes called a *closure*). If the callback function is defined in the same scope as a variable whose value is the RPC object, the function can access the variable when it is called.

Example 17-2 demonstrates the use of a nested function as a callback. The `create_callback()` function creates a function object, a `lambda` expression, that calls another function with the RPC object as an argument. This function object is assigned to the `callback` property of the RPC object.

Example 17-2. Using a nested function as a callback to access the RPC object

```
from google.appengine.api import urlfetch

def process_results(rpc):
    try:
        results = self.rpc.get_result()
        # Process results.content...

    except urlfetch.Error, e:
        # Handle urlfetch errors...

def create_callback(rpc):
    # Use a function to define the scope for the lambda.
    return lambda: process_results(rpc)

# ...

    rpc = urlfetch.create_rpc()
    rpc.callback = create_callback(rpc)
    urlfetch.make_fetch_call(rpc, 'http://api.example.com/catalog_feed')

    # ...

    rpc.wait()
```

If you've used other programming languages that support function objects, the `create_callback()` function may seem unnecessary. Why not create the function object directly where it is used? In Python, the scope of an inner function is the outer function, including its variables. If the outer function redefines the variable containing the RPC object (`rpc`), when the inner function is called it will use that value. By wrapping the creation of the inner function in a dedicated outer function, the value of `rpc` in the scope of the callback is always set to the intended object.

Someone still needs to call the `wait()` method on the RPC object so the callback can be called. But herein lies the value of callbacks: the component that calls `wait()` does not have to know anything about what needs to be done with the results. The main routine can query its subcomponents to prepare and return RPC objects, then later it can call `wait()` on each of the objects. The callbacks assigned by the subcomponents are called to process each result.

 If you have multiple asynchronous service calls in progress simultaneously, the callback for an RPC is invoked if the service call finishes during any call to `wait()`—even if the `wait()` is for a different RPC. Of course, the `wait()` doesn't return until the fetch for its own RPC object finishes and its callbacks are invoked. A callback is only invoked once: if you call `wait()` for an RPC whose callback has already been called, it does nothing and returns immediately.

If your code makes multiple simultaneous asynchronous calls, be sure not to rely on an RPC's callback being called only during its own `wait()`.

Visualizing Calls with AppStats

AppStats is a tool to help you understand how your code calls services. After you install the tool in your application, AppStats records timing data for requests, including when each service call started and ended relative to the request running time. You use the AppStats Console to view this data as a timeline of the request activity.

Let's take another look at our contrived URL Fetch example from earlier in this chapter:

```
ingred1 = urlfetch.fetch('http://store.example.com/products/molasses')
ingred2 = urlfetch.fetch('http://store.example.com/products/sugar')
ingred3 = urlfetch.fetch('http://store.example.com/products/flour')

combine(ingred1, ingred2, ingred3)
```

Figure 17-3 is the AppStats timeline for this code. It's clear from this graph how each individual call contributes to the total running time. In particular, notice that the Grand Total is as large as the RPC Total.

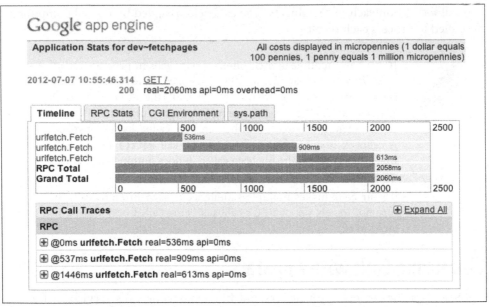

Figure 17-3. The AppStats Console illustrating three synchronous calls to urlfetch.Fetch

Here's the same example using asynchronous calls to the URL Fetch service:

```
ingred1_rpc = urlfetch.make_fetch_call(
    urlfetch.create_rpc(), 'http://store.example.com/products/molasses')
ingred2_rpc = urlfetch.make_fetch_call(
    urlfetch.create_rpc(), 'http://store.example.com/products/sugar')
ingred3_rpc = urlfetch.make_fetch_call(
    urlfetch.create_rpc(), 'http://store.example.com/products/flour')

combine(
    ingred1_rpc.get_result(),
    ingred2_rpc.get_result(),
    ingred3_rpc.get_result())
```

Figure 17-4 shows the new chart, and the difference is dramatic: the URL Fetch calls occur simultaneously, and the Grand Total is not much larger than the longest of the three fetches.

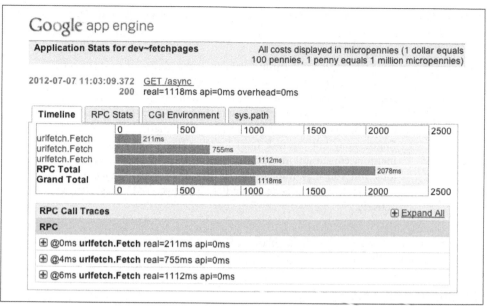

Figure 17-4. The AppStats Console illustrating three overlapping asynchronous calls to urlfetch.Fetch

AppStats has two parts: the event recorder and the AppStats Console. Both parts live within your app, and are included in the runtime environment.

Once installed, you can use AppStats in both the development server and your live app. Running in the development server can give you a good idea of the call patterns, although naturally the timings will not match the live service.

The event recorder hooks into the serving infrastructure for your app to start recording at the beginning of each request, and store the results at the end. It records the start and end times of the request handler, and the start and end times of each remote procedure call (RPC) to the services. It also stores stack traces (and, for Python, local variables) at each call site.

The recorder uses memcache for storage, and does not use the datastore. It stores two values: a short record and a long record. The short record is used by the AppStats Console to render a browsing interface for the long records. Only the most recent 1,000 records are retained. Of course, memcache values may be evicted more aggressively if your app uses memcache heavily. But in general, AppStats is able to show a representative sample of recent requests.

The performance overhead of the recorder is minimal. For typical user-facing requests, you can leave the recorder turned on for live traffic in a popular app. If necessary, you can limit the impact of the recorder by configuring it to only record a subset of traffic, or traffic to a subset of URLs. AppStats records and reports its own overhead.

 AppStats accrues its timing data in instance memory during the request, and then stores the result in memcache at the end of the request handler's lifetime. This works well for user-facing requests, even those that last many seconds. For non-user-facing task handlers that last many minutes and make many RPC calls, App Engine may kill the task (and log a critical error) due to excess memory consumption. AppStats can be useful for optimizing batch jobs, but you may want to watch carefully for memory overruns, and disable it for large task handlers when you're not testing them actively.

In the next few sections, we'll walk through how to install the event recorder and the Console. Then we'll take a closer look at the AppStats Console.

Installing AppStats

AppStats for Python includes two versions of the event recorder, one specifically for the Django web application framework, and another general-purpose WSGI recorder.

If you're using Django, edit your app's *settings.py*, and find MIDDLEWARE_CLASSES. Add the AppStatsDjangoMiddleware class, with an entry like this:

```
MIDDLEWARE_CLASSES = (
    'google.appengine.ext.appstats.recording.AppStatsDjangoMiddleware',
    # ...
    )
```

For all other Python applications, you install the WSGI middleware, using an *appengine_config.py* file. This file is used to configure parts of the App Engine libraries, including AppStats. If you don't have this file already, create it in your application root directory, and add the following Python function:

```
def webapp_add_wsgi_middleware(app):
    from google.appengine.ext.appstats import recording
    app = recording.appstats_wsgi_middleware(app)
    return app
```

App Engine uses this middleware function for all WSGI applications, including those running in the Python 2.7 runtime environment.

Regardless of which method you use to install the recorder, you can specify additional configuration in the *appengine_config.py* file.

Three settings control which handlers get recorded. The first is a global variable named appstats_FILTER_LIST that specifies patterns that match environment variables. For example, to disable recording for request handlers on a particular URL path:

```
appstats_FILTER_LIST = [
    {
        'PATH_INFO': '/batchjobs/.*',
    },
]
```

`appstats_FILTER_LIST` is a list of clauses. Each clause is a mapping of environment variable names to regular expressions. If the environment variables for a given request match all the regular expressions in a clause, then the request is recorded. Do a Google search for "WSGI environment variables" for more information on the variables you can match. Also note that the regular expression matches from the beginning of the environment variable (a "match"-style regular expression).

The `appstats_RECORD_FRACTION` configuration variable sets a percentage of requests not already filtered by `appstats_FILTER_LIST` that should be recorded. The default is 1.0 (100%). To only record a random sampling of 20 percent of the requests:

```
appstats_RECORD_FRACTION = 0.2
```

If you need more control over how requests are selected for recording, you can provide a function named `appstats_should_record()`. The function takes a mapping of environment variables and returns `True` if the request should be recorded. Note that defining this function overrides the `appstats_FILTER_LIST` and `appstats_RECORD_FRACTION` behaviors, so if you want to retain these, you'll need to copy the logic that uses them into your function.

The `appstats_normalize_path(path)` configuration function takes the request path and returns a normalized request path, so you can group related paths together in the reports. It's common for a single handler to handle all requests whose URL paths match a pattern, such as `/profile/13579`, where 13579 is a record ID. With `app stats_normalize_path()`, you can tell AppStats to treat all such URL paths as one, like so:

```
def appstats_normalize_path(path):
    if path.startswith('/profile/'):
        return '/profile/X'
    return path
```

Other settings let you control how AppStats uses memcache space, such as the number of retained events or how much stack trace data to retain. For a complete list of AppStats Python configuration variables, see the *sample_appengine_config.py* file in the SDK, in the *google/appengine/ext/appstats/* directory.

The last step is to install the AppStats Console. Edit *app.yaml*, and enable the `appstats` built-in:

```
builtins:
- appstats: on
```

The AppStats Console lives on the path `/_ah/stats/` in your application. The Console works in the development server as well as the live app, and is automatically restricted to administrative accounts.

Using the AppStats Console

The AppStats Console is your window to your app's service call behavior. To open the Console, visit `/_ah/stats/` in your app, or if you configured it, use the link you added to the Cloud Console sidebar. AppStats works in your development server as well as your live app.

Figure 17-5 shows an example of the AppStats Console. (A very small app is shown, to limit the size of the example.)

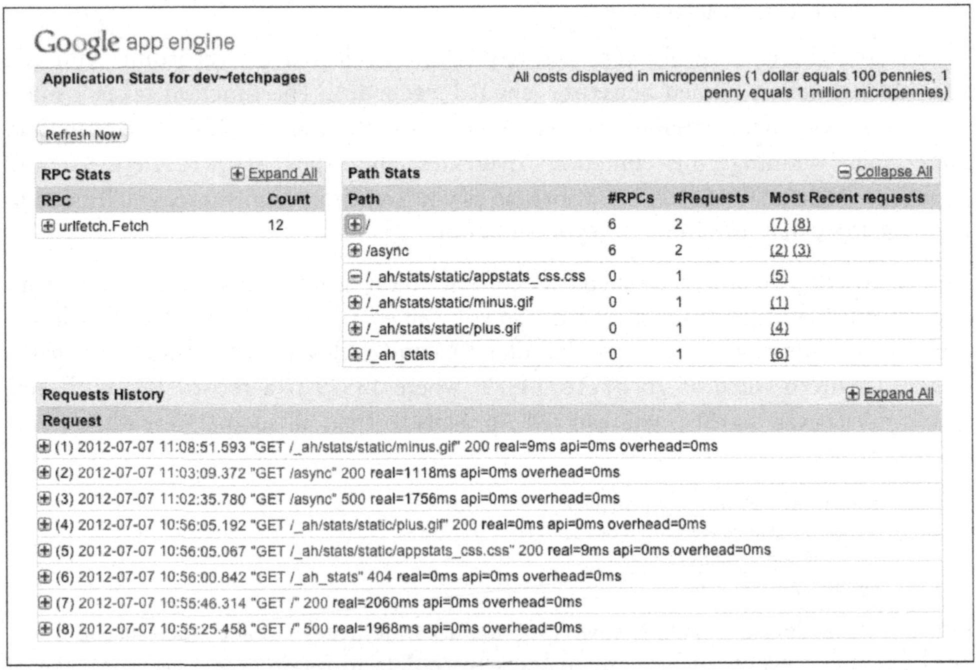

Figure 17-5. The AppStats Console front page for a small app

The front page of the Console shows a summary of recent service calls. RPC Stats is a summary of calls by service, with the most popular service at the top. Click to expand a service to see which recent request URLs called the service. Path Stats shows the same information organized by path, with the URL with the heaviest total number of calls at the top. Click to expand a path to see a summary of the path's calls per service. The Most Recent Requests column references the Requests History table at the bottom of the screen.

The Requests History table at the bottom lists all recent requests for which AppStats has data, up to 1,000 recent requests, with the most recent request on top. Click the + to expand the tally of service calls made during the request.

To view the complete data for the request, click the blue request date and path in the Requests History table. Figure 17-6 shows an expanded version of an example we saw earlier.

Figure 17-6. The AppStats Console request details page, Python version with stack trace

The centerpiece of the request details page is the timeline. The timeline shows the history of the entire request, with a separate line for each service call. From this you can see when each service call began and ended in the lifetime of the request, the total (aggregate) time of all service calls (the RPC Total), and the actual amount of time spent handling the request (Grand Total). As we saw earlier, the Grand Total can be less than the RPC Total if you use simultaneous asynchronous requests.

When running on App Engine (not the development server), the timeline also includes red bars on top of the blue ones. This represents an estimate of the monetary costs of the call, including API and bandwidth costs. (The unit, "API milliseconds," is not always useful, except in comparison to other red bars in the graph.)

The RPC Call Traces table below the timeline lets you examine each RPC call to find out where in the code it occurred. In the Python version, each element in the stack trace also includes the local variables at the call site at the time of the call.

The request details pages include another tab that shows the service call tallies (RPC Stats). The Python version also has tabs for the environment variables as they were set at the beginning of the request (CGI Environment), and the Python package load path as it is currently set in the AppStats Console (sys.path). (The sys.path is not the exact load path of the request being viewed; it is determined directly from the AppStats Console environment itself.)

The interface to the datastore is a library built on top of a more rudimentary service interface. The correspondence between library calls and datastore RPCs is fairly intuitive, but you'll notice a few differences.

The most notable difference is how the datastore libraries fetch query results. Some features of the query APIs, such as the != operator, use multiple datastore queries behind the scenes. Also, when results are fetched using iterator-based interfaces, the libraries use multiple datastore RPCs to fetch results as needed. These will appear as RunQuery and Next calls in AppStats.

Also, the local development server uses the RPC mechanism to update index configuration, so it'll sometimes show CreateIndex and UpdateIndex calls that do not occur when running on App Engine.

You can use stack traces to find where in the datastore library code each call is being made.

## CHAPTER 18

The Django Web Application Framework

As with all major categories of software, web applications have a common set of problems that need to be solved in code. Most web apps need software to interface with the server's networking layer, communicate using the HTTP protocol, define the resources and actions of the application, describe and implement the persistent data objects, enforce site-wide policies such as access control, and describe the browser interface in a way that makes it easily built and modified by designers. Many of these components involve complex and detailed best practices for interoperating with remote clients and protecting against a variety of security vulnerabilities.

A *web application framework* is a collection of solutions and best practices that you assemble and extend to make an app. A framework provides the structure for an app, and most frameworks can be run without changes to demonstrate that the initial skeleton is functional. You use the toolkit provided by the framework to build the data model, business logic, and user interface for your app, and the framework takes care of the details. Frameworks are so useful that selecting one is often the first step when starting a new web app project.

Notice that App Engine isn't a web application framework, exactly. App Engine provides scaling infrastructure, services, and interfaces that solve many common problems, but these operate at a level of abstraction just below most web app frameworks. A better example of a framework is webapp2, a framework for Python included with the App Engine Python SDK that we've been using in examples throughout the book so far. webapp2 lets you implement request handlers as Python classes, and it takes care of the details of interfacing with the Python runtime environment and routing requests to handler classes.

Several major frameworks for Python work well with App Engine. Django, Pyramid, web2py, and Flask work well, and some frameworks have explicit support for App Engine. These frameworks are mature, robust, and widely used, and have large thriving support communities and substantial online documentation. You can buy books about some of these frameworks.

Not every feature of every framework works with App Engine. Most notably, many frameworks include a mechanism for defining data models, but these are usually implemented for relational databases, and don't work with the App Engine datastore. In some cases, you can just replace the framework's data modeling library with App Engine's ndb library. Some features of frameworks also have issues running within App Engine's sandbox restrictions, such as by depending upon unsupported libraries. Developers have written adapter components that work around many of these issues.

In general, to use a framework, you add the framework's libraries to your application directory and then map all dynamic URLs (all URLs except those for static files) to a script that invokes the framework. Because the interface between the runtime environment and the app is WSGI, you can associate the framework's WSGI adapter with the URL pattern in *app.yaml*, just as we did with webapp2. Most frameworks have their own mechanism for associating URL paths with request handlers, and it's often easiest to send all dynamic requests to the framework and let it route them. You may still want to use *app.yaml* to institute Google Accounts–based access control for some URLs.

Django is a popular web application framework for Python, with a rich stack of features and pluggable components. It's also large, consisting of thousands of files. To make it easier to use Django on App Engine, the Python runtime environment includes the Django libraries, so you do not have to upload all of Django with your application files. The Python SDK bundles several versions of Django as well. App Engine includes Django 1.5 as a third-party library that you can request from *app.yaml*. You can use a newer version by downloading it and adding it to your application directory.

Django has its own data modeling library that is typically used with relational database as its backing store. Some Django components rely on this modeling library and don't work without it. On App Engine, an easy option is to use Google Cloud SQL (introduced in Chapter 11) as the backing store for the Django library, though this doesn't have the automatic scaling features of Cloud Datastore. Alternatively, you can use an adapter layer, such as djangae (*https://github.com/potatolondon/djangae*) (currently only for Django 1.6 and 1.7), which uses Cloud Datastore as the backing store for Django and works with most components. Many features of Django don't need its native data modeling facility at all, and you can always use App Engine's ndb library directly in your own app code to access Cloud Datastore.

The official documentation for Django is famously good, although it relies heavily on Django's own data modeling features for examples. For more information about Django, see the Django project website (*http://www.djangoproject.com/*).

In this chapter, we discuss how to use Django 1.5 via the provided libraries, and discuss which of Django's features work and which ones don't when using Django this way. We'll also take a quick look at how to use Django with Cloud SQL.

Using the Bundled Django Library

The App Engine Python SDK provides Django 1.5 in its *lib/django-1.5/* subdirectory. With Django, you use a command-line tool to set up a new web application project. This tool expects *lib/django-1.5/* to be in the Python library load path, so it can load modules from the `django` package.

One way to set this up is to add it to the `PYTHONPATH` environment variable on your platform. For example, on the Mac OS X or Linux command line, using a bash-compatible shell, run this command to change the environment variable for the current session to load Django 1.5 from the Python SDK located at *~/google-cloud-sdk/platform/google_appengine/*:

```
export APPENGINE_PATH=~/google-cloud-sdk/platform/google_appengine
```

```
export PYTHONPATH=$PYTHONPATH:$APPENGINE_PATH/lib/django-1.5
```

The commands that follow will assume the SDK is in *~/google-cloud-sdk/platform/google_appengine/*, and this `PYTHONPATH` is set.

The Django library is available in the runtime environment by using a `libraries:` directive in *app.yaml*, just like other libraries. We'll see an example of this in a moment.

Django 1.5 is the most recent version included with the Python runtime environment as of App Engine version 1.9.18. Later versions of Django are likely to be added to the runtime environment in future releases.

Instructions should be similar for later versions, although it isn't clear whether all future versions of Django will be added to the Python SDK. All previously included versions must remain in the SDK for compatibility, and the SDK might get a little large if it bundles every version. You may need to install Django on your local computer separately from the Python SDK in future versions. Django will likely be included in the runtime environment itself, similar to other third-party Python libraries. If you install Django yourself, you do not need to adjust the PYTHONPATH, and can run the Django commands without the library path.

You can install Django in your Python environment (or virtual environment) using pip:

```
pip install Django==1.5
```

Check the App Engine website for updates on the inclusion of future versions of Django in the runtime environment.

Creating a Django Project

For this tutorial, we will create an App Engine application that contains a Django project. In Django's terminology, a *project* is a collection of code, configuration, and static files. A project consists of one or more subcomponents called *apps*. The Django model encourages designing apps to be reusable, with behavior controlled by the project's configuration. The appearance of the overall website is also typically kept separate from apps by using a project-wide template directory.

You create a new Django project by running a command called django-admin.py startproject. Run this command to create a project named myproject in a subdirectory called *myproject/*:

```
export DJANGO_DIR=~/google-cloud-sdk/platform/google_appengine/lib/django-1.5

python $DJANGO_DIR/django/bin/django-admin.py startproject myproject
```

This command creates a project root directory in the current directory named *myproject/* with several starter files. This root directory contains a subdirectory, also named *myproject/*. The starter files are as follows:

manage.py
 A command-line utility you will use to build and manage this project, with many features

myproject/__init__.py
> A file that tells Python that code files in this directory can be imported as modules (this directory is a Python package)

myproject/settings.py
> Configuration for this project, in the form of a Python source file

myproject/urls.py
> Mappings of URL paths to Python code, as a Python source file

myproject/wsgi.py
> Code that sets up the WSGI middleware

The `django-admin.py` tool has many features, but most of them are specific to managing SQL databases. This is the last time we'll use it here.

If you're following along with a Django tutorial or book, the next step is usually to start the Django development server by using the `manage.py` command. If you did so now, you would be running the Django server, but it would know nothing of App Engine. We want to run this application in the App Engine development server. To do that, we need a couple of additional pieces.

Hooking It Up to App Engine

To connect our Django project to App Engine, we need a short script that instantiates the Django WSGI adapter, and an *app.yaml* configuration file that maps all (non-static) URLs to the Django project.

Create a file named *main.py* in the application root directory (the outer *myproject/* directory) with the following contents:

```
import os
os.environ['DJANGO_SETTINGS_MODULE'] = 'myproject.settings'

import django.core.handlers.wsgi

application = django.core.handlers.wsgi.WSGIHandler()
```

The first two lines tell Django where to find the project's `settings` module, which in this case is at the module path `myproject.settings` (the *myproject/settings.py* file). This must be set before importing any Django modules. The remaining two lines import the WSGI adapter, instantiate it, and store it in a global variable.

Next, create *app.yaml* in the application root directory, like so:

```
application: myapp
version: 1
runtime: python27
api_version: 1
```

```
threadsafe: yes

handlers:
- url: .*
  script: main.application

libraries:
- name: django
  version: "1.5"
```

This should be familiar by now, but to review, this tells App Engine this is an application with ID myapp and version ID 1 running in the Python 2.7 runtime environment, with multithreading enabled. All URLs are routed to the Django project we just created, via the WSGI adapter instantiated in *main.py*. The libraries: declaration selects Django 1.5 as the version to use when importing django modules.

Our directory structure so far looks like this:

```
myproject/
  app.yaml
  main.py
  manage.py
  myproject/
    __init__.py
    settings.py
    urls.py
    wsgi.py
```

We can now start this application in a development server. Start the development server from the command line, using the current working directory as the application root directory:

```
dev_appserver.py .
```

Load the development server URL (http://localhost:8080/) in a browser, and enjoy the welcome screen (Figure 18-1).

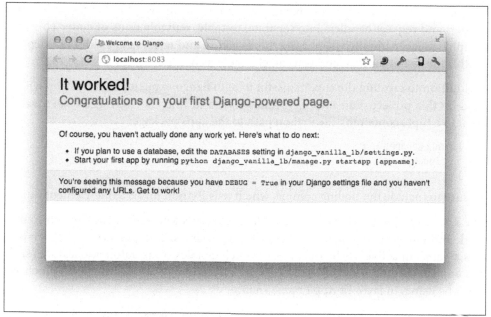

Figure 18-1. The Django welcome screen

Creating a Django App

The next step is to add a Django "app" to the Django project. You create new Django apps by using the project's manage.py script, which was generated when you created the project. (You can also use django-admin.py to create apps.)

With the current working directory still set to the application root, create a new app named bookstore for this project:

```
python manage.py startapp bookstore
```

This creates the subdirectory *bookstore*, with four new files:

__init__.py
> A file that tells Python that code files in this directory can be imported as modules (this directory is a Python package)

models.py
> A source file for data models common to this app

tests.py
> A starter file illustrating how to set up automated tests in Django

views.py
> A source file for Django views (request handlers)

This layout is Django's way of encouraging a design philosophy that separates data models and request handlers into separate, testable, reusable units of code. This philosophy comes naturally when using the datastore and ndb. Django does not depend on this file layout directly, and you can change it as needed.

In addition to creating the app, it's useful to tell Django explicitly that this app will be used by this project. Edit *myproject/settings.py*, and find the INSTALLED_APPS value. Set it to a tuple containing the Python path to the app's package:

```
INSTALLED_APPS = (
    'bookstore',
)
```

Be sure to include the trailing comma, which tells Python this is a one-element tuple.

The *settings.py* file is a Python source file. It contains settings for the Django framework and related components, in the form of variables. The INSTALLED_APPS setting lists all apps in active use by the project, which enables some automatic features such as template loading. (It's primarily used by Django's data modeling tools, which we won't be using, in favor of App Engine's ndb.)

Let's define our first custom response. Edit *bookstore/views.py*, and replace its contents with the following:

```
from django import http

def home(request):
    return http.HttpResponse('Welcome to the Book Store!')
```

In Django, a view is a function that is called with a django.http.HttpRequest object and returns a django.http.HttpResponse object. This view creates a simple response with some text. As you would expect, the HttpRequest provides access to request parameters and headers. You can set headers and other aspects of the HttpResponse. Django provides several useful ways to make HttpResponse objects, as well as specialized response classes for redirects and other return codes.

We still need to connect this view to a URL. URLs for views are set by the project, in the *myproject/urls.py* file. This allows the project to control the URLs for all of the apps it uses. You can organize URLs such that each app specifies its own set of mappings of URL subpaths to views, and the project provides the path prefix for each app. For now, we'll keep it simple, and just refer to the app's view directly in the project's URL configuration.

Each Django app defines its own URL patterns. Create a new file in the *bookstore/* directory named *urls.py*, and give it the following contents:

```
from django.conf.urls import patterns, url

from bookstore import views
```

```
urlpatterns = patterns('',
    url(r'^$', views.home),
)
```

Add a reference to the *bookstore/urls.py* file from the project's main *myproject/urls.py*, like so:

```
from django.conf.urls import include, patterns, url

urlpatterns = patterns('',
    url(r'^books/', include('bookstore.urls')),
)
```

The entry in the project's *myproject/urls.py* file maps all URL paths that begin with books/ to the bookstore Django app. The entry in *bookstore/urls.py* matches subpaths of this path. The pattern r'^books/$' matches books/, and this is followed by the pattern r'^$', which matches the empty string.

With the development server still running, load the /books/ URL in your browser. The app calls the view to display some text.

You may notice that, now that you have defined a URL pattern, the URL / no longer displays the Django welcome screen. Eventually, you will want to add an entry to *myproject/urls.py* to associate the root URL path with an appropriate view.

Using Django Templates

Django includes a templating system for building web pages and other displayable text. The Jinja2 templating library we've used throughout the book so far is based on the Django template system. Their syntaxes are mostly similar, but you'll notice minor differences between the two systems. As just one example, Jinja2 lets you call methods on template values with arguments, and so requires that you use parentheses after the method even when not using arguments: {{ someval.method() }}. In Django, templates can call methods of values but cannot pass arguments, and so the parentheses are omitted: {{ someval.method }}.

Django templates are baked into the Django framework, so they're easy to use. It's possible to use Jinja2 templates with a Django application, but Jinja2 does not automatically support some of the organizational features of Django.

Let's update the example to use a Django template. First, we need to set up a template directory for the bookstore Django app. In the *bookstore/* directory, create a directory named *templates/*, and a subdirectory in there named bookstore:

```
mkdir -p bookstore/templates/bookstore
```

(The -p option to mkdir tells it to create the entire path of subdirectories, if any subdirectory does not exist.)

By default, Django knows how to look for templates in each app's *templates/* subdirectory. We create another subdirectory named after the app (*templates/bookstore/*) so that bookstore templates all have a common path prefix.

Inside the *bookstore/templates/bookstore/* subdirectory, create the file *index.html* with the following template text:

```
<html>
  <body>
    <p>Welcome to The Book Store! {{ clock }}</p>
  </body>
</html>
```

Finally, edit *bookstore/views.py* to look like this:

```
from django.shortcuts import render_to_response
import datetime

def home(request):
    return render_to_response(
        'bookstore/index.html',
        { 'clock': datetime.datetime.now() },
    )
```

Reload the page to see the template displayed by the new view.

The render_to_response() shortcut function takes as its first argument the path to the template file. This path is relative to *bookstore/templates/*. The second argument is a Python mapping that defines variables to be used within the template. In this example, we set a template variable named clock to be the current datetime.datetime. Within the template, {{ code }} interpolates this value as a string.

The behavior of the template engine can be extended in many ways. You can define custom tags and filters to use within templates. You can also change how templates are loaded, with template loader classes and the TEMPLATE_LOADERS setting variable. The behavior we're using here is provided by the django.template.loaders.app_directories.Loader class, which appears in the default settings file created by Django.

Using ndb with Django

In Chapter 9, we discussed several powerful automatic behaviors of the ndb library. To support these features, ndb needs an opportunity to clean up pending operations when a request handler is finished. Django needs to be told to give ndb this opportunity. ndb provides a class that Django knows how to call at the beginning and end of each request. Django calls this class *middleware,* because it lives in the middle of the call stack.

Edit *myproject/settings.py*, then locate MIDDLEWARE_CLASSES. At the *top* of this list, insert an entry for the ndb middleware, like so:

```
MIDDLEWARE_CLASSES = (
    'google.appengine.ext.ndb.django_middleware.NdbDjangoMiddleware',
    # ...
)
```

You don't have to think too hard about how this works. Just remember to include it when using ndb and Django together. If your app doesn't use the ndb library, you don't need the middleware.

Using WTForms with ndb

One of the many arduous tasks that web frameworks can do well is forms, those pages of data entry fields that users fill out and submit, and applications store away for processing later. A good framework makes it easy to describe forms and their corresponding data models, and takes care of HTML rendering, data validation, error reporting, and security. Django includes a forms framework, but it only works with Django's data modeling library, and doesn't work with App Engine's ndb.[1] Instead, you can use a work-alike library called WTForms. You don't need Django to use WTForms: it works just as well with webapp2, Flask, or any other framework.

We won't go into the details of how WTForms works—see the WTForms documentation (*https://wtforms.readthedocs.org/en/latest/index.html*) for a complete explanation —but let's walk through a quick example to see how the pieces fit together. Our example will use the following behavior for creating and editing Book entities:

- An HTTP GET request to /books/book/ displays an empty form for creating a new Book.

- An HTTP POST request to /books/book/ processes the book creation form, and either creates the book and redirects to /books (the book listing page) or redisplays the form with errors, if any.

- An HTTP GET request to /books/book/1234 displays the form to edit the Book entity, with the fields filled out with the current values.

---

1 In the old ext.db library, this compatibility was provided by the google.appengine.ext.db.djangoforms module, which wrapped the Django forms interface. There is no equivalent adapter for Django and ndb, but WTForms is a capable substitute.

- An HTTP POST request to /books/book/1234 updates the book with that ID, with the same error-handling behavior as the book creation form.

WTForms is a third-party library that is not provided by App Engine, so it must be added directly to the application code. From the application root directory, run the following command:

```
pip install -t lib WTForms WTForms-Appengine

# Clean up unnecessary installation control files.
rm -rv lib/*-info
```

This creates a *lib/* directory, and installs the WTForms library and its App Engine ndb plug-in. When you deploy your app, these files will be deployed with it and will be available to the app.

To make libraries in *lib/* available for import, we must add it to the lookup path. Edit *main.py*, and add these lines near the top:

```
import sys
sys.path.append('lib')
```

Let's set up the new form URLs. Edit *bookstore/urls.py* to use a new view function named book_form() to handle these URLs:

```
from django.conf.urls.defaults import patterns, url

urlpatterns = patterns('myproject',
    url(r'^book/(\d*)', views.book_form),
    url(r'^$', views.home),
)
```

The regular expression '^book/(\d*)' captures the book ID in the URL, if any, and passes it to the view function as an argument.

Edit *bookstore/models.py* and replace its contents with the following ndb model definitions:

```
from google.appengine.ext import ndb

class Book(ndb.Model):
    title = ndb.StringProperty()
    author = ndb.StringProperty()
    copyright_year = ndb.IntegerProperty()
    author_birthdate = ndb.DateProperty()

class BookReview(ndb.Model):
    book = ndb.KeyProperty(kind='Book')
    review_author = ndb.UserProperty()
    review_text = ndb.TextProperty()
    rating = ndb.StringProperty(choices=['Poor', 'OK', 'Good',
                                         'Very Good', 'Great'],
```

```
                          default='Great')
        create_date = ndb.DateTimeProperty(auto_now_add=True)
```

No surprises here. These are just ndb models for datastore entities of the kinds Book and BookReview.

Now for the views. Edit *bookstore/views.py*, and replace its contents with the following:

```python
from django import template
from django.http import HttpResponseRedirect
from django.shortcuts import render_to_response
from google.appengine.ext import ndb
from wtforms_appengine.ndb import model_form

from bookstore import models

def home(request):
    q = models.Book.query().order('title')
    return render_to_response('bookstore/index.html',
                              {'books': q})

BookForm = model_form(models.Book)

def book_form(request, book_id=None):
    if request.method == 'POST':
        # The form was submitted.
        if book_id:
            # Fetch the existing Book and update it from the form.
            book = models.Book.get_by_id(int(book_id))
            form = BookForm(request.POST, obj=book)
        else:
            # Create a new Book based on the form.
            book = models.Book()
            form = BookForm(request.POST)

        if form.validate():
            form.populate_obj(book)
            book.put()
            return HttpResponseRedirect('/books/')
        # else fall through to redisplay the form with error messages

    else:
        # The user wants to see the form.
        if book_id:
            # Show the form to edit an existing Book.
            book = models.Book.get_by_id(int(book_id))
            form = BookForm(obj=book)
        else:
            # Show the form to create a new Book.
            form = BookForm()

    return render_to_response('bookstore/bookform.html', {
```

```
      'book_id': book_id,
      'form': form,
   }, template.RequestContext(request))
```

We've updated the home() view to set up a query for Book entities, and pass that query object to the template. Edit *bookstore/templates/bookstore/index.html* to display this information:

```
<html>
  <body>
    <p>Welcome to The Book Store!</p>
    <p>Books in our catalog:</p>
    <ul>
    {% for book in books %}
      <li>{{ book.title }}, by {{ book.author }} ({{ book.copyright_year }})
      [<a href="/books/book/{{ book.key.id }}">edit</a>]</li>
    {% endfor %}
    </ul>
    <p>[<a href="/books/book/">add a book</a>]</p>
  </body>
</html>
```

Finally, create the template for the form used by the new book_form() view, named *bookstore/templates/bookstore/bookform.html*:

```
<html>
  <body>

  {% if book_id %}
    <p>Edit book {{ book_id }}:</p>
    <form action="/books/book/{{ book_id }}" method="POST">
  {% else %}
    <p>Create book:</p>
    <form action="/books/book/" method="POST">
  {% endif %}
      {% csrf_token %}
      <p>
        {{ form.title.label|safe }}: {{ form.title|safe }}
        {% if form.title.errors %}
        <ul>
          {% for error in form.title.errors %}
          <li>{{ error }}</li>
          {% endfor %}
        </ul>
        {% endif %}
      </p>
      <p>
        {{ form.author.label|safe }}: {{ form.author|safe }}
        {% if form.author.errors %}
        <ul>
          {% for error in form.author.errors %}
          <li>{{ error }}</li>
          {% endfor %}
```

```
            </ul>
            {% endif %}
        </p>
        <p>
            {{ form.copyright_year.label|safe }}: {{ form.copyright_year|safe }}
            {% if form.copyright_year.errors %}
            <ul>
              {% for error in form.copyright_year.errors %}
              <li>{{ error }}</li>
              {% endfor %}
            </ul>
            {% endif %}
        </p>
        <p>
            {{ form.author_birthdate.label|safe }}: {{ form.author_birthdate|safe }}
            {% if form.author_birthdate.errors %}
            <ul>
              {% for error in form.author_birthdate.errors %}
              <li>{{ error }}</li>
              {% endfor %}
            </ul>
            {% endif %}
        </p>
        <input type="submit" />
      </form>

    </body>
  </html>
```

BookForm is a class generated by the model_form() function, based on the models.Book ndb model. You can also define form classes manually by subclassing wtforms.Form. A form model is very similar to an ndb data model, using class members to declare typed fields. Because form data is typically stored in a datastore once it is submitted, it is convenient to define the form model in terms of the underlying data model, so you don't have to describe the same thing twice and keep both models in sync.

The form class has useful default rendering and processing behavior for each of the default property declaration types, and you can customize this extensively. For now, we'll use the defaults produced by model_form(). An instance of the form class is responsible for storing the form data entered by the user, keeping track of validation errors, and populating the ndb.Model instance when we're ready to store the data.

The book_form() view function takes the HTTP request object and the book_id captured by the regular expression in *urls.py* as arguments. If the request method is 'POST', then it processes the submitted form. Otherwise it assumes the method is 'GET' and just displays the form. In either case, the form is represented by an instance of the BookForm class.

If constructed without arguments, the BookForm represents an empty form for creating a new Book entity. If constructed with the obj argument set to a Book object, the form's fields are prepopulated with the object's property values.

To process a submitted form, you pass the dictionary of POST parameters (request.POST) to the BookForm constructor as its first positional argument. If you also provide the obj argument, the instance sets the initial values—including the entity key—and the form data overwrites everything else, as provided.

The BookForm object knows how to render the form based on the model class and the provided model instance (if any). It also knows how to validate data submitted by the user, and render the form with the user's input and any appropriate error messages included. The validate() method tells you if the submitted data is acceptable for saving to the datastore. If it isn't, you send the BookForm to the template just as you would when displaying the form for the first time.

If the data submitted by the user is valid, the BookForm knows how to produce the final entity object. The populate_obj() method takes an entity instance and populates its properties based on the submitted form data. In this example, a successful create or update redirects the user to /books/ (which we've hardcoded in the view for simplicity) instead of rendering a template.

To display the form, we pass the BookForm object to the *bookstore/templates/bookstore/bookform.html* template. Methods on the object generate HTML for the labels and form fields for each property. Our template also tests for validation errors, in case the form is being redisplayed because of a data entry error, and prints error messages as needed.

Restart the development server, then load the book list URL (/books/) in the browser. Click "add a book" to show the book creation form. Enter some data for the book, then submit it to create it. Because the development server may try to display the book list prior to updating the global datastore index, you may need to reload the book list after creating a book to see it appear.

 The default form widget for a date field is just a text field, and it's finicky about the format. In this case, the "author birthdate" field expects input in the form YYYY-MM-DD, such as 1902-02-27.

Continue the test by clicking the "edit" link next to one of the books listed. The form displays with that book's data. Edit some of the data and then submit the form to update the entity.

Also try entering invalid data for a field, such as nonnumeric data for the "copyright year" field, or a date that doesn't use the expected format. Notice that the form redisplays with your original input, and with error messages.

The main thing to notice about this example is that the data model class itself (in this case Book) completely describes the default form, including the display of its form fields and the validation logic. The default field names are based on the names of the properties. You can change a field's name by specifying a verbose_name argument to the property declaration on the model class:

```
class Book(ndb.Model):
    title = ndb.StringProperty(verbose_name="Book title")
    # ...
```

With WTForms, you can customize the display, the error messages, and the validation routines in many ways. See the WTForms documentation for more information.

Cross-Site Request Forgery

Cross-site request forgery (CSRF) is a class of security issues with web forms where the attacker lures a victim into submitting a web form whose action is your web application, but the form is under the control of the attacker. The malicious form may intercept the victim's form values, or inject some of its own, and cause the form to be submitted to your app on behalf of the victim.

Django has a built-in feature for protecting against CSRF attacks, and it is enabled by default. The protection works by generating a token that is added to forms displayed by your app, and is submitted with the user's form fields. If the form is submitted without a valid token, Django rejects the request before it reaches the view code. The token is a digital signature, and is difficult to forge.

This requires the cooperation of our example code in two places. The *template/bookstore/bookform.html* template includes the {% csrf_token %} template tag somewhere inside the <form> element. Also, the render_to_response() function needs to pass the request to the template when rendering the form, with a third argument, template.RequestContext(request).

The blocking magic happens in a component known as *middleware*, similar to the middleware we added for ndb support. This architectural feature of Django lets you compose behaviors that act on some or all requests and responses, independently of an app's views. The MIDDLEWARE_CLASSES setting in *settings.py* activates middleware, and django.middleware.csrf.CsrfViewMiddleware is enabled by default. If you have a view that accepts POST requests and doesn't need CSRF protection (such as a web service endpoint), you can give the view the @csrf_exempt decorator, from the django.views.decorators.csrf module.

This feature of Django illustrates the power of a full-stack web application framework. Not only is it possible to implement a security feature like CSRF protection across an entire site with a single component, but this feature can be provided by a library of such components. (You could argue that this is a poor example, because it imposes requirements on views and templates that render forms. But the feature is useful enough to be worth it.)

See Django's CSRF documentation (*https://docs.djangoproject.com/en/1.8/ref/csrf/*) for more information.

Using a Newer Version of Django

The versions of the Django library that are available in the App Engine runtime environment tend to lag behind the latest releases. As of App Engine 1.9.18, App Engine provides up to Django 1.5, while the latest release of Django is 1.8. There are good reasons to use newer versions, and it's usually not a problem to do so.[2] Instead of using a built-in version, you add Django to your application files.

You can add Django 1.8 to your app just as we did earlier with the WTForms library. Run these commands from the application root directory:

```
pip install -t lib Django==1.8
rm -rv lib/*-info
```

If you haven't already, add these lines near the top of *main.py*:

```
import sys
sys.path.append('lib')
```

Remove django from the libraries: section of *app.yaml*.

We must make one small change to *main.py* to upgrade to Django 1.8's method of setting up the WSGI application instance. The complete file looks like this:

```
import os
os.environ['DJANGO_SETTINGS_MODULE'] = 'myproject.settings'

import sys
sys.path.append('lib')

from django.core.wsgi import get_wsgi_application

application = get_wsgi_application()
```

Restart the development server, and confirm that the app is still working.

---

2 If you intend to use Django with Google Cloud SQL, stick with Django 1.5. As of App Engine 1.9.18, the google.appengine.ext.django.backends.rdbms custom driver is not compatible with Django 1.8.

If you ever need to run the `django-admin.py` command, or if you just want to start a new project from scratch using the new version, be sure to use the new installation, like so:

```
export DJANGO_DIR=.../myproject/lib/
```

```
python $DJANGO_DIR/django/bin/django-admin.py startproject newproject
```

A complete installation of Django contains nearly 4,000 files. Be aware that App Engine imposes a file count limit of 10,000 application files per version per app. You may be able to remove components from *lib/django/contrib* that you are not using to reduce the number of files. For example, in Django 1.8, GeoDjango (*lib/django/contrib/gis*) contributes 608 files.

Using Django with Google Cloud SQL

While Django as we've seen it so far is already quite useful for App Engine apps, the framework really shines when paired with a relational database. You can configure Django to use Google Cloud SQL from App Engine to take advantage of a rich collection of database-backed features and plug-ins.

If you haven't already, perform the setup steps described in Chapter 11 to install MySQL and the MySQLdb library on your local computer, set up a Cloud SQL instance, and create a database.

You configure Django to use a database with settings in the *myproject/settings.py* file. With App Engine and Cloud SQL, you can use the `django.db.backends.mysql` driver included with Django, setting the `'HOST'` parameter to be the `/cloudsql/` socket path for the Cloud SQL instance.

Continuing the example from the Cloud SQL chapter, with a project ID of `saucy-boomerang-123`, an instance name of `mydb`, a database named `mmorpg`, and a user named `app`, the configuration that would work when running on App Engine to connect to Cloud SQL looks like this:

```
DATABASES = {
    'default': {
        'ENGINE': 'django.db.backends.mysql',
        'HOST': '/cloudsql/saucy-boomerang-123:mydb',
        'NAME': 'mmorpg',
        'USER': 'app'
    }
}
```

When testing the app locally, we need different configuration to tell Django to use the local MySQL test database. The *settings.py* file is Python code, so we can use conditional logic to select database configuration based on the environment:

```
import os

if os.environ.get('SERVER_SOFTWARE', '').startswith('Google App Engine'):
    # This is App Engine.
    DATABASES = {
        'default': {
            'ENGINE': 'django.db.backends.mysql',
            'HOST': '/cloudsql/saucy-boomerang-123:mydb',
            'NAME': 'mmorpg',
            'USER': 'app'
        }
    }
else:
    # This is a development server.
    DATABASES = {
        'default': {
            'ENGINE': 'django.db.backends.mysql',
            'HOST': '127.0.0.1',
            'NAME': 'mmorpg',
            'USER': 'app',
            'PASSWORD': 'p4$$w0rd'
        }
    }
```

In addition to the application code, Django's command-line tools use this configuration to create and manage table schemas. These tools run locally, and during development you use these tools to update your local MySQL database. You also use these tools to update the live database prior to deploying new software.

For this to work, the configuration needs to support a third case: connecting to the live database from the local machine. The App Engine SDK includes a custom driver to support this case, called `google.appengine.ext.django.backends.rdbms`. The custom driver uses `gcloud` authentication to access your app's databases. Here is one way to set this up in *settings.py*:

```
import os

if os.environ.get('SERVER_SOFTWARE', '').startswith('Google App Engine'):
    # This is App Engine.
    # ...

elif os.environ.get('MANAGE_DATABASE_MODE') == 'live':
    # The administrator is running a command-line tool in "live" mode.
    DATABASES = {
        'default': {
            'ENGINE': 'google.appengine.ext.django.backends.rdbms',
            'INSTANCE': 'saucy-boomerang-123:mydb',
```

```
            'NAME': 'mmorpg',
            'USER': 'app'
        }
    }

else:
    # This is a development server.
    # ...
```

The App Engine SDK must be on the PYTHONPATH library lookup path for the command-line tools to find and use the custom driver. If you haven't already, add ~/google-cloud-sdk/platform/google_appengine (where ~/google-cloud-sdk is the path to your Cloud SDK installation) to this path in your environment. The yaml library is also needed, and is included with the SDK. If you're using the version of Django distributed with the SDK, add the path to this library to PYTHONPATH as well.

For example, if using the *bash* shell, add this to your .bashrc file:

```
export APPENGINE_PATH=~/google-cloud-sdk/platform/google_appengine

export PYTHONPATH=$PYTHONPATH:$APPENGINE_PATH
export PYTHONPATH=$PYTHONPATH:$APPENGINE_PATH/lib/yaml/lib
export PYTHONPATH=$PYTHONPATH:$APPENGINE_PATH/lib/django-1.5
```

The MANAGE_DATABASE_MODE environment variable is just an environment variable you can set when you run a Django tool. In Mac OS, Linux, or Windows with Cygwin, you can set this environment variable when you run a command, like so:

```
MANAGE_DATABASE_MODE='live' ./manage.py syncdb
```

To use your local database, simply leave the environment variable unset:

```
./manage.py syncdb
```

The ./manage.py tool was created in your application root directory when you ran the django-admin.py startproject command. You use this to update and manage your database.

With all of this set up, you can now perform every step of the official Django tutorial (*https://docs.djangoproject.com/en/1.8/intro/tutorial01/*). As before, use dev_app server.py . instead of ./manage.py runserver to start the development server.

The `manage.py` tool needs enough database privileges to create, update, and drop tables. In Chapter 11, we created the `app` account and gave it specific privileges that did not include creating and dropping tables. To expand the privileges on this account, connect to the database using your `root` account:

```
mysql -h ... -u root -p
```

At the `mysql>` prompt, grant all privileges to `app`:

```
GRANT ALL ON mmorpg.* TO 'app';
```

You may want to create a separate `admin` database account that is used exclusively by `manage.py`, then either modify `manage.py` to modify `settings.DATABASES`, or use the environment variable technique to select this account in *settings.py*.

## CHAPTER 19

Managing Request Logs

Activity and message logs are an essential part of a web application. They are your view into what happens with your application over time as it is being used, who is using it and how, and what problems, if any, your users are having.

App Engine logs all incoming requests for your application, including application requests, static file requests, and requests for invalid URLs (so you can determine whether there is a bad link somewhere). For each request, App Engine logs the date and time, the IP address of the client, the URL requested (including the path and parameters), the domain name requested, the browser's identification string (the "user agent"), the referring URL if the user followed a link, and the HTTP status code in the response returned by the app or by the frontend.

App Engine also logs several important statistics about each request: the amount of time it took to handle each request, the amount of "CPU time" that was spent handling the request, and the size of the response. The CPU time measurement is particularly important to watch because requests that consistently consume a large amount of CPU may be throttled, such that the CPU use is spread over more clock time.

Your application code can log the occurrence of notable events and data by using a logging API. Logging a message associates a line of text with the request that emitted it, including all the data logged for the request. Each message has a *log level* indicating the severity of the message to make it easier to find important messages during analysis. App Engine supports five log levels: debug, info, warning, error, and critical.

You can browse your application's request and message logs, using the Cloud Console, under Monitoring, Logs. You can also download your log data for offline analysis and recordkeeping. An app can query log data programmatically using the log service API.

In this brief but important chapter, we'll look at all of these features of the logging system.

 If you're new to web programming, you can ignore the advanced features of the logging system for now. But be sure to read the first couple of sections right away. Writing log messages and finding them in the Cloud Console are important methods for figuring out what's going on in a web application.

Writing to the Log

App Engine writes information about every request to the application log automatically. The app can write additional messages during the request to note application-specific details about what happened during the request handler.

An application log message has a *log level* that indicates the importance of the message. App Engine supports five levels: debug, info, warning, error, and critical. These are in order of "severity," where "debug" is the least severe. When you browse or query log data, you can filter for messages above a given log level, such as to see just the requests where an error condition occurred.

App Engine will occasionally write its own messages to the log for a request. Uncaught application exceptions are written to the log as errors, with traceback information. When a handler exceeds its request deadline, App Engine writes an explicit message stating this fact. App Engine may also write informational messages, such as to say that the request was the first request served from a newly started instance, and so may have taken more time than usual.

In the development server, log messages are printed to the terminal. During development, you can use log messages to see what's going on inside your application, even if you decide not to keep those log messages in the live version of the app.

Python applications can use the `logging` module from the standard library to log messages. App Engine hooks into this module to relay messages to the logging system, and to get the log level for each message. Example 19-1 shows this module in action.

Example 19-1. The use of the logging Python module to emit messages at different log levels

```
import logging

# ...
        logging.debug('debug level')
        logging.info('info level')
        logging.warning('warning level')
```

```
logging.error('error level')
logging.critical('critical level')

sys.stderr.write('stderr write, logged at the error level\n')
```

In addition to messages logged with the logging module, each line of text written to the standard error stream (sys.stderr) is logged at the "error" level. (Because Python uses CGI, anything written to the standard output stream becomes part of the response data.)

In a traditional application using the logging module, you would configure the module to output only messages above a given level of severity. When running on App Engine, log messages are always recorded, at all log levels. You can filter messages by severity after the fact in the Cloud Console, or when downloading logs with appcfg.py.

When running in the development web server, log messages are written to the Console, and data written to sys.stderr is written to the server's error stream.

The development server sets its log level to INFO by default. You can change this to DEBUG by giving the server the command-line argument --debug.

Viewing Recent Logs

You can browse and search your application's request logs and messages from the Cloud Console. Open the Monitoring top-level section, then select the Logs panel. Figure 19-1 shows the Logs panel with a request opened to reveal the detailed request data.

The Logs panel features a rich dynamic interface for browsing and searching recent log data. You can load more results in real time by scrolling to the ends of the list. You can filter this display by module, version, and log level.

You can also apply textual filters to labels and other request metadata. There are two ways to specify a filter: as a regular expression, or as a set of labels and patterns. When you specify just a regular expression, the Logs panel shows all requests where any field or application log message matches the expression.

You can use labels and patterns to match more specific fields of the request. Each field filter is the field name followed by a colon, then the regular expression for the pattern. Field filters are delimited by spaces. Some useful examples of fields are path (the URL path, starting with a slash) and user (a user signed in with a Google Account; the pattern matches the Google username). For example, this query shows requests by the user dan.sanderson for paths beginning with /admin/:

```
path:/admin/.* user:dan\.sanderson
```

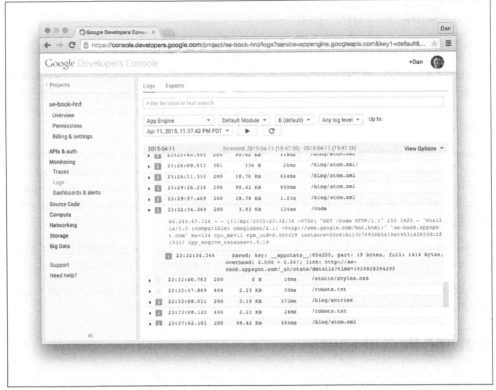

Figure 19-1. The Logs panel in the Cloud Console

The Logs panel shows log data for the application version currently selected in the drop-down menus. If you're having a problem with a live app, a useful technique is to deploy a separate version of the app with additional logging statements added to the code near the problem area, and then reproduce the issue using the version-specific URL (or temporarily make the new version the default, then switch it back). Then you can view and search the logs specific to the version with the added logging messages.

If a specific long-running instance appears to be having trouble, you can view logs just for that instance. Open the Compute top-level section, App Engine, then the Instances panel, then find the Logs column and click the View link for the instance you wish to inspect.

The Logs panel is useful for digging up more information for problems with the application code. For broader analysis of traffic and user trends, you'll want to download the log data for offline processing, or use a web traffic analytics product like Google Analytics (*http://www.google.com/analytics/*).

Downloading Logs

You can download log data for offline analysis and archiving by using the AppCfg command-line tool. To use it, run `appcfg.py` with the `request_logs` command, with the application directory and log output filename as arguments.

The following command downloads request logs for the app in the development directory *clock*, and saves them to a file named *logs.txt*:

```
appcfg.py request_logs clock logs.txt
```

This command takes many of the same arguments as `appcfg.py update`, such as those used for authentication.

The command fetches log data for the application ID and version described in the application config file. As with `appcfg.py update`, you can override these with the `--application=...` and `--version=...` arguments, respectively.

By default, this command downloads request data only. To download log messages emitted by the application, include a minimum severity level specified as a number, where 0 is all log messages ("debug" level and up) and 5 is only "critical" messages, using the `--severity` argument:

```
appcfg.py request_logs clock logs.txt --severity=1
```

Application messages appear in the file on separate lines immediately following the corresponding request. The format for this line is a tab, the severity of the message as a number, a colon, a numeric timestamp for the message, then the message:

```
1:1246801590.938119 get_published_entries cache HIT
```

Log data is ordered chronologically by request, from earliest to latest. Application messages are ordered within each request by their timestamps.

Request data appears in the file in a common format known as the Apache Combined (or "NCSA Combined") logfile format, one request per line (shown here as two lines to fit on the page):

```
127.0.0.1 - - [05/Jul/2009:06:46:30 -0700] "GET /blog/ HTTP/1.1" 200 14598 -
"Mozilla/5.0 (Macintosh; U; Intel Mac OS X 10_5_8; en-us)...,gzip(gfe)"
```

From left to right, the fields are:

- The IP address of the client
- A - (an unused field retained for backward compatibility)
- The email address of the user who made the request, if the user is signed in using Google Accounts; otherwise a - appears here
- The date and time of the request

- The HTTP command string in double quotes, including the method and URL path
- The HTTP response code returned by the server
- The size of the response, as a number of bytes
- The Referrer header provided by the client, usually the URL of the page that linked to this URL
- The User-Agent header provided by the client, usually identifying the browser and its capabilities

By default, the command fetches the last calendar day's worth of logs, back to midnight, Pacific Time. You can change this with the --num_days=... argument. Set this to 0 to get all available log data. You can also specify an alternative end date with the --end_date=... option, whose value is of the form YYYY-MM-DD (such as 2009-11-04).

You can specify the --append argument to extend the log data file with new data, if the logfile exists. By default, the command overwrites the file with the complete result of the query. The append feature is smart: it checks the data file for the date and time of the most recent log message, then only appends messages from after that time.

Logs Retention

By default, App Engine stores up to 1 gigabyte of log data, or up to 90 days worth of messages, whichever is less. Once the retention limit is reached, the oldest messages are dropped in favor of new ones.

You can increase the maximum amount and maximum age in the Compute, App Engine, Settings panel of the Cloud Console. Locate the Logs Retention setting, enter new values, and then click Save Settings.

The first gigabyte and 90 days of retention are included with the cost of your application. Additional storage and retention time is billed at a storage rate specific to logs. See the official website for the latest rates. If you're paying for log storage, you can retain logs for up to 365 days (one year).

Querying Logs from the App

App Engine provides a simple API for querying log data directly from the application. With this API, you can retrieve log data by date-time ranges, filter by log level and version ID, and page through results. You can use this API to build custom interactive log data inspectors for your app, or implement log-based alerts.

This is the same API that the Cloud Console uses to power the Logs panel. You'll notice that the API does not include filters based on regular expressions. Instead, the

Logs panel simply pages through unfiltered results, and only displays those that match a given pattern. Your app can use a similar technique.

The development server can retain log data in memory to help you test the use of this API. In the Python server, you must enable this feature with the `--persist_logs` flag:

```
dev_appserver.py --persist_logs
```

You fetch log data by calling the `fetch()` function in the `google.appengine.api.log service` module. The function takes query parameters as arguments:

`include_app_logs`
> `True` if the log records returned should include application messages.

`minimum_log_level`
> The minimum severity a request's application log messages should have to be a result. The value is an integer from 0 (debug) to 4 (critical), represented by constants named like `logservice.LOG_LEVEL_INFO`. The default is to return all requests; specifying a log level limits the results to just those requests with application log messages at or above the specified level.

`start_time`
> The earliest timestamp to consider as a Unix epoch time. The default is `None`, no starting bound.

`end_time`
> The latest timestamp to consider as a Unix epoch time. The default is `None`, no ending bound.

`version_ids`
> A list of version IDs whose logs to fetch. The default is `None`, fetch the calling app's version.

`include_incomplete`
> If `True`, include incomplete requests in the results. (For more information, see "Flushing the Log Buffer" on page 414.)

`batch_size`
> The number of results to fetch per service call when iterating over results.

`offset`
> The offset of the last-seen result, for paging through results. The next result returned follows the last-seen result.

The function returns an iterable that acts as a stream of log results. Each result is an object with attributes for the fields of the request data, such as `method`, `resource`, and `end_time`. See the official documentation for the complete list of fields.

If application log messages are requested (`include_app_logs=True`), the `app_logs` attribute of a result is a list of zero or more objects, one for each log message. The attributes of this object are `time` (an epoch time), `level` (an integer), and `message`.

Here's a simple example:

```
import time
from google.appengine.api import logservice

# ...
        self.response.write('<pre>')

        count = 0
        for req_log in logservice.fetch(include_app_logs=True):
            # Stop after 20 results.
            count += 1
            if count > 20:
                break

            self.response.write(
                '%s %s %s\n' %
                (time.ctime(req_log.end_time),
                 req_log.method,
                 req_log.resource))

            for app_log in req_log.app_logs:
                self.response.write(
                    '   %s %s %s\n' %
                    (time.ctime(app_log.time),
                     ['DEBUG', 'INFO', 'WARNING',
                      'ERROR', 'CRITICAL'][app_log.level],
                     app_log.message))

        self.response.write('</pre>')
```

Each result includes an `offset` attribute, a web-safe string you can use to make a "next page" button in a paginated display. Simply pass the `offset` of the last result on a page to the `fetch()` function, and the first result returned will be the next result in the sequence.

Flushing the Log Buffer

In the log fetch API, an "incomplete request" is a request that has not yet finished, but may have written some messages to the log. The API lets you optionally fetch log data for incomplete requests, such as to include the logged activity of a long-running task in the log data.

Application log messages accrue in a log buffer. Typically, the contents of the buffer are written to permanent log storage when the request handler exits. Because most request handlers are short-lived, this is sufficient for capturing log data in real time. For long-running request handlers (such as task handlers), you may wish to flush the log buffer periodically to make log messages available to the fetch API.

To flush the log buffer manually, you can call the `flush()` function in the `google.appengine.api.logservice` module:

```
from google.appengine.api import logservice

# ...
        logservice.flush()
```

You can also enable automatic log flushing for the duration of the request. To do this, you modify global variables in the `logservice` module. To flush the logs after a certain number of seconds:

```
        logservice.AUTOFLUSH_ENABLED = True
        logservice.AUTOFLUSH_EVERY_SECONDS = 10
```

To flush the logs after a certain number of bytes have been accrued in the buffer:

```
        logservice.AUTOFLUSH_ENABLED = True
        logservice.AUTOFLUSH_EVERY_BYTES = 4096
```

To flush the logs after a certain number of lines have been accrued in the buffer:

```
        logservice.AUTOFLUSH_ENABLED = True
        logservice.AUTOFLUSH_EVERY_LINES = 50
```

You can combine these settings. The flush occurs after any limit is reached. To disable a limit, set it to `None`.

## CHAPTER 20

Deploying and Managing Applications

Uploading your application to App Engine is as easy as clicking a button or running a command. All your application's code, configuration, and static files are sent to App Engine, and seconds later your new app is running.

Easy deployment is one of App Engine's most useful features. You don't have to worry about which servers have which software, how servers connect to services, or whether machines need to be rebooted or processes restarted. Other than your developer account, there are no database passwords to remember, no secret keys to generate, and no need to administer and troubleshoot individual machines. Your application exists as a single logical entity, and running it on large-scale infrastructure is as easy as running it on your local computer.

App Engine includes features for testing a new version of an app before making it public, reverting to a previous version quickly in case of a problem, and migrating the datastore and service configuration for the app from one version to another. These features let you control how quickly changes are applied to your application: you can make a new version public immediately to fix small bugs, or you can test a new version for a while before making it the version everyone sees.

Service configuration is shared across all versions of an app, including datastore indexes, task queues, and scheduled tasks. When you upload the app, the service configuration files on your computer are uploaded as well, and take effect immediately for all app versions. You can also upload each configuration file separately. This is especially useful for datastore indexes, as new indexes based on existing entities take time to build before they are ready to serve datastore queries.

Notice that service configuration is separate from the application configuration, which includes URL mappings, runtime environment selection, and inbound service activation. Application configuration is bound to a specific app version.

App Engine provides rich facilities for inspecting the performance of an app while it is serving live traffic. Most of these features are available in the Cloud Console, including analytic graphs of traffic and resource usage, and browsable request and message logs. You can also use the Console to inspect and make one-off changes to datastore entities.

You also use the Cloud Console to perform maintenance tasks, such as giving other developers access to the Console, changing settings, and setting up a billing account.

In this chapter, we discuss how to upload a new app, how to update an existing app, and how to use App Engine's versioning feature to test a new version of an app on App Engine while your users continue to use the previous version. We look at how to migrate the datastore and service configuration from one version to another. We also look at features of the SDK and the Cloud Console for inspecting, troubleshooting, and analyzing how your live application is running. And finally, we discuss other application maintenance tasks, billing, and where to get more information.

Uploading an Application

We introduced uploading an application way back in Chapter 2, but let's begin with a brief review.

You can upload the app with the AppCfg command-line tool from the SDK. The tool takes the update action and a path to your application root directory (the directory containing the *app.yaml* file):

```
appcfg.py update clock
```

Using Versions

The upload tool determines the application ID from the appropriate configuration file. This is the application element in the *app.yaml* file.

The tool also uses this file to determine the version ID to use for this upload, from the version element. If App Engine does not yet have a version of this app with this ID, then it creates a new version with the uploaded files. If App Engine does have such a version, then it replaces the existing version. The replacement is total: no remnants of the previous version's code or static files remain. The new app has only the files present in the project directory on your computer at the time of the upload. Of course, data stored by the services for the app remain, including the datastore, memcache, log data, and enqueued tasks.

The version of the app that is visible on your app's primary domain name—either app-id.appspot.com or your custom domain—is known as the *default version*. When you upload your app for the first time, the initial version becomes the default version automatically. If you subsequently upload a version with a different version ID, the original version remains the default until you change the default using the Cloud Console.

Recall from Chapter 3 that each version has its own `appspot.com` URL that includes the version ID as well as the application ID:

```
version-id.app-id.appspot.com
```

 Remember that there are no special protections on the version URLs. If the app does not restrict access by using code or configuration, then anyone who knows an unrestricted URL can access it. If you don't want a user to be able to access a version other than the default, you can check the `Host` header in the app and respond accordingly. You can also upload the nondefault version with configuration that restricts all URLs to administrators. Be sure to upload it again with the real configuration before making it the default version.

When you replace an existing version by uploading the app with that version ID, App Engine starts using the uploaded app for requests for that version within seconds of the upload. It is not guaranteed that every request after a particular time will use the new code and static files, but it usually doesn't take more than a few seconds for the App Master to update all the frontend servers. (It can take longer for apps with many instances and long warmup requests, as App Engine waits for new instances to be ready before diverting traffic from the previous version.) The App Master ensures that all the files are in place on a frontend server before using the new files to handle requests.

If you upload the app with the same version ID as that of the version that's currently the default, your users will start seeing the updated app within a few seconds of uploading. This is fine for small, low-risk changes that don't depend on changes to your data schemas or datastore indexes.

For larger changes, it's better to upload the app with a new version ID (in the application configuration file), test the app with the version URL, then switch the default version to direct traffic to the new version. To switch the default version, go to the Cloud Console, Compute, App Engine, then select the Versions panel. Select the radio button next to the desired version, and then click the "Make default" button. This is shown in Figure 20-1.

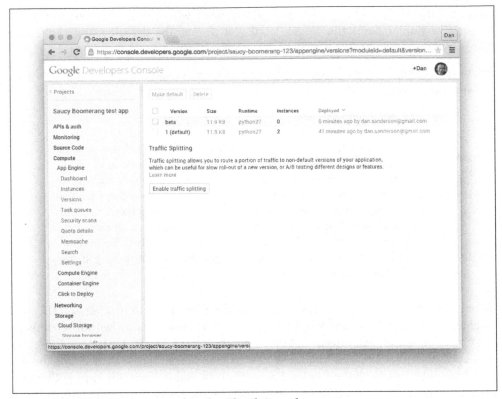

Figure 20-1. The Versions panel in the Cloud Console

App Engine can host up to 60 different version IDs per app at one time, across all modules. You can delete unused versions from the Cloud Console by clicking the Delete button on the appropriate row.

Many actions in the Cloud Console refer to a specific version of the app, including usage statistics and the log viewer. You can control which version you're looking at by selecting it from the drop-down menu in the top-left corner of the screen, next to the application ID. The version ID only appears as a drop-down menu if you have more than one version of the app.

Instead of updating the default version in Cloud Console, you can do this via the `appcfg.py set_default_version` command. This makes it easy to include this last step in your automated deployment workflows:

```
appcfg.py set_default_version --application=myapp --version=rel-20141231
```

Managing Service Configuration

All versions of an application use the same services. Service configuration and application data are shared across all versions of the app.

An app can have several service-related configuration files:

index.yaml
> A description of all the required datastore indexes

queue.yaml
> Configuration for task queues

cron.yaml
> The schedule for scheduled tasks (cron jobs)

Whenever you upload the app, these configuration files are uploaded from your computer to the services and take effect for the entire app, replacing any configuration that was once there. This is true regardless of whether the app version ID is new or already exists, or whether the version ID is the default.

You can update the configuration for each service without uploading the entire app by using the AppCfg tool. To update just the index configuration, use the `update_indexes` action, with the project directory (e.g., `app-dir`):

```
appcfg.py update_indexes app-dir
```

To update just the task queue configuration, use `update_queues`:

```
appcfg.py update_queues app-dir
```

And to update just the pending task schedule, use `update_cron`:

```
appcfg.py update_cron app-dir
```

App Engine Settings

There are various App Engine–specific settings for projects that are important but don't justify their own entry in the sidebar nav. You can find these in the Settings panel, under Compute, App Engine. This panel has multiple tabs to further organize these settings.

Under the Application Settings tab, you'll find your daily budget. This is where you set the maximum daily expenditure that you want to allow for the application. If the app ends up consuming resources whose cost is covered by the full amount, App Engine stops serving the app to avoid charging you more than you're willing to spend. This is a safety catch. Once you have an idea of how much your app's resource usage costs during a typical day, it's best to add a significant amount to this for your budget to accommodate unexpected traffic.

The "Google login cookie expiration" time is the amount of time a user signed in with a Google account will remain signed in. If the user signs in to your app, he will not have to sign in again from the computer he is using until the expiration time elapses.

The "Google authentication" setting refers to how Google account authentication works for apps running on a Google Apps domain. When set to "Google Accounts API," all Google users can sign in, and it's up to the app to decide which user is authorized to perform certain actions. When set to "Google Apps domain," only Google accounts on the domain are allowed to sign in, and other domain account management policies apply.

This is also where you set the amount of log data to retain for the app. If you retain more than the default 1 GB, you may be billed for additional storage. See Chapter 19.

The Settings panel also provides the Custom Domains tab, which you can use for setting up a domain name for the app. (Refer back to "Domain Names" on page 62.)

Managing Developers

When you register an application ID, you become a developer for the application automatically. You can invite other people to be developers for the application from the Permissions section of the Cloud Console. (This is a project-wide panel, under the project name.)

To invite a developer, click the Add Member button, then enter the person's email address in the dialog that opens. You can select from several levels of access, including ownership, edit-only privileges, or read-only privileges.

App Engine sends an email to the developer inviting her to set up an account. If the email address you invited is for a Google account, the developer can use the existing account to access App Engine, although she must still accept the invitation by clicking on a link in the invitation email message. If the email address does not have a corresponding Google account, the developer can create a Google account for that address by following the instructions in the message. The developer cannot accept the invitation from a Google account with a different address; you must invite the alternative address explicitly.

An invited developer who has not yet accepted the invitation appears in the list with a status of "Pending." After the developer accepts the invitation, she appears with a status corresponding to her level of access.

You can remove any developer from the list by clicking the Remove button for the developer. The developer loses all access immediately. You can also adjust the permission level from this screen.

Developers with view permissions can see the Console for the project, but cannot make changes or deploy code. Developers with edit permissions can do everything except manage project permissions for other people, billing, and disabling or deleting the app. Edit access includes deploying new versions, changing the default version, accessing logs, and inspecting and tweaking the datastore. All developers, including read-only developers, can access application URLs configured as administrator-only, and are recognized by the Users API as adminsitrators.

Quotas and Billing

The Cloud Console provides a detailed summary of the App Engine resources your project is using via the App Engine "dashboard." You can locate this dashboard in the sidebar navigation: Compute, App Engine, Dashboard. This handy screen provides a visual overview of your app's traffic, resource usage, and errors.

The topmost chart displays time-based data over the past 24 hours. You can select from several data sets to view via the drop-down menu, including requests per second, clock time or CPU time per request, bandwidth, errors, and quota denials. You can adjust the period for this chart by clicking on the buttons (such as "6 hr").

Below the chart is a graph showing how much of the billable quotas have been consumed for the calendar day, and how much of your daily budget has been spent for each quota. A message at the upper-right of the chart indicates how much of the calendar day is remaining. If any of the bars look like they might fill up before the next reset, you may need to increase your budget for that quota to avoid quota denials.

Near the bottom of the dashboard are lists of popular URL paths and URLs that are returning errors. You can click on a URL to view the detailed request logs for that URL path.

The dashboard's time-based chart and URL traffic lists show data for the version of the app selected by the drop-down menu in the upper-left corner of the screen. When you first sign in to the Console, the default version is selected. To view data for a different version of the app, select it from the drop-down menu.

You can view a more comprehensive chart of how the app is consuming resources with quotas from the Quota Details section of the Cloud Console. This chart shows billable quotas as well as several fixed quotas, such as API calls and service bandwidth. If your app is having quota-denial errors, check this screen for information on how the app is consuming resources.

The resource usage chart on the dashboard and the quota details screen show the total of all resource usage for all versions of the app. All versions of an app share the same budget and quotas.

When your app is ready to outgrow the free quotas, you can set a budget for additional resources. App Engine allocates more resources as needed according to the budget you establish, and you are only billed for the resources actually consumed.

You probably set up a billing account when you created the project. If you need to adjust which account is associated with the project select the Billing & Settings panel in the Cloud Console. The owner of the billing account is solely responsible for setting the budget and paying for resources consumed.

Getting Help

If you have questions not answered by this book, you may find your answers in the official documentation on Google's website:

> *https://cloud.google.com/appengine/*

The documentation includes complete references for the APIs and tools for the Python runtime environment; a list of frequently asked questions and answers (the FAQ); and a large collection of articles describing best practices, interesting features, and complete working examples.

You may also want to browse the contents of the App Engine libraries as installed by the Cloud SDK. The source code for the Python SDK serves as supplementary documentation, and includes several undocumented (and unsupported) features and extensions. The SDK also includes a set of functional example applications.

All App Engine developers should subscribe to Google's App Engine downtime mailing list. This low-traffic, announcement-only list is used by the App Engine team to announce scheduled times when services are taken down for maintenance, and also to report the status of unexpected problems:

> *http://groups.google.com/group/google-appengine-downtime-notify*

You can check the current and past health of App Engine and its services by consulting the system status site:

> *https://code.google.com/status/appengine*

By far the best place to ask questions about Google App Engine is Stack Overflow. Post your question with the `google-app-engine` tag, and it'll be seen by the App Engine developer community, as well as the App Engine team at Google. As you learn more, you can answer other people's questions and build your reputation as an App Engine expert. You can also use Google to search through past answers, which may have what you're looking for:

http://stackoverflow.com/questions/tagged/google-app-engine

If you believe you have found a bug in App Engine, the SDK, or the Cloud Console, or if you have a feature you'd like to request, you can post to the App Engine issue tracker. You can also see features others have requested, and vote for your favorites. (The App Engine team does indeed consider the highly requested features in this list when determining the product road map.)

http://code.google.com/p/googleappengine/issues/list

Google has a general discussion group for App Engine developers and an IRC channel, and also does regular live-streamed video question-and-answer sessions with the team. This page has more information on community resources:

https://cloud.google.com/appengine/community

Index

Symbols

!= (not equal) operator, 147, 150, 172, 186
character, 53
* (asterisk), 56, 119, 311
** (double asterisk), 138
-dot-, 69, 118
. (dot), 25, 46, 56, 64, 69, 118
.* pattern, 24, 42
.yaml files, 120
/ (forward slash), 56, 119
/.* (catchall pattern), 57, 79
404 Not Found Error, 51
500 generic error, 84
< operator, 147, 150, 158
<= operator, 147, 150, 158
= (equality) operator, 158
== (equality) operator, 147, 150
> operator, 147, 150, 158
>= operator, 147, 150, 158
@ (at) symbol, 311, 316, 318
@csrf_exempt decorator, 401
@db.transactional() decorator, 202
@ndb.transactional() decorator, 203-212, 352
[] (square brackets), 135

A

abstractions
    datastore as, 5, 126
    instances as, 81
    request handler, 92
    runtime environment as, 4
access, restricting, 54, 419
Activation policy, 265
allocate_ids() method, 141

ancestor paths, 137
ancestors
    ancestor paths, 195, 197
    ancestor queries, 199
    kindless queries and, 164
    root ancestors, 197
AND clauses, 148
Apache Combined logfile format, 411
App Engine Python, 19, 21
app masters, 52
app.yaml file, 23
appcfg.py command
    adjusting instance number with, 120
    appcfg.py delete_version, 121
    appcfg.py request_logs, 411
    appcfg.py set_default_version, 420
    appcfg.py stop_module_version, 120
    appcfg.py update, 46, 114
    appcfg.py update counter.yaml, 124
    appcfg.py update_cron, 362, 421
    appcfg.py update_dispatch, 119
    appcfg.py update_indexes, 249, 421
    appcfg.py update_queues, 337, 421
    appcfg.py vacuum_indexes, 249
    deleting versions with, 55
    downloading logs with, 409
    instance shutdown with, 110
    managing versions with, 109
    uploading apps with, 418
application exceptions, 408
    (see also warning messages)
application IDs, 54
applications, configuring, 49-80
    access restrictions, 54

About the Author

Dan Sanderson is a software engineer at Google. He has worked in the web industry for over 15 years as a software engineer and technical writer for Google, Amazon, and the Walt Disney Internet Group. He lives in Seattle, Washington. For more information about Dan, visit his website at *http://www.dansanderson.com*.

Colophon

The animal on the cover of *Programming Google App Engine with Python* is a four-lined snake (*Elaphe quatuorlineata*), found mainly in Italy and the Balkan Peninsula.

This creature's name derives from four dark stripes that extend from the eye to the corner of its mouth. These lines become more prominent as the snake matures. Adults are light brown with white bellies, and can grow to be as long as 8.5 feet. This gives it the distinction of being Europe's largest nonvenomous species from the Colubridae family, which encompasses two-thirds of all living snake species.

The four-lined snake occupies a variety of habitats, primarily woodland areas and bushes in rocky areas. Rodents account for most of its diet, as well as lizards and small birds.

Many of the animals on O'Reilly covers are endangered; all of them are important to the world. To learn more about how you can help, go to *animals.oreilly.com*.

The cover image is from *Wood's Animate Creation*. The cover fonts are URW Typewriter and Guardian Sans. The text font is Adobe Minion Pro; the heading font is Adobe Myriad Condensed; and the code font is Dalton Maag's Ubuntu Mono.

Get even more for your money.

Join the O'Reilly Community, and register the O'Reilly books you own. It's free, and you'll get:

- $4.99 ebook upgrade offer
- 40% upgrade offer on O'Reilly print books
- Membership discounts on books and events
- Free lifetime updates to ebooks and videos
- Multiple ebook formats, DRM FREE
- Participation in the O'Reilly community
- Newsletters
- Account management
- 100% Satisfaction Guarantee

Signing up is easy:

1. Go to: oreilly.com/go/register
2. Create an O'Reilly login.
3. Provide your address.
4. Register your books.

Note: English-language books only

To order books online:
oreilly.com/store

For questions about products or an order:
orders@oreilly.com

To sign up to get topic-specific email announcements and/or news about upcoming books, conferences, special offers, and new technologies:
elists@oreilly.com

For technical questions about book content:
booktech@oreilly.com

To submit new book proposals to our editors:
proposals@oreilly.com

O'Reilly books are available in multiple DRM-free ebook formats. For more information:
oreilly.com/ebooks

O'REILLY®

CPSIA information can be obtained at www.ICGtesting.com
Printed in the USA
BVOW11s1255260615

406266BV00002B/2/P